IN THE
WHIRLWIND
OF JIHAD

MARTHA BRILL OLCOTT

IN THE
WHIRLWIND
OF JIHAD

CARNEGIE ENDOWMENT
FOR INTERNATIONAL PEACE

WASHINGTON DC ▪ MOSCOW ▪ BEIJING ▪ BEIRUT ▪ BRUSSELS

© 2012 Carnegie Endowment for International Peace. All rights reserved.

No part of this publication may be reproduced or transmitted in any form or by any means without written permission from the Carnegie Endowment.

Carnegie Endowment for International Peace
1779 Massachusetts Avenue, N.W., Washington, D.C. 20036
202-483-7600, Fax 202-483-1840
www.ceip.org

The Carnegie Endowment does not take institutional positions on public policy issues; the views represented here are the author's own and do not necessarily reflect the views of the Endowment, its staff, or its trustees.

To order, contact:
Hopkins Fulfillment Service
P.O. Box 50370, Baltimore, MD 21211-4370
1-800-537-5487 or 1-410-516-6956
Fax 1-410-516-6998

Cover design by Jocelyn Soly
Composition by Zeena Feldman
Printed by United Book Press

Library of Congress Cataloging-in-Publication Data
Olcott, Martha Brill, 1949-
In the whirlwind of jihad / Martha Brill Olcott.
pages; cm
Includes bibliographical references and index.
ISBN 978-0-87003-259-2 (paperback) – ISBN 978-0-87003-260-8 (cloth)
1. Islam and state–Uzbekistan–History–20th century. 2. Islam and state–Uzbekistan–History–21st century. 3. Islam–Uzbekistan–History–20th century. 4. Islam–Uzbekistan–History–21st century. 5. Islamic renewal–Uzbekistan. 6. Islam and state–Soviet Union. 7. Islam–Asia, Central–History–20th century. 8. Islam–Asia, Central–History–21st century. I. Title.

BP63.U9O43 2011
297.09587 – dc23   2011047617

TABLE OF CONTENTS

FOREWORD — vii

PREFACE — ix

NOTE ON TRANSLITERATION — xiii

1 AN INTRODUCTION TO ISLAM IN UZBEKISTAN — 1

2 ISLAM AND THE STATE BEFORE SOVIET RULE — 27

3 ISLAM AND THE STATE IN THE SOVIET UNION — 51

4 RELIGIOUS LEADERS OF THE SOVIET ERA — 75

5 MUHAMMAD SODIQ MUHAMMAD YUSUF— UZBEKISTAN'S THEOLOGIAN — 107

6 ISLAM IN THE COMMUNITIES — 135

7 ISLAMIC REVIVAL IN THE UZBEK COMMUNITIES — 159

8	"MANAGING ISLAM" SINCE INDEPENDENCE	191
9	THE RISE OF RADICAL ISLAM IN UZBEKISTAN	223
10	THE ISLAMIC MOVEMENT OF UZBEKISTAN IN TAJIKISTAN AND AFGHANISTAN	253
11	THE POST-9/11 WORLD	287

NOTES	321
GLOSSARY	377
BIBLIOGRAPHY	385
INDEX	407
ABOUT THE AUTHOR	415
ABOUT CARNEGIE	416

FOREWORD

From the time of the Arab Conquest in the seventh century, Islam has been an ever-present factor in the lives of the peoples who have lived in modern-day Uzbekistan—and a force that political leaders must contend with to secure their authority.

A center of learning in philosophy, science, and the arts during the centuries of the Islamic Empire, for most of modern history, Central Asia's population has accepted a fusion of religious authority with political power. Since the Russian Conquest, however, Islam has been subordinated to the will of secular authorities. Throughout Soviet rule, the relationship was a contentious one, but one that most believers felt powerless to alter. As the Kremlin's power waned, the region experienced a strong religious revival. This revival was far-reaching enough to convince the government of newly independent Uzbekistan, particularly Islam Karimov, Uzbekistan's first and, to date, only president, that bringing Islam back under state control had to be done in a way that did not antagonize the majority of believers.

In her comprehensive volume, *In the Whirlwind of Jihad*, Carnegie Endowment Senior Associate Martha Brill Olcott examines the evolving role of Islam in Uzbekistan and the intertwined nature of religion, the state, and society in the country. She details the religious revival in Uzbekistan over twenty years of independence—introducing readers to the varied cast of clerics and officials as well as to the competing interpretations of Islam, including the region's traditional Hanafi school of Sunni Islam, Salafi (fundamentalist) critics, and the teachings of Sufi masters who originally came from this land. She also examines the potential for conflict and the very real confrontations that have occurred since independence, such as the rise of the Islamic Movement of Uzbekistan that is now part of the al-Qaeda network, and the tragic confrontation between citizens and Uzbek authorities in Andijan in 2005. Her analysis draws on the implications of these events for the peaceful coexistence of Islam and the Uzbek state.

Uzbekistan's government continues to negotiate the balance between the religious and the secular—a challenge made more difficult in a globalized, post-9/11 world in which communication and exposure to external forces can be very broadening but are fraught with risks of conflict, and even terrorism. The latter is no empty threat for Uzbekistan, which shares a border with Afghanistan. Finally, there is the question of what will happen after Karimov's inevitable departure and what role Islam will likely play in the period of transition and in the legitimation of his successor.

Uzbekistan is Central Asia's most populous nation, thirty million strong, sharing borders with the other four former Soviet republics and with Afghanistan. Its choices in the next phase in its national history will affect the security of all of its neighbors, increasing tensions and risks in an already troubled region. Understanding developments in this country is more critical than ever, and Olcott's book shines a needed light on this intriguing and timely topic.

—JESSICA T. MATHEWS
President
Carnegie Endowment for International Peace

PREFACE

The title of this book, *In the Whirlwind of Jihad*, comes from the struggle that the Quran enjoins believers to engage in if they are to live lives that are in accordance with the will of Allah. While most of the social science literature about jihad focuses on *jihad bil saif*—when believers engage in an armed struggle in defense of Islam—the Quran terms this a "lesser jihad," as it is the product of the circumstances in which a believer finds himself. But every Muslim believer must engage in *jihad al-nafs*, "the greater jihad," as it is a struggle to rid evil from within oneself.

This book looks at the intertwined nature of religion, the state, and society in Uzbekistan and the evolving relationships among them. It focuses on the impact of Islam's legacy on the nature of the religious revival that occurred from the late 1980s through 2001 and the policy implications of this revival, both for the Uzbek state and for the international community more generally. These years encompass the period from the collapse of the Soviet Union to the launching of the U.S.-led "war on terror" in neighboring Afghanistan.

From the time of the Arab Conquest in the seventh century to the present day, Islam has been an ever-present factor in the lives of the people who live in the territory that is now Uzbekistan and a force that political leaders have had to contend with as they sought to assert their authority. For this reason, jihad, in at least one of its two forms, has always been a feature of life in Uzbekistan.

This book looks at some of the battles over ideas in Islamic thinking in Central Asia and shows a trajectory of development that crosses national boundaries within the region, including the ways in which the area's Islamic community responds to global Islamic influences.

It describes the evolving role of religion in Uzbekistan, concentrating on the legacy of the late colonial and especially Soviet periods, in helping to shape the way that Islam has developed since independence. It is likely to continue to evolve over the next decade or so as Uzbekistan completes the transition from Soviet rule by bringing to power a leadership that has been raised under the conditions of independence.

Much of the literature on religion in Uzbekistan, and on Central Asia before it, has created the impression that this region was somehow removed from the rest of the Muslim world. While this book does not attempt to be a comprehensive history of Islam in Central Asia, or Islam in Uzbekistan, it seeks to contribute to the growing literature written in Western languages, Russian, Uzbek, and Tajik, which tries to give a strong sense of the religious continuity that has existed in Central Asia. The book describes the restrictions that were placed on religious believers during the Soviet period and the ways in which both the practice of religious rituals and the teachings of the faith were preserved.

The interactions between religion and the state in independent Uzbekistan are dealt with extensively. While such restrictions exist in all secular societies, the control of the Uzbek state over Islam (and religion more generally) has fallen short of the standards of religious freedom set by the U.S. government[1] and the European Union (EU).[2] Nonetheless, there has been a religious dynamism since the late Soviet period unknown in Central Asia for decades, and—given mass literacy and global communications—probably never before reaching so far down into society.

This book seeks to provide information about why the revival developed, to show what forms the revival is taking, and to indicate how the current policies of the Central Asian governments, and of their neighbors, are likely to influence the evolution of this revival.

While each of the Central Asian states is an independent country, with its own trajectory of development, Uzbekistan is the region's most populous country. The cities of Uzbekistan—Bukhara (Bukhoro), Khiva (Khorazm), Kokand (Quqon), Andijan (Andijon)—have been the religious centers of

Central Asia throughout its history, along with the heavily Uzbek cities just beyond Uzbekistan's borders in southern Kazakhstan, as well as Osh in Kyrgyzstan and Khujand in Tajikistan.

In addition to the impact one country's policies can have on neighboring states, developments in one country can resonate beyond its borders, too. This was made clear during Tajikistan's civil war in the mid-1990s, and again when interethnic clashes in Osh in June 2010 caused over 100,000 ethnic Uzbeks to take temporary refuge in Uzbekistan. Developments within the region resonate much more quickly than do those in Afghanistan—not to mention Iran, Turkey, or the Middle East. All have played a role in the way Islam has developed in Uzbekistan in recent decades.

I chose to concentrate on Uzbekistan because I have been privileged to view many of the developments there firsthand. In the past twenty-five years, I have been able to travel (mostly by road) the length and breadth of the country. In these travels, and in my analysis, I have been able to benefit from the help of a number of talented Uzbek scholars who have conducted interviews for me in Uzbek and sometimes in Arabic, shared their own unpublished materials, and extended to me access to ordinary citizens and religious leaders alike that a Western woman (even a fluent Russian-speaking one) could never gain on her own. I have been able to interview many of the country's leading religious figures, including both those who have served at the behest of the state and those who have worked to restrict the state's role in religious affairs. Working with a team of Uzbek scholars, I also conducted interviews with some hundred ordinary Uzbek citizens from four different regions of the country in 1992.

These experiences, combined with the decades of research that preceded them, make me feel a sense of obligation to offer my version of the role Islam has played in Uzbekistan in the recent past and what role it might play in the near future. While what is offered is by no means a definitive answer, it will hopefully serve as something of a starting point for those interested in exploring the relationship between religion and the nation-building policies of the Uzbek government.

This book would not have been possible without the assistance of a great many people. First and foremost I wish to thank Professor Bakhtiyar Babadjanov of the Institute of Oriental Studies of the Academy of Sciences of Uzbekistan. He was responsible for collecting many of the materials used in this book, and I benefited from his interpretation of the materials he collected with me and for this project. He has no responsibility for the current text, although his contributions are cited throughout. I also want to give special thanks to Abdujabar Abduhvahitov, who introduced me to many of the clerics in Tashkent, Namangan, and Andijan in the early 1990s, and continued to talk through many of my questions on Islam in Uzbekistan while he was a visiting scholar at Carnegie in 2002, and later when he was Rector of Westminster University in Tashkent. The number of friends I met in Uzbekistan over the years are too numerous to name, but I am grateful for the hospitality shown to me by countless Uzbeks throughout the dozens of trips to Uzbekistan that I have made over the past twenty years of research. I also want to thank the many members of the staff at the Embassy of Uzbekistan in Washington for their help in facilitating all of these trips. My research also benefited from the counsel of two Tajik scholars of Islam, Muzaffar Olimov and Saodat Olimova, who run Sharq, an independent think tank in Dushanbe and whose research helped inform the comparative aspects of this work. David Abramson and El'yor Karimov read through the entire manuscript and offered detailed comments.

Most of all I want to thank my colleagues at the Carnegie Endowment, and its administration, who afforded me the opportunity and the time to do this complex project. Several assistants made major contributions to verifying all the facts in this book, including Diora Ziyaeva, who also was responsible for collecting a lot of material on education, as well as Diana Galperin and Jane Kitaevich. We also brought on two consultants, Aaron Platt and Ibrat Usmanov, who helped with the Uzbek language materials. I want to give special thanks to Alyssa Meyer, who went over the manuscript with a fine-toothed comb to ensure all the spellings were accurate, conformed to modern Uzbek usage, and that there were no historical mistakes that slipped through the cracks.

—MARTHA BRILL OLCOTT
Washington, D.C.
May 2012

NOTE ON TRANSLITERATION

This book uses sources in multiple languages and materials that span several centuries, when no standard transliteration guidelines existed. Therefore, I decided to follow a format that would make the reading of this work most acceptable to a broad audience. Whenever possible I have used the most common spelling for an English speaker. In most cases, this has taken the form of common English; for religious Islamic terminology, however, I used transliterated Arabic (for instance, Quran), and for terms in which transliterated Russian is the most accepted, I used its spelling (for example, *chaikana*).

For terms not easily recognized by an English-speaking audience, I made exceptions. First, names of individuals living prior to 1920 (the introduction of modern Uzbek) who have not been significantly covered in the English-language press are written in transliterated Russian. For names of individuals living after the introduction of modern Uzbek, Uzbek transliteration (Latin alphabet and standard language with no local dialects) is used. I have also included frequent alternative names for individuals in parentheses immediately following the individual's name, as in the case of Baha-ud-Din Naqshaband (al-Bukhari), for example. Additionally, to keep transliterations more accessible, I have decided to avoid the use of apostrophes in the Uzbek and Arabic transliterations and where possible I have substituted "kh"s for "x"s in the Uzbek transliteration. I also used the English plural format of adding an "s" to Arabic and Uzbek plural terms rather than changing the word; for example, the plural of *maktab* is written as *maktabs*.

IN THE **WHIRLWIND** OF **JIHAD**

In any case where common English is used, I have also included the Uzbek transliteration in parentheses at the term's first mention.

—MARTHA BRILL OLCOTT

1

AN INTRODUCTION TO ISLAM IN UZBEKISTAN

THE CHALLENGE OF GOVERNING UZBEKISTAN

When Uzbekistan received its independence in late 1991, the question of whether the country would remain a secular society was a relatively open one. Uzbekistan experienced an Islamic revival starting in the 1980s, which became more widespread when the Soviet Union collapsed, especially during the early years of independence when the Uzbek state was weak. Religious groups competed with secular authorities but as the state grew stronger, and more autocratic, it was better able to channel the course of Islam's development. But even then, the state was not able to fully define Islam's development, as opportunities for contact with the wider Islamic world increased dramatically. Events in late 2001 once again changed the playing field, introducing a powerful international presence in the form of NATO troops, initially even based in Uzbekistan, bent on destroying al-Qaeda's presence in the region. Equally as important, the declaration of the "war on terror" led to increased international wariness about groups that might be labeled Islamic extremists. This deepened the Uzbek government's commitment to combat any groups that might potentially pose such a threat. The criteria that the government applied not infrequently put it at odds with its U.S. and European partners.

More than 90 percent of Uzbekistan's roughly 28 million people are at least nominally Muslim, and of the Hanafi[1] school, although the teachings of the Shafi school, whose founder[2] is buried near Tashkent, have also influenced Central Asia's Hanafi traditions. About 1 percent of the population is Shii and is mostly found in the Samarkand (Samarqand) and Bukhara regions, and about 6 percent of the population is of ethnic Russian or other European ethnic origin.

While outside observers may see the territory that is now Uzbekistan as part of a Muslim periphery, from the time of the Samanids (819–999), the local Iranian dynasty that was part of the Abbasid Empire through to the present, the indigenous population that lived in Transoxiana (Mawarannahr)[3] saw their history and culture as intertwined with Islam, as a faith and as the definer of their way of life.

By 652 some fifty thousand Arab families were settled in Mary (in present-day Turkmenistan), from which Arab armies made repeated attempts to capture Bukhara and Samarkand. Bukhara finally fell under Arab control in 709 and Samarkand in 712. By 750 Arab rule was established up to the Syr Darya (Sirdaryo, *daryo* meaning river). Moreover, no matter what the political ideology of the ruling authorities or their attitude toward religion, the Uzbeks and their ethnic predecessors have always viewed themselves as Muslims, and as part of the Muslim world, seeking to preserve this faith.

The Central Asians, though, did not see themselves solely as subjects of the faith, but as definers and innovators of it. Under the Samanids, the last half of the ninth century was a time of religious innovation, during which the six recognized canons (*sahihs*) of (Hanafi) *hadith*[4] studies in Central Asia were compiled. The first was compiled by Muhammad ibn Ismail al-Bukhari (810–870).

It was also a time of the flowering of philosophy and the sciences, as Central Asia lays claim to such great Islamic thinkers as philosopher and mathematician al-Khorazmi (Muhammad ibn Musa al-Khorazmi) (780–850), said to have been born in Khiva and viewed as a founder of algebra; the logician and philosopher al-Farabi (Abu Nasr Muhammad al-Farabi) (872–950/951), claimed by some to have been born near Otrar (earlier Farab) in southern Kazakhstan; and ibn Sino (Abu Ali al-Husayn ibn Abdullah ibn Sino), also known as Avicenna (980–1037), born near Bukhara, renowned philosopher and poet and regarded by many as the father of modern medicine.

The history of Sufism, an important trend of spiritual revival that has been part of Sunni Islam for more than a millennium, also has deep roots in Central Asia. The Kubrawiya, Yasawiya, and Naqshabandiya originated in the region, and the Qadiriya,[5] which originated in Baghdad, also has been prominent in Central Asia.[6]

The Karakhanids, a Turkic dynasty, defeated the Samanids in Bukhara in 992. During Karakhanid rule, some 60 compilations of *fura al-fiqh* (judgments) were written that used Islam to regulate everyday life. Ismaili Islam also came to the region in the tenth and eleventh centuries. Roughly contemporaneously, the Seljuks, another Turkic dynasty, emerged in the Turkmen lands. The Seljuks took Baghdad in 1055 and ruled from Khurasan as well as from Khorazm. Under the Seljuks, there was an increase in both Hanafi and Shafi mosques and madrasas and an increase in the role of Sufism as well. Yasawiya, founded by Khoja Ahmad Yasawi (1106–1166) in what is now the city of Turkestan, in Kazakhstan, dates from this period. The Karakitais invaded from China in the middle of the twelfth century, defeating the Karakhanids, and then the Seljuks.

Like the Karakhanids before them, the Mongols who ruled next allowed Muslim religious leaders to regulate the lives of their believers even though their conquest of Central Asia in 1220 led to the temporary decline of many of the region's leading cities. One leader, Khan Berke (ruled 1255–1266), and his descendants Tudemengu and Uzbek accepted Islam. Berke's conversion is attributed to a Kubrawiya sheikh (*shaykh*) (Sayf ah-Din Baharzi, died 1263). Uzbek, who took the Muslim name Sultan Muhammad Uzbek Khan, made Islam the state religion. From this point on, Islamic rituals began to predominate over previous non-Muslim ones. Baharzi was a disciple of Najm ad-Din al-Kubra (d. 1221), founder of the Kubrawiya. The Kubrawiya remained an important force until the seventeenth century, and many of its rituals were adopted by other Sufi groups in the region.

Mongol (Chingizid) rulers remained in power in Central Asia until the time of Emir Timur (1370–1405), who established the Timurid dynasty that ruled until the sixteenth century. Timur introduced the institution of *sheikh ul-Islam* (the head cleric, or leader of Islam) in Central Asia, which established the head of Islam as an advisor to the ruler, but effectively made religion subordinate to state power.

The Timurid period was also one in which Sufism flourished. Emir Timur personally ordered that the grave of Ahmad Yasawi be turned into a major commemorative complex in 1389. Baha ud-Din Naqshaband (d. 1390) greatly strengthened the movement developed by Yusuf Hamadani (d. 1143) and his disciple Yasawi. The best known disciple of Naqshabandiya, Khoja (Khwaja) Ahror Vali (whose real name was Ubaydalla), died 1490, is said to have given the infant Babur his Muslim name. Babur (1483–1531) went on to establish the Mughal Dynasty in India. Khoja Ahror's son and grandson were with Babur in India and then both returned to Central Asia, where the family preserved vast holdings (belonging to the order) near Samarkand, through the nineteenth century.

A Turkic dynasty, the Shaybanids, defeated Babur in 1500, marking the beginning of the modern Uzbek nation. The Shaybanids were succeeded by another Turkic dynasty, the Astrakhanids, in 1599, and they in turn were replaced by the Mangits in Bukhara (1785) and the Qunrats in Khiva (1804). In general, these centuries were marked by little religious innovation.

This did not affect the standing of Sharia law, as until the Russian conquest of Central Asia in the mid-nineteenth century,[7] the land and peoples of Uzbekistan had been part of *dar al-Islam*, the world of Islam, in which Sharia law dominated. From that time on, until 1991, the population of the region was part of *dar al-kufr* or *dar al-harb*, in which the status of Sharia law was determined by non-Muslims. After the Bolshevik Revolution in the Soviet Union, from the 1920s on, Sharia lost all formal status.

Since independence, which was declared by the Uzbeks on September 1, 1991, and recognized by the international community after the Soviet Union's demise four months later, it is no longer clear whether or not Uzbekistan is part of "the world of Islam." Many Muslims living in the country consider themselves as living in *dar al-Islam* because they are independent, ruled by an Uzbek, and Islam has been restored to a public place in society. They are not troubled by the fact that the constitution declares Uzbekistan to be a secular state; indeed, many of them consider that to be appropriate. For others, though, who consider themselves to be devout Muslims, Uzbekistan is still seen to be a part of *dar al-kufr* or *dar al-harb*, because Sharia has no standing in the country. The overwhelming majority of these people are willing to accept the situation, or to use the strength of their faith to push for an expanded role for Islam in peaceful ways. For a small minority, though, this situation is not acceptable, and they are willing to use force, or consider the use of force, to change it. Uzbekistan has spawned small jihadist movements over the past two decades. The best known is the Islamic Movement of Uzbekistan (*Uzbekiston islomiy haraqati*), or IMU, which has become part of the al-Qaeda network.[8]

Even during the Soviet period, a large proportion of Central Asians considered themselves Muslims. They were taught atheism in school, but what they were taught in those courses had as much credibility as what they were taught in a whole range of other Soviet courses, such as history, philosophy, economics, and communist theory. Many practiced the age-old rituals of the Islamic community: circumcision, Islamic marriage, and burial. Few were aware that these practices were illegal; even professional atheist lecturers in Muslim republics were sometimes unaware that circumcision, save in instances of medical necessity, was a violation of Soviet law.

In addition, there was a much smaller group of devout Muslims who had at least a limited traditional religious education, and from the mid-1940s on, when Soviet authorities reestablished Muslim Spiritual Administrations,[9] a tiny number of Islamic clerics were trained, traveled abroad, and showed the same mastery of religious themes at international religious symposia as Muslim leaders from other parts of the world. They were but one source through which those living in the Soviet Union remained aware of developments in a broader Islamic community.

The collapse of the Soviet Union transformed Islam from a minority faith, a largely suppressed religion of a colonized population, to the majority religion of newly independent populations. Long used to hiding their religious practices, millions of Muslims now felt free to follow the dictates of their conscience, and the leaders of new nations had to figure out how to embrace this in ways that did not threaten their hold on power. So the relationship of Islam to the state remains as contentious a question as ever throughout Central Asia, nowhere more so than in Uzbekistan.

No one has been more focused on this issue than Islam Karimov (Islom Karimov), Uzbekistan's first and, to date, only president. He was quick to recognize the challenge of bringing Islam back under state control, but sought to do so in a way that did not antagonize the majority of believers. Karimov was appointed head of the Communist Party of the Uzbek Soviet Socialist Republic in June 1989, just days after deadly riots in Uzbekistan's Ferghana Valley (Fargona vodiysi).[10] He was chosen as president by the republic's parliament in March 1990 and voted in by the population on December 29, 1991,[11] just four days after the Soviet Union was formally dissolved. While the election was flawed, in these days of turmoil, winning any sort of elite and popular support was a real challenge; party leaders in Kyrgyzstan had been ousted by a Soviet-era parliament,[12] and those in Tajikistan had been dispatched by angry crowds.[13]

What happened in the neighboring countries brought home the message to Karimov that he had to enjoy the support of a substantial portion of his population if he were to remain in power. That strengthened his conviction that political and religious freedoms must be carefully doled out and closely supervised.

Karimov feared that if Uzbekistan "tilted" too far toward Islam, he would be vulnerable to ouster by those who still identified him with the atheist Communist Party that he had long served. He also feared that Islamic appeals were alienating local European and Europeanized populations, many of whom were already leaving the country and whose departure deprived it of desperately needed skills; equally troubling, they might also frighten away potential foreign investors.

Uzbekistan, like the rest of Central Asia, was experiencing a religious revival; new mosques and religious schools opened weekly, and the general popular observance of religious traditions was increasing, even among intellectuals who long had scorn for their more observant rural cousins.

The state was but one of the many actors interested in influencing the development of Islam. Religion was always a major force in Central Asian society, but now it had grown to such proportions that it had begun to acquire political dimensions as well, raising the risk that proponents of "fundamentalist," "Wahhabist,"[14] "radical," or "extremist" Islam would seek control of the state.

These terms have all been invoked imprecisely, both by those with a lot of knowledge about the role Islam plays in Central Asian societies and those with limited knowledge. The specter of an "Islamic" Central Asia—whether one in which Islamic parties actually rule, or just one in which Islamic groups share power peacefully—frightens many inside and outside of the region.

Most interested foreign actors, as well as the leading political figures tied to the Uzbek government, want to tilt events in ways that favor secular actors in Central Asia. This has certainly been the intent behind many of the policies pursued by the Karimov regime, both the socializing efforts designed to portray the state as religion friendly, as long as Islam is properly understood, and the harsh treatment accorded to those who reject the state's right to set these limits.

In this regard, Karimov has much in common with many of his predecessors throughout the region's long history. Traditionally, Central Asia's rulers used Islam more to justify the will of the ruler rather than as the source of their power. While history does not dictate the future, the heritage of Islam in Central Asia suggests that the current wave of Islamic revival is likely to continue and to produce religious figures who will seek to expand the role of Islam in the state.

The behavior of religious believers is difficult to predict because religious belief dictates that people use their conscience as their guide, and individual conscience is a notoriously unpredictable phenomenon. Conscience can drive some to disobey laws, while it persuades others to obey them and bide their time.

Islam is a dynamic faith, and a global one. Theological tensions within the community of believers remained a constant presence throughout the region's Islamic history as fellow clerics termed each other "conservative," "corrupt," or "heretical." At times, this tension came from Sufi leaders; other times from reformist or fundamentalist clerics. Sometimes the center of attack was the state. But always the focus was on bringing believers back to the faith, a faith that was practiced "as it should be."

These debates, however, made no distinction based on the ethnicity or territorial origin of the cleric. This is because Islam, not ethnicity, was the defining identity for the population of the region, until—and for most purposes through—the end of the Russian empire.

When Soviet rule supplanted the Russian colonial administration in Central Asia, religion was viewed as a competing ideological system to communism. If not stamped out, religion at least required firm control. The Bolsheviks were determined that national identity would replace religious identity, and they sharply cut back on the legal status of religion and religious institutions.

By the late 1920s, the mosques and madrasas in Central Asia were closed, if not destroyed. All religious lands were seized by the state. Prominent clerics who weren't jailed or killed went into hiding. The idea that culture in the Soviet Union was "national in form and socialist in content" became an oft-repeated mantra. During World War II, the Islamic and Russian Orthodox religions were allowed to introduce a sharply restricted and well-supervised form of practice; state institutions that monitor religious organizations have survived into independence.

Nonetheless, some people managed to get religious training, and some Central Asians gained access to religious materials written outside of the country. Many of the religious debates going on in other Muslim countries were replicated in Uzbekistan, or at least some Uzbeks were aware of them.

Local religious leaders emerged and influenced religious thinking. Muhammadjon Hindustani (Rustamov) (1892–1989) was a major figure during the Brezhnev years, teaching pupils privately without the permission of the Soviet authorities. One of his contemporaries was Shaykh Muhammad Sodiq Muhammad Yusuf (Muhammad Sodiq ibn Muhammad Yusuf ibn Muhammad Ali), the last Soviet-era *mufti* and the first to lead Uzbekistan's believers after independence. He remains an influential figure and his writings are discussed at length in later chapters. Another religious leader, Shaykh Abduvali qori (Mirzaev), disappeared mysteriously in 1995, but his writings still inspire Uzbek jihadists and his sermons continue to get thousands of downloads on YouTube.[15]

The sermons of each of these men give testimony to the very different understandings about Islam that were being taught in the region and offer very different prescriptions about what is the "right path" for religious believers to pursue. Some of this is the result of the varying experiences that each man had, but there are also fundamental theological differences that separate them. Hindustani believed that principles of tolerance were inherent in Hanafi teachings and placed primacy on the survival of Islam under adverse conditions. Abduvali qori, termed a fundamentalist or Salafist,[16] focused on what he saw as the corruption of local Hanafi practice. Maintaining that he is true to the teachings of the Hanafi school of law, Sheikh Muhammad Yusuf preaches that Muslims must strive toward reconciliation within the faith, reaching out beyond borders. And all three of these men criticized "everyday" or folk Islam, including those of many self-trained Sufis, as little more than superstition.

As Uzbekistan continues to develop in the post-Soviet era, already the majority of its population[17] has no conscious recollection of Soviet rule.

This new generation has been educated in a society that allows for the practice of Islam, teaches respect for Islamic values as part of a secular education, and allows relatively unfettered contact with the broader Islamic world. It was not always so.

RELATIVE ISOLATION: CENTRAL ASIA FROM COLONIZATION TO SOVIET RULE

Until the period of the Russian conquest in the middle of the nineteenth century, territorial boundaries had little meaning in Central Asia. Competing feudal states existed—the Khanates of Khiva and Kokand, as well as the Emirate of Bukhara—in what the Russians termed "Turkestan." Each had a walled city that was shut to outsiders at night and depended on allied nomadic tribesmen for security. But many of their territories were under only nominal control, sometimes encompassing little more than tax collectors coming by to extract feudal dues.

Though no longer serving as centers of religious innovation, the seminaries of Bukhara and Samarkand continued to draw students from Balkh and Herat (in Afghanistan) as well as the more distant cities of Osh and Jalalabad (in Kyrgyzstan) and Turkestan (present-day Kazakhstan), as well as from the Volga region. The Sufi brotherhoods in Central Asia had ties with fellow *murids*[18] and *pirs*[19] in Afghanistan and in Xinjiang, the latter being a very important source of the Naqshabandiya revival in the nineteenth century. Sufi pilgrims would try to visit the various shrines associated with their order—and especially, those associated with their own teachers, if possible—and would enjoy hospitality from the local religious house.

Ties with the more distant Islamic community were limited. Wealthy Central Asians, and many others who were simply devout, made the pilgrimage to Mecca and naturally brought back news of the larger Muslim world, at least insofar as they had access to it through other pilgrims. Most Central Asian pilgrims, however, spent their time with other Central Asians, staying at *kanaqas*[20] run by Sufis from the region[21] or in guest houses of various Central Asian mosques that were part of their *waqf*[22] holdings.

The Central Asians also made contact with a broader community through trade, though most of that trade was of a relatively local character. While some trade existed with India and the Middle East (mostly through India, rather than overland through Iran), trade across the region into Russia and Europe was relatively limited, given the inhospitable conditions in the area. Because convoys of all sorts were subject to attack across the territory of the Emirate of Bukhara, especially the lands inhabited by Turkmen tribes, trade facilitation was an early justification for Russia's incursions into the area.

After the Russian conquest, physical obstacles to travel within Central Asia and beyond the borders of the Russian empire eased. As trade increased, regularly secured routes came into use between India and Central Asia, between China and Central Asia, across Turkestan into Iran, and across the Caucasus and down into Turkey. Pilgrims to Mecca were able to take advantage of these new opportunities. The number of pilgrims traveling on *hajj* increased 130 to 135 percent between 1870 and 1904.[23]

These pilgrimage journeys served as a systematic form of contact between Central Asians and the broader Islamic community. Travel restrictions during this time were physical rather than political, as they were to become during the Soviet period. Because the pilgrims were gone for months (and often even a year or more), the barrier for most potential pilgrims was economic. Although the trip cost less to go overland to India and then by boat to Arabia, the richer Central Asians favored traveling there via Turkey, as it took them through the Caliphate (in Istanbul) and the world's leading center of modern Islamic thinking.

The Russian colonial administration believed that foreign Muslims were a potentially seditious influence, be they English spies in Afghanistan or Ottoman spies in Istanbul, so they planted their own spies among the pilgrims from Russia. Although the literature brought back into the Russian empire could not be distributed legally without passing through censorship, it was not difficult for most materials published in other Muslim countries to pass into local Central Asian hands. A greater challenge to the spread of ideas was the relatively low number of readers.

Central Asians, Azerbaijanis, and Tatars had relatively unimpeded access to the growing forces of Islamic intellectual modernism through the mosques, madrasas, and universities in Istanbul, through pilgrims and traders—the latter more numerous than the former—and from upper-class Turkic speakers who were able to travel from Russia to the Ottoman Empire (and more rarely to Europe) on various forms of personal business. These travelers played a major role in shaping the content and development of the Jadid movement,[24] a movement to reform Islamic education that gained popularity in Central Asia and throughout the Muslim regions of the Russian empire in the late nineteenth and early twentieth centuries. The ideas of Jamal ud-Din Afghani (1838–1897) were obviously very important for the Jadid reformers, although those of Muhammad Abduh (his protégé and founder of the Salafiya), which also came to Central Asia largely through Istanbul, served to influence another group of Central Asian clerics.[25] They were more concerned with reclaiming the teachings of Islam than with the secular political activism that was necessary to reform society.

The Muslims of the Russian empire exchanged ideas among themselves in the mosques and madrasas in St. Petersburg and, to a lesser extent, in Moscow, in Kazan, and even in a more remote and conservative city like Bukhara. They also developed a literary culture in these years and published books and periodicals that discussed religious themes and debated them from the point of view of intellectual modernism. Many of these discussions were about ways to make their tradition-bound Islamic communities more competitive with the rest of the empire, not to mention the world beyond Russia's borders. For many, religion, in one form or another, was understood as the source of the problem. Where they clashed was over whether Islam could be reformed or had to be relegated to a circumscribed position in society.

This divide, rather than the question of ethnicity, was the most fundamental one during the last years of the Russian empire, and it remained the case in the years the first two Dumas (parliaments) were in session (1906–1910). The ethno-territorial principle that applied for representation in the Duma inadvertently served to stimulate the development of ethno-religious agendas among the Muslim communities of the empire.

All this, of course, existed alongside the more traditional Islamic establishment, which continued to teach according to the largely unchanged Hanafi texts. The bulk of the pilgrims coming home simply served to reinforce the influence of Central Asia's clerical establishment.

Some of the people who traveled to Arabia via India were also exposed to more radical teachings, including followers of Sufi Sheikh Shah Waliullah (1703–1762/63) or former students at the "Dar al-Islam" (House of Learning) Madrasa in Deoband. While the Central Asian Islamic elite—especially the younger generation of quasi-Russified intellectuals—were influenced by developments in the Ottoman Empire, ordinary Central Asians were more affected by religious currents in India and Pakistan. Even into the first decade of Soviet rule, students from Central Asia still traveled east or southeast for religious training, going to madrasas in Afghanistan or India where they had contacts. Both the Ottoman Empire and the madrasas of Afghanistan and India offered a wide variety of ideas and religious interpretations for the Central Asians.

These foreign contacts would help save the lives of some of the Central Asian clerical and feudal establishment as they fled Bolshevik rule during the Russian Revolution and Civil War in its aftermath. They were able to take refuge in Afghanistan, and through more difficult passage to Turkey, even on to Arabia (now Saudi Arabia). In addition, the Soviet borders with Afghanistan and China remained penetrable by local residents well into the 1930s, with people in border villages able to smuggle family members back and forth long after that as well.

CLOSING OFF CENTRAL ASIA: STALIN AND THE SOVIET SYSTEM

World War I introduced new and very serious restrictions on contacts between Central Asians and the outside world. More importantly, the Imperial Russian Army's participation in the Triple Entente strained the Russian empire's resources to the breaking point.

Competing authorities were seeking control in Turkestan, but most of the small middle and upper class, including Jadid reformers, supported the Kokand Autonomy government, which was formed during the period of the Provisional Government in St. Petersburg in 1917.[26] This government opposed the Bolshevik Revolution, although many Jadid reformers supported the pro-Bolshevik "people's republics"—which briefly replaced the Emir of Bukhara and the Khan of Khiva—in the areas that had been

Russian protectorates.²⁷ Some even stayed with the Bolsheviks in 1918 when these territories were absorbed into the Turkestan ASSR, which then became part of the Uzbek SSR in 1924.²⁸ In the end, enticed in part by promises of amnesty, most of the reformists sought to make peace with the Soviet system. A few decided to back the *basmachi* (or Freemen's Movement), whose disparate armies were largely defeated by a unified Red Army force that took control of most of Central Asia by 1922.

Many Jadid reformers served in posts in the Soviet education system in particular during the first major education campaigns of the early 1920s. By 1928, however, virtually all were pushed out of the government and prominent posts in the education system. Most were later arrested during Stalin's purges in the 1930s.²⁹

During the anti-religious drives of 1929–1938, even "former" clerics who had lost their mosques and the madrasas were nonetheless classified as "enemies of the people" and treated as such. In general, the clerical establishment was decimated. Some survived, especially those in more remote places, thanks to local protection or their chameleon-like qualities. While maintaining anything resembling even a semiformal *hujra* (from the term for cell or classroom in a madrasa) was too dangerous, small study circles did continue to operate, teaching traditional Hanafi Islam as well as Salafi-style teachings. The latter, represented by the *Ahl-i Hadith* movement—meaning "adherents of *hadiths*"—focused on neglected early texts and rejected the scholastic approach of Central Asia's traditional Hanafi seminaries and the Hanafi school of law in its entirety. It was founded by Shami domulla al-Tarabulsi (Said ibn Muhammad ibn Abd al-Wahid ibn Ali al-Asali al-Tarabulsi), (born in Tripoli, that is, Tarabulus, in 1860, died in 1932, after his arrest). The *Ahl-i Hadith* movement strongly influenced the thinking of Ziyauddin Bobokhon[30] in the 1930s. He eventually served as the second *mufti* of SADUM (the Spiritual Administration of the Muslims of Central Asia and Kazakhstan, or DMU, as it was renamed).

Mufti Ziyauddin Bobokhon remained committed to the belief that the teachings of the prophet were best understood not from his literal words but from the spirit of his writing, through *bil-ray* and *qiyas*.³¹ This was best achieved through study of *hadiths*, particularly in Arabic, a language that Ziyauddin is said to have spoken beautifully.³² The *Ahl-i Hadith* version of Salafism was similar to that of Muhammad Abduh, rather than that of later disciples of his intellectual descendant, Hassan al-Banna (1906–1949). It was purification of Islam for the purpose of the survival of the faith, survival in accommodation to secular society, rather than the kind of politicized Salafism of the last half of the twentieth century. Islam was presented as an integrated whole, while for Hindustani and other traditional clerics of Hanafi teachings, Islam and its local presentation were somehow inseparable.

In the last decades of his life, Hindustani became an adamant defender of local interpretations of Hanafi law, including many of the traditional practices that had derived from it in Central Asia. He argued that modernism and Salafiya fundamentalism both stemmed from conditions quite different from those of Central Asia, where the imperative was ensuring the survival of Islam under the political conditions of the Soviet Union.

His pragmatic argument was derived by practicing *taqlid*, reason based on the imitation of legal precedent. Hindustani's argument was that these "foreign" religious teachings, which rejected the traditional schools of law, be they fundamentalist or modernist, were also derived from local conditions in other countries.

THE OUTSIDE WORLD BEGINS CREEPING IN

A window to the Muslim world was opened slightly with the creation of the Spiritual Administration of the Muslims of Central Asia and Kazakhstan in 1943 and the Mir-i Arab Madrasa in Bukhara in 1945. SADUM was headed by Eshon Bobokhon ibn Abdulmajidkhon from 1943 to 1957.

Although SADUM was created by Soviet authorities, they remained suspicious of its leaders, and so riddled the official religious establishment with spies and kept close watch over the sermons delivered in legally registered mosques. Still, tiny numbers of Soviet citizens, all with ties to SADUM, were allowed to make *hajj*, study abroad, and represent the Soviet Union at international religious conclaves. At the same time, Islamic tracts published abroad found their way into the libraries run by SADUM.

More materials came in from Central Asians working in Soviet embassies and trade missions in Middle Eastern countries. In addition, materials were brought in by exchange students from the Arab world and other

Islamic countries who were attending Uzbek institutions of higher education when the Soviet Union, under Nikita Khrushchev and then Leonid Brezhnev, began to pursue policies of engagement in the Middle East and developing world more generally.[33]

These students apparently brought multiple copies of the literature that was shaking up the Middle East and large parts of the Islamic world, among them the writings of Sayyid Qutb (1906–1966) and Sayyid Abul Ala Maududi (1903–1979),[34] including the former's commentary on the Quran (*fi Zilal al-Quran*).

Muhammad Sodiq Muhammad Yusuf himself wrote about the influence of students from Palestine, Syria, and Egypt in his book *Ixtiloflar haqida*[35] and Abduvali qori as well as others are said to have regularly made trips to Tashkent in the 1970s, five or six times per year, to participate in student-led study groups.

Those organizing these study circles, as well as the burgeoning number of *hujras* offering unsanctioned religious education, kept a low profile. Chance brought me in contact with Fahmi Awadi, reputed to be a Muslim Brotherhood leader, at an international conference in 1992; he spoke of the great frustration he had felt when traveling through Central Asia as a journalist in the late 1970s and early 1980s, that he had found so few Muslims who were able to read contemporary Arabic literature, and far fewer who were knowledgeable about or sympathetic to the literature of the Brotherhood.[36] For his efforts to disseminate this literature, Awadi was declared persona non grata by the Moscow authorities and deported. A great irony is that he admitted to me that he was not aware that study circles existed in Tashkent.

Similarly, I made several trips to Dushanbe when Hindustani was still teaching, but while my local hosts had direct contact with him (he still had ties to the manuscript collection of the Academy of Sciences), they also made it clear that he would have no contact with foreign specialists. Like others running *hujras*, Hindustani took care in selecting his students, realizing that the instruction he was giving them put him and them at risk from local authorities in case any of them reported him or each other to the local security services.

This was a period of religious ferment in the countries just beyond Central Asia's borders, Iran and Afghanistan, and from the late 1970s on it became easier for Central Asian youth to access religious materials. Ordinary citizens were also finding it easier to get information about religion. Foreign radio broadcasts were reaching Soviet audiences with greater frequency, including Radio Gorgan from Iran, which was particularly active throughout the 1980s. Even before the Soviet invasion of Afghanistan, U.S. intelligence seems to have believed that the Islamic republics were the "weak underbelly" of the Soviet Union and tried to disseminate materials (in printed formats as well as on U.S.-sponsored radio broadcasts) about the Central Asian republics' rich Islamic heritage which, these materials emphasized, had been suppressed by their Soviet rulers.

The Iranians also continued to target Central Asia with religious materials even after their own Islamic revolution occurred in 1979. This mostly took the form of Radio Tehran broadcasts; printed materials that were deemed potentially suitable for a Sunni audience were also smuggled in. The Iranians obviously had no help from Washington in these efforts.

Of course, Afghanistan itself was the most ready source of materials on Islam, as nearly a hundred thousand Soviet troops and tens of thousands of support technicians were stationed there for most of the 1980s. That war put thousands of Central Asian servicemen and technical specialists in direct contact with Afghans from both sides, in a society that was not too dissimilar, ethnically or religiously, from their own. Some literature also came from Moscow or other European cities of the Soviet Union and illegal Russian-language translations of Sayyid Qutb's pamphlet "Some Lessons on Islam" and Sayyid Abul Ala Maududi's short "The Basis of Islam" also made their way to Central Asia.

These texts, despite their rather imperfect translations, were read with great interest in the Soviet Union, not only by religious activists, but also by those eager to learn about developments in the Arab world and South Asia more generally. Moreover, given the relative paucity of foreign materials, it is likely that there was considerable appeal attached to "forbidden" literature smuggled into the Soviet Union.

There is no question that the ideas of these writers had a radicalizing effect on that small group of young Central Asians who were interested in learning about religion and religious ideas in the late 1970s and early 1980s. The message was simple: imperialism, colonialism, and communism were all harmful, and a return to the simplicity and purity of Islam in its founding period would be cleansing. The Soviet education system had long stressed that colonialism and imperialism were bad, and the young Central Asians themselves had firsthand experience with some of communism's weaknesses. Thus, if the communists were so vehemently opposed to Islam, then surely there was an implicit purity in Islam that was antithetical to communism—or so these young Central Asians seem to have thought.

At the same time, the "contagion" from contact with Islamists in Afghanistan was nowhere near what many U.S. experts had expected or hoped for. Afghanistan, however, did serve as a source of contemporary literature on Islam, and of Salafist literature in particular.

There were, of course, some who were profoundly affected by this experience. Juma Namangani[37] (born Juma Khojaev, 1969–2001), one of the founders of the Islamic Movement of Uzbekistan, had always claimed that the books he brought back from Afghanistan were the source of his new attraction to Islam. This, in turn, led him to study with Abduvali qori and then go to Tajikistan and fight in the civil war there.

Some Central Asians among the Soviet troops and support personnel did defect to the Afghan cause (as did some ethnic Russians), and these men did get to radical madrasas in Pakistan. They were rather small in number, however. Most seemed to have stayed in Pakistan or Afghanistan until after the fall of the Soviet Union, coming back only in the mid-1990s to lead trainees in Tajik and Afghan terror camps. Small groups of young Muslims were formed, especially among Uzbeks and Tajiks in the Ferghana Valley. They called themselves *Mujaddidiys* (those for renewal) or *Javononi islomi* (the Youth of Islam).

CENTRAL ASIA IN THE PERIOD OF COLLAPSE OF SOVIET RULE

When the iron curtain began to crumble, there was a real hunger to learn about what was going on in the world. For many Central Asians, there was special interest in what was going on in the Islamic community beyond their borders, as many continued to identify themselves as Muslims, even if they were not devout or rarely considered themselves to be devout.

In most communities there were no mosques or madrasas, but frequently an elder was able to teach small groups of young boys how to read the Quran, and sometimes a woman was able to instruct interested young girls as well.

But people wanted more. Hanafi Islam had survived in a kind of intellectual hibernation for much of Soviet rule. In Central Asia, theologians, not to mention ordinary intellectuals, had never grappled with the challenge of trying to adapt Islam to modern life. By definition, it could not be adapted because in the context of the Soviet Union, "modernity," as defined by the state, rejected the very premise that religion had a role in modern society. While few in Central Asia fully subscribed to this view, they ordinarily saw their obligations to their religious heritage as being met by practicing many of Islam's rituals, such as circumcisions, weddings, funerals, and other major life cycle events.

Religion had reemerged semi-clandestinely during the late Brezhnev era, as the state became weaker internally. Eventually, popular pressure effectively forced Mikhail Gorbachev to increase the role of religion in what proved to be a futile effort to restore public support for the Soviet regime.

But initially, only the Russian Orthodox Church was restored to public life. Gorbachev, and even more so his wife, Raisa, was increasingly engaged in a highly public campaign to pour Russian cultural values into the moral and spiritual vacuum created by the years of Soviet misrule. No similar sensitivity was shown toward Islam; indeed, the opposite was true. At a time when Moscow was preparing to celebrate the millennium of Russia's conversion to Orthodoxy, official animus toward Islam even went so far as to prevent sons from attending the funerals of their parents.

The last Soviet census, taken in January 1989, showed that the birthrates of the Central Asian nationalities were still very high and that in a decade Central Asians would account for roughly a quarter of the Soviet Union's population. Soviet sociologists noted that the majority of Central Asians did not know Russian fluently and did not wish to move from their rural homes, where jobs were scarce, to work in the labor-deficient regions of Russia. Many argued that the cause of this reluctance was Islam, the practice of which was more pervasive than was previously thought. Islam was said to breed a form of mental parochialism that led those under its "influence" to prefer to not learn Russian, to serve poorly in the military, and to be potentially disloyal to the Soviet state.[38]

Islamic rituals became more widely practiced, but public instruction in the faith was often relegated to those whose formal religious training was limited. That was something that bothered the clerics associated with SADUM almost as much as it did the authorities in the Kremlin.

This period brought a new generation of clerics to prominence, including Muhammad Sodiq Muhammad Yusuf, who took over as *mufti* of SADUM in 1989. He studied in a *hujra* and in registered Islamic institutions and abroad, as did his colleagues Sayid Abdulloh Nuri and Muhammad-Sharif Khimmat-zoda in Tajikistan and Sodikjon qori Kamalludin (Kamalov)[39] in Kyrgyzstan. They all wanted to raise the level of religious education in Central Asia, and to do so were willing to work within Soviet institutions, at least at first.

From the time of the convening in early 1990 of the popularly elected new Congress of People's Deputies[40] (in which Muhammad Sodiq served), long-held policies were first criticized and then overthrown. At first these legislative debates were covered live, then on a delayed basis, on the second all-USSR television channel. None of these actions had the effect that the Soviet leadership around Gorbachev had desired: the Soviet population was not appeased; new non-governmental organizations kept forming.

While Central Asia's religious revival was quick to develop and rapidly gained momentum, political protests developed much more slowly in Central Asia than in the Baltic republics, Ukraine, or the South Caucasus. There was some ethnic violence in this region; localized disturbances between local Meskhetian Turks and Uzbeks in the Ferghana Valley in 1989, some clashes over water between Kyrgyz and Tajiks in the mountains between the two republics, and fighting between local Chechens and Kazakhs in western Kazakhstan. There were also riots in Dushanbe in early 1990 amid rumors that Armenian refugees from Karabakh would get new housing (ahead of locals long waiting for their new apartments) in Tajikistan's overcrowded capital.

More serious violence occurred the following year, in June 1990, when clashes broke out virtually simultaneously between Uzbeks and Kyrgyz in a number of communities in southern Kyrgyzstan. Had the Uzbek leader, Islam Karimov, not put the full force of the republic's resources under his control, the situation could have deteriorated into all-out war, much as what occurred between the Armenians and Azerbaijanis in the fight over

Karabakh. Political power in Kyrgyzstan was crumbling, and there were all sorts of rumors that nefarious forces in Moscow (from the Communist Party and various security forces) were fomenting the unrest rather than seeking to end it.

In the aftermath of Osh, in particular, Karimov would not have wanted to further rile the already seriously unnerved Uzbek population. At the time, there were no borders separating the Uzbek and the Kyrgyz republics, just traffic outposts, and many Uzbeks had wanted to go into Kyrgyzstan to defend their relatives. Karimov made many trips to the region to try to keep the population from getting too agitated.

The Islamic revival of the late Soviet period appeared virtually unstoppable. Mosques were opening in every *mahalla* (neighborhood community within a city) in Uzbekistan, and in villages, towns, and cities throughout Central Asia. Unsanctioned madrasas were springing up, particularly throughout the Uzbek and Tajik regions.

Public interest in religion grew to an almost insatiable level, with hundreds of unsanctioned locally organized madrasas and mosques appearing seemingly overnight. There was a demand for Qurans in Uzbek. Other religious books sold quickly as well, even if the purchaser was unable to understand much of the argument. Some, including many young people, began experimenting with religion by adopting Islamic dress, beards, no ties for young men, and the *hijab*, or some modification of it, for women. Public observance of religious holidays increased, including the fast at Ramadan, when whole communities would gather at *iftar* celebrations[41] at nightfall all month.

TOLLING THE WARNING BELL: THE TAJIK CIVIL WAR AND THE RISE OF JIHADIST GROUPS IN UZBEKISTAN

As the Soviet Union dissolved, Islam Karimov clearly recognized that he had to make some accommodation to religion in an effort to speed up the process of popular legitimization of both independence and his own rule. He could see that the environment was well-suited to the spread of Islamic fundamentalist ideas. Small numbers of Central Asians had some knowledge of radical Islamic thought, whether it was the ideas of the Muslim

Brotherhood, the teaching of clerics from Pakistan, or the ferment in Iran. Moreover, there was an appeal to trying out these ideas in Central Asia, a kind of desire to appear intellectually fashionable.

Many Hanafi clerics opposed his approach, claiming, as Muhammad Sodiq did in his subsequent writings, that these ideas were fine in the cultural and religious milieu in which they had developed but were not suited to the conditions of Central Asia.[42]

Others, though, sought to increase their own numbers as rapidly as possible to reap the benefits of the changing political environment before they lost control over the growing community of believers (which, incidentally, was becoming more affluent as well, given the legalization of limited forms of private property). Even the subsequent comments of Muhammad Sodiq regarding what was suitable and not suitable to Muslims in Central Asia were more moderate than his attitudes of the late 1980s. During my first meetings with him in 1990 and 1991, he was angrier at the popularity of Obidkhon qori (Nazarov) than he was at odds with his teachings. Obidkhon qori was then the senior imam at the Juma mosque in the old city of Tashkent.[43]

But the advent of the bloody civil war in Tajikistan caused the pendulum to shift in the opposite direction. All of Central Asia's rulers became convinced that secular states had to wield more control over the Islamic communities in their respective countries or risk that secular power would eventually be subordinated to religious authority.

The Tajik civil war was a very divisive event at home, although it created a degree of unity, and a sense of common purpose, among most other Central Asian state rulers, who were willing to contemplate anything short of armed intervention (and had no opposition to Russia's) to contain the unrest in this neighboring state. It also created greater unity among the more radical elements of the region's Islamic leadership.

Many people in the Ferghana Valley, in particular, knew Sayid Abdulloh Nuri as well as the other leaders of the Islamic Renaissance Party (IRP) and wanted to aid them without compromising their position in either Uzbekistan or Kyrgyzstan. Abduvali qori was said to have sent flour and arms from Penjikent (the border with Samarkand Oblast) and through Khujand (in the Ferghana Valley) to Muslims fighting in Tajikistan.

Money was collected in mosques, and clerics offered their blessings to students going off to fight. Dozens, if not hundreds, of young men who had studied in the Islamist (unsanctioned) madrasas in Andijan, Namangan, and Kokand traveled to Tajikistan, some with letters of recommendation from their imams, to swell the ranks of the IRP. Many of them stayed on, forming the first nucleus of the Islamic Movement of Uzbekistan.

After Emomali Rahmon's presidential victory in Tajikistan in 1994, much of the leadership of the IRP fled to Afghanistan with their families. Afghanistan had been a historic site of exile, and the IMU eventually made much of this in its recruiting films, recorded videos, and cassettes that were smuggled into Uzbekistan. One of these films ("The Call") shows a meeting between descendants of Muhammad Alim Khan (the last emir of Bukhara) and the IMU leadership.

Tens of thousands of Tajiks—including whole communities and some families as well as unaccompanied children—initially fled, and a small percentage of them were relocated under sponsorship to Pakistan, where their children were sometimes exposed to neo-Deobandi and other forms of radical Islamic education.[44] Most Tajiks gradually returned home, but the leadership of the IRP remained abroad until the period of intense negotiation and the signing of the agreement of national reconciliation, which took effect in 1997.

Most of the Uzbeks who fought with them also returned home, but a core group of IMU leaders "hid" in the area of Tavildara. They were forced to leave, fleeing to Afghanistan in March 2000 after a year of hard pressure exerted by Uzbek authorities. Most remained there until the U.S.-led bombing attack was imminent, following the attack on the World Trade Center and the Pentagon on September 11, 2001. The IMU ranks regularly thinned and were augmented by recruits from Central Asia, mainly Uzbekistan, some of whom signed up for the promise of regular salaries. Material assistance to the IMU (by that time, the bulk of the former Tajik fighters had been reintegrated into their society) increased substantially after 2000, presumably largely from the group's growing ties to al-Qaeda.

Uzbek authorities have blamed the IMU or its splinter organizations for all of the terrorist attacks on Uzbek soil in 1999, 2000, 2001, 2004, 2005, and 2009, and for incursions into Kyrgyzstan as well.[45] However, the largest unrest, in Andijan, could be said to have only the most tenuous connections with the IMU, through some of the gunmen who participated in the prison attack that set it off. The focus was the Akramiya movement, named for its leader Akrom Yuldoshev, who left Hizb ut-Tahrir in 1993 and never had any relationship with the IMU. On May 12, 2005, a prison holding 23 businessmen allegedly tied to Akramiya was "liberated" by armed gunmen who were seemingly supported by popular demonstrations that were broken up by Uzbek authorities with a high loss of life.

"OUR" ISLAM OR NATIONAL ISLAM IN UZBEKISTAN?

From the first days of independence, it was clear to Uzbekistan's ruling elite that religion would by definition be an important, albeit potentially fluid, component in the evolving state ideology. But the content of the message about Islam and who is empowered to deliver this message has changed over time, depending upon Uzbek leaders' perception of the threat that uncontrolled or unregulated Islamic actors are believed to constitute.

Uzbekistan's religious leaders also are seeking to define the role of religion in Uzbek society. Their focus on the spiritual gives them more all-encompassing goals than those of the government. The clerics have seen *davat* (Islamic missionary work—literally a "call/summons to the faith") as the central focus of their religious responsibility. Some religious leaders define religion and the obligation of believers in ways that enhance the role of religion in the state, while others make religion the yardstick by which state actions are judged.

Some religious leaders have been more vocal than others and even aggressive in pursuing their mission of *davat*, preparing recordings of their sermons or appearing on radio and television in addition to their normal appearances at weddings, circumcisions, funerals, and religious services in mosques.

The growing public role of Islamic leaders is seen as threatening not just by the government but also among many in the secular elite who worry that the implicit link between morality and religion will lead to the ouster of secular figures from leading social and economic roles. This creates a dilemma for Uzbek authorities, who fear using religious leaders to spread their messages, but at the same time realize that securing public loyalty will be impossible without a measured use of religious leaders.

Because of this, the Karimov regime has always sought to identify and then work with sympathetic clerics whom the government believes will espouse a message fully supportive of the state. This would be a message that draws on Hanafi[46] traditions that have long been popular in Central Asia, traditions that are generally associated with religious tolerance and with the need of Muslim believers to obey leaders who come from outside their own religious traditions, as long as those leaders respect Islam.

Government initiatives are also designed to discredit what are deemed to be dangerous religious messages. This is achieved through supervising the licensing or accreditation of religious institutions and those who serve in them, the publication and distribution of religious literature, the content of media, and the commemoration of historical figures. The idea is to do battle against the ideas of the so-called Wahhabis—those who preached a politicized form of Islam, by reemphasizing the importance of "Our [Uzbek] Islam" or such slogans as "Let's protect our religion!" (*Uz dinimizni himoya qilamiz!*), "Let's protect our religion from all enemies!" (*Dinimizni yot kuchlardan saqlaylik!*), and "We shall never give up our sacred religion!" (*Biz muqaddas dinimizni hech kimga bermaymiz!*).[47]

THE GLOBAL ENVIRONMENT CAN'T BE KEPT OUT, NOR IS IT ALL-ENCOMPASSING

The idea that the nature of Hanafi Islam as practiced in Uzbekistan is uniquely national is at odds with the global forces that independence has helped empower.

Uzbeks enjoy greater access to a broader Muslim world than was the case at any time under Soviet rule, as a result of direct ties between Uzbekistan and Muslim majority states, both near and more distant. Turkey was the most aggressive about building ties with the Central Asians. But while President Turgut Ozal spearheaded the effort to present Turkey as an attractive secular model, a wide range of Islamic actors in that country, including the Sufis, traditional Hanafi clerics, Islamists, and representatives of the *Tablighi* movement all became actors on the Uzbek stage as well. Tens of thousands of Uzbeks have made *hajj* since independence, partly funded by the Saudi government. Saudi Islamic philanthropic organizations, some with and some without Saudi government support, sent representatives to the region. Uzbeks were also invited to these countries.

Uzbek clerics get—and regularly accept—invitations to participate in international meetings, and madrasa students have opportunities to study in other Islamic countries.

Foreigners seeking to come to Uzbekistan are subject to more scrutiny now than in the early 1990s. But religious activists are able to slip through, especially if they have bona fide commercial interests to bring them to the country. Uzbeks are now much more careful than they were several years ago about monitoring students who go off to study in the seminaries outside of the Central Asian region; their funding sources in particular are scrutinized. But young Uzbeks who are determined can find other legitimate excuses for leaving the country and arrange funding upon arrival. Supervision of those going on *hajj* has also increased markedly since 2001, but Uzbeks who are concerned that they will be denied a place on Uzbekistan's formal quota of *hajjis* can go to Kyrgyzstan and travel with Kyrgyz pilgrims.

For all these differences, though, today's community of believers has many of the same divisions as in Soviet times. The tension between "folk Islam"—popular practices—and religious teachings continues, but within a religious landscape that is much more complex than it was in Soviet times despite the continued presence of a state that seeks to "guide" religion in the service of state goals.

In some ways, freed of Soviet-era ideologically based social restrictions, Uzbekistan has become a more traditional society, and one that is more tied to its Muslim heritage than was true for most of the twentieth century. Yet at the same time, it is a country living in the twenty-first century, where Uzbeks regardless of their political ideology are able, if they are so inclined, to find links to a global community through the Internet, television and radio, and travel. Establishing these links can be costly, and differential economic opportunity plays a much greater role in Uzbekistan today than it did at any time during Soviet rule.

How this will all play out in post-Karimov Uzbekistan remains to be seen. Much will depend on what will happen during the last years of Karimov's rule, whether the state holds in neighboring Kyrgyzstan, whether peace and stability are introduced in Afghanistan, and whether economic opportunities for Uzbeks begin to catch up with their economic expectations.

2

ISLAM AND THE STATE
BEFORE SOVIET RULE

RELIGIOUS AUTHORITY AND THE STATE BEFORE COLONIAL RULE

Since the introduction of Islam, Central Asia's rulers have had to contend with Islam and its understanding of "just rule" as they have sought to bolster their own authority. Rulers from within the region have sought to co-opt Islam to serve their own purposes, either through the choice of a *sheikh ul-Islam* or by favoring clerics of one theological school or Sufi order over those of another. Conquerors from outside of the region, such as the Russians or the Soviets after them, sought to sharply limit Islamic authority or attempt to make it fully subservient to secular rule.

Central Asia's religious leaders became important mediators between state and society. The task of secular rulers has been made somewhat easier by the teachings of the Hanafi theological-juridical school, which have dominated in this region as early as the writing of *Al-Aqaid* (Dogmatics) by Najm ad-Din Abu Hafs Umar ibn Muhammad ibn Ahmad an-Nasafi (1068–1142).[1] Hanafi-Maturidi theologians in Central Asia accepted the idea that Muslims could be ruled by someone who was either a non-believer (*ghayr-i din*) or an infidel (*kafir*), so long as that ruler did not close the mosques and madrasas, and as long as he allowed Muslims to observe their rituals and be judged by Sharia.[2] Rulers gained further flexibility as the Hanafi school allowed a large role for customary law (*adat*) and for ritual (*salat-namaz*), although local clerics have periodically attempted to curb this practice in favor of emphasis on the Quran and *hadiths*.

Central Asia's Sufi leaders made a unique contribution to the religious debate on state-society relations. They often rejected or distanced themselves from their rulers and the legalistic formalism of worship sanctioned by pro-establishment clerics. The degree of politicization of Sufi movements varies from setting to setting. The history of some Sufi orders has been characterized more by open political confrontation, but there is a contestation of religious authority that is implicit in all Sufi movements, which makes them tacitly political.

From the eighteenth century on, Sufi-led protest movements were often found in societies that were confronted with the encroachment of Western ideas or colonialism. Central Asia under the Russians was no exception. Small Sufi-led revolts took place in the nineteenth century, and Sufi *ishans* (*eshons*) led some of the guerrilla fighting against Bolshevik rule during the civil war. But throughout most of Uzbekistan's history Sufism was closely identified with the state.

Many of the attitudes toward the relationship between church and state date from the time of Timur (lived 1336–1405; ruled 1370–1405). Timur sought to use religion as a critical part of the ideological glue that held his disparate empire together. He also took definitive steps to begin institutionalizing Islam, and in so doing, he subjugated it to the control of what was effectively temporal power. While Timur ruled as "Sultan zul Allah" (the shadow of Allah on earth), he created the institution of *sheikh ul-Islam*, who named the *qadi kalan* (senior judge), the imams of the main mosques and madrasas, and even the heads of the Sufi *tariqas* (orders), whether or not the *sheikh ul-Islam* was a Sufi. The institution of *sheikh ul-Islam* was preserved until the time of Soviet rule.

The establishment of the Muslim Spiritual Administration, first by the Russians and then by the Soviets, was in part an effort to redefine the institution of *sheikh ul-Islam* so it would facilitate non-Muslim rulers governing Muslim populations. This institution continues through to the present day, now as the Muslim Spiritual Administration of Uzbekistan. Also persisting is the tension it created for Muslim religious leaders, not all of whom are willing to be convinced that their acceptance of rule by a *kafir* is consistent with their religious obligations. The teachings of

Hanafi Islam make this proposition more acceptable but do not ensure that the secular ruler will be viewed as just.

CENTRAL ASIA'S SUFI LEGACY[3]

In the period before Timur, some seminal Sufi leaders played a major role in defining state-society relations. A number of Kubrawiya leaders left a distinctive mark in the history of the region through their political and economic activities. One example is Sheikh Sayf ad-Din Baharzi of Bukhara, who died in 1263. He was a well-known and much respected figure of the period just after the Mongol conquest. A disciple of Najm ad-Din al-Kubra, he remained in Bukhara after it was ravaged by the Mongols. Baharzi played a key role in the economic revival of the city and used his and others' restored economic fortunes to fund the city's spiritual revival, finding funds for the building of new madrasas. Moreover, he reached out to the local Chingizid governors, and his surviving correspondence with them records his efforts to appease them and to avoid other attacks on the city and the vicinity.

The Kubrawiya remained an important force in what is now western Uzbekistan and eastern Turkmenistan until the seventeenth century. By that time, its structural cohesion (the linkage between religious doctrine, economic power, and political support) was almost fatally weakened. By the nineteenth century, the Kubrawiya had almost disappeared, but by then most of its teachings and many of its ritualistic practices had been adopted by other Sufi groups in the region.

The Yasawiya, another significant religious force at this time, was composed of "common Turks" whose ritual practices were often borrowed from their cultural and religious traditions. The movement was founded by Khoja (Khwaja) Ahmad Yasawi, who died in 1166 in the city of Turkestan (in Kazakhstan).[4] The emphasis of Yasawi's followers was focused even more than the other Sufi groups in the region on the use of mysticism and the need for abstention from worldly pleasures, and Yasawiya *ishans* largely insulated themselves from politics.

One exception was the period of political activity by Yasawiya sheikhs in Transoxiana in the sixteenth century, when their behavior was strongly influenced by the leaders of the traditionally more active Naqshabandiya. Even that did not last long, and by the eighteenth century, the Yasawiya had largely disappeared from Central Asia as an organized political force, although some Yasawiya groups remained in Turkey.[5]

Central Asia's politically most influential Sufi movement has been the Naqshabandiya, which is based on the teachings of Abu Yusuf Hamadani (Hazrat Abu Yaqub Yusuf Hamadani), a twelfth-century figure who built on the teachings of Yasawi, and whose disciples were called Khwajagan. They included most prominently Abd al-Khaliq Ghijduvani[6] (d. 1179), and later Baha ud-Din Naqshaband (who died in 1389, came from Kasr-i Hinduvan near Bukhara, and is buried just outside that city). The latter's contribution was so significant that his followers were then referred to as Khwajagan-Naqshabandiya and eventually just Naqshabandiya. It took some five or six generations for the Naqshabandiya to reach beyond the Bukharan oasis.[7]

Although there is little historical evidence to support this, the Naqshabandiya tradition holds that Sheikh Sayyid Amir Kulal (d. 1371), a teacher of Baha ud-Din Naqshaband, helped inspire Timur to set off on his conquests. Naqshaband himself is also reputed by the Naqshabandiya's teachings to have been in communication with Timur.

Baha ud-Din Naqshaband's most famous statute allows for "seclusion in society" (*khalwat dar anjuman*). In other words, adherents are not required to leave the society or to isolate themselves from it, but to seek seclusion within their hearts as they strive for spiritual purification. Even more important for shaping the political and economic roles that the movement played in the history of the region, adherents are urged to actively participate in the life of the community—trading, manufacturing, farming—while contemplating God constantly in their hearts.

The Naqshabandiya's process of initiation was less rigorous than that of others. Rather than a complex series of spiritual exercises and lengthy seclusion, initiation for Naqshabandiya involved only "extending one's hand" to the sheikh and repenting of one's sins; this was followed by completing a lesson on how to commemorate God. After joining, new brothers were sworn to continue to perform *zikr* (an act of remembering God) and could continue to take direction from their teacher while remaining part of society and carrying on their business.

After Baha ud-Din Naqshaband, the next most influential person in the history of the movement is Khoja Ahror Vali (lived 1404–1489 or –1490). Khoja Ahror served as the role model of a Sufi sheikh who was also a politically influential leader.[8] All modern Naqshabandiya sheikhs in Central Asia, Turkey, and elsewhere begin the chain of their spiritual succession (*silsila*) with Khoja Ahror, who is associated with the idea of a "just Sharia." His tomb in Khwaja-yi Kafshir, a village about four kilometers east of Samarkand, has always been a popular pilgrimage destination. Even under Soviet-imposed atheism, the mosque adjacent to his tomb was never closed because the authorities feared the public outcry that would have resulted from such an action.[9] Since independence, Khoja Ahror has been granted an honored and public status.

Bakhtiyar Babadjanov maintains that Khoja Ahror's religious justification for politicization of the brotherhood's activity was clear. He writes, quoting Khoja Ahror:

> The times have worsened, and therefore, the best deed is to be with the court of the ruler, so that one can help the people and the repressed.

And:

> One should go to the rulers having raised the religion of the prophets to its limits, so that their throne and crown appeared insignificant compared to the eminence of the faith.[10]

Khoja Ahror also introduced what has been an enduring debate in Uzbekistan through to the present day, in his criticism of the Chingizid and Timurid practice of elevating *adat* law (customary law, law of the steppe) as the law of the state, as well as its dominion over Islamic laws (based on the Quran and the *hadiths*).

According to Bakhtiyar Babadjanov, Khoja Ahror was the first spiritual authority to push for the submission of state and legal norms to Islamic laws and for the establishment of a state order based on religious, or Sharia, rules. To achieve this, he believed a ruler should be well versed in Islamic laws, and, more importantly, should follow them.

Khoja Ahror also introduced to Naqshabandiyas the concept of a single regional leader of the brotherhood (*Pishva-ye tariqat*). With all small brotherhoods unified under the control of a single leader, the creation of this position strengthened the order institutionally, giving it the characteristics of a well-organized order, with a clearly defined hierarchy. Any attempts at independence by petty sheikhs were severely punished.

Babadjanov maintains that Khoja Ahror also introduced a new ethical norm, stipulating that the sheikh and members of the brotherhood could and should be wealthy. At the same time, however, they should have "their hearts not tied to their wealth." Khoja Ahror himself had extensive *waqf* properties that he acquired sometime after 1470. He left a mosque and madrasa in Tashkent, a madrasa in Samarkand, and the *kanaqa* shrine complex outside of Samarkand where he was buried. He increased the value of these holdings by setting up deeds for the purchase of property to revert to *waqf* holdings upon his death. Jo-Ann Gross notes that as late as 1884, the Ahrori *waqf* trust earned income from 800 tenants living in houses that the trust controlled in Tashkent.[11]

Babadjanov argues that Khoja Ahror most often used "pacification from the position of force," supported by his own economic might and that of his supporters as well as his authority as a spiritual leader. Khoja Ahror was also a spokesman for a group of clerics who seemed to have enjoyed the wide support of merchants, craftsmen, and other strata of the population.

From the late fifteenth century on, the history of the Naqshabandiya became more like a narrative of the political activities of the heads of Sufi clans than of a spiritual and philosophical movement. Under the influence of the Naqshabandiya, from the sixteenth century on, leaders of other Sufi brotherhoods started to get actively involved in politics, leading to competition among brotherhoods or orders. Even in Khoja Ahror's lifetime, there was a struggle among his sons for the title of "Head Sheikh," each son with his own armed supporters.

Babadjanov argues that the new political role played by prominent Sufi sheikhs also led to the deterioration of the movement and to the introduction of the very element of spiritual decay that these orders were created to root out from Islam.

As politically influential Sufi dynasties—which included the lines that followed Khoja Ahror and Makhdumi Azam (d. 1542) as well as the Juybariya sheikhs in Bukhara, whose progenitor was Khoja Islam (d. 1563)—

started to develop close personal ties with the families of ruling dynasties, they ceased being capable of independent political activity.

It is the opinion of Bakhtiyar Babadjanov that the politicization of Sufism in Transoxiana led to its becoming a state-like structure, and that, as in the Central Asian states of the sixteenth and seventeenth centuries themselves, this ensured that the Sufi movements would suffer the same kind of stagnation that characterized the khanates.[12]

By contrast, Annemarie Schimmel, in her landmark study *Mystical Dimensions of Islam*, simply notes that the Naqshabandiya played a major role in Central Asian politics in the seventeenth and eighteenth centuries, not characterizing it as either stagnating or innovative.[13]

The Naqshabandiya experienced a spiritual revival in the middle of the eighteenth century, due largely to the vibrancy of its Indian branch, The Mujaddidiya, and its leader, Ahmad Sirhindi (d. 1624), who was known as "Mujaddad alf i-sani" or "Reformer of the Second Millennium" (he lived at the beginning of the second millennium of the Muslim chronology). Sirhindi studied with the Transoxianian Naqshabandiya and with the sheikhs of the Qadiriya in India, and he combined their ritual practices. He borrowed the traditions of social and political activity and links of basic spiritual succession from the Transoxianian Naqshabandiya. The Mujaddidiya was effectively a reformed version of the Naqshabandiya.

The Naqshabandiya then simplified its rituals, widened its social base, and re-engaged in the political and economic life of the community. But then, in turn, the creation of a broader, more diverse group led to the relaxation of the established strict ethical norms and Sufi statutes. That created a widening gap between the leaders and disciples and set off a struggle for power within the brotherhood, which quickly became fused with the competitions among the ruling dynasties.

RELIGION AND THE STATE IN THE KHANATES

Adeeb Khalid writes of how Shaybani Khan's successor, Ubaydulla Khan (d. 1540), traveled to the shrine of Ahmad Yasawi in Turkestan in the early days of Uzbek rule and promised to rule according to Sharia precepts if victorious against Babur.

In Khalid's opinion, Ubaydulla Khan thus restored the Timurid relationship between religion and state authority. He commissioned Faizullah Ruzbihan, a scholar from Shiraz (Iran), to compose his *Suluk ul-muluk* (conduct of kings), which set forth the idea that "political authority is an absolute necessity and therefore a religious obligation." A just ruler, according to Faizullah, protects Sharia by appointing properly learned men to serve as *sheikh ul-Islam* and *alem al-ulama* (learned of the learned).[14]

This structure continued as the Uzbek dynasty split into three competing khanates: the Khanates of Khiva and Kokand and the Emirate of Bukhara. Claims of descent from Chingis Khan were still the most important source of political legitimacy. Hence the "Emirate" of Bukhara, as the ruling Mangit dynasty, could not claim descent from Chingis Khan, and so was not a Khanate. At the same time, though, rulers often attached honorifics to their name, such as Emir al-Muminin (Commander of the Faithful), to convey a high religious status.

Religious institutions were at the core of all social institutions as well. In the 1860s, when Tashkent fell to the Russian troops, there were said to have been some 600 functioning mosques and about 120 madrasas in the old city of Tashkent.[15] Most of them were small and were called *mahalla*. The larger mosques also served as centers and meeting places for elders and religious leaders and were called *qurultoy*. Similarly, in the mid-nineteenth century, the city of Kokand had 300 mosques, 120 religious (primary) schools, and 40 madrasas for some ten thousand households.[16]

The interpretation of Sharia that was common in Central Asia at this time had been seriously eroded by local customary practices (*urf wa adat*), especially those associated with surviving practices of some of the early Sufi orders, whose leaders strongly opposed efforts to make judicial decisions better reflect traditional Hanafi teachings.[17] The influence of *urf wa adat* was so strong that Bakhtiyar Babadjanov complains that intellectual Sufism had been almost completely overshadowed by folk Sufi practices, such as *ziyorats* (visits or pilgrimages) to shrines of distinguished Sufis, and that the Naqshabandiya had effectively become one with the institutions of the state.

As a result, Babadjanov argues, from the eighteenth century on, jurisprudence and, more important, the local system of education and theological debate, looked too far inward, becoming scholastic rather than staying in touch with the needs of the Islamic community. For this reason, Babadjanov says, it became common for commentators in the first half of the nineteenth century to claim that "the spring of the Sharia has dried up."[18]

These kinds of concerns were the preoccupation of Central Asia's elites, both religious and quasi-secular. For the population in Central Asia, there was no uncertainty; they believed themselves to be living in *dar al-Islam*, the world where they placed their trust in their religious elders to guide their spiritual lives. When the Russians began their Turkestan campaign in the mid-1860s, the Emir had mobilized his troops to fight a "holy war." But Adeeb Khalid argues that this was only because clerics in Bukhara and Samarkand had pressured the Emir to go to battle to avenge the defeat of the armies of the Khan of Kokand by Russia in nearby Jizzakh.[19]

The Emir's forces proved no match for those of the Russians, and in 1868 he capitulated, accepting protectorate status. Once defeated, he tried to "play the religion card" to his own advantage, seeking to convince his own population that he was a defender of their traditional faith and arguing to the Russians (who installed a political agent/resident) that he was all that separated them from a "fanatical" population.[20] (This strategy was repeated, after a fashion, by the leaders of the Central Asian republics a century later in the Brezhnev period, as they sought to persuade Moscow to accept their weak enforcement of social policies that targeted religion.)

The Emir's policies of accommodation to the Russians led to periodic expressions of hostility by some of the country's clerics. Some clerically inspired unrest in April 1871 even made it onto the pages of the *New York Times*, albeit with some delay until July 1871.[21] Generally, though, the *sheikh ul-Islam* appointed by the Emir in consultation with leading *ulama* (class of local clerics) managed to keep control over the situation.

The Russian conquest served to open up Bukhara and Khiva to outside influences almost as much as in the rest of Central Asia.

Students from Central Asia and elsewhere in the empire were free to travel to study in Bukhara, and in fact in some ways it was more conducive to do so now, as the trip between the Muslim regions of Russia and Bukhara was much safer given Russian control of the now expanded trade routes. But Adeeb Khalid reports that by the turn of the twentieth century, the number of madrasas in Bukhara had dropped to 80 with only 22 offering religious instruction. The others were little more than dormitories that generated income for the *waqfs* that owned them.[22] This, too, was evidence of the religious decline that Babadjanov reports.

RELIGION AND THE STATE IN RUSSIAN TURKESTAN

The Russian authorities wanted to rule, but not necessarily "civilize," these new Muslim populations. This was a switch from the sixteenth and seventeenth centuries. When the Russians conquered the Tatar khanates, they had been quite aggressive in their treatment of the Muslim populations, banning the construction of new mosques, other times razing mosques and even forcing conversions of the Muslim population.

But by the time of Catherine the Great (reigned 1762–1796), Russian authorities had decided to largely ignore Islam, allowing the Islamic community to be partly self-regulating under the administration of a head cleric who was appointed, nominally by a body of clerics but in reality by Russian authorities. The Spiritual Administrations answered to the Ministry of Internal Affairs (after 1832) generally through the local administration. They chose *qadis* (*qozis*) (the judges of Sharia) and had responsibility for overseeing the maintenance of mosques, madrasas, and the publication of religious materials.

The first Muslim Spiritual Administration was established in Kazan at the end of the eighteenth century. It served as a prototype for regulating the affairs of Muslims throughout the empire. The Orenburg Spiritual Administration (located in Ufa) was created as the governing body for the Muslims of the Volga region and Siberia in 1788. Central Asians living in the Steppe region[23] were made subject to it as well. Those in Turkestan[24] fell under the authority of the local *qadi kalan*.

There is no question that the Russian colonial authorities sought to limit the role of Islamic institutions in Turkestan, but at the same time they had no interest in replacing them with Russian institutions. The Russian authorities also sought to avoid the prolonged struggle for control that they had experienced in the north Caucasus in the first decades of the nineteenth century.

To the Russian bureaucratic mind, the Central Asians, or Turkestanis and *sarts* (urban dwellers) as they were then known, represented an "alien" population. For that reason, they believed that order would best be maintained through the use of traditional "intermediaries," in this case religious authorities, who had long served as the pillar of moral and judicial authority in the community. These "intermediaries" were authorized to exercise their traditional authority at the behest of the colonial administration.

The Russian authorities restricted the application of Sharia to social and family affairs, and only if both parties to a dispute were Muslim. All of the indigenous population was considered to be Muslim,[25] regardless of whether people were religious or professed their faith. Not all Turkestanis were happy with this situation and on occasion turned to the Russian authorities to review or annul decisions made by the Sharia courts, but the overwhelming majority of the indigenous population did in fact consider themselves to be Muslim.

The biggest restriction to be introduced was the elimination of the *zakot*, the alms that Muslims were expected to offer to religious institutions. Muslims could make voluntary religious donations, but mandatory taxation became the exclusive right of the colonial government. This meant that religious institutions became even more dependent upon the earnings of *waqf* holdings, which were essentially frozen by the colonial authorities. *Waqf* holdings, grants of land, and other forms of property made to ecclesiastic institutions could not be expanded although they retained their tax-exempt status. Traditionally these awards were made by the rulers. Colonial authorities would not make such awards, and they also restricted the religious institutions from expanding their holdings with their own funds. In addition, the administrators of the *waqf* holdings had to be appointed, or their appointment approved, by local Russian authorities. The same was true of Sharia court judges and the faculty at madrasas. In much of Turkestan, the procedure for appointment seems to have been left in the hands of clerics themselves, constituted in committees, and their choices ratified by local authorities.[26]

Waqf land included property deeded to religious orders by their followers, both gifts and in-kind payment of *zakot*, as well as the lands on which mosques, schools, and other religious buildings were situated. As a result, many religious orders held agricultural lands equal in size to those of large individual landowners, but unlike the individual landowners, their property and the income it produced was tax-exempt. Not only did the clerical establishment lose the right to accumulate new land, over time, but the status of the existing lands also began to be scrutinized. This was accomplished through the "Revision of *Waqf* Properties." Many mosques lost their *waqf* possessions. Moreover, construction of new religious establishments and *waqf* provision were not allowed unless a special resolution was obtained from the commission with a governor-general.[27]

The income of the existing *waqfs* was very much dependent on how they fared from the changing economic conditions that resulted from Russian policy. The policy introduced cotton cultivation and seriously expanded trade but at the same time sharply restricted the production of food crops—and *waqfs* often owned farmland, houses, businesses, and warehouses. Robert Crew's research highlights the sharply divergent fates. In Andijan, *waqf* revenue in support of local madrasas came close to tripling from 1892 to 1908. But Crew also reports that Russian officials in Ferghana—concerned that many of the Islamic schools were too poor to function properly, putting social discipline at risk—suggested levying a one percent tax on *waqf* income to be used to support the poorer *waqf* endowments.

Russian authorities had introduced so many restrictions on Islamic institutions that it was a legitimate question as to whether the Turkestanis were still living in a Muslim society. This question was not a minor one for devout Muslims, for if they were not, religious injunctions might impel them to resist Russian rule and oppose the will of the colonial authorities.

This seems to have been a question of real concern to influential Central Asian intellectuals. Hisao Komatsu, an expert in nineteenth-century Islam, cites the example of Muhammad Yunus bin Muhammad Amin Taib (1830–1905). Taib, who was appointed as a *qadi* in Kokand in 1886 and had earlier served as commander in the Kokandi army in the campaigns against Russia, wrote to admonish Turkestanis against rebelling, claiming that Turkestan was part of the *dar al-Islam*. Taib had traveled to Afghanistan, Russia, and England as an emissary of the Khan of Kokand. He is quoted by Komatsu as writing that:

> At present, the population of the Ferghana Valley and Turkestan should make use of their positive conditions as much as possible. This country can be con-

sidered Dar al-Islam, where Muslim qadis and officials work. Islamic law, Sharia, is enforced by those in power. It is a great situation for them to be able to solve any legal issues according to Sharia. They should give thanks....

For Taib, the deciding factor is whether Muslim clerics and judges continue to exercise their authority. The choice in effect, is theirs. Taib continues:

... it is known that if [Muslim, KH] officials neither undertake work nor accept the responsibilities of their offices, and Christian governors who rule these countries leave legal matters in the hands of Christian judges, and other civil affairs in the hands of Russians, then this province would become Dar al-Harb.[28]

Overall, most of Central Asia's religious leaders accepted the terms offered them during the period of Russian colonization; though it left their power structure weakened, it remained essentially intact. As a result, a kind of religious aristocracy was able to perpetuate itself in Central Asia, and its membership came heavily from the traditionally powerful Sufi families.

Most local Sufi figures of authority of the nineteenth and twentieth centuries were descendants of Sufi family clans; in the Ferghana Valley, for example, they were descendants of Makhdum Azam; in Samarkand and Bukhara, they were descendants of Khoja Ahror and the loud *zikr* sheikhs. Some smaller groups (Mujaddidiya, Qalandariya, and Qadiriya) remained active in Bukhara and in Surkhandarya (Surkhandaryo), Karategin, Hisar—territories that had been transferred to the Emirate of Bukhara when protectorate status was negotiated. A number of highly regarded Sufi figures remained, including Mavlana Imlavi and Khoja Kirmani in Bukhara and Ishan It-Yimas and Abdurahmanjon in Tashkent. In Andijan, a group was led by Malana Makhdum, himself a descendant of Makhdum Azam. One of its members, Madamin Bek, later headed the longest armed resistance to the Red Army troops, as part of the so-called *basmachi* movement. But Madamin Bek himself was not a Sufi leader of any particular spiritual standing.

Descendants of these families and clans were called *khoja* (*khwaja*), *khoja zadeh* or *ishans*, as they are still called today. They were and still are considered heirs of their ancestral traditions. They were privately tutored, usually in their relatives' homes, and were educated in Sharia studies (Quran, *hadith*, dogma, *fiqh*[29]). These clans were secluded, married only within similarly high-ranking families, and were considered "blue-blooded" (*Oq suyak*, or white bone). Now, as in the past, most prominent clerical families in Central Asia, whether or not the current generation of leaders are themselves adherents of the Sufi way, also are "White Bone."[30] This tightly integrated family structure has allowed them to continue to play a significant role in the preservation of Sufism, its traditions and rituals in Soviet times.

RELIGIOUSLY INSPIRED UNREST IN CENTRAL ASIA

In many countries, Sufism provided anti-colonial movements with an organizational structure, formed over Sufism's centuries-long existence and based on the absolute submission of a disciple to his teacher. Sufism never successfully played that role in Central Asia, however, perhaps because the colonial experience was not long enough, perhaps because the economic crises that Central Asian society experienced as a result of colonial economic policy were not dire enough. Most important, perhaps it was because of the Russian administration's relatively hands-off policy toward the Muslim population, which allowed most social issues to be decided by local judges according to Islamic law.

In times of unusual stress, tempers flared, such as during the 1892 cholera epidemic. Residents of Tashkent's old city protested required sanitary inspections and quarantine measures, seeing them as a Russian plot to poison their water. The Russians had long opposed the local practice of placing cemeteries in densely populated residential areas, and so many old city residents saw the new health measures as an excuse to drive them out of their homes. A peaceful protest by the local population became violent when Cossack troops and local Russian residents of the new city turned on the protesting old city residents. But there was no clear religious subtext to the protests.

Nor was there a clear religious subtext to Central Asia's deadliest riots: the draft riots of June 1916, when local Russian garrisons were emptied of troops in an effort to put down protests by local Central Asians (mostly Kyrgyz and Kazakhs) in the Ferghana Valley, and in the Chu River valley. These protests were provoked by an order calling for the raising of troops to serve in labor battalions alongside the Russian Imperial forces on the German front. Many Central Asians believed that the draft was simply an excuse to free up more farmland for Russian and Ukrainian settlers who were taking up the offer of government-provided homesteads.[31] The Kyrgyz refer to this as the *urkhun*, or exodus, as several hundred thousand Central Asians were forced from their homes, many fleeing to Xinjiang and some then to Turkey, while untold numbers—maybe even 100,000—were killed. While those fleeing sought refuge in *dar al-Islam*, the causes and the way the uprising manifested itself had little to do with religion.

The one Sufi-inspired uprising in Central Asia occurred in May 1898 in Andijan, the very city that more than a century later, in May 2005, was the site of the largest protest ever to have been made against Uzbek President Islam Karimov. Although its causes may also have been primarily economic, the Andijan Uprising of 1898 was the only significant violent event during the Russian colonial period that had an explicitly religious tone. And like the 2005 events, suppression of the protest had a lingering political effect.

The 1898 uprising was organized by Dukchi Ishan (Muhammad-Ali [Madali] Sabir),[32] a disciple of a provincial Naqshabandiya-Mujaddadiya sheikh, Sultan Khan-tura. Dukchi Ishan was born in 1850 or 1851 in the Shahidan settlement, near Margilan (Margilon), to a family of a hereditary manufacturer of spindles (a *dukchi*), from which he took his nickname. In his youth, he accompanied his father to Samarkand and Bukhara, where he was left with local *mullahs* (Islamic clerics) and taught the basics of Arabic grammar. While there, he also read the Quran. When he was about fifteen or sixteen, he became a disciple of the Naqshabandiya sheikh Sultan Khan-tura in a settlement called Tajik.

Dukchi Ishan wrote that at the age of twenty-six, his *pir* granted him the right to begin training others. Two years later, he was "raised to a white felt" by the closest followers of Ishan Sultan Khan-tura, a well-regarded Naqshabandiya-Mujaddidiya sheikh,[33] which meant that Dukchi Ishan was recognized as *khalifa* (spiritual successor) of his teacher and that he acquired a spiritual connection with the sheikhs of the brotherhood. Dukchi Ishan moved to Mingtepa (35 kilometers southeast of Andijan) with several disciples of his late *pir*, as well as the remains of Ishan Sultan Khan-tura.

When he was around thirty-four years old, Dukchi Ishan went on *hajj*. After a year of living in Mecca, he returned to Mingtepa, where he set up his *kanaqa*, which included a mosque, school, library, a room for guests, a kitchen, and a stable. These were built with the help of resources of his *murids*. The *kanaqa* became a magnet for many who were critical of the Russian colonial authorities and those who served in the local bodies of "self-administration" (including *qadi* courts).

Initially Dukchi Ishan was against any call to immediate action or suggestions that local Russian settlers should be attacked. In fact, at the outset, he pressed hard for order, claiming that only universal *ghazavat* (holy war) would change the political situation. With time, and in the absence of other political outlets, support for Dukchi Ishan grew in other cities and villages of the Ferghana Valley, and he appointed formal deputies to manage the "affairs of brothers" (*yaran*). Gradually, in the face of deteriorating economic conditions that were caused by the transformation of the centuries-old subsistence economy, his position toward *ghazavat* began to change.

Bakhtiyar Babadjanov collected archival information about a meeting of *murids* in Osh district (of which the Andijan region was a part), held in early 1898, in which Dukchi Ishan was announced a successor of Allah's messenger with a right to declare *ghazavat* and duties of "decreeing the right conduct and banning reprehensible conduct" (*al-amr bi-l-maruf va-n-nahii an al-munkar*). This document was then changed by Dukchi Ishan, who named himself "*khalifa* of master Umar ibn al-Khattab (Al-Faruk)," to signify that he, too, was intending to "wage justice."

Using this document, Dukchi Ishan made an appeal to elders of Uzbek and Kyrgyz clans, and even to several officials of the organs of local government, to invoke *ghazavat*. But while many expressed sympathy with the notion, most who received the document either demanded more time for the preparation of *ghazavat* or rejected the appeal altogether.

There is no question about the political nature of Dukchi Ishan's message. The community around him consisted mostly of peasants, victimized by the colonial administration's land policy, under which Russians arrived from other parts of the empire and were awarded farms on what had always been locally held lands. He urged his followers to use the Sufi promise to "defend Sharia" to seek religious recourse and protection against the Russians. Dukchi Ishan also aspired to stimulate a sense of struggle among his supporters, the *ghazi*, not only "for the land and pastures of fathers and grandfathers," but also "for the beliefs of ancestors."

Babadjanov writes of such matters as how knowledge of the fundamentals of Islam was limited, including of the basic rituals of daily prayer and fasting. He considers that those who gathered around Dukchi Ishan reflected the major transformations that had occurred in Sufism, especially in the Naqshabandiya-Mujaddidiya, during the hundreds of years of its existence. This change drove society in only one direction: turning Sharia into the cornerstone of Sufism and the only law that pervaded all aspects of Muslim life.[34]

Most of the clerical elite in the Ferghana Valley seem to have taken issue with what Dukchi Ishan was trying to do. Mirza Sami, one of the local historians of the time, wrote that the hasty speech of Dukchi Ishan "violated the *fatwa*[35] on peace with the White Tsar," and in so doing "brought much harm to Muslims and became a root of unrest and disorder among them."[36]

Dukchi Ishan drew his supporters from economically distressed nomads and from the poorer sectors of the agricultural population of the Ferghana Valley (the Kyrgyz, Uzbeks, and Uighurs). They appear to have identified more with the economic arguments Dukchi Ishan was making than with his religious arguments, and so they were less concerned with the objections of more establishment-oriented clerics. For his part, Dukchi Ishan openly criticized representatives of local "new bourgeoisie," the *bais* (large landowners), the *ulama* and representatives of hereditary spiritual clans and clergy (*eshons*, *khojas*, and *sayyids*[37]). Without broad support from the religious elite, the scale of the protest was limited from the onset.

There is no question, though, that Dukchi Ishan sought to communicate a sense of religious legitimacy to the local population. His *murids* conducted a ceremony of Dukchi Ishan's "ascension to khan" (*khon kutarilish*) a day before setting out (May 17, 1898), reflecting the aspirations of his supporters to constitute an Islamic state in place of the Kokand Khanate that had been defeated by the Russians in 1876. And in the tradition of earlier Islamic warriors, Dukchi Ishan personally took part in attacks on Andijan's Russian army barracks.

The uprising quickly failed. Its organizers, including Dukchi Ishan, tried to flee to Kashgar but were captured en route. The Naqshabandiya leader was tried and then hanged, along with six of his closest supporters. The authorities also gathered up the library of Dukchi Ishan's *kanaqa* (about 300 volumes of manuscripts and lithographic editions), which eventually made their way to the Institute of Oriental Studies of the Academy of Sciences of Uzbekistan. Today, contemporary scholars have access to Dukchi Ishan's library and, with it, the ability to learn about the level of religious learning in the Naqshabandiya of Central Asia in the late colonial period.

These books include literary works on Islamic law and books on madrasas, Sufi hagiography, and the divans of Bedil and Mashrab. The library also contains Dukchi Ishan's own *Ibrat al-Ghafilin*, written in rhymed prose in the Ferghana dialect of Uzbek. The text focuses on the moral decline of Muslims, who stopped following religious injunctions and forgot about Sharia in favor of the unsanctioned innovations (*bidat*) that had become more popular than the "beliefs of fathers." *Ibrat al-Ghafilin* is one of the final works of Naqshabandiya-Mujaddidiya writings from the fifteenth through the nineteenth centuries. Collectively, their authors sought to turn Sharia into a single law and the norm of life of Muslims.

The uprising caused the Russian colonial administration to consider tougher policies toward Islam. While most of the recommendations in a review undertaken by Governor-General S. M. Dukhovskoy (1898–1904) were not implemented, the Russians were afraid of new uprisings under Sufi banners, and so tried to further weaken Sufi groups economically. This was done largely through reviewing the tax-exempt status of *waqf*, land property that belonged to religious institutions and individuals. It caused many Sufi *kanaqas* to lose *waqf* holdings, including Khoja Ahror's descendants in Samarkand, and some prominent Sufi leaders lost their formal posts. As a result, on the eve of the Russian Revolution, Sufism was no longer a united and structurally solid movement, even in the Emirate of Bukhara and the Khanate of Khiva, which as protectorates were not directly administered by the Russians.

THE RISE OF THE JADID REFORMERS

After Russian colonization, theological innovation in most of the seminaries of Central Asia further declined,[38] or at least it appeared to do so, compared with the kind of vibrant intellectual debate that was taking place in some of the Muslim intellectual circles in Moscow, St. Petersburg, Kazan, and elsewhere.

The younger group of theologians from the Volga region of Russia, who had lived in close proximity with Russians for centuries, was grappling with how to counter what many believed were the pernicious consequences of theological stagnation for Islamic communities, a stagnation that they believed centered on the system of confessional education that had developed in the madrasas. For some Central Asians, this meant a turn toward the secular world.

Others sought answers within religion. One group turned to fundamentalist ideas, *al-Islahiyah*, or what would later be termed *Salafiya*, where the answers to contemporary challenges largely centered on the interpretation of the Quran and Sharia. A second group, more prominent at that time, was the *usul-isautiyya jadidiyya*, better known as the Jadid movement. Its members were concerned with revitalizing religious and general education of the Turkic nations to empower and support them in their quest for cultural self-preservation within the Russian Empire.

The two groups were not wholly distinct, for both sought to return to what were the forgotten innovative beginnings of earlier Muslim theologians, writers, and thinkers, and to try and reconcile Islam with technological innovations and scientific discoveries of the Western world. In seeking these answers, they drew on examples from a broader Muslim world.

While a handful of Central Asians were exposed to these "modern" ideas through travel to Istanbul, the introduction of Russian rule in Turkestan and protectorate status in Khiva and Bukhara opened opportunities for travel and exchange of ideas for first hundreds, and then thousands, of young people who journeyed throughout the empire in the fifty-odd years between the introduction of colonial rule and the Russian Revolution.

Russian rule also made travel safer, and eased access to Istanbul, for those in Bukhara and Khiva with the means to travel as well as for those in the colonially administered territories of Turkestan. A fortunate few went there to study; still others gained contact through publications, such as the Turkish language journal *Sirat-i mustakim* (The Righteous Path), which included the writings of Muhammad Abduh[39] and his circle.

Some of the first Central Asian religious reformers studied at the Tatar new method[40] madrasas inside Russia, something that was not difficult for Turkestani, Bukharan, or Khivan youth from prominent families. Many of these were children of the growing merchant and smaller entrepreneurial class, as those from noble or clerical families were far more likely to be sent for training at the traditional Hanafi madrasas in various Central Asian cities.

Ismail Gasprinski (1851–1914) was one of the most influential figures in the reform of the madrasa system and the creation of new method schools. While Gasprinski, a Crimea-born and Moscow-educated Tatar from a noble family, was raised in circumstances that were socioeconomically largely different from those of his Turkestani peers, his genuine interest in the fate and development of Turkestan emerged early on in his life. His revolutionary thoughts on the importance of reforms in the education system in Turkestan began during his stay in Moscow. As a student of the famous Milutin Gymnasium and a habitué of gatherings and salons of Russian intellectuals,[41] he became acquainted with the disdainful attitude shared by the members of the Russian nobility and intellectuals toward the people of Turkestan for their limited knowledge of secular subjects, low literacy rates, and preservation of traditional lifestyle. Gasprinski realized that the ethnic communities of Turkestan could fend off such accusations of "backwardness" only by dramatically changing the existing education system—revising the curriculum at madrasas and introducing their students to secular subjects. At the earliest opportunity, Gasprinski put his theoretical model to practice; while working at the Zindjirli Madrasa near Yalta, he challenged the madrasa system by creating a European class structure and included in the daily curriculum such subjects as math, geography, and Russian language. In addition to raising the quality of education at madrasas, Gasprinski attempted to stir civic awareness in the Muslim-dominated communities by launching a newspaper in the Tatar-Crimean dialect, which was later supplemented by the newspaper *Tercuman* (Translator), published both in Russian and Tatar.[42] Despite an initially limited circulation,[43] *Tercuman* soon enjoyed unparalleled popularity, serving and enlightening readers from Crimea to China. In his newspapers, Gasprinski contemplated the nature of the political and economic situation in the world and the region, introduced his readers to local and Western literary works, and offered a platform to Central Asian intellectuals to voice their concerns and exchange ideas. *Tercuman* thus became a "brain factory" of Turkestan and the wider Muslim community, attracting and cultivating the best and the brightest minds, all of whom later came to play a pivotal role in the transformation of Turkestan.

Similar to Gasprinski's print activities, which knew no geographical bounds, his educational initiatives soon traversed the borders of Crimea, paving their way into the emirates of Turkestan. In 1893, Gasprinski was invited to visit Bukhara by the Emir, and held discussions on the possibility of opening a new method school in Bukhara. The idea was received enthusiastically by local intellectuals and civil activists. Letters written by Russian authorities attempted to denigrate Gasprinski's name, accusing him of devising seditious activities and breeding pan-Islamic sentiments among the Turkic nations. Despite these numerous setbacks and obstacles, Gasprinski's method appealed to many progressive thinkers in Turkestan, and by 1903, according to Shoshanna Keller's research, some 20 method schools were operating in Tashkent, most through the efforts of Munavvar qori Abdurashidkhanov, and in Bukhara, through the efforts of Mahmud Khoja Behbudi.[44]

In recent decades, Uzbek scholars have placed more attention on the contributions made by Munavvar qori and Behbudi, for unlike the Tatar Gasprinski, both were from Turkestan.

Meanwhile, only a small portion of the religious community had contact with Gasprinski's educational reforms, and *qadimist* (traditionalist) clerics sometimes went so far as to denounce reformers to Russian authorities, claiming that their new method ideas were seditious.

Although these schools served only a fraction of the number of students who attended the traditional Quran schools, their graduates had a disproportionate influence in the region, organizing some of Central Asia's first newspapers and political parties.[45] The traditional Islamic institutions were still much more deeply entrenched in Bukhara, as it was a protectorate, rather than under a formal colonial administration. The institution of *sheikh ul-islam* was preserved, as was that of the *qadi kalan*, although their jurisdiction was now limited to the reduced territory of the emirate, and the power of this office (with the support of many local clerics) was exerted against the first new method schools in Bukhara. When a new emir[46] ascended to the throne in 1910, new Jadid schools were established in Bukhara; by 1914, they had an enrollment of some 170 students.[47]

The Jadid approach, the reformers argued, would bring more rigors to religious education because of a new emphasis on the mastery of materials, including a much more thorough study of language. These techniques, they maintained, would also be applied to a broad range of courses, in a new kind of madrasa to be called *muhandislik madrasas*, or technical madrasas.

Despite some similarity in curriculum between these "technical madrasas" and the state schools, most Russian authorities remained suspicious of the movement to reform madrasa education, believing that it could become a source of spreading seditious political ideas, like those of Pan-Turkism or Pan-Islamism, ideas that were also supported by many Jadid reformers.

In fact, the new style madrasas proposed by the reformers were quite close to the Russian "Russian-native" schools, as they were termed, which also combined education in secular subjects—in the humanities, languages, and basic mathematics—with religious studies. Of course, in these state schools, the curriculum was set by state educational officials, who were Russian, and not by the clerical establishment.

The period of 1905 to 1917 was marked by political ferment in Russia evolving into political activism. Parts of Russia's Muslim community sought to participate in new political institutions such as the Duma by creating the *Ittifak ul-Muslimin* (Muslim Congress Party), which competed in Duma elections with the Constitutional Democrat (Kadet) faction. Among other things, the party called for cultural autonomy for the Muslim population and support of the Jadid reformist agenda in education.

Influenced by the ideas in one of Ismail Gasprinski's newspapers, *Tercuman*, and Sayyid Jamal al-Din Afghani's newspaper, *Qanun* (Law), both of which circulated in Turkestan, Jadid reformers also sought to engage elite debate through the publication of their own journals and newspapers but were hampered by restrictions on publications. However, during the relative political liberalization of 1906–1908, Munavvar qori and other Jadids from Tashkent published some new periodicals, including *Shuhrat* (Glory), *Khurshid* (Sun), and *Asiya*.[48] Another wave of publications followed from 1912 to 1915.[49]

Mahmud Khoja Behbudi, the founder of Samarkand's first "new method" school, was the son of a traditional Hanafi *qadi*. He had been exposed to Gasprinski's ideas when he traveled to Istanbul and through his subscription to *Tercuman*. Behbudi, who is considered by Adeeb Khalid to be Turkestan's leading Jadid reform figure,[50] sent a lengthy draft document outlining his ideas on education to the Muslim faction of the Duma.

Turkestan, in Behbudi's opinion, should be an autonomous part of the Empire in which the settlement of non-Muslims is to be prohibited, and it should be ruled by a *sheikh ul-Islam* elected for a five-year term by a distinguished *ulama*. In the preface to his 74-article proposal, he writes:

> It is necessary to provide much more autonomy to Turkestan than to Muslims in European Russia because Turkestanis long ago conducted local administration by themselves and are much more eager to enjoy it than their brothers in European Russia. Turkestanis' only desire is to organize a Muslim ecclesiastic and local administration and to have men of insight as the officials. This administration is not only for ecclesiastic affairs. It should cover also civil and local administration as well as jurisdictions that are now at the disposal of *qadis*.[51]

The Jadidis and the Salafists both saw themselves as modernizing forces within Islam. They shared the conviction that Islamic learning should focus on the Quran and the *hadiths*, rather than the centuries of supporting commentary. But for many Salafists, the emphasis was on opening the sacred texts of Islam to ordinary Muslims, which had the added benefit of freeing them from the conservative influence of the *qadimists* and their perpetuation of precedence and the "older ways." Many Jadid reformers, meanwhile, put their emphasis on teaching Islam in ways that supported education and progress more generally.

This kind of tension among conservatives, modernists, and "fundamentalists"—those who argued for going back to the strict adherence to one's own *mazhab*—was a normal feature of life in a Muslim society. And increasingly in Central Asia, since the late nineteenth century, the demands of reformist elements had been added to this mixture.[52]

The interplay between these forces would likely have remained a feature of Central Asian religious life as long as Sharia served as a basis of jurisprudence, even if its scope in society continued to be reduced. While serving to reduce access to Islamic ideas, the Russian colonization rather abruptly ended the general intellectual isolation of the Central Asian region from secular teachings. By so doing, colonization undermined the respect that some religious students held for their clerical elders, who previously served as mediators between the Central Asian intellectual establishment (such as it was in the eighteenth and early nineteenth centuries) and a wider foreign and—prior to the Russian conquest—largely Muslim world.

The Bolshevik Revolution fundamentally redefined the debate over the relationship between religion and the state, eventually forcing into subterfuge or silence all advocates of a revered place for Islam in society. Yet most of the questions posed by clerics and intellectuals in the late nineteenth and early twentieth centuries would be raised again when the USSR began to dissolve, when there was once again debate about the proper relationship between religion and state authority, and how to balance secular values with Islam and Islamic teachings.

3

ISLAM AND THE STATE IN THE SOVIET UNION

THE BOLSHEVIK REVOLUTION, CIVIL WAR, AND THE PEACE THAT FOLLOWED

The years 1917 through 1923 were a period of real turmoil in Central Asia in which power shifted frequently. There was no uniformly accepted authority in Turkestan between the February and October revolutions in 1917, and after the Bolshevik Revolution there were competing authorities in Tashkent (the Soviets, almost entirely Russian) and in Kokand (a government of local nationalists, with support of the local council of *ulama*). In 1917, Jadid reformers, referring to themselves as "Young Bukharans" in the style of the Young Turks of the Ottoman Empire, pushed unsuccessfully for the Emir of Bukhara to introduce political reforms within the emirate.

Throughout much of 1918, there was no effective power center in Turkestan, and the Emir of Bukhara rebuffed an effort by the pro-reform Young Bukhara Party who, with support from Bolshevik forces, tried to take control of the Emirate. In the relative power vacuum, various Islamic institutions, such as Sharia courts and councils of religious leaders, were able to assert strong influence. That made it even more incumbent upon the Bolshevik forces, when they seized control in 1919 and 1920, to seek ways to work with these religious groups as they attempted to placate the population.

From the beginning, Soviet leaders always saw religion as an enemy of the state, and when they first came to power the Bolsheviks tried to stamp it out. With vast lands, mosques, and religious schools under its control, the Islamic establishment had been almost as great a target as was the Russian Orthodox Church. In 1918 and 1919, local Bolshevik Soviets seized *waqf* lands, mosques, and madrasas, stripping *qadis* of all judicial powers, and from this point onward, state agencies (including security forces), took charge of supervising religious believers.

The Bolsheviks were quick to seize lands belonging to religious institutions as they consolidated their territorial control during the Civil War, but they backed off some of the restrictions on religion relatively quickly in an effort to pacify the population. Nonetheless, in much of the country, Islamic leaders urged resistance to the Bolsheviks, and in the North Caucasus in particular Sufi *tariqas* formed the backbone of resistance to the Red Army. In the mountain regions, the Bolsheviks encountered pockets of resistance throughout most of the 1920s. Most of the fighting in Central Asia was over by late 1922.

Before the Russian Revolution, Khiva and Bukhara had clearly been viewed by believers as part of the *dar al-Islam* and most considered the rest of Turkestan so as well, in spite of the restrictions placed on some Islamic institutions. The Bolsheviks' ideology targeted religion as the enemy, thrusting the region into the *dar al-harb*.

The decision to resist Bolshevik rule, and for how long to resist it, was a complicated one. In the immediate aftermath of the Civil War in Central Asia untold thousands of believers fled, made *hijra*, migrating from their homes in order to live in *dar al-Islam*.

Those with economic means faced more difficult choices, for fleeing the region involved a lot of risky and arduous travel, going through Afghanistan or China to the Ottoman lands or elsewhere in the Middle East. Although few succeeded, the goal of many was to get all the way to Saudi Arabia to join the small Central Asian community that served as overseers of the *waqf* holdings in the holy cities.

Ordinary Central Asians had little choice but to stay in the region and put their energies toward survival—no simple task during the revolutionary years. For those who stayed the issue was to resist, submit, or try to suborn the regime from within—something that seemed quite possible during the first years of Soviet rule. Many of the reformers who went to work for the Soviet authorities seem to have done so with the firmly held belief that, as with the Russian rulers before them, the Soviet authorities would prove somewhat malleable and would accommodate themselves to the traditional institutions that had shaped the lives of Central Asians for centuries.

Moreover, moves against religious institutions, such as threatening to close all religious schools or seize all *waqf* properties, furthered popular resistance to Bolshevik rule. The resistance, termed *basmachi* by the "Reds," a pejorative term denoting a raider or plunderer, lasted until the late 1920s.[1] By 1924, when the Soviet authorities formally reorganized Turkestan into the Uzbek Soviet Socialist Republic and created distinct Tajik, Turkmen, and Kyrgyz political units, the resistance was more of a nuisance to the state than a threat to its survival.

Central Asian Muslims often made much of the religious element in the *basmachi*'s resistance to the introduction of Bolshevik rule, and the Islamic Movement of Uzbekistan celebrates the movement as a major part of the history of Jihad in Central Asia. But while religion might have been a key element in stimulating the resistance, only a few of the military leaders came from Sufi orders. Most leaders of large *basmachi* troops came from ordinary families. More often, leaders of resistance groups added "Emir al-Muminin" to their names, emphasizing that they were marching under the banner of Jihad—although it was certainly true that the *basmachi* fighters enjoyed a great deal of support, both moral and financial, from Central Asia's religious establishment. A number of prominent Sufis helped organize fighters, and in a few instances members of *tariqas*, such as Madamin Bek,[2] became leading resistance leaders.

A number of Jadid reformers, as well as the nationalists, thought that they might be able to take advantage of Soviet rule to achieve many of their principal goals while the Soviets decided to make use of the Jadid reformers in their initial efforts to transform the educational system into a wholly secular one. The main *waqf* administration of the People's Commissariat of Education of the Turkestan Autonomous Soviet Socialist Republic, or ASSR, was created, and it existed as well in the Uzbek Soviet Socialist Republic from 1923 to 1926. Educational institutions that opposed reforms were deprived of their *waqf* properties or were simply closed. Parallel to the state efforts were those of moderate Jadid clerics, such as Munavvar qori Abdurashidkhanov, who sought to reform the local system of confessional education. He was executed in 1931.

But those charged with running the early Soviet governments in Turkestan also quickly realized that they needed to pursue a more nuanced policy if they were going to get firm control of the local population. For a short time after the Civil War, the new Soviet rulers sought a partial accommodation with religion. *Waqf* lands were sharply reduced—only property held by Medina and Mecca escaped nationalization—but mosques and some religious schools were permitted to continue to operate, as were religious courts that accepted the primacy of Soviet law.

Shoshana Keller has written an excellent book, rich in archival material, which details the policies toward Islam in Uzbekistan that Soviet authorities pursued during their first two decades in power. She very convincingly argues that through 1922 most Soviet authorities felt that they had little choice but to work through Islamic institutions, such as Sharia courts and clerical councils, always trying to promote the most "progressive" clerics and push out the most conservative, or face a situation in Turkestan in which there was a virtual absence of institutions of social control among the local population.[3]

Waqf holdings that had been seized in the chaotic early days after the revolution began to be returned, especially from 1920 on, when the Turkestan Commission of the Central Committee of the Communist Party came to the region to try to create order. The return of *waqf* lands, which continued through 1922, was part of a more general effort to reverse the first land seizures and to try to develop popular support for the new Soviet government.[4]

In the early years, religious institutions still had significant economic reach. Keller writes of the *waqf* holdings in Bukhara in 1921, under the Bukharan People's Republic, when some 200 *waqf* endowments held 500 to 700 desyatins (a desyatin is 2.7 acres), more than 1,400 shops, some 18 mills, and 133 houses, producing in total some million gold rubles per year.[5]

Islamic judicial institutions were also initially suppressed, then partially reinstated, only to be once again closed down in the late 1920s. In late 1917, the Council of People's Commissars (SOVNARKOM)[6] embarked with zeal on a sweeping campaign aimed at uprooting and abolishing all judiciary institutions and replacing them with more modern courts staffed by democratically elected judges. But Soviet authorities' badly crafted strategy, lack of resources, poor knowledge of the nuances of local judiciaries, and adverse circumstances soon forced them to change direction. In the subsequent years (1919–1923), the Bolsheviks made persistent, albeit often unsuccessful, attempts to restore the role of the local Islamic law and harmonize it with early Soviet legislation.

In his detailed account of the fate of Sharia courts in Turkestan in the aftermath of the Bolshevik Revolution, Paolo Sartori discusses in great length the schemes and machinations of the SOVNARKOM to integrate the local judicial system into the Soviet legal framework.

Sartori posits that reinstating Sharia courts was more than just a provisionary measure for the Bolshevik authorities; supporting the functioning of an Islamic legal system, he suggests, was a strategic tool to ingratiate themselves with the local population and have a functioning judiciary in the region (as the Soviets themselves lacked the necessary resources to establish one of their own).

According to Sartori, the Soviet legal reforms failed because those who planned them were poorly versed in Sharia law, thus often unwittingly giving *qadis* carte blanche to circumvent the SOVNARKOM's restrictions.

For instance, he argues that although the *qadis* were allowed to render judgments solely on civil cases, their resourcefulness and knowledge of various legal tools often allowed them to adjudicate cases of landed property and circumvent the imposed restrictions. They did this by instructing the parties to reach "amicable" settlements on their own or with the intervention of the third party or other forms of reconciliation. Such settlements made it unnecessary to bring the case to the Soviet Committee for Land and Water, which would probably resolve the litigation by taking away the land from the parties.[7]

When the early idealism of the revolution wore off and the challenges of governing began to sink in, Soviet authorities also quickly realized that they would face an almost unmanageable task of educating the population if they closed all the religious schools and made no use of teachers who had themselves been trained in madrasas.

For the first years, they concentrated on trying to modify the curriculum in the *maktabs* and madrasas and requiring that instruction in religious subjects (as well as secular ones) be conducted in the local languages, either Uzbek or Tajik (that is, the vernacular), utilizing the new system of Arabic orthography, *usul-u jadid*, instead of the traditional Persian or Chagatai.

In general, the challenges of introducing Soviet rule were greater in Bukhara and Khiva, because those two cities had never been fully incorporated in the Russian Empire. For that reason, the Bolshevik authorities took a two-step approach to incorporation. Shoshana Keller reports that in Khiva in mid-1923 there were some 29 Soviet schools with 1,500 students and 282 madrasas with 2,000 students.[8] In fact, Keller argues that in October 1923 when the Khorazm People's Republic was reorganized as the Khorazm Soviet Socialist Republic, Islam was the still the sole form of recognized authority in the republic. One of the solutions that was then tried was to get pro-communist teachers (many of whom came from Tatar cities) to teach secular subjects alongside those offering instruction in religious subjects, with an eye to the former replacing the latter in a few years.[9]

In many ways the situation in Bukhara was more complex. The transitional government there, the Bukharan People's Republic, was much more of a coalition government, with large representation of local elites, than was the government in Khiva, which was much more of Moscow's choosing. In Bukhara, clerics were more assertive about trying to set the political agenda. In January 1924, they held the First Congress of Ulama of the Bukharan People's Socialist Republic, at which they endorsed a largely reformist religious agenda.[10] The *qurultoy* (congress) was also quick to condemn the *basmachi* as "thieves, murderers and robbers of the poor," which makes apparent the rift among clerics between those who were willing to work with the new authorities (the majority) and those who supported the opposition. According to Keller, seven clerics served in the Central Executive Committee of this government, and five of them were Communist Party members.[11]

Even before the formal incorporation of Bukhara and Khiva into a single Uzbek Soviet Socialist Republic, authorities in the Turkestan Autonomous Soviet Socialist Republic (the juridical structure that preceded it and that was subordinated to Russia) began seeking to cut back on the power bases of religious authorities. It started with the Sharia courts, which as of February 1924 ceased to receive government funding and were forced to exist through the fines they collected, thus threatening their existence.[12]

The question of controlling *waqfs* in particular became an imperative when the Soviets turned to land reform in 1925, and their desire to control the economic basis of Central Asian society effectively doomed religious institutions from being self-perpetuating. But, as Keller points out, first the Bolshevik authorities had to figure out a way to finance education, because eliminating the *waqf* holdings would effectively close all the madrasas, and until a better functioning secular school system could be established, efforts to educate young people (especially women) who were generally not sent to state schools would be threatened.

By the end of 1925, most of the earlier concessions were revoked: madrasas were required to register and meet all the standard secular school guidelines or, failing that, to close. Islamic values also became more of a target with the Soviet goal of fully integrating women into society. In 1927 the "Hujum" campaign[13]—the drive to "unveil" women and get them to end their physical seclusion and take on public economic roles—was resisted by many clerics and other traditional leaders as well as by most women.[14]

THE STALINIST SYSTEM OF THE 1920s AND 1930s

The drive against religious institutions took on a new intensity when land reform policies were introduced, for party workers in the ideological sector risked being held responsible for the resistance that land reform projects were encountering. By the time the purges were in full force in the late 1930s, more party workers were being arrested for lack of vigilance than clerics remaining in the republic.

In the end Stalin's economic program served as the driver for ending the institution of the *waqf* and with it the clerics and the religious schools that *waqf* holdings sustained. Once Soviet authorities moved against private land ownership, which they began in earnest by 1927, the *waqf* was doomed to extinction. Virtually all the religiously held property was formally nationalized in January 1929 with the introduction of the collectivization drive. Some *waqf* holdings managed to survive until the collectivization drive was completed in the mid-1930s, but they were rare exceptions. This also dealt a fatal blow to Sufi cloisters, whose *kanaqas* were closed down when *waqf* holdings were restricted, leading many Sufi sheikhs to flee the country or to go into hiding in remote regions of Central Asia.

In mid-1927 a decision was made to close all the remaining "old method" religious schools in Uzbekistan, and the number of madrasas dropped dramatically between 1926 and 1928, from eighteen to two in Kokand and from four to two in the old city of Bukhara. Not a single madrasa remained in Samarkand and the old city of Tashkent.[15] Another decision was made to convert new method schools to an all-secular curriculum, although that proved difficult to implement and was eventually abandoned. By the early 1930s, all education was conducted in secular schools that were organized and run by the state. Furthermore, teaching Uzbek in the Latin alphabet, instead of in Arabic script, reduced the advantages of using religious schools as a base upon which to build secular education. By 1940, Soviet authorities had decided to switch written Uzbek to the Cyrillic alphabet.

Leaving the country also became more difficult after 1926, but until then small groups of clerics attended international Muslim gatherings in Turkey, Saudi Arabia, and Egypt, and religious leaders with economic means were able to find ways to leave permanently.[16]

At roughly the same time, Soviet authorities started to close local spiritual administrations and began subjecting clerics to more aggressive forms of taxation.[17] Although Sharia courts were not banned until 1929, new restrictions were introduced that effectively forced them underground, as many Central Asians preferred to use these traditional institutions to adjudicate family and other social matters rather than rely on the frequently poorly organized and always seemingly alien Soviet civil court system. Many of the remaining Jadid reformers began losing their posts in the educational system.

In 1928 Uzbek officials began a much more aggressive campaign to close mosques. Until a new national law on religious associations was introduced in 1929, the closure of mosques required some formal approval of the community, which retained the right to reclaim its possessions from within the mosques. But many local officials were unwilling to back down when communities resisted, and Shoshana Keller dates the beginning of a campaign of terror against clerics to this period.[18] The use of terror was resisted by some in Uzbekistan's leadership, because it made the Communist Party's goal of getting large numbers of ethnic Uzbeks into positions of political responsibility, the so-called "nativization" policy, difficult. In addition to scaring away people from working in the government and communist party, it also increased popular resistance to the new economic policies.

On April 8, 1929, the Russian Federation adopted a comprehensive "Law on Religion Associations"[19] that served as the model for laws passed by the supreme soviets of all the other union republics. It remained largely unmodified for the next sixty years, and it was this law, rather than the more lenient and never enforced provisions of the 1936 USSR constitution,[20] that regulated religious affairs. This law put all religious institutions under firm state control and required that all existing religious communities secure registration (not many managed to do this successfully). It also charged the Ministry of Internal Affairs with enforcing the law.[21] From this time on, religious institutions could no longer own property. Registered religious communities could rent property, although they were liable for payments for communal services and taxes and had to raise all the money for their operation from their members. All forms of missionary work were made illegal, and only registered religious schools could teach about the faith. Private religious instruction became a crime, even within the confines of the family unit. The law gave the state full license to close down all surviving religious institutions and turned into criminals anyone who worked in them or accepted any sort of personal religious mission. This set the stage for mass arrests of clerics and those who protected them. Very little published material is available about popular resistance encountered by the drive against the mosques, as it was impossible to access the archival materials that related to it until Uzbek independence.

While in earlier years uses for mosques and madrasas were devised with some respect for local sensibilities, such as turning them into state schools, now the opposite was the case. During the 1930s, thousands of mosques were declared decrepit, then closed. Many were destroyed or, worse, used for some kind of sacrilegious purpose. The Jome (Gumbaz) Mosque in Namangan, for example, was made into a wine factory. This particular example came back to haunt local authorities in the 1980s when local radicals took over the building, rededicated it, and used it as the central mosque for the region.

The takeover of mosques began slowly, and the 1929 legislation specified a formal procedure to be followed. Keller describes how local citizens or authorities had to petition the Commission on Cults to begin the process.[22] The existence of such a procedure slowed down the closings, so that approximately 3,000 mosques were reported as functioning on January 1, 1936, making it clear that Islam had far from disappeared.[23] And the government seems to have been especially troubled by the fact that the mosques drew large crowds during Ramadan, when Soviet authorities would have preferred that workers be on the job.

Some clerics tried to flee, and a relatively small number seem to have become itinerant preachers.[24] Keller writes of a 1935 campaign against these "horseback *ishans*," when 32 of them were executed, allegedly for seeking to spread the idea of "the Komsomol for this world, the *murid* for the next."

The waves of purges from 1936 through 1938 made any public observance of religion very dangerous. Until that time, the goal of the policy was to close mosques and religious schools. The killing of clerics was a more logical by-product of Stalin's purges than of a Moscow-dictated policy to destroy the religious elite in Central Asia. This came about when local party officials were charged with rooting out enemies of the state, and clerics and those with a religious education made convenient targets. Jadid reformers who had served in the early Soviet governments were targets as well; in fact, by the mid-1930s, most of the leadership of these governments were themselves labeled as traitors. In the first years of the purge there was some recognition that the educated class and those with religious education were one and the same group and that the survival of the Soviet system depended upon preserving at least part of this class.

In the last years of the purges, those responsible for the mechanism of the purges seemed concerned first and foremost with arresting, imprisoning, and killing enough people to save themselves. In Uzbekistan, most people grew too scared to practice Islam or to protect those who did. The Uzbeks interviewed in the early 1990s still recalled the trauma from this repression, which left many too frightened to secure religious education. That, of course, had been the intent of the purges.

Despite the best efforts of Stalin's terror machine, hundreds if not thousands of clerics survived—if people with systematic religious education are to be included. They were sufficient in number to allow illegal—*hujra*—schools to once again be organized when conditions liberalized somewhat. These schools were not always fully operational; sometimes they consisted of nothing more than someone with a religious education teaching his child or a few young people how to read the Quran and what few religious tracts remained hidden in his possession. The importance of these schools is the subject of a later chapter.

THE STATE "RETURNS" ISLAM

In the 1940s, thinking that religion might play a useful role in the war effort, Stalin relaxed his persecution of religion slightly, ordering the creation of state-supervised Religious Councils. Among these was the Spiritual Administration of the Muslims of Central Asia and Kazakhstan, which was opened in 1943 in Tashkent and headed by Eshon Bobokhon ibn Abdulmajidkhon (1859–1957). SADUM in turn was permitted to open the Mir-i Arab Madrasa in Bukhara and eventually the Imam al-Bukhari Institute in Tashkent.

The creation of SADUM was a mixed blessing for Central Asia's Muslims. It permitted Islam to enjoy an officially sanctioned place in public life, but it simultaneously put under direct official scrutiny believers who studied, served, or prayed in the SADUM-sanctioned mosques and religious schools. The Soviet authorities never intended that SADUM should meet the needs of all of Central Asia's believers. Indeed, they used their gesture toward Islam as an excuse for a new crackdown on all unlicensed religious schools, mosques, and prayer houses.

According to archival data collected by Yaacov Roi, 2,274 former mosques were still standing in Uzbekistan in late 1944. Of those, 208 were empty—not being used as schools, storehouses, or for some other function—and fourteen were being used as mosques.[25]

The most important fact about SADUM was that it was intended to be a largely symbolic body, creating a legal basis of religion, but doing so in a way that was not ever intended to serve the basic needs of the population. For example, Roi notes that in 1956 there were only 72 registered mosques and 132 registered clerics (excluding *muezzins*[26]) in Uzbekistan and that the distribution of mosques by republic, oblast, and city was completely arbitrary and largely random.[27] The number of legally registered mosques increased for a while after Nikita Khrushchev took power. But in the early 1960s, ideological controls grew stronger after Khrushchev set the goal of building communism on the socialist foundations of the Soviet Union.[28] For roughly a decade, until controls grew more lax under the stewardship of Leonid Brezhnev, it was harder to open mosques, and practicing religious believers more easily fell afoul of local party officials.

According to the Uzbek Information Agency, by 1980 the number of registered mosques in Uzbekistan had increased to 89. At this time, according to the 1979 USSR census, the population of the republic was 15.4 million. By 1989, there were 300 registered mosques[29] and a population of 19.9 million.[30]

SADUM was designed to create a vertically integrated system of religious accountability. But the institution never functioned as its Soviet creators intended, and neither does the current Uzbek equivalent (the Spiritual Administration of Uzbekistan). The idea was that the *mufti* appointed a *qadi* to head each of the regions of the republics under the *mufti*'s control. The *qadis* were responsible for the imams who headed the mosques in their area. Hanafi Islam has never supported a strong hierarchical structure, and individual clerics have always viewed themselves as spiritual leaders competent to guide those who gather in their mosques based on Islam as they had been taught to understand it.

This led to splits, described at length in a later chapter, between those who saw the perpetuation of traditional ritual practices as a good thing and those who saw them as taking away from the spirituality of the faith. The latter were better able to present their ideas as consistent with Soviet economic and social policies, which helps explain why they found favor with the state leaders who supervised religious affairs. While SADUM had the authority to determine the content of Friday and holiday sermons, it was unable to influence the context in which these remarks were delivered.

Roi found a great deal of archival material that argued that the system never really created the degree of control that was desired.[31] *Qadis* viewed themselves as figures of religious authority, and local imams and *mullahs* also were self-selecting about what instructions (which came from SADUM in the form of *fatwas*) they felt bound to follow.

This was certainly consistent with what I saw when I began to travel throughout the Ferghana Valley beginning in 1990. The one difference was that in the Soviet period, recalcitrant clerics—technically the responsibility of SADUM to remove—risked falling afoul of local Soviet state and security officers who could order these clerics' arrest. The vigilance of the state and security authorities tended to vary, depending on Moscow's relative interest in pursuing anti-religious policies.

The decision to open or register mosques was not made with any intention to serve the needs of religious believers. The intent was to allow the state to monitor the practice of those who were most devout, as there was an expectation that such people would play an active role in the legally registered mosques. Some did, while others—especially in times in which Soviet officials were less vigilant in their ideological campaigns—opted for a more private and self-contained form of existence.

Registered mosques were expected to be financially self-supporting, as was SADUM, and fees were collected for the performance of *nikoh toys* (weddings), *jinazs* (religious burials), and other rites. In addition, believers offered *sadaqa-fitr* donations during Ramadan, and the largest single source of funds came from donations from the community made at the time of *Ramazan hayit*[32] and *Qurbon hayit*.[33] The donations at this time of year often came from a broader community. The money collected went to the upkeep of the mosques, the administrative costs of SADUM and its madrasas, and the salaries of all concerned, which could not exceed guidelines set by the state. There were also "voluntary" donations to the Soviet Peace Fund, and funds for the preservation of historical buildings.[34] The practice of religion was not expected to be profitable.

More people attended services in the mosques during *Ramazan hayit* and *Qurbon hayit*, but attendance figures are notoriously unreliable: It did local party officials no good to report high numbers, for then they were admitting their lack of vigilance. During the holiday season, mosques were generally filled to overflowing, and the size of the crowds served as a form of protection for those attending services. Thousands, and in some cases tens of thousands, of "pilgrims" went to holy sites within Central Asia during the Islamic festivals as well, such as the Throne of Suleiman in Osh, Shah-i Zinda (where Timur is buried) in Samarkand, the mausoleum of Baha ud-Din Naqshaband near Bukhara, and Shah-i Mardan in Ferghana Oblast.

All of these were eventually removed from the jurisdiction of SADUM and given over to state agencies responsible for the administration of historical monuments, in an effort to eliminate such pilgrimages.

Unlike Friday services, on feast days it was virtually impossible for authorities to record the presence of all in attendance at the mosques. But many party officials had little interest in engaging in such activities. For that reason, absentee figures during those holidays should also be presumed to be lower than was in fact the case, and party workers had a vested interest to underreport late arrivals and early departures during Ramadan. If people were fasting or engaging in religious observances, those charged with their ideological supervision might also be faulted.

Roi also reports that the *upolnomochennye* (authorized) workers of the state committees on religion regularly toured the rural (and urban) regions to find and report unregistered religious groups and congregations and the perpetuation of religious traditions and customs but often showed little enthusiasm for executing these tasks. He cites, for example, archival data from Turkmenistan from the mid-1960s in which an inspection tour revealed that only one boy in the surveyed population was uncircumcised. Similarly, 80 percent of the boys surveyed in a questionnaire distributed a few years later in three rural regions of Uzbekistan said that they were circumcised.[35] But unable to stamp out such practices, most anti-religious workers just seem to have contented themselves with leaving them unreported. As we will see in later chapters, the public celebration of such rituals did come under attack, but if people celebrated quietly most got away with it, and Roi reports that household visits by *mullahs* were generally not considered a form of "proselytizing the faith."

Party officials also often had little interest in reporting the number of unregistered mosques or unregistered *mullahs*. There were also many cases when the counting seemed more or less accurate—such as the archival report reproduced by Roi from Bukhara in 1954 when one inspector reported that each of the 250 *kolkhozes* (collective farms) in his region had at least one, and in several dozen cases more than one, *mullah*. More typical was the 1974 report cited by Roi that there were no unregistered clerics in Andijan and Khiva, a manifestly absurd claim.[36]

In fact, the archival materials reproduced by Roi suggest that the number of unregistered congregations might be as much as ten times as large as those registered. Roi also found reports in the archives of clerics from SADUM enlisting the assistance of unregistered clerics to help them minister to believers during holiday seasons or in distant regions.[37]

SADUM was also supposed to be the sole source of training for clerics who served in the officially registered mosques. In reality, the two training institutions, which were designed to prepare Muslim clerics for the entire USSR, could not accomplish this task. As a result, even legally registered mosques were sometimes led by people who had only informal training, or those who had been taught in *hujras*.

Initially about a third of all registered clerics had served as clerics before 1941, and roughly a tenth had been working clerics before the revolution. Roi reports that by 1963, the majority were over sixty years of age, and the majority had also trained as *mullahs* after 1941.[38] Roughly half of the clerics had formal religious education; the remainder were either self-trained or had been taught in more informal circumstances.[39]

The Mir-i Arab Madrasa (formally known as the Islamic Special Secondary School) in Bukhara, well known in the Muslim world for preparing qualified theologians, was established by Sheikh Mir-i Arab in 1530–1536 with financial support from Ubaydulla Khan, the Emir of Bukhara. The school was re-established in 1945 and once again began admitting students in 1946.

The school was named for Sheikh Mir Arab Said Abdulla al-Yamani, a famous Sufi figure, and its mausoleum holds the graves of Sheikh Mir-i-Arab and Emir Ubaydulla Khan, among others. While Mir-i Arab trained a very small number of students in its first years of existence, turning out only 85 graduates between 1945 and 1970,[40] virtually all *muftis* of the Soviet Central Asian Republics pursued their education at this academic institution.

The school, located in ancient Shahriston in the central part of Bukhara, occupies a two-story building with 144 *hujras*. Nonetheless, the confessional education offered at the Mir-i Arab Madrasa in Bukhara in the early years of its re-establishment was relatively limited. Many on the teaching staff were only minimally qualified. The curriculum included the introduction of Jadids' methods of combining secular and religious sciences, unacceptable in the confessional education system, plus the even more problematic lectures in the pseudo-patriotic principle of "faithfulness to socialist ideals."

In fact, in the first years of its existence, the quality of religious education at Mir-i Arab was lower than education offered in the unsanctioned *hujras*, leaving intact the authority of those who had received this illegal education, at least those from certain *hujras*, as is discussed in a later chapter.

Attempts were made to raise the quality of education offered within the SADUM system. Studies of the Quran and its interpretations were augmented with courses on famous collections of *hadiths* by Imam al-Bukhari (d. 870) and Imam Muslim (Muslim ibn al-Hajjaj) (d. 875), although the courses of instruction reflected the theological preferences of Mufti Ziyouddin Bobokhon (1957–1982). He went so far as to try to adopt courses offered at Al-Azhar[41] or other Muslim universities.

SADUM had received authorization to open a second madrasa in Tashkent. From 1956 to 1961, there was also an effort to launch a supreme madrasa of "a new kind," which was established in the building of the old Barak Khan Madrasa. The Imam Ismail al-Bukhari Islamic Institute in Tashkent, though, did not commence its activities until 1971, and it was designed to train *ulama*. While the institute started by accepting only 20 applicants a year, the number of students gradually increased.

But contact with the greater Islamic community was all but impossible save through the mediation of SADUM and the state-regulated religious establishment. In Soviet times, going on *hajj* was almost impossible. A maximum of 20 could go each year, with the first pilgrims making the trip to Mecca in 1953.[42]

They were the channel for dissemination of Qurans and other religious texts, all of which were in very short supply, given the general unwillingness of the government to permit these materials to be printed.[43]

It was impossible to go abroad to study Islam, except with the approval of SADUM, and this privilege was granted to only a handful of graduates of SADUM's own religious academies, Mir-i Arab, and the Imam Ismail al-Bukhari Institute in Tashkent.

SADUM regulated official Soviet relations with the foreign Muslim world, sent delegations of clerics on foreign goodwill tours, and reciprocated the hospitality that they received, always with an eye to gaining positive publicity for the Soviet Union.

During the Khrushchev years, it also became harder for Central Asians to practice what some have called everyday or household Islam—religious rituals that surround the life cycle of birth, circumcision, marriage, and death. But at the same time, Khrushchev's policies opened the door for more linkages between the official Islamic institutions and the greater Muslim world, as well as more informal contacts between Central Asian Muslims and their brethren in the Middle East.

Soviet citizens who participated in officially sponsored exchanges went through elaborate scrutiny. They were required to pass background checks and evaluations of their mental health as well as of their political loyalty. When not traveling in large, shepherded groups, they traveled in pairs, each person charged with the responsibility of informing on the other. However, no security system is flawless; some travelers who had left the USSR as "agents" discovered a genuine faith while abroad, while others were "double agents" all along, religious believers who had simply outwitted their controllers.

The Soviet students and clerics who went to study abroad were viewed as "authentic" by their co-religionists and were not seen as having been compromised by their potential or alleged association with the organs of state security (something that made these same clerics the object of potential distrust by some believers in their home republics and the object of criticism by scholars in the West).

The Soviet-era clerics who received foreign training, especially those who went abroad during the Brezhnev years or later, were exposed to the intellectual ferment going on in Islamic seminaries of the Middle East. They were exposed as well to the teachings of the other traditional schools of Islamic jurisprudence, all of which were more conservative than Central Asia's own Hanafi tradition. While they could not put these teachings into practice upon their return to the Soviet Union, these ideas clearly had an influence on such figures as Muhammad Sodiq Muhammad Yusuf (and Akbar Turajonzod, the Tajik cleric and civil war figure), which became apparent in later years.

ISLAM AND THE CRUMBLING SOVIET STATE

Toward the end of Leonid Brezhnev's[44] life, a halfhearted effort was made to improve the quality of anti-religious propaganda. The Islamic Revolution in Iran and the Soviet military effort to attempt to save socialism from

Islamic rebellion in Afghanistan led Moscow to view Soviet Muslims with greater wariness. Even so, the Muslim population of the USSR was not seen to be politically susceptible. Soviet Muslims served in Afghanistan (with mixed success), as they did almost everywhere, and technical specialists from Central Asia were the major source of auxiliary civilian personnel in the Afghanistan campaign.[45]

Anti-religious propaganda was undermined by the corruption that surrounded most ideological work in these years. Reports were more important than deeds, so many fewer lectures criticizing religious practices were reported than were in fact given. During the 1980s, I met many scholars who went to Central Asia as lecturers for the "*Znanie*" (knowledge) society. While formally responsible for much of the propaganda work, they signed up for free travel to the region to earn a little extra money, and generally spent their time doing ethnographic or archeological research in the communities in which they were supposedly lecturing.

To many in Moscow, it was "Islam" that made the Central Asians more clannish, self-protective, and closed to outside influences, and it was Islam that pressured them to marry young and have enormous families that were fed at Moscow's expense.[46]

Anxious to escape dismissal—or, worse yet, jail—party leaders demonstrated their vigilance by turning on each other. This was particularly true in Uzbekistan, where the party organization had come under special scrutiny because of the abuses in the cotton industry under longtime Uzbek party boss Sharaf Rashidov (Sharof Rashidov) (who had died in 1983).[47] Central Asia had been singled out for special criticism because of the prevalence of Islam and family-based cronyism; of the two, Islam was the easier target, because each of Central Asia's rulers was a product of the old patronage system and thus understood how difficult it would be to eliminate cronyism, even if a leader were inclined to try.

Each of Central Asia's leaders demonstrated his qualities of leadership by attacking the religious believers in his republic; the more the local party was under attack by central authorities, the more Islam became the focus of local repression.

But the anti-religious campaign that was launched in the 1980s soon ran afoul of more important Kremlin priorities. It was the belief that the USSR was "stagnating"—to use the term chosen by Brezhnev's successors to describe his rule—that propelled first Yuri Andropov, and then far more aggressively, Mikhail Gorbachev, to endorse an ever-expanding program of economic, political, and social reforms. The primary goal of these reforms was to spur an economic recovery, but the systemic economic reforms that this required inevitably also demanded personal sacrifices by most of the population; to make sacrifice more palatable, the Soviet leadership looked for ways to make loyalty more appealing.

Needing a new unifying ideology to replace the one they were modifying beyond recognition, the Soviet leaders reached into the national past to restore to the population many of the intangible virtues that communism had failed to give them. Their intention was to find a replacement but still Leninist ideology in a collective past. But the way in which they went about this search ended up also legitimating the re-examination of individual, regional, and republic pre-Soviet pasts.

This process of re-examination had unexpected results. Gorbachev's bewilderment at the time of the USSR's formal dissolution in December 1991 suggests strongly that not even the parade of recently loyal republics declaring their independence in the aftermath of the failed August coup had prepared the last Soviet leader for the impending death of his homeland.

To Gorbachev, for most intents and purposes, Russia and the Soviet Union were one and the same. Russia's past included the achievements of prerevolutionary history, which was strengthened by Lenin's adoption of socialism, but which then was warped through the obsessive behavior of Lenin's successor. Russia's future was that of the entire Soviet Union, an indivisible whole that would be held together through a more rational economic integration of the country, as well as by the spiritual renewal of the Russian people themselves.

That non-Russians would seek their own spiritual renewal, let alone that this would put them at odds with Russians, was unthinkable to Gorbachev. It was even more unthinkable to his wife, Raisa Gorbacheva, who for the first time since the Lenin era sought to play a public role as "first lady." Raisa Gorbacheva was a professional "Soviet philosopher" and used her husband's position to surround herself with a nineteenth-century style *salon* of Russian intellectuals who, the Gorbachevs assumed, would preside over this process of Russian renewal.

In the mid-1980s, Raisa Gorbacheva and her colleagues in the Soviet Culture Fund sponsored the rehabilitation of Russia's purged intellectuals, the rewriting of Russian history, and the restoration of the Russian Orthodox Church to an honored place in public life. Other Soviet nationalities were quick to demand the same rights the Russians were gaining—that their purged writers and poets be reprinted, that their suppressed national heroes once again be awarded public recognition, and that they be free to practice and transmit their religious faiths. In addition, the other Soviet nationalities demanded what Russians had no need to demand: that their languages be pulled back from what for some cultures was near extinction, for others simple banishment to the kitchen, and be given their proper prominence in public life.

The last nations to be conquered were the first to protest, but political movements for expanded cultural and religious rights quickly spread from the Baltic republics and western Ukraine to other republics, Muslim as well as European. In December 1986, in Kazakhstan, nationalist demonstrations turned deadly, when thousands were wounded and more than 50 killed after special troops attacked the crowds of young people who had taken to the streets to protest the replacement of long-term Kazakh party boss and Politburo member Dinmukhamed Kunaev by a Russian from outside of the republic.[48]

The Uzbek elite was itself growing tired of what it saw as the disproportionate punishment that was being inflicted upon Uzbekistan's Communist Party, many of whose members had been jailed in the years following Rashidov's death. Although Uzbekistan's cotton scandal was widely assumed to have reached deep into the Politburo, and many powerful Russians must have benefited from it, no one outside of Uzbekistan was punished for that malfeasance. So they, too, began pushing for more national autonomy, in cultural as well as economic and political arenas.

The national sensitivities that Gorbachev's policies unintentionally reawakened created security challenges that were greater than at any time since the civil war years. Only the presence of special security forces kept Armenians and Azerbaijanis apart in Karabakh (and not always successfully), while other troops had been sent to Georgia, to several places in the North Caucasus, to Uzbekistan's Ferghana Valley, and to Osh in Kyrgyzstan.[49]

Instead of revitalizing and fine-tuning a basically functioning political engine, as Gorbachev seems to have expected, his reforms instead had rebounded in all sorts of unexpected, even fantastic, ways. By March 1989, Gorbachev was facing large legislatures in each of the republics whose members had been elected in at least partially democratic ways and were now demanding much greater autonomy in republic-level economic and political decisionmaking. In the case of the Baltics, a demand for republic sovereignty was even beginning to be made.

To try to salvage the situation, as well as to attempt to placate the nationalist movements that were beginning to swell in several of the various republics, the Politburo of the Communist Party began to grant republic leaders increased discretionary powers, including greater control over ideology, which included policies covering religion.

The whole nature of government was changing in the USSR, which further accelerated the decentralization of nationality policy. In spring 1989 an all-union Congress of People's Deputies was elected, many of whose members (though not the Central Asian ones) had been selected on a partially democratic basis. Elections were also set for late 1989 to select new republican legislatures, which were designed partially to supplant some functions of the republic communist organizations. These elections were intended to transform the various republic-level supreme soviets into semi-sovereign legislatures, no longer the rubber stamps of local communist parties.

As part of this shift to popular empowerment, laws governing public organizations were changed as well. The permitted degree of freedom varied from republic to republic, but in general Soviet citizens were now more or less free to form voluntary associations and interest groups that could participate in public life through organizing public lectures, petitioning for legislation, and even backing candidates for election.

In Central Asia, most of these "informals," as such nongovernmental public organizations were called, developed to support changes in policy that were already acceptable to the local party leadership, including pressing for an increased public role for the eponymous language, which became an official language in Uzbekistan. Groups were also formed to support the rehabilitation of "repressed" historical figures of both the pre- and post-revolutionary periods and to rewrite each republic's history.

Far more significant was the change in official policy toward religion. For the first time since the revolution, people were free to engage in organized and personal religious observance with only the most minimal official supervision. Restrictions against political activities by religious groups remained in place, though. Groups with explicitly religious agendas were still banned; the forbidden groups included the Islamic Renaissance Party, which had begun in Russia and had attempted to form a branch in Uzbekistan.

The first and most immediate beneficiary of this change in official attitudes toward Islam was the Central Asian Spiritual Administration of Muslims. Although Uzbekistan did not pass a law on freedom of conscience until July 1991, SADUM policies began to change dramatically after the February 1989 appointment of a new *mufti*, Muhammad Sodiq Muhammad Yusuf, who defined the revitalization of the practice of Islam as his primary task.

Muhammad Sodiq came to power on February 6, 1989, as the result of what almost was a coup; Mufti Shamsuddin Bobokhonov, the grandson of SADUM's founding Eshon Bobokhon ibn Abdulmajidkhon, was ousted after several days of demonstrations around Tashkent's main mosque by demonstrators protesting Bobokhanov's alleged drinking and womanizing, a charge he strongly denied.[50]

There were now new incentives to ally with SADUM. *Mullahs* who submitted to SADUM's authority gained access to "pilgrimage passes" for themselves and their followers. Yearly charter flights funded by Saudi Arabia were organized beginning in 1990 and were turned over to SADUM for administration. Technically pilgrimage was open to anyone, but in practice travel abroad required an exit visa, which could be denied those who did not have tickets for the official *hajj* flights. Clerics who did not seek direct affiliation with SADUM were free to run their mosques but were forced to raise their own funds for maintenance and construction activities. Moreover, their congregants could not participate in official delegations to Mecca or SADUM-sponsored trips.

Clerics were now encouraged openly to preach the faith and to attempt to attract as many new believers as possible. SADUM also endorsed some of the social programs of the fundamentalists, urging the population to live lives shaped by Sharia. SADUM officials also became strong advocates of increased Arabic language education and argued against others in Uzbekistan who maintained that Uzbek should return to the Latin script it once used, scrapping its Cyrillic-based alphabet. SADUM officials initially sided with the fundamentalists and unofficial clergy that Uzbek should be written in neither Cyrillic nor Latin, but rather in its original Arabic script, so that Uzbeks would no longer be cut off from their prerevolutionary religious heritage.

One result of this confluence of opinion was that *Islom nuri* (The Light of Islam), a newspaper that began in May 1990 as SADUM's first uncensored publication, was printed in Uzbek's Latin alphabet, with parallel columns of Arabic and Cyrillic script. Ironically, at that same time the language of instruction in the Tashkent Islamic Institute was still Russian (as well as Arabic), rather than Uzbek, since Russian was the only language that the seminarians, still drawn from throughout the USSR, had in common.

For many clerics, SADUM remained suspect, whereas others, in the tradition of the Hanafi faith that had long been practiced in the region, were willing to be loyal and grateful for the improved conditions.

One of these communities, Namangan, gradually slipped almost completely out of the control of the secular authorities. In 1989, a group of young men formed *Adolat* (Justice), which began introducing Islamic "justice" based on their own interpretations of Islamic law, which included the occasional public execution. This group worked with those in *Tavba* (Repentance), organized in 1991, and served as the precursors of the Islamic Movement of Uzbekistan.

Karimov was determined that Uzbekistan would not repeat the situation that was occurring in Tajikistan, where the Communist Party chief (Kakhar Makhamov) was driven from power in September 1991 after crowds, including hundreds with green flags, camped in the main downtown square, chanted "jihad," toppled a large statue of Lenin, and called for his resignation. Earlier in the day protesters in Dushanbe had seized the television tower and relay station and were broadcasting the events throughout the republic, and even beyond. The failed Communist Party coup had occurred just two weeks earlier, and for the last few years since 1989, the seemingly impossible had become commonplace.

I was in Tashkent that day and watched as some film concluded, and channel four went automatically to the live protests in Dushanbe, as if channel four was preprogrammed to alternate between the Central Asian republics on a fixed schedule. The live coverage ended abruptly a few hours later, and Uzbek folkloric singers and dancers filled the screen, presumably after a senior security official, or maybe even Karimov himself, came home and turned on his TV set.

Karimov saw his own Islamists close up when he campaigned for president in the Ferghana Valley in the autumn of 1991, and he clearly did not like what he saw. Determined to right the balance between Islamic institutions and those of the secular state, Karimov turned against Muhammad Sodiq Muhammad Yusuf in the last days of the Soviet Union. Concerned that Muhammad Sodiq was becoming too independent and that he was too close to radical elements, Karimov had him removed shortly after Uzbekistan achieved its independence. He thereupon began putting slowly into place a set of policies that were designed to assert the primacy of secular values over Islamic ones and gave enhanced powers to security agencies to make sure that the writ of the state was obeyed.[51]

RELIGIOUS LEADERS OF THE SOVIET ERA

My goal in this chapter is not to write an exhaustive history of religious life throughout the Soviet period, but to try to give some suggestion as to how complicated things were during that time. The task of writing a complete history of Islam in this period will rest with another generation, as it requires that the archives of the Spiritual Administration of the Muslims of Central Asia and Kazakhstan as well as Soviet archives be exhaustively researched, preferably by a scholar with little stake in the outcome of the findings. In the current environment, access is still restricted, and most who enjoy access are themselves concerned about how their findings might work to the benefit of one or another group of clerics, or hinder the ability of the state to control Islam.

My intent here is to introduce most of the major, and some of the minor, religious figures who had a formative influence on the subsequent development of Islam in Uzbekistan. So it is possible that some Soviet-era religious figures have been inadvertently excluded from my commentary, or alternatively there are some whose influence is overstated. One religious figure, Muhammad Sodiq Muhammad Yusuf, is the subject of a separate chapter, which follows.

There is an equally rich (and overlapping) history of Islam in Tajikistan. I have included only a handful of the most important figures from Tajikistan, those who had the greatest impact on Uzbek religious thought. But in framing my discussion on Uzbek Islamic religious leaders, I have benefited from being able to read the unpublished interviews done by Muzaffar Olimov and

Saodat Olimova with clerics and their children who were active in the last six decades of the twentieth century in Tajikistan. This chapter also depends very heavily on the research that Bakhtiyar Babadjanov carried out at the request of the Carnegie Endowment for International Peace.

No matter how rapacious Stalin's henchmen had been, the decimation of the class of clerics was never complete. Even in the 1920s and 1930s, not only did religion survive, but there were theologians seeking to teach Islam and engage in theological disputations designed to introduce innovations in local practices. Their efforts had an impact on the religious environment in Tashkent.

While the numbers of such people dropped sharply, there were still enough surviving students of these people, as well as people with madrasa education more generally, to pass on Central Asia's Islamic heritage when political conditions loosened somewhat, toward the end of Stalin's life. Despite the illegal status of many theologians, Islamic clerics continued to have a special status in society and the respect of their communities, although they did not occupy the same central social roles that they had when religious institutions had been legal.

Even when all the madrasas were closed, the existence of *hujras* created the conditions necessary for at least a small number—hundreds, and even maybe a few thousand—of devout Muslims living in the Soviet Union to meet their obligation by the laws of Sharia to transmit their knowledge of Islam and its laws, to be engaged in *davat*. While this system of education represented an obvious decline from even the colonial era religious education, it did represent sufficient theological vitality to keep Islam alive in the region's religious centers. And, once restrictions were loosened, first in the Soviet period and then following independence, Islam was able to interface with a larger religious world.

Given the targeted campaign against religious institutions and the clerics associated with them in the centers of Muslim confessional learning (Bukhara, Samarkand, and Khiva), Tashkent began to emerge as a center of religious learning, albeit one that was much smaller and more semi-clandestine than its predecessors.

The Stalin years were the grimmest, from the point of view of religious education, and virtually none of the surviving clerics were willing to take on pupils until conditions eased somewhat after World War II. Even then, most were willing to work only with students who were either relatives or drawn from a circle of close family friends.

Our elderly and religious interlocutors in Uzbekistan were unable to remember the existence of any *hujra* in the 1930s through late 1940s, and until 1943 through 1944 virtually all mosques and all madrasas were closed as well. The religious leaders who escaped persecution mostly fled to remote areas such as Surkhandarya in Uzbekistan and Batken in Kyrgyzstan, or to the mountain regions of Tajikistan.

What religious education continued was done in families in what was termed *qori pochcha hujras* (run by a relative able to read the Quran). This instruction was generally restricted to learning some basic prayers and some *ayats* (verses) from the Quran, normally the first *sura*[1] (*al-Fatiha*), the last *ayats* from *Ayat ul-Kursi* (Quran, 2:251), and some prayers (*duas*) of personal supplication. This same kind of religious instruction continues to be carried out in the old cities of most Uzbek urban centers.

Parents who wanted their children, primarily boys, to continue education tried to place them with religiously educated people. Because this method of education was illegal, there were fewer and fewer *hujras* as time went by. Groups were limited to six or seven children. By the beginning of the 1980s, only three *hujras* were left in the old city of Tashkent. This situation could not help but have an impact, and the level of religious literacy in the old city sharply declined. However, by 1987 the number of *hujras* in the old city increased by several times. *Hujras* were mostly attended by young men ages 16 to 25 or 26. By the end of the 1980s, many *hujras* in the old city of Tashkent transformed into *jamoas* (communities) for spreading the faith, whose initiator and main influence was Obidkhon qori Nazarov (to be discussed later). In Soviet times *hujra* education was generally limited to rote learning of the Quran and laying the basis of other religious studies—*tajwid*, *tafsir ul-Quran*, *hadith*, *usul al-fiqh*, *fura al-fiqh*, and *ilm ul-faraid*. The best of the students were able to achieve an understanding of the texts of Arab grammar, philology, and, of course, theologians' essays and works, but their level of mastery was significantly less than had been true of those trained in colonial days, not to mention earlier. Nonetheless, those trained in the Soviet-era *hujra* schools were accepted by the community as *ulama*.

The religious divisions that were present in pre-Soviet Central Asia also continued to be represented in the world of underground, and then aboveground, Islam, once SADUM came into being, with one of the main points of contention being the role of *taqlid*.

Taqlid has formed the basis of religious decisionmaking in Central Asia for more than a half millennium, and the practice has come under strong criticism from reformist elements, from the time of the Jadids through to the present. The term comes from the Arabic words *taqlidid/taqlidiya*, meaning to follow or to imitate and, thus, means following the authoritative decisions already made when writing a *fatwa* or in one's reading of the Quran or the *hadiths*. *Taqlid* is generally practiced in one form or another in each of the four Islamic schools of religious law, making each of the four traditions different from the other three. This explains why the Hanafi tradition in Central Asia could be kept alive despite the repressive political conditions of Soviet rule. But there were always critics of this practice, termed Salafi here but often called "Wahhabi" by their Hanafi critics.

By definition Sufi *hujras* were Hanafi in orientation, because the exaggeration of ritual that helps define them is wholly absent and anathema to Salafi tradition. The Sufi *hujras* or *khalqas* (circles or chains of religious believers) were generally found in provincial or remote areas, where they would be virtually invisible to representatives of the Ministry of Internal Affairs and KGB (State Security Committee). Because of these organizations' secrecy and concealment, members of the Sufi *hujras* were not as readily recognized as the other theology students from metropolitan areas. As a result, the leaders and members of Sufi *hujras* never had the same relatively public clashes as the Hanafi clerics and their Salafi or "Wahhabi" critics.

The majority of Sufi sheikhs have come from traditional Sufi family clans, and the sheikhs were the center of a highly individualized approach to their education. That is in keeping with the nature of the Sufi intellectual tradition, which places the teacher as guide to Sufi-style worship, and not simply the teacher as source of introduction to religious text.

For much of Soviet rule, well-organized or structured study groups were rare, but teachers took on students as they saw fit and taught them independent of a structured program of study. The common curriculum incorporated the studies of Sharia and some rituals. This program was traditionally delivered only to those who themselves aspired to become sheikhs. From the mid-1980s on (beginning with the Gorbachev reforms), the role and presence of Sufi *khalqa* increased; by now there are *khalqas* and *hujras* with some thirty thousand students (for example, Ibrahim Hazrat's *khalqa*, which is described in a later section).

These theological divisions were much more important than whether a cleric or teacher received a salary from SADUM and worked in a state-recognized religious institution or worked outside of the formal system. There were never really "two" Islams, parallel and official, as was often depicted in Western writings about religion in the Soviet Union.[2] Rather, there was Islam, a single faith with important theological distinctions dividing clerics who propagated it. SADUM's clerics not only interacted with those who were providing religious education that was not sanctioned by the SADUM, they sometimes even advanced the careers of those working outside of it. Being inside or outside of the SADUM system, and sometimes conducting unsanctioned activities while earning salaries from the SADUM, was less important than supporting certain sides of the major theological questions of the day.

The term "Wahhabi" is obviously a contentious one, and whether it is properly applied in the Central Asian context is less important than the degree of anger within the clerical community that its use clearly implies. And (although this is skipping ahead in the story a bit) Muhammadjon Hindustani (Rustamov) seems to have invoked it in his anger at Ziyauddin Bobokhon, who responded to Hindustani's public rebuke of him for deviating from traditional Hanafi teachings in his *fatwas* by removing Hindustani from the Council of Ulama of SADUM.

This created a religious life that reproduced in a reduced scale the kinds of complexities that existed in most other Islamic communities. The number of religious institutions in the region was a small fraction of those that had been in place prior to the Soviet rule, when in Bukhara alone there were several hundred madrasas. Similarly, the *fatwas* issued by the official religious hierarchy were scrutinized by ideological workers in the state and Communist Party apparatuses, to ensure that they were not potentially seditious in content. Islamic clerics were prohibited from delivering sermons or anything else that might be construed as performing missionary work among the population. The clerical establishment also included individuals with close ties to state security, both informers and actual employees of the security services.

At the same time, SADUM was an instrument of religious enlightenment, albeit on a highly restricted stage. The two madrasas were authentic religious institutions, staffed by clerics with religious education, including, with time, increasing numbers of individuals with foreign training. Their existence restored traditional Hanafi religious education in the region.

This created a new context for a deepening of debate between those who advanced centuries-old Hanafi teachings and those who sought their reform.

The interpretative tilt of these years was that of accommodation to the secular (and in the case of the Soviets, atheistic) rulers who served as Central Asia's overlords. However, in the context of Islam, the atheism of the Soviet authorities was not of doctrinal interest, no more than that of any unbelievers would have been. The focus, instead, was on the state's attitude toward Islam, and that was much improved over the decades of the 1920s and 1930s.

The fact that SADUM clerics did not largely view those who ran *hujras* as "enemies" helps explain why the institution of *hujras* was able to survive for so long. One of our major correspondents, a retired KGB officer, A. Kamilov, who led operations in Andijan for much of the 1980s and early 1990s, explained this situation. He noted that thanks to a well-developed network of informants throughout the region, the KGB was very aware of where the *hujras* were, and who was studying there, but that the *hujras* were not perceived as primary threats to the state. Rather, when the anti-religious campaigns of the 1980s were launched by Andropov, expanded by Konstantin Chernenko and then by Mikhail Gorbachev, the KGB's attention was focused on "everyday" or "household" Islam, on traditional life-cycle rituals and pilgrimages to local tombs, and not on religious education. The former was seen as a source of the "backwardness" of Central Asian peoples and their alleged relative failures in social and economic development. By contrast, theological teachings of Islam were the source of intellectual strength, and when Gorbachev allowed the reintroduction of religion, as represented by the Russian Orthodoxy, back into Soviet public life, Komsomol activists and even Communist Party workers also sought to rediscover their religious roots, giving further legitimacy to the *hujras*.

SHAMI DOMULLA, *AHL-I HADITH*, AND OTHER EARLY SALAFI *HUJRAS*

In the first decades after the revolution, Salafi teachings continued to serve as a source of religious innovation in Uzbekistan, led in large part by clerics who came to Central Asia from outside of the region and brought with them a broader context of religious thought in general and religious reform in particular.

The most influential of these was Shami (domulla) al-Tarabulsi, who was educated in Al-Azhar in Cairo. He traveled to Iran, Afghanistan, and Kashmir before settling in Central Asia in 1919, where he remained until his death in 1932, following his arrest in Khiva.[3] Shami (domulla) al-Tarabulsi lived in Xinjiang for fifteen to twenty years, and it is there where he seems to have deepened his commitment to Salafi thinking.[4] The movement was particularly strong in Xinjiang, focused on drawing the population away from Sufi practices.[5]

Shami (domulla) al-Tarabulsi is considered by some to be the "father" of modern Central Asian Salafi thought. He was a proponent of achieving the purification of Islam by relying on the teachings of the *hadiths* and eliminating local practices that lacked doctrinal sanction. His preaching brought him to the attention of the Russian consul in Kashgar, who seems to have facilitated his travel westward in the hopes that the cleric would be a positive influence on the "medieval" practices of Russia's Central Asian population. Shami (domulla) al-Tarabulsi arrived in Tashkent in February 1919, after Russian colonial authorities were no longer in control.

In these conditions of near political anarchy, though, Shami (domulla) al-Tarabulsi seems to have quickly established himself as one of the leading religious authorities in Tashkent by besting a leading local cleric (Sheikh Maksud qori) in a theological dispute. As a result of this, he went from the insignificant post he had arranged for himself in a *mahalla* mosque to the Dasturkhonchi Madrasa in the old town of Tashkent. From this setting he wrote and preached against traditional Hanafi and Sufi clerics, complaining of the poor or nonexistent doctrinal bases for most religious practices in the region—such as pilgrimages to holy sites, wedding ceremonies, and burial rites The only solution, according to Shami (domulla) al-Tarabulsi, was to base religious practice on the Quran and any *hadiths* that could reliably be linked directly to the Prophet.[6]

When Islamic institutions were closed, Shami (domulla) al-Tarabulsi and his supporters organized their own *hujra* that was located in the old city of Tashkent (at first, in the "Mu-yi Mubarak" Madrasa, then at Shami (domulla) al-Tarabulsi's house). People started to call them "*Ahl-i Hadith*" because they based their *fatwas* solely on the Quran and *hadiths*. Consequently, they rejected the spirit and teachings of local traditions based on the teachings of the Hanafi school and the concordant decisions of local theologians of the past (*ijma*). They viewed their activities as a kind of Quranic study circle, rather than a *hujra*. The *Ahl-i Hadith* rejected most textbooks of Hanafi education, and Sufi texts were completely rejected. Shami (domulla) al-Tarabulsi taught the Quran, the collections of *hadiths* "al-Jami as-Salih" of Imam Bukhari, the works of Imam Muslim, and those of their commentaries. He also taught some Salafi texts, mainly those of Sheikh ul-Islam ibn Taymiya. He emphasized Arab language instruction, mainly using poetry collections that were popular in the Ottoman Empire.

As Shami (domulla) al-Tarabulsi wrote:

> ... It will be enough for us to mention from them his sublime words directed to honorable spouses and true believing mothers—may Allah be pleased with them—where he said, "Remember what is read in your homes from the ayats of Allah, the sign of wisdom"; that is, from the Quran and the Sunna of the Prophet, as well as his words from the hadith—may Allah bless and welcome him: "The Heaven sent the book and together with it that which is similar to it," that is, the Quran and the hadith. That which is not mentioned in the Quran is put into the hadith. ... And from thence his (that is, the Prophet's) words, may Allah bless him and greet: "O God! Take pity upon my successors." And it was asked: "Who are your successors, o Messenger of Allah?" He answered, "Those who follow me, who tell my hadiths, and explain them to new people." Or, as he said, may Allah bless him and greet him, and he also called in his hadiths to bless the muhaddithes, named them his successors (*khalafa*), his amirs and deputies (*nuwwab*) in communicating the knowledge of the Sharia and saving her from deviation, change, and replacement, and showed them greater respect than caliphs, amirs, and governors.[7]

Shami domulla and his followers supported some of the early anti-religious policies of the Soviets, which they saw as helping Central Asians return to the purity of their faith, including the destruction of shrines around burial places (*mazars*) of revered Central Asian theologians and other esteemed figures (but of course not the destruction of the *mazars* themselves). For that reason initially Shami (domulla) al-Tarabulsi and other such theologians' religious purism suited the new authorities of that time, who were trying to put together a fight against "remnants of the past," relying on some loyal theologians.[8]

Certainly, the choices before Shami domulla and his followers were difficult: they were willing to work with Soviet authorities to root out superstitious practices, while still condemning Soviet organized violence against religious believers and clerics.

In the 1920s and 1930s, some of the *Ahl-i Hadith* members split off to create another fundamentalist group, the *Ahl-i Quran* (adherents of the Quran), because they saw *Ahl-i Hadith* as too accepting of Soviet rule and its clerics as too complicit in it.

The *Ahl-i Quran* movement was also known as *uzun soqolis* (literally "long-beards"), and it organized *hujras* in Tashkent and in the Ferghana Valley (in Margilan and Kokand), and in Khujand in Tajikistan. They, too, opposed many local "religious" practices, especially the *ziyorats* to the graves of "saints" that were a central part of local Sufi ritual. These theologians accepted only the Quran as a legitimate basis of religious law, and they believed that the *Ahl-i Hadith* clerics were putting too much faith in the validity of the *hadiths*. One of the unusual features of the group was its advocacy of using an Uzbek, rather than Arabic, translation of the Quran.

According to Bakhtiyar Babadjanov, most of the members of this group (as opposed to those in *Ahl-i Hadith*) had poor Arabic language skills and, thus, were pushing reliance on the Uzbek language translation of the Quran. This was a rather unusual phenomenon for Islamic fundamentalists, most of whom advocated the use of the vernacular Quran solely for self-education. The *Ahl-i Quran* also advocated the reciting of *namaz*[9] twice a day, rather than the prescribed five times daily. In recent years other schismatic groups have made similar claims, including the Akramiya[10] movement, whose jailed leader Akrom Yuldoshev was blamed by the Uzbek government for triggering the unrest in Andijan in May 2005.[11]

The movement, though, also included figures who were noted for their religious learning, including its founder, Sabircha domulla. He had been a student of Mullah Abd as-Samad (who studied with Shami (domulla) al-Tarabulsi), Baduh Hazrat, and also of Hazrat Hasan (whose full name was Hazrat Hasan Akhmadajanovich Ponomarev al-Kizildjari).[12]

Hazrat Hasan was considered one of the most influential clerics in Uzbekistan in the 1920s, after being exiled to Tashkent from his birthplace in Petropavlovsk (northern Kazakhstan). Bakhtiyar Babadjanov maintains that Hazrat Hasan was a critical link between Central Asian Islam and the early Salafi thinkers in the Arab world, having become familiar with their teachings as a result of trips to the Middle East.[13]

Ashirbek Muminov credits Hazrat Hasan with an even larger role, seeing him as a link with Shihab ad-Din al-Marjani (1818–1889),[14] the Tatar reformer who was influential in the development of the Jadid movement and who served as Hazrat Hasan's mentor as well. Muminov depicts Hazrat Hasan as a masterful interpreter of Quranic texts, and he, too, saw only the Quran and the *hadiths* as an acceptable basis of religious teachings. Muminov maintains that al-Kizildjari was close to Jamal Khoja Ishan, and through him with the members of both the *Ahl-i Hadith* and *Ahl-i Quran* movements.[15]

By the late 1920s and early 1930s a balancing act was no longer possible, and members of the *Ahl-i Hadith* movement were either arrested or went into hiding. Several clerics managed to survive and return to teaching, especially in the old city of Tashkent when conditions became more favorable.[16] Ashirbek Muminov writes that a group of some 3,000 followers were still in Tashkent in 2007, with the death or incapacitation of a member leading to a son or another close relative taking his place, and that their meetings were at traditional Uzbek *gaps* (male social gatherings).[17] The much respected Yunus qori (Khakimdjanov) was also tied to this movement. In the Khrushchev and Brezhnev years, he had his own *hujra* in the Ferghana Valley, which he maintained until his death in the mid-1970s. He is credited with being a formative influence for Abdulhakim qori Margiloniy (or Hakimjon qori, born Abdulhakim Vosiev), who trained a subsequent generation of Islamic fundamentalists in Margilan (in the Ferghana Valley).

THE BOBOKHON FAMILY AND SADUM

Shami (domulla) al-Tarabulsi's students and followers included many of the most influential clerics of Soviet Uzbekistan during the decades just before and after World War II.[18] His most important pupil was Ziyauddin Bobokhon (1908–1982), who first served as deputy and then *mufti* of SADUM (1957–1982). In that post, he was able to introduce some of Shami (domulla) al-Tarabulsi's teachings both through the curriculum of SADUM's madrasas and in the *fatwas* that were issued.

While there is no doubt that the seven decades of Soviet rule transformed the development of Islam in Uzbekistan and in Central Asia more generally, it did not deal it a death blow. As noted above, a handful of prominent clerics survived and were able to maintain study circles that, while small in size, were enough to allow for religious continuity. And so when Soviet policies changed, there were at least a few clerics of sufficient learning necessary to serve as religious leaders in the community and to be accepted as such as they traveled throughout the Muslim world representing the Islamic community of the Soviet Union.

In this regard the Bobokhon(ov) family, as they were known during Soviet rule, is worthy of a detailed introduction. As already noted, the first three *muftis* all came from the same family, Eshon Bobokhon ibn Abdulmajidkhon (1943–1957);[19] his son, Ziyauddin Bobokhon (1957–1982); and Ziyauddin Bobokhon's son, Shamsuddin Bobokhonov (1982–1989).

The Bobokhon family was a well-known religious family before the Soviet takeover. According to Vitaly Naumkin, director of the Institute of Oriental Studies of the Russian Academy of Sciences, Eshon Bobokhon ibn Abdulmajidkhon's grandfather, Ayub Khan ibn Yunus Khan, was a well-known *faqih* (an expert on Islamic law) and a teacher in the Mu-yi Mubarak Madrasa in prerevolutionary Tashkent and was granted the honorary title Sheikh-ul-Islam.[20]

Ziyauddin Bobokhon (1908–1982), who first served as deputy and then *mufti* of SADUM, was the more influential religious figure of the three. He is generally viewed as having been strongly influenced by his time spent studying with Shami (domulla) al-Tarabulsi. He was in exile for much of his youth. Fearing for his safety because of the company he was keeping, in 1933 or 1934, Ziyauddin Bobokhon fled to relatives in Sayram (in southern Kazakhstan), then to Bekobod city southwest of Tashkent, then to Khujand where he worked as a cook in a *kolkhoz*. He returned to Tashkent only after his father, Eshon Bobokhon ibn Abdulmajidkhon, was appointed as the first *mufti* of SADUM in 1943.

Salim Hajji Khujandi (born in the 1890s, and died in 1983) ran a *hujra* in Bekobod, now a small industrial city some 40 kilometers west of Khujand, on the Uzbek side of the border. He took up residence there in 1931, four years after fleeing Bukhara to avoid arrest, and in 1933 to 1934 he offered sanctuary to Ziyauddin Bobokhon.

Salim Hajji, who taught his students from a traditional Hanafi curriculum, later told his students that though he was "bowled over by Ziyauddin's Wahhabi[21] arrogance," he couldn't turn him in to state security, choosing to fight to purge his soul of his Wahhabi ideas, to turn him away from the teachings of *Ahl-i Quran*. It was a task at which Salim Hajji apparently failed.

The Bobokhon family seems to have remembered the favor. Eshon Bobokhon ibn Abdulmajidkhon appointed Salim Hajji imam of Bekobod's only mosque, in 1948, and in 1954 he opened his *hujra*, teaching both Uzbeks and Tajiks. Salim Hajji maintained close ties with Hindustani and seems to have taken advice from him on various theological matters, with the course of instruction in his *hujra* being close to that in Hindustani's. Both focused on medieval Hanafi texts and both excluded texts of Sufi mysticism.

Salim Hajji wrote several theological essays. The best known, "Regarding the limits of matters on reading the prayer *sunnat* in homes," was written in the 1960s. Although not published, this 20–22 page essay was circulated in manuscript form and highlighted the theological rift between Hanafi tradition and its critics. The topic of the essay, *sunnat*, is a prayer read before the beginning of the formal prayer session in the mosque. Hanafi Muslims believe that this prayer is mandatory, while their Salafi critics believe that it should be omitted.

Although we do not possess a copy of this text, Bakhtiyar Babadjanov has had it explained in detail to him by a number of Salim Hajji's students.[22] The best known of these students, Sallohiddin Mahsum-domla, the imam of the Katartal Mosque in Tashkent at the time of Babadjanov's interview, characterized his teacher Salim Hajji as belonging to the old generation of "*taqlidchis*," those who revered tradition.

The need to respect tradition is underscored in Salim Hajji's writing. The introduction to the text (*muqaddima*) apparently makes open reference to local clerics who are termed "Wahhabis," possibly the first such reference in Soviet Uzbekistan, calling them aliens (*yots*) to local Muslims. Salim Hajji apparently wrote that opinions of local Wahhabis were formed under the influence of apostates (*malun*) from the Arab world, such as Hassan al-Banna, Sayyid Abul Ala Maududi, and Sayyid Qutb. Although few read the essay, it was nonetheless well known to local believers, attesting to the way that ideas and materials were able to circulate, and to the fervor with which religious divisions were perpetuated even when the teaching of Islam was allegedly restricted by a watchful government eye.

Returning to the story of Ziyauddin Bobokhon, his father's pre-revolutionary position as *qadi* of Tashkent may have been a source of protection of the younger Bobokhon. It is rumored that in 1938, the People's Commissariat of Internal Affairs was preparing to arrest him, but did not because his father agreed to cooperate with local security forces. Similar charges were made against Eshon Bobokhon during his tenure at SADUM. But, as the latter's defenders maintain, the compromises the elder Bobokhon may have made were in the interests of ensuring the perpetuation of Islam.

In 1947 Bobokhon went to travel and study in the Middle East for a year, going to Al-Azhar in Cairo and then to Saudi Arabia. The religious practices there seem to have deepened his antipathy to local Hanafi practices, which, at least according to Vitaly Naumkin, Bobokhon termed "pagan" in some of his *fatwas*.[23]

Ziyauddin Bobokhon's approach to the formulation of *fatwas* was similar to that of his theological mentor, which is to say, they should be based on the Quran and *hadiths*, which gave him a theological grounding from which to attack traditional local "religious" practices, "household" or "everyday" Islam. For Bobokhon it was an issue of doctrinal purity, but like Shami (domulla) al-Tarabulsi, the Soviet *mufti* understood that this made his *fatwas* seem more in line with the regime's social policies.

While Bobokhon was often viewed as a "compromised" figure for his support of Soviet social policies, his position can be just as easily explained as being driven by a commitment to seek the purity of religious practices. Bakhtiyar Babadjanov singles out a series of 1952 *fatwas* on "muridism" and "ishanism" (terms used for customary Sufi practices), which he attributes to Ziyauddin Bobokhon. Though Ziyauddin might appear to be appeasing Soviet authorities by endorsing Soviet social goals, at the same time he made a strong case that such practice violated Sharia through the use of examples from local Hanafi teachings on *hadiths* and the Quran.[24]

In any case, his theocratic approach made the mission of SADUM more consistent with that of the Soviet state. But while the Soviets saw this as promoting atheism, some in SADUM at least saw it as promoting the "true" faith of Islam. A more traditional Hanafi approach to social customs might well have produced real tension between SADUM and the Soviet state authorities.

Ismail Sattiev (d. 1976) was quite close to Eshon Bobokhon as well as to Ziyauddin Bobokhon, who was closer to Sattiev's theocratic orientation. Sattiev was born in Namangan, where his father, Mullah Sotti Okhund, was an imam. Ismail Sattiev studied with Ghofur qori and with Sobit Khon-tura Saghuni (d. 1976 in Mecca). In 1927, Sattiev joined the *Ahl-i Quran* and from the 1930s until 1942 was hiding in Kara Suu and Batken. Muhammad Sodiq Muhammad Yusuf married Ismail Sattiev's daughter, in the way that religious dynasties sought to intermarry to preserve something of a religious class.

Sattiev ran a Salafi *hujra*, as well as worked for SADUM. Sattiev was part of the first delegation, headed by Eshon Bobokhon, which was sent to a 1943 reception in Moscow with Kalinin and Molotov to discuss the creation of SADUM and establishment of a number of mosques. Although the group obtained permission to establish these institutions, it needed to comply with certain conditions. Eshon Bobokhon apparently said in a private conversation that "although signing the document undermined our consciences, it served the interests of Islam and Muslims,"[25] emphasizing the dilemma that has always confronted Muslim leaders who are subject to secular authorities for establishing the rules by which they are permitted to work.

In 1956, Sattiev was appointed director of the Mir-i Arab Madrasa in Bukhara, where he is said to have had the opportunity to benefit from bribes and other financial resources. The extent of this is unclear, but the Central Archives contain letters written by the madrasa students complaining about "someone" taking advantage of his authority. The complaints included facts about Sattiev's replacing nearly all of the teaching staff with friends from the Ferghana Valley, and especially from Namangan. He openly demanded kickbacks and, according to other complaints that could not be independently verified, had a passion for pedophilia. Nevertheless, Sattiev maintained his position for a long time, perhaps because of his close friendship with Ziyauddin Bobokhon. Yet another explanation—widely believed but never proven—could be that Sattiev, in fact, worked for the KGB.

It would be a real mistake to cast Bobokhon as a politicized religious figure. He had no problem helping to protect some people whose views he disagreed with, even while trying to limit the influence of these same people in SADUM.

One noteworthy person who fits in this category was Nodirkhon domla Aloutdinov (1899–1975)[26] from Tashkent, who established an important *hujra* that existed from the early 1960s through the middle of the 1970s. Nodirkhon domla was a descendant of the well-known Ala ad-Din family of clerics and went to primary and secondary religious schools before beginning a period of self- and directed study with leading religious figures in Tashkent. Nodirkhon domla's specialty was Sufi mystical poetry, and he was considered a poet of some distinction in his later years.

Nodirkhon domla taught in Jadid schools from 1920 until the last part of the decade, and then in 1928 or 1929 fled to a remote part of Syr Darya Oblast, finding work in a railcar repair shop. His reputation for religious learning, especially of classical Sufi poetry, was such that he was one of the initial organizers of SADUM in 1943 and was reported as largely responsible for collecting the manuscripts to form the Barak Khan Madrasa library where SADUM was housed. He worked in SADUM until his death, initially heading the department of *fatwas* and running a public outreach department for giving religious advice to the lay population. Bakhtiyar Babadjanov reports that his responsibilities were diminished after Ziyauddin Bobokhon took over, largely because the two clashed on the content of the *fatwas* that derived their content from traditional Hanafi interpretations of social law.[27]

In addition to his work in SADUM, Nodirkhon domla established a *hujra* in the old city of Tashkent in 1962 that he ran through the mid-1970s. Babadjanov considers him to have been the most learned of the clerics of traditional Hanafi teachings in Tashkent during these years and that he had a number of notable students and supporters.[28] Nodirkhon domla believed that most local religious rites and rituals, including the cult of "saints," the cult of ancestors, and the worship of their graves, largely conformed to Sharia.

HINDUSTANI AND HANAFI "TRADITIONALISM"

The Hanafi thinker who most influenced Uzbek and other Central Asian clerics of the generation of the 1970s and 1980s was Muhammadjon Hindustani. He seems to have trained more students over the course of his lifetime in his Dushanbe *hujra* than did any other figure in Central Asia. There is no question that officials in Moscow, at least at some level, knew of his existence. I, too, knew of his existence and traveled to Dushanbe in 1983 in the hopes of meeting him. But as one senior scholar at the Institute of Oriental Studies Manuscript Archives (a colleague of Hindustani's) explained to me, I might want to meet Hindustani, but there was no reason at all why Hindustani should want to meet me. Hindustani's ability to continue to train students came in part because of the caution with which he proceeded, and this caution helped him maintain the support of the local power structure in Dushanbe, where he lived and worked.

Hindustani was an ethnic Uzbek; his students were Uzbek and Tajik. But maybe Hindustani was able to succeed because he was sitting quietly in Dushanbe, a very remote part of the Soviet Union, and not teaching in Tashkent, a city of international importance in Soviet times—Moscow's Asian showplace.

Hindustani was able to use his position at the Institute of Oriental Studies as a *krysha* (place of protection)[29] as he sought to educate a new generation of Islamic theologians in Central Asia. For these extensive efforts Hindustani received a number of honorific titles and was known as Domla Hindustani, Hindi domla, Hajji domla, Mawlavi, and to his students, Hajji dada. His full name was Muhammadjon Rustamov. He was born in 1892, in the village of Chorbog, not far from Kokand. At age eight his father, Rustam Hajji Kokandi (who taught at madrasas in Kokand and Samarkand), sent him off to study. For four years Hindustani studied with two well-known local clerics (Muhammad Amin and Toshbolta domla) and then, in 1904, he went to Kokand to study Quran syntax and Arabic grammar and syntax (*sarf va nahu*) with Zikriye qori and Mullah Eshonqul. He then pursued formal religious education at the Ming-ayim Madrasa in Kokand and the Khanakah Eshon Sayakhshin Madrasa in Bukhara. He was studying there when World War I broke out, causing him to flee the country to avoid being drafted into the labor detachments of the Russian Army.

Hindustani was one of a number of students who left Bukhara for Balkh, in Afghanistan, where his teacher was Hazrat Muhammad Gavs Said-zade. He studied a wide variety of disciplines, including Islamic law and the mystical poetry of Rumi, Hafiz, and Bedil. But the deteriorating political situation in Afghanistan led Hindustani to return (with his teacher) to Bukhara in 1916, and both then went on to Tashkent, where Hazrat Muhammad Gavs Said-zade began teaching at the Kukaldosh Madrasa. The two left Tashkent for Jalalabad, Afghanistan, shortly after the October Revolution, and in 1919, Hindustani went to India to complete his studies in the Usmaniya Madrasa in Kashmir, which explains why he is known as "Hindustani." While in India, Hindustani is said to have mastered both Hindi and Urdu, and also went on *hajj* to Mecca (with his father, who died during the pilgrimage).

Hindustani then returned to his home village of Chorbog in 1929, allegedly as part of a promise to his dying father, and then settled in Kokand at the height of the Stalinist repression. His effort to evade arrest through hiding out in a small village (Abligh, in the Akhangaran region), proved fruitless, and he was arrested in 1933 and sentenced to two years of forced labor. Later, in 1937, he was arrested again while living in a settlement outside of Tashkent and was sentenced to three years in Siberia. He returned to Kokand in 1940, working in an oil processing factory for three years until he was drafted and sent to the front. Severely wounded in battle, he was not sent home until 1947, when he moved to Dushanbe to take up an appointment as *imam-hatib*[30] of the Mawlana Yaqub Charkhy Mosque in Dushanbe. He was arrested after just over a year at this post and spent four and a half years in prison, but was fully rehabilitated after Stalin's death in March 1953.

After his release, Hindustani took up a post in the Institute of Oriental Studies of the Academy of Sciences in Dushanbe, teaching Urdu and producing annotated manuscripts of Arabic language texts. He also was appointed the *imam mecheti* (Russian term for "imam of a mosque"), serving at the mosque in Charkhi (Dushanbe). It was at this point that Hindustani began offering illegal religious instruction in a *hujra* that was located inside of Mavlan Charkhi Mosque, with the tacit approval of some local authorities. During this period he also began work on the six-volume *tafsir*.

Unlike many of the illegal religious schools that were organized in Central Asia, Hindustani's followed a formal and extensive curriculum, quite similar to what might be offered at a normal madrasa. Dozens, and possibly hundreds, of young men studied with Hindustani.

Hindustani's better students spent several years in study with him, receiving lectures on the Quran, studying the *hadith*, learning about Islamic jurisprudence, the doctrinal system of Islam (*Fiqh al-akbar*, "Aqida an-Nasafiy"), ethics (*adab*), oratory (*nutq*), Islamic cosmology and narrative history, Islamic medicine, astrology, astronomy, and of course advanced Arabic grammar, syntax, and morphology. This course of study was designed to parallel what students would have received in a madrasa. While for some it was their only religious education, for others it was a form of preparation for more formal instruction, either in SADUM's madrasas or in other *hujras*, under teachers with different specialties.

Some who studied with Hindustani decided to break with the Hanafi tradition that he taught them. Among those were Hakimjon qori, who created what could be seen as a competing *hujra* in Margilan, and Rahmatulla-alloma and Abduvali qori, both of whom went to study with Hakimjon qori. Hindustani also taught Sayid Abdulloh Nuri, leader of the Islamic Renaissance Party of Tajikistan, and Hikmat-zade, of the same organization. All of these individuals eventually rejected what they saw as Hindustani's excessively conciliatory attitude toward the secular authorities.

Even more significant are the clerics trained by Hindustani who both continue to exemplify Central Asia's Hanafi tradition and seek to extend it. These include Ismoil qori Ququoni, the imam of a major mosque in Kokand, whose opposition to the "Wahhabis" in 1992 was so strong that they held him captive, and Muhammad Sodiq Kasymov Andijoni, who has sought to position himself as a defender of Hanafi orthodoxy against Muhammad Sodiq Muhammad Yusuf's more dynamic interpretation of this tradition. Muhammad Sodiq Kasymov Andijoni's brother, Abdulatif

Kasymov Andijoni, a well-known critic of "Wahhabism" in Uzbekistan, as well as of the Hizb ut-Tahrir movement, is another Hindustani student, as is Kimsanbai-azhi, the imam of the main mosque in Shymkent (Kazakhstan), and formerly the main spiritual leader of Kazakhstan.[31]

For this group of Hanafi clerics in particular, Hindustani's writings remain a source of inspiration. His best known theological writings are his extensive commentaries and translation of the Quran into Uzbek (six volumes in all), which he completed in 1984, as well as his series of philosophic essays (*Isharat as-Sabbaa, Pand-nama-iy Hazrat Mawlavi*), and various religious translations and commentaries. As already mentioned, Hindustani's *hujra* was just one of many that trained young Central Asians during these years. There were also several others worth mentioning in or near Dushanbe that often tried to support one another or work in concert. Many date from the mid-1950s, the period of the Khrushchev thaw. During this time, the Communist Party first secretary, Bobojon Gafurov,[32] took over as director of the Institute of Oriental Studies of the Tajik Academy of Sciences, and this seemingly offered protection from a high-ranking person to those "deviating" from Soviet ideological norms.

Qozi domla (Abdurashid domla)[33] also ran a *hujra* in Dushanbe. He was a student of Islamic law and was considered by some to be a theologian of even greater accomplishment than Hindustani. Qozi domla was born in the city of Ferghana and grew up there. When he died in 1978, he was buried in Dushanbe. He, too, studied in Bukhara and returned to Ferghana after the revolution, fleeing to Hissar in the early 1930s, when arrests of clerics increased. In 1949 he moved to the outskirts of Dushanbe, with the support of Hindustani—where he was known as Qozi Tajikistan. There he was named *qadi* of the Republic of Tajikistan, a post he held for two years, until Ziyauddin Bobokhon took over SADUM and removed him. Qozi domla then served as imam in a small mosque on the outskirts of Dushanbe.

He began teaching in 1956. Bakhtiyar Babadjanov argues that Qozi domla's curriculum, though, was less rigorous than that of Hindustani, a conclusion contested by Muzaffar and Saodat Olimov, who have interviewed many students of both religious leaders.[34] Qozi domla's curriculum included an introduction to Arabic syntax and grammar, and dogma "*Sharh Aqaid an-Nasafi*," using commentaries of the well-known work "*al-*

Aqaid," written by a local Hanafi theologian, Abu Hafs an-Hasafi (died 1147). He taught *fiqh*, on the basis of "*Hidaya al-furu*," a well-known work by the noted Hanafi author Burhan ud-Din al-Margilani (died 1197 in Samarkand), and he also taught commentaries to the Quran (for example, "Baydavi"). In various years his students included Turajonzoda, Hikmatulla, and Sayid Abdulloh Nuri from Tajikistan, and Hojji Ahmadjon Makhdum, a noted Sufi figure from Uzbekistan who is described at some length below.[35]

This same Hojji Ahmadjon Makhdum was sent to Hindustani by Hazrat Bobo Muhammad, who ran an important *hujra* in Surkhandarya, in Sarasiya, in the southeastern part of the oblast near the Tajik border, where he was born and where, in 1968, he died. This is another indication of the kind of teaching network that had emerged.

Hazrat Bobo Muhammad al-Khorazmi (Muhammad ibn Musa al-Khorazmi) studied in Bukhara before the revolution, returning home and seeking work in a *kolkhoz* to blend into the community. During those years he briefly offered Hindustani safe haven. For a short time after World War II, Bobo Muhammad served as imam of Surkhandarya's only legally sanctioned mosque, which was in Termez (near the Afghan border and a stone's throw from Tajikistan and its capital, Dushanbe).

After Stalin's death, Bobo Muhammad began a small *hujra*, initially gathering pupils solely from among his friends and relatives. His curriculum was limited to instruction in "*ilm ul-faraid*" (the laws on inheritance), on the preparation of specific kinds of *fatwas*, and on the methodology of *fiqh* (*furu al-Fiqh*). Bobo Muhammad generally sent his advanced students on to study with Hindustani, and Hindustani reportedly also sent students to study *fiqh* with Bobo Muhammad, his particular strength.

Bobo Muhammad seems to have gotten into trouble because he was publicly critical of the well-known Tajik writer Sadriddin Ayni, who had been a Jadid reformer before the revolution. Bobo Muhammad was quoted as saying that Sadriddin Ayni "sold religion for a good and wealthy life," with Bobo Muhammad accusing him of "becoming an apostate." That was a major mistake, as Ayni was something of a favorite of Stalin, who had even met with the Tajik memoirist and playwright.[36]

Even in Soviet times, someone interested in getting a religious education might go to study in several *hujras*. The same Hojji Ahmadjon Makhdum, referred to above, also went to study with Makhdum Bobo-vi Andaqi (Abd ar-Rahmanjon Bobo)[37] in the village of Andaq, some 40 kilometers northeast of Samarkand. There he learned as well the ritual bases of internal or silent *zikr* (*zikr-i batin*), which he practiced.

For a Hanafi traditionalist like Hindustani, the Sufi tradition was an acceptable one, and Sufi teachings formed an important part of the training of some of his students. Bakhtiyar Babadjanov asserts that Hindustani was himself a practitioner of the Sufi way,[38] although the *domla* (*domulla*) (teacher) defined his life's work as preserving the basic tenets of the Hanafi legal tradition in the face of the constraints placed on religious teachings by Soviet authorities.

Certainly, Hindustani's circle included a number of important Sufi figures. These included Eshon Abdurahmonjon, another important Soviet-era Sufi Mujaddidiya leader. Abdurahmonjon was born in the Kala-ji nav (Qala-ji naw) settlement near Dushanbe and died there in 1984 at the age of 99. Abdurahmonjon studied in the Kukaldosh Madrasa in Bukhara at the same time as Muhammadjon Hindustani and remained in contact with him throughout his life.

In about 1956, Abdurahmonjon established his own *hujra*, refusing admission to all students who lacked a basic knowledge of Sharia. This differentiated him from populist Sufi figures who sought to use Sufism to bring the masses to Islam. Abdurahmonjon's *hujra* offered studies of the rituals ("silent *zikr*"—"*Khafi*," "psycho-physical concentration"—*tavajjuh* prayers), as well as studies of mystical poetry, including works of Jalal ad-Din Rumi (or Jalal ad-Din Muhammad Balkh)[39] and Bidel.[40] Studies of manuscripts of well-known Sufis were also included in the curriculum. For Abdurahmonjon, who was himself the author of traditional Sufi compositions, the only path to the practice of Sufism lay through strictly following the rules of Sharia first, and he is said to have trained his students to forsake exposing their knowledge of Sufism among the crowd.[41]

Abdurahmonjon was not unique. Sheikh Asadullah (d. 1976), another famous Sufi from Kalai Nav (Tajikistan), accepted Muhammadjon Hindustani's former students although he limited his teachings to exercises of the rituals (for example, *zikr*).

SUFI LEADERS

Sufism is an inseparable part of Central Asian Islam, very much a part of the Hanafi tradition in general and of Islam's development in what is now Uzbekistan. Like so much else relating to Islam, the history of Sufism during the Soviet period has yet to be written. One of the challenges in deciding about its significance is in the nature of Sufism itself and its complexity. Thousands of people went to worship at Sufi shrines, especially on holy days.

Although the authority of Sufi sheikhs among believers in the Soviet Union was relatively high, experts like Bakhtiyar Babadjanov believe that Sufism went through a much deeper and more profound degradation during the Soviet period, much greater than under colonial rule or in the centuries preceding it. This was because, whatever their social status, almost without exception, Soviet-era sheikhs could not create a fully functioning group with a traditional center again, for fear of the authorities. Sufism, like most other aspects of Islam, was actually adapting to its surroundings.

Babadjanov believes that for the most part the level of historical learning of most Sufi sheikhs was average and even mediocre, limited mostly to the knowledge of rituals and some theoretical statutes of classical Sufism. This, though, was often sufficient to give them public followings, and for many to be willing to formally train *murids*, although no *kanaqas* with publicly held property were able to be created during Soviet times.

Given the constraints placed on religious leaders who sought to disseminate their faith, some of those who devoted themselves to studying the Sufi way felt that they were unable to claim or formally transmit to their students the status of having mastered the Sufi way. As a result, many of the lines of descent from generations of Sufi sheikhs were disrupted, while in other cases they were passed on to men who lacked the level of religious learning of their predecessors.

Even under these difficult conditions, there were at least a handful of spiritual leaders who achieved a higher level of religious learning and sought to preserve or even in some way to contribute to the understanding of earlier Sufi thinkers.

Three Naqshabandiya sheikhs in particular are worthy of consideration: Ravnaqi, his nephew Faqiri, and Ahmadjon Makhdum. Good biographical material about the first two of these men is available in Stanislav Prozorov's four-volume work on Islam.[42] Material on Hojji Ahmadjon Makhdum comes from his autobiography.[43]

The first on these men, Faizallah Ravnaqi Makhdum Khodjaev Shakhrisabzi (1892–1978), also known as Faid Allah, was a lawyer, poet, and author of essays on the history of the Sufi brotherhoods.[44] He was born into a family of *qadis* from Shakhrisabz (Shahrisabz) and was educated in the Kukaldosh Madrasa (which he completed in 1919 or 1920), after which he was appointed *qadi* of Shakhrisabz. Ravnaqi was a gifted poet. His early poems, written under the pseudonym Ramzi, were included in a collection of poems by prominent poets of Bukhara, published on the eve of the Russian Revolution.

After the liquidation of the Sharia courts, Ravnaqi took various jobs in the new Soviet judicial bodies that had employed *qadis* in an effort to popularize Soviet law while trying to embed some norms of Sharia in it. During the anti-religious campaigns of the 1930s, Ravnaqi hid his archive and library and fled to a remote region of Tajikistan, where he made a living through odd jobs and traditional healing.

He returned to Shakhrisabz in the late 1950s, when he was able to turn his attention to his religious writings. Then in the 1960s, he organized his own *hujra* and gave private lessons on reading the Quran (*qiraat*), on poetry writing, and on calligraphy. He also continued to practice traditional methods of healing, relying on medieval medical treatises, with the success he enjoyed contributing to his reputation as a holy man.

Ravnaqi died in Shakhrisabz in 1978 and is buried in the suburban cemetery of Arslanbob. His burial spot has become a place of pilgrimage, and today the street where he lived is named for him, attesting to the official favor with which Uzbekistan's Sufi tradition is viewed.

Ravnaqi is unique in the volume of his written legacy. He is the author of about ten books of essays of various kinds, including several small treatises on the history of Sufi brotherhoods, the best known of which are *Risala-yi tarikat-i Ishkiya*, *Risala-i Chishtiya*, and *Risala-yi Jakhriya-yi Yasawiyas*, which focuses on the technique of Sufi rituals. His essays on *fiqh* are especially well regarded.

Ravnaqi also had an extraordinary library, which was opened to scholars and disciples in 1997. It includes more than one hundred volumes of manuscripts on various issues of theology and *fiqh*; Sufi treatises; and poetic collections, including many that Ravnaqi rewrote with his own calligraphy; as well as books of legal decisions from the office of the Shakhrisabz *qadi*, and from other cities of the Bukhara emirate. Finally, it contains some 500 lithographs from India, the Middle East, Russia, and various cities in Central Asia on the same subjects that were issued in India, Arab countries, Samarkand, Novo-Bukhara (Kagana), Tashkent, and Russia.

Ravnaqi's nephew, Ismail bin Ibrahim (1910–1980), was the Sufi poet better known by his pseudonym Faqiri. Faqiri also left a copy of his own genealogy.[45] Faqiri's father, Ibrahim Hajji (d. 1914) simultaneously served as *imam-hatib* in Jome Mosque in Shakhrisabz (which had been built by Ulugbek in 1432–1436), as a representative of the emir in the city administration (*uraq*), and as head (*mudarris*) of the local madrasa at which Faqiri began his studies.[46]

After Soviet authorities closed the madrasa, Faqiri continued his education initially with his grandmother, an *otin oyi*, then with his uncle, Ravnaqi. At the beginning of the 1930s, Faqiri became a *murid* of Katta-hajji Dahbidi (Muhiy ad-Din Dahbidi),[47] a popular Naqshabandiya sheikh whose spiritual legacy went all the way back to Sheikh Makhdum Azam (d. 1542).[48] Faqiri continued his training with Katta-hajji through correspondence, after local authorities banned Katta-hajji from gathering *murids*. The determination with which Faqiri pursued his training speaks both to the drive with which he pursued his faith and the lengths to which clerics and their students went in those years to pass on age-old texts and their interpretations.

Some of the letters between the two men are preserved in Faqiri's archives, providing a window on the Sufi instructions (*tanbih*) that were offered at the time. Faqiri's archives also include correspondence from the 1960s and early 1970s and his correspondence with a number of Central Asia's most authoritative *ulama*, including Hindustani. These letters include dogmatic questions, sequence of performing some Sufi rituals, and their mandatory or voluntary interpretations, which were mandatory for members of concrete Sufi communities.

Faqiri was an adherent of the Naqshabandiya-Mujaddidiya tradition of quiet *zikr* (*khafi*),[49] and had a few disciples to whom he taught theoretical problems of Sufism as well as the ritual practice (such as *zikr* and *tavajjuh*).

However, because of his interrupted education, he believed that he was barred from gaining a solid spiritual connection (*nisbat*), and so while he could teach he had no right to judge that his disciples had completed their spiritual path. This decision on Faqiri's part meant that he was unable to spread Katta-hajji Dahbidi's legacy to another generation. Late in life, Faqiri became blind and a recluse. He died in his native Sarasia, where he was buried in a local cemetery. His grave almost instantly became an object of pilgrimage for the local population.

Faqiri's known writings include a collection (*divon*) of mystical poems in the Tajik and Uzbek languages; Sufi treatises (*risolas*),[50] which are mainly dedicated to the peculiarities of a ritual in various local brotherhoods or their history; and his own versions of folk tales told at women's ritual gatherings. Faqiri also had an extensive library, which has been partially preserved by his descendants.[51]

Hojji Ahmadjon Makhdum, mentioned briefly above, is another noted Sufi. Born in 1939 in the village of Zarkon (or Zar-i Kon), in the Sarasia region of Surkhandarya Oblast, he was mentioned in passing in the section on Hindustani. He came from a distinguished family of Sufi sheikhs.[52] Hojji Ahmadjon was said to have had a prodigious intellect and began his religious studies at a very young age, learning to read Arabic at age six. He studied Sufi rituals with his father and also received formal religious instruction. While completing only six years of secular schooling, he is said to have mastered a full madrasa curriculum of higher education. He seems to have devoted much of his life to learning. Studying with Hazrat Bobo Muhammad in Sarasia, and, as already noted, with Qozi domla and Muhammadjon Hindustani in Dushanbe, as well as with a number of other well-known Sufis, such as Eshon Abdurahmanjon[53] and with Eshon Shaykh Asadulloh, both from the village of Qalay-i just outside of Dushanbe.[54] Again, this testifies to how the region's clerics managed to create something of a training network during the last three decades of Soviet rule.

While he accepted students to whom he taught the Mujaddidiya traditional *zikr*, including the currently very popular Ibrahim Hazrat, Ahmadjon Makhdum left no formal disciples. He, too, felt unable to do so because of what he viewed as his own incomplete Sufi training. But he was well regarded because of the depth of his knowledge of classical Sufism, which was reflected in his writings, and for this reason he was sought after by a generation of young clerics from Tajikistan and the Surkhandarya region of Uzbekistan (north of Dushanbe). Ahmadjon Makhdum's reputation was such that Sheikh Zulfikar Ahmad came from Lahore to visit him at home in 1992.[55]

PRESERVING UZBEKISTAN'S SUFI LINEAGES

While Ahmadjon Makhdum, Ravnaqi, and Faqiri were too humble to train formal disciples, others were not so modest. For example, many of the most prominent Naqshabandiya-Mujaddidya Sufis in Uzbekistan were trained by Abd al-Wahid Turkestani or one of his disciples.

Sheikh Abd al-Wahid Turkestani (d. 1940/1941) was the founder of the largest Naqshabandiya-Mujaddidiya *tariqa* in contemporary Central Asia. The brotherhood claims its origin from the Indian sheikh and Naqshabandiya Ahmad Sirhindi (d. 1624), also known as Mujaddid Alf Thani, and from well-known Bukhara sheikh and Naqshabandiya-Mujaddidiya *khalifa* Husayn (d. 1833/34).

The Sufi lineage of Abd al-Wahid Turkestani is somewhat contested;[56] there are few written resources on which to reconstruct his life story, and most accounts of his life seem to liberally mix fact with fiction in ways designed to enhance his spiritual authority. For example, some maintain that the Bolsheviks failed to arrest Turkestani because at key moments he was able to render himself invisible.

What is known is that Abd al-Wahid Turkestani came from the Kushata village, an Uzbek village just over the border in Kazakhstan;[57] that he belonged to the Mujaddidiya-Husayniya, one of the local Naqshabandiya *tariqas*; and that sometime before 1910 he received *irshad* (guidance) from Bukhara Sheikh and Mujaddidiya *khalifa* Muhammad Amin.

Like his teacher, Abd al-Wahid Turkestani did not participate in political activities, even during the Soviet period, and warned his students and relatives to stay away from politics as well. This helped him avoid being swept away in the purges, and his leadership allowed the Husayniya to survive Soviet rule. Helpful, too, was that Turkestani accepted only a limited number of students to teach the rule of *zhiq*,[58] which is still part of the basic practices of the Husayniya.

Turkestani named Qori Abd Allah (d. 1976)[59], as his successor. Qori Abd Allah lived with his teacher for approximately thirty-three years and was buried next to him in Kushata.

Although Qori Abd Allah found himself under pressure from the authorities to abandon teaching, he continued to accept new *murids* and trained them very cautiously. He never addressed his students in written form (*irshad-namas*) as was traditional, but limited himself to giving simple oral instructions during private meetings. He also persistently warned his followers that they were at risk of arrest and recommended that they not accept more than two or three *murids* at a time. Many of these men went on to accept *murids* and since independence to establish *kanaqas* in various parts of Uzbekistan, Kazakhstan, and Russia. Ibrahim Hazrat of Kokand is considered the most authoritative of Abd Allah's followers. Without Abd Allah, it is hard to imagine that the Husayniya could have had the rapid revival it has enjoyed since the late 1980s.

The Yasawiya and Qadiriya Sufis practiced loud *zikr* (known as *jahr*) and, thus, were known as the Jahriya. Gulom ota Nurmat, born in 1916 in Ku-yi Girvan[60] near Namangan, was one of the dominant figures who preserved this tradition. He received his religious education from his father, Nurmuhammad ota, who also introduced him to the Sufi rituals. He took up further Sufi training and practice when he returned home in 1943 after being badly wounded at the front.

Gulom ota entered the Namangan group of the Yasawiya, consisting of some nine sheikhs, which held unsanctioned gatherings in houses of participants or in remote villages.[61] Bakhtiyar Babadjanov reports that the number of participants or observers of the loud *zikr* rituals could range from one hundred to some two thousand people. One of the best known leaders of this group was Muhammad Siddiq Pasha, who died in 1988, after which the group was effectively dissolved. Gulom ota was the last surviving sheikh of this group. After Muhammad Siddiq Pasha's death, Gulom ota began to take part in meetings of other Yasawiya groups, as the Yasawiya do not subscribe to the same rigid hierarchical practice as the Naqshabandiya. The former are united only by a collective ritual practice. Gulom ota, though, is said to have accepted only a small group of students, two or three per year, to whom he taught basic Sufi practices, primarily *zikr*.[62]

Dovudkhon Ortikov, also from the Qadiriya, opened his *hujra* in Namangan in 1983 with a curriculum that included lectures on the proper manner of reading of the Quran; on mystical poetry from a Persian poetry collection, including works of Abd al-Qadir al-Jilani; and on Sufi rituals. Dovudkhon is said to have been more learned than Gulom ota and had a more classical religious education. He believed that *zikr* and ritual dance (*raqs*) gave him both physical and spiritual strength,[63] and unlike all of the Sufi leaders written about in this section, he sought to inspire his students to engage in political activism. Dovudkhon and some of the people he trained found natural allies in the students of Hakimjon qori.

HAKIMJON QORI AND THE YOUNG RADICALS

As Hindustani sought to leave his imprint on the generation of Hanafi clerics, he faced a rebellion organized by some of his former students. These individuals were trained by and grouped around Abdulhakim qori Margiloniy, a native of Margilan, who is considered "the father" of political Islam in Uzbekistan.

Hakimjon qori claimed to have been born in 1890, which is questionable given his longevity, as he lived roughly a decade after independence. He studied in a small local madrasa, acquiring the rudiments of a religious education, then from 1927 until 1930, he studied at a *hujra* organized by *Ahl-i Quran* in Tashkent and was the last surviving member of his study group. From 1933 to 1945, he was in hiding, moving from Osh to Uzgen and then Batken. In 1945, he returned to Uzgen, and later went back home to Margilan. In 1955, he started a *hujra*, but felt constrained by his own limited education, which led him to study at Muhammadjon Hindustani's *hujra* in Dushanbe from 1957 to 1959, where he paid special attention to increasing his Arabic skills.

Hakimjon qori then returned to Margilan and reopened his *hujra*. He developed a curriculum that mirrored what was taught earlier in the study circles organized by members of *Ahl-i Quran*. Like them, he explicitly rejected the idea that Islam was defined by ritual or "folk" practices; took special exception to the "residues" of Sufism, such as worshipping at graves or other shrines; and, from the beginning of 1960s, was one of first to discuss the issue of purifying Islam.

Hakimjon qori's library included a collection of essays by ibn Taymiya (1263–1328) and Sayyid Abul Ala Maududi (1903–1979), as well as commentaries on the Quran by Sayyid Qutb ("*Fi Zilali Quran*"). It also contained works of contemporary authors, primarily Salafis of the Arab world. These books were given to him by *hajjis*, whom he had provided with financial support.[64] Those who studied with him have noted that the writings of medieval Salafi and contemporary Arab writers strongly influenced Hakimjon qori's understanding of Islam.

Many of the younger generation of students from the Ferghana Valley who came to study with him in the 1970s were attracted by Hakimjon qori's apparent engagement with ideas and trends that were happening in other Muslim countries. By contrast, they found Hindustani to be hidebound, tied to local Central Asian teachings and in their minds too obsequious in his behavior toward Soviet authorities.

Hakimjon qori shaped a generation of famous Central Asian theologians, including several who went on to create their own *hujras*. Young Tajik radicals, such as Sayid Abdulloh Nuri, came to study with him, and he had a great influence on the development of radical Islamic thought in the Ferghana Valley. This was largely through Rahmatulla-alloma[65] and Abduvali qori; both came to Hakimjon qori after breaking with Hindustani.

Both of these men had been introduced to Palestinian, Syrian, Lebanese, and Algerian students studying at Tashkent State University and at the Polytechnic Universities of Tashkent and Andijan. In addition to advancing their Arabic language skills, Rahmatulla-alloma and Abduvali qori received religious literature from these Middle Eastern students, including essays by Hassan al-Banna (1906–1949) and Sayyid Qutb (1906–1966). Rahmatulla-alloma and Hakimjon qori were already versed in the writings of ibn Taymiya.

Rahmatulla-alloma established a *hujra* in 1978, and Abduvali qori served as his assistant. In addition to main lectures on Arabic language, Quranic studies, *hadiths*, and basics of *fiqh*, the curriculum at the *hujra* included essays by ibn Taymiya, Maududi, and Quran *tafsirs* by Sayyid Qutb (*Fi Zilali Quran*). The curriculum, though less complete than that offered by Hindustani, encouraged students to critically reassess their attitudes toward the local practice of Islam. Like those in *Ahl-i Quran* before them, they proclaimed advantages of a stricter implementation of the ideas of the Quran and *hadiths* in the everyday life of devout Muslims and disputed local traditions, especially those that allowed Muslims to adapt to changing conditions. The curriculum stressed that Muslims were to be bound by Sharia principles. The most trusted students were allowed to study politics, the status of Islam in the world, and the religious history of local khanates. Textbooks on the history of Islam, brought by the Arab students, gradually became a part of the curriculum.

Rahmatulla-alloma described his religious philosophy in an essay, "Musulmon-obod"[66] (the country of Muslims' prosperity), which offered his interpretation of holy Muslim texts. His perspective was unacceptable to Hanafi traditionalists because it paid no heed to traditional interpretation, of Islamic texts (*ijtihad*[67]), yet it supported the general agreement of legal experts on Islamic law.

After Rahmatulla-alloma's death in an automobile accident in 1981, Abduvali qori continued the work of the *hujra* and soon became the major voice in the radical Islam movement in Uzbekistan, occupying that role even posthumously since the mid-1990s.

Bakhtiyar Babadjanov believes that the standards that Abduvali qori maintained were as high as those of Hindustani. Following the example of Sayid Abdulloh Nuri, Abduvali qori introduced the history of Islam's caliphate into his *hujra*'s curriculum. According to a student, Ayubkhon Homidov,[68] many textbooks contained overtly anti-Soviet messages and supported the reestablishment of an Islamic government, continuing the tradition of "political lessons" started by Rahmatulla-alloma. Homidov added, however, that while these textbooks did not describe any direct plan for an Islamic revolution, they did include medieval Islamic proverbs that encouraged believers to trust in Allah for provision of victory.

As the USSR collapsed, Abduvali qori began to more publicly spread his message, talking to crowds at midday prayers and in mosques. He preached the religious principles found in his foundation work, *tafsir*,[69] focusing on key doctrinal and social issues. His lectures were attended not only by his students, but also by many devout Muslims who wanted to know more about Islam. His *hujra* also began to offer training in karate and kung fu, as if to train students in struggles that may lie ahead.

Abduvali qori's perspective on Islamic doctrine was very similar to that of Hakimjon qori, with both men opposing pilgrimages to graves of "saints" and evening prayer gatherings (*tahajjud*),[70] except during Ramadan. Abduvali qori also objected to most Sufi rituals, and for this reason most of his followers were characterized as "Wahhabis" by local Hanafis.

A number of other prominent Uzbek clerics passed through the *hujras* of Hakimjon qori, Rahmatulla-alloma, and Abduvali qori. Obidkhon qori, the imam of Tashkent's Kukcha Mosque who fled Uzbekistan in the mid-1990s, is probably the most influential of the radical Uzbek clerics who went through the *hujra*, while more establishment figures, such as Abdulaziz Mansurov, who was a friend of Shamsuddin Bobokhon's and briefly served as an adviser to the president on religious affairs, also studied with these radical clerical figures.

While the ideas of Rahmatulla-alloma and Abduvali qori found support among countless young people, their numbers were insignificant in comparison to the resurgence in traditional religious rituals and practices, such as pilgrimages to graves of "saints" and saints' tombs. And the revival of religious practices encouraged both Islamic radicals and traditional Hanafi clerics to try to compete for the souls of the population.

5

MUHAMMAD SODIQ MUHAMMAD YUSUF— UZBEKISTAN'S THEOLOGIAN

INTRODUCTION

One figure was omitted from the previous chapter, Muhammad Sodiq Muhammad Yusuf (also known as Muhammed Sadik Mamayusuf or Mamayusupov), the former *mufti* of the Spiritual Administration of Central Asia, and Uzbekistan's first *mufti* after independence. He was earlier omitted because he merits a chapter of his own.

Many consider Muhammad Sodiq Uzbekistan's unofficial spiritual leader. His following reaches into southern Kazakhstan and among Uzbeks in Khujand, although outside of Uzbekistan the respect he enjoys is mostly from fellow clerics. Most Muslims, including most official imams and many politicians, agree with the positions he takes. His wide support makes him capable of influencing the broad population, and, if necessary, of leading it.

Experience has taught Muhammad Sodiq to be careful. Having endured exile, and knowing so many clerics who were on the losing side in Tajikistan, he has sought to minimize any potential conflict with authorities and avoid questions that could split the Muslim community into competing factions. He has managed to do this while remaining a prolific and original writer. In recent years, he has developed a substantial and very modern presence on the internet as well.[1] On his Internet sites in particular he focuses on trying to address ordinary problems that believers face and on providing access to contemporary as well as traditional Hanafi teachings on Islam. The Russian language materials on his websites are designed not just for observant Muslims but also for a broader audience of people interested in Islam.*

While a new generation of clerics is beginning to emerge, Muhammad Sodiq remains the most charismatic figure of all religious leaders in Uzbekistan, indeed, in Central Asia.[2] He is the only religious figure in Uzbekistan who has enough authority to retain an independent voice on religious affairs while still living in Uzbekistan. His critics see him as too accommodating to the state, while supporters see him as a counterweight to official positions.

Muhammad Sodiq himself would likely admit that he is willing to make accommodations to state policy when core religious values are not threatened by his concessions. As he has explained in our meetings,[3] his goal is to make Uzbekistan a more congenial place for believers, but the only way to do this is to bring more of the country's citizens back to their faith. He is seeking to use his writings and sermons to try to create the conditions for a religious revival in Uzbekistan—a revival that would bring together traditional Hanafi teachings with more contemporary understandings of Islam that are circulating throughout much of the Muslim, and especially Arab, world. Muhammad Sodiq stays current through his active participation in the Organization of Islamic Cooperation and through travels in the Middle East and beyond.

While some of Muhammad Sodiq's followers liken him to Iran's Ayatollah Khomeini, the "Uzbek Sheikh" (as he terms himself) does not encourage this comparison, fearing it would anger Uzbek authorities and so impede his religious mission. Inappropriate analogies aside, Muhammad Sodiq's status is such that arresting, "disappearing," or exiling him would alienate believers against the Uzbek state and risk serious damage to Uzbekistan's reputation in much of the Arab world.

---

* The materials in this section draw heavily on materials prepared by Bakhtiyar Babadjanov for the Carnegie Endowment for International Peace project on Islam. He is responsible for all of the translations from Uzbek, but while I made substantial use of the interpretive materials that he prepared, all of the judgments contained here are my own, and he bears no responsibility for the conclusions offered.

BIOGRAPHICAL SKETCH

Muhammad Sodiq was born in Andijan on April 15, 1952, into a family of distinguished clerics. He was the youngest son of Muhammad Yusuf qori (d. 2004), who taught him the basics of Islam. His father's father was Muhammad-Ali domulla Andijani, who died before the Bolshevik Revolution and was a teacher in an Andijan madrasa. Muhammad-Ali's ancestors came from a family of Naqshabandiya-Mujaddidiya sheikhs, but neither grandfather, father, nor son was a practicing Sufi.

Muhammad Yusuf qori was invited by Eshon Bobokhon to serve as a lecturer on the Quran and to deliver Quranic commentary at Mir-i Arab Madrasa in Bukhara in 1950. In 1953, he was appointed head sheikh and keeper of the shrine to Baha ud-Din Naqshaband, just outside of Bukhara. He served there until the shrine was closed in 1957 and continued working in the madrasa until his retirement in 1960, when he returned to his hometown of Andijan.

Muhammad Sodiq received his primary religious education from his father while also pursuing Soviet secular education. He also spent a year studying at the Hanafi *hujra* number one of Mansur Hajji[4] from Andijan. After he finished middle school, Muhammad Sodiq was accepted into the Mir-i Arab Madrasa in Bukhara, and then studied at the Higher Islamic Institute in Tashkent, finishing with distinction in 1975. In 1975–1976, he worked as an editor of SADUM's official magazine *Muslims of the Soviet East (Sovet musulmonlari)*.[5]

By this time Muhammad Sodiq had married into the Sattiev family, a prominent religious family from Namangan. The father of his wife, Ismail Sattiev, was a close friend of Muhammad Yusuf qori, and the marriage was thus a union of two prominent families. Sattiev, described briefly in the preceding chapter, was a close associate of Eshon Bobokhon, who appointed him to be the director of the Mir-i Arab Madrasa in Bukhara. Sattiev held the post until 1962, when he was named head of the *fatwa* department of SADUM, a move that seemed to have occurred because he was suspected of favoring students and job applicants from his home region.

His ties to the Sattiev family proved very useful when Muhammad Sodiq got into trouble with the Uzbek authorities. The Sattiev family is said to have helped keep Muhammad Sodiq from being jailed in 1992 and 1993, negotiating his exile instead. Then a sister-in-law allegedly used her high position in the Ministry of Justice to secure permission from President Islam Karimov for Muhammad Sodiq to return from exile in 1999 in order to assist in the government's fight against terrorism.

Earlier in Muhammad Sodiq's career, his in-laws were said to have helped him get sent to Libya. He was admitted to ad-Dawa al-Islami National Islamic University in Libya in 1976. The time spent in Libya was critical to the development of Muhammad Sodiq's religious worldview, as well as establishing ties to a cohort of Muslim clerics, mostly from the Arab world, but reaching throughout the larger Muslim world.

In 1980 Muhammad Sodiq returned to Uzbekistan and worked in the Department of International Communications for SADUM and simultaneously lectured on *tafsir*, *hadith*, and *fiqh* at the Higher Islamic Institute in Tashkent. During Muhammad Sodiq's years there, his organizational skills became evident and he further strengthened his international connections. He actively participated in the organization of a series of international conferences that took place in Tashkent in the 1980s.

During that time Muhammad Sodiq was named assistant director of the Higher Islamic Institute and then became its director. Under his leadership, he achieved a sweeping reorganization of the teaching methodology used at the institute, developed a curriculum for self-education, and introduced educational programs for modern Islamic educational centers. Some have speculated that Shamsuddin Bobokhonov, who took over as *mufti* in 1982, appointed Muhammad Sodiq to the posts at the Higher Islamic Institute to weigh his rival down with administrative responsibility and take him out of the international limelight.

MUHAMMAD SODIQ'S CAREER AS A *MUFTI*

Muhammad Sodiq was elected *mufti* by the SADUM in March 1989, and in the same year he was elected deputy to the Supreme Soviet of the USSR. While serving in both positions, he sought to build his prestige on these two very different stages simultaneously in order to advance his goal of spreading Islam in Uzbekistan.

Muhammad Sodiq believes that he was able to positively influence Mikhail Gorbachev's negative views about Islam. He says that Mikhail Gorbachev always deferred to him personally when questions arose that were connected with decisions about religion or about sensitive diplomatic relations with Arab countries. Muhammad Sodiq served as Gorbachev's personal translator on a number of occasions when the Soviet leader received delegations from Syria and Saudi Arabia. Early in 1991 Muhammad Sodiq was sent to Islamabad to negotiate with Afghan leader Gulbuddin Hekmatyar[6] about the return of Soviet prisoners of war. Demonstrating his independence, Muhammad Sodiq published his favorable impressions of this Afghan leader, who was still fighting to seize power from the pro-Soviet president, Muhammad Najibullah.[7] Muhammad Sodiq further claims that Gorbachev once attempted to use him to prod OPEC, the Organization of Petroleum Exporting Countries, to raise slumping oil prices, a vital means of survival for the USSR with its failing economy.

It is clear that Muhammad Sodiq took advantage of opportunities to demonstrate his loyalty to Moscow. Appointed in February 1989, Muhammad Sodiq was confirmed as *mufti* at a full congress of SADUM representatives and foreign guests the following month. He delivered a major address at the time of his appointment devoted to the importance of recent changes in Moscow's policies, such as the return of the Caliph Usman's Quran to Tashkent (it had been taken by the Russians at the time of the conquest of Turkestan), and the restoration of the Abu Isa Muhammad at-Termizi Mausoleum, the Baha ud-Din (Naqshaband) Mausoleum and Mosque, the Kalyan Mosque in Bukhara, and the Jami Mosque in Kokand. But while praising Moscow, he pushed for more change, stressing that Islam could not be returned to a condition of vitality without more mosques and better trained clerics, and he praised Uzbek authorities for building new dorms and academic buildings at SADUM's two madrasas.[8]

Publicly, the *mufti* was always an enthusiastic supporter of Gorbachev, and of *glasnost* and *perestroika*, making speeches in support of Moscow's campaigns against alcohol abuse and against bribery and corruption. He used the podium of the USSR Congress of People's Deputies to speak in favor of the Soviet Union's foreign policies in the Middle East, as well as of Gorbachev's domestic initiatives.[9] But in his writings Muhammad Sodiq maintained a more critical tone, voicing displeasure with official policy toward Islam, stressing that believers have always been treated as second-class citizens in Soviet life, in violation of the "naturalness" of religion.[10]

Muhammad Sodiq did use his status as a USSR deputy to advance the agenda of SADUM. He got permission for Soviet Muslims be allowed to travel to Saudi Arabia for the *hajj*. In June 1990, some 500 Central Asian pilgrims traveled to Saudi Arabia, following a well-publicized state visit by Saudi clergy to Tashkent. Muhammad Sodiq also used his platform in Moscow to press the case for foreign religious study, to call for limiting restrictions on the opening of new mosques and Islamic educational institutions, and on the publication of religious newspapers and periodicals, as well as the importing of religious literature. While Muhammad Sodiq was *mufti*, the number of madrasas in Uzbekistan increased from two to fourteen, and the number of registered mosques from 188 to 5,000.

In general, the new *mufti* was no friend of advocates of secular nationalism, stressing in his speech before the second session of Uzbekistan's Supreme Soviet, in June 1990, that historically Uzbeks, Kazakhs, Kyrgyz, and Tajiks were one Muslim people and that efforts to drive them apart should be viewed with suspicion.[11] At the same time, though, he opposed the creation of religious parties and for that reason was against the registration of the Islamic Renaissance Party in Uzbekistan. Muhammad Sodiq argued that such parties fracture the community of believers, because Islam itself was a "party,"[12] or at least had an indivisible set of aims.

Muhammad Sodiq's successes on these broader stages, Moscow and the global Islamic community, likely added to his problems at home, making his early ouster as *mufti* somewhat inevitable. He had powerful enemies within SADUM's hierarchy from his first days in office. He had come to power as the result of a demonstration of believers against SADUM, the first such demonstration since its founding.[13] Several hundred people, some with banners saying "Remove the corrupt *mufti*!" marched from SADUM to the Lenin monument in the center of Tashkent and sent representatives to meet with the head of Uzbekistan's Communist Party. Shortly thereafter, at a hastily called meeting of SADUM's ruling council, Muhammad Sodiq was elected *mufti*.

The demonstrators were mainly from Andijan and Namangan, where Muhammad Sodiq's support was strongest, and he and his supporters seem to have been responsible for the planning of the demonstration, which was designed to bring him to power. Abduvali qori was rumored to have hired buses to bring people to Tashkent.

As a result, many Uzbek state officials held Muhammad Sodiq responsible for "letting the cat out of the bag" so to speak, and they believed that the precedent of organizing demonstrations of believers helped to legitimize future demonstrations (in the early 1990s) by anti-regime Islamic groups in Namangan and Andijan.

He also clashed with state authorities more directly, opposing the desire of the Committee on Religious Cults to edit published *fatwas* and using his *fatwas* to address issues of social importance, including state policies of encouraging birth control.

Muhammad Sodiq took responsibility for regulating the social and spiritual life of Uzbek believers, seeking to expand the traditional teachings of the local Hanafi school of law by introducing the works of popular Arabic authors into the curriculum of SADUM's madrasas and expand religious debate to include some of their ideas.

But the inclusion of religion in public life that occurred in these years made it very difficult for any single person, even one who is an accomplished and well-respected religious leader, to monopolize or direct the discussion. The change in state policy toward religion had made the post of head of SADUM considerably more powerful than it had been in the past, in financial as well as social and political terms. Revenue collected by SADUM increased dramatically as the number of mosques and schools under its jurisdiction grew, and this increased the value of the "prize" that being *mufti* entailed. Despite its numerous advantages, though, the position of *mufti* was not an easy one to handle. The swelling of the ranks of religious authorities that occurred in these years created a much larger constituency that a *mufti* had to appease. At the same time, it did not change the fact that since SADUM itself was a government creation, the *mufti*, though chosen by an assembly of Islamic believers, served at the behest of the president of Uzbekistan.

The population now felt free to practice their faith largely as they wished, and many felt drawn to spiritual leaders who emphasized the simple recitation of *namaz* and traditional rituals, such as pilgrimages to graves rather than prodding believers to embrace systematic religious learning.

This was something that was potentially quite disturbing to Muhammad Sodiq, who did not want to see the practices depart from formal Hanafi teachings. In addition to issuing a number of *fatwas* with his attitude toward Islam management and behavior at these shrines, a special imam was assigned by SADUM to each shrine. The job of these imams was to explain Hanafi teachings on *ziyorat*, as part of an effort to ensure that those practicing rituals would learn their dogmatic foundations. In addition, orders were sent to all the mosques requiring that local imams offer similar guidance to those attending their services. Under Muhammad Sodiq's direction, SADUM also sought to limit the various polytheistic practices that were still associated with "saint" worship, and of course rejected the notion that any "saints" were buried in Central Asia. Practices to be discouraged included material offerings left at graves, lighting of candles on graves, and the grinding of "holy dust" from the graves of local "saints."

This kind of spiritual challenge was one that was relatively easily handled by Muhammad Sodiq, who certainly did not want these graves closed, in that the voluntary money donations given by Muslims or left at the shrines were one of the sources of SADUM's income. Instead, Muhammad Sodiq successfully persuaded the government to transfer control of all such "holy places" to SADUM.

A far more difficult issue was how to handle the ideological divide between the radical Muslims of the Ferghana Valley and those clerics who supported the dominant Hanafi tradition.[14] Not only did the former differ from the latter on how Islam should be taught and practiced, but the radicals were also pressing hard for the state to cede power to religious groups. By late 1991, radical Islamic groups in Namangan were usurping state functions, especially in the area of security, and had even occupied some government and former Communist Party property.

In the period just before and after independence was granted, the jockeying for authority was acute, and no one could be certain how it would end. Would secular forces reassert control? Would religious groups prevail? Or would conflicting elite groups push matters to the point of civil war, as occurred in Tajikistan?

The situation that Muhammad Sodiq confronted was complex and fraught with danger. Added to these concerns were his own theological predilections, which made him critical of Hanafi traditionalists while also unwilling to embrace the radical position. His complaints with the radicals were more tactical than substantive, although Muhammad Sodiq accepted far more of the Hanafi theological tradition than they did.

Muhammad Sodiq believed that Abduvali qori's commentary on the Quran could not be included in even the most strict constructionist interpretation of Hanafi Islam, because it allowed no real role for pre-Islamic norms and customs. Abduvali's stance was akin to that taken by Sayyid Qutb in his *tafsir*, and Muhammad Sodiq did not consider this Egyptian social thinker to be a theologian. Given his own theological inclinations, Muhammad Sodiq undoubtedly viewed himself as an honest broker through his various efforts to reconcile traditionalists and radicals.

Controversy, though, dogged Muhammad Sodiq from the time he took power. Abduvali qori appears to have set his sights on replacing Muhammad Sodiq as *mufti*, and even entered a short-lived pact with Shamsuddin Bobokhonov, the former *mufti*, who sought to return to power.

Muhammad Sodiq's opponents organized a *qurultoy* of the *muftiyat* (council of *muftis*) that was held at the Panorama movie theater in Tashkent in 1990. Speakers included both Bobokhon and Abduvali qori. The focus of the meeting was on the alleged misconduct of Muhammad Sodiq in his handling of a gift of a million Qurans, presented in 1989 by Saudi Arabia to the (then still Soviet) SADUM for free distribution. Both then and now, it was considered very prestigious for an Uzbek family to have a Quran, be they a practicing Muslim family or not.

However, Muhammad Sodiq decided that the cause of Islam in Uzbekistan would be better served through the sale of a large portion of these Qurans. After sending copies to Tatarstan, Bashkortostan, and Moscow, he decided to sell the rest of the Qurans for 50 rubles apiece (at a time when books of similar quality were selling for 40–60 rubles). He made no secret of what he was doing, including mentioning in television interviews that money from the sale of the Qurans would go toward the restoration of old mosques and the construction of madrasas in various parts of Uzbekistan.

Muhammad Sodiq successfully defused the crisis in 1990, producing documents from the Saudis that granted him the right to sell the Qurans if the proceeds went to the restoration or construction of religious institutions. He also offered detailed financial accounting of how the money collected from the official sale of Qurans was dispensed.

But many of Tashkent's religious leaders in particular believed that Muhammad Sodiq and his closest allies[15] were directing the attention of foreign benefactors interested in supporting the revival of Islamic institutions to donate money in the cities of the Ferghana Valley at the expense of Tashkent.[16] They wanted him to be replaced by a *mufti* from Tashkent.

Rumored to have been directed by Bobokhon, one of the key members of this group[17] was Abdurashid qori Bahromov, the imam of Tilla Sheikh Mosque, who was himself appointed as *mufti* in 1995, a post he continues to hold. The Tashkent clerics sensed that they did not have enough power to remove the *mufti* and tried to entreat Abduvali qori to support them, dangling the possibility that he might be named *mufti*.

Muhammad Sodiq's opposition sought to use a July 1991 *qurultoy* to pave the way for his removal and planned a boycott. However, when Muhammad Sodiq learned of their plans, he got his supporters from the cities in the Ferghana Valley to travel to Tashkent, where they filled the square in front of the headquarters of the Spiritual Administration (the Barak Khan Madrasa building) and the blocks beyond it,[18] while his opponents gathered in front of the Tilla Sheikh Mosque and in the direction of the Kukcha neighborhood of the "old city." As the day (July 6) went on, both crowds increased in size and began denouncing each other through portable microphones.

Bakhtiyar Babadjanov reports that the *mufti*'s opponents started chanting: "We shall disembowel this Muhammad Sodiq and stuff his body with straw," while those from the Ferghana Valley called on the crowd to inflict carnage on the "corrupt Kukcha." Both sides proclaimed, "Allahu akbar" ("God is great"). Stones were thrown, and people in the crowd began arming themselves with sticks and iron rods from fences around them. Just when it seemed that bloodshed was inevitable, some *mahalla* elders came out to try to negotiate between the two camps, accompanied by the state adviser on religious affairs and some of his colleagues. State media outlets blamed the unrest on the *mufti* and his supporters,[19] while religious journals, controlled by the *mufti*, published the opposite version of the events, calling the group that opposed the *mufti isyonchilar* (insurgents).[20] But Muhammad Sodiq's legitimacy as *mufti* remained in question.

While the protests ended in Tashkent, Islamic radicals were making significant gains in the Ferghana Valley, especially in Namangan. Muhammad Sodiq traveled to the region in October 1991. Several months later, I met some of the religious activists whom he had addressed while in Andijan, and they reported that Muhammad Sodiq had endorsed their call to bring religious instruction to Uzbekistan's schools from kindergarten through college, to make jobs in state schools available to those with religious education, to grant religious figures increased access to media outlets, to have Friday made the official day off, and to get Islam declared the state faith.[21]

Abduvali qori, though, never fully accepted Muhammad Sodiq's authority. While I never managed to meet the Andijan cleric (he was traveling outside of Uzbekistan during the two occasions I visited his mosque and madrasa), I spent several hours with his deputy, at the mosque and at his home. The modesty with which the Andijan radicals comported themselves was a striking contrast to the pomp and ceremony that characterized Muhammad Sodiq at the time.

Muhammad Sodiq has always liked his creature comforts and had enough money to have a very large house. It is located on the outskirts of Tashkent in close proximity to his entourage's estates, all built since Uzbekistan's independence. He also was able to support himself and those working with him in exile for several years. He is said to earn the necessary funds from commercial activities derived from contacts that he has made during all of his travels.

Although the two men's styles clearly clashed, it is argued that Abduvali qori had concluded that Uzbek state security services were supporting the opposition because they were displeased with Muhammad Sodiq's independence. Abduvali qori was pressing for even greater independence for religious authorities, thus making a change of *mufti* seem quite risky for him and his followers. With time, Abduvali qori's ambition seems to have shifted from taking over as *mufti* to finding a way to reunify the Islamic community within Central Asia and possibly forge permanent links among like-minded Muslims throughout the former Soviet Union.[22] These goals seemed more attainable under Muhammad Sodiq than with anyone else.

Shamsuddin Bobokhonov once again sought to oust Muhammad Sodiq at a January 1992 session of the *muftiyat* (now the Muslim Spiritual

Administration of Uzbekistan). But Muhammad Sodiq countered by demanding that a meeting of the full membership be held.

This was convened the following month, with more than a thousand people in attendance, including guests from Turkey and Saudi Arabia, as well as two senior Uzbek government officials.[23] Those gathered, which included clerics representing both the traditional and radical wings of Uzbekistan's religious community, voted to give Muhammad Sodiq a five-year term as *mufti*.

Uzbek authorities were undoubtedly dissatisfied with Muhammad Sodiq, given that radical Islamic groups were increasing in strength in both Tashkent and the Ferghana Valley and that the *mufti* had been unable or unwilling to slow down this trend. But Uzbek authorities' priorities lay elsewhere, with breaking the political power of secular nationalists, who were seen to be behind massive student demonstrations at Tashkent University in mid-January. The demonstrations were broken up by force, two students were killed, and thousands were sent home for an extended vacation.[24]

The authorities began moving against Muhammad Sodiq in early 1993. His house was mysteriously bombed, and in mid-January 1993, he was "asked" to write a request to be relieved of his duties because of health difficulties (the traditional Soviet style of resignation). The entire Spiritual Administration was dissolved, and a substantial part of the archives was seized and confiscated. Muhammad Sodiq's supporters began demonstrating in protest, but the *mufti* was able to get them to disperse before they clashed with law enforcement officials.

He then set about negotiating terms for self-imposed exile, which seemed the only alternative to eventual arrest. Muhammad Sodiq was formally removed as *mufti* in April 1993, nominally for misappropriation of funds.

In the end, Muhammad Sodiq's "centrist" position did not satisfy either side. He was too moderate for the radicals, and too radical for the conservatives. Looking back on the events of the early 1990s, Muhammad Sodiq says that he should have been more flexible at some moments and less flexible at others. He seems to feel he should have been more defiant when he was accused of having personally benefited from the sale of Qurans provided by the Saudis for free distribution, but he also believes that he should have more forcefully defended the interests of the Uzbek state when radical Islamists seized the administration building in Namangan in December 1991.[25]

In reality, though, Uzbek authorities wanted a *mufti* who would be tough on Islamic radicals, or Wahhabis, as they were termed. Muhammad Sodiq was replaced by Mukhtar Abdullaev, who had ties to the Naqshabandiya in Turkey. It was hoped that these connections would direct the Islamic revival in a different and more innocuous direction. When this failed to happen, he, too, was replaced, in 1995, by Abdurashid qori Bahromov, who was at least as much a bureaucrat as a spiritual leader. His longevity in this post is clear evidence of his ability to toe the official line, however it may change.

MUHAMMAD SODIQ OUT OF OFFICE

Muhammad Sodiq has had the luxury and the opportunity to reflect on these events for nearly twenty years, and he has woven his conclusions into his ever-growing body of religious writings. In January 1993, his friends in Libya and Syria helped him get settled and obtain a residence permit in Libya. He traveled widely in the Arab world and continues to do so since his return to permanent residence in Uzbekistan.

He created a position of some importance for himself in the Arab world, speaking with some authority about the state of Islam everywhere in the former Soviet Union. In Uzbekistan, he maintained close ties through his sons, who kept traveling to and from their homeland, as well as through his meetings with Uzbeks making *hajj* or just traveling in the Arab world.

His expertise was recognized by the Rabita al-Alam al-Islami (Muslim World League), an international Islamic organization in Saudi Arabia, which put him in charge of Muslim countries and federations of the Commonwealth of Independent States (CIS) in 1997 and made him a permanent member of the governing council of the organization.

Some of his time was spent in commercial activities, but most of the money that he accumulated seems to have been through trade or investments done by relatives (who had access to contacts that Muhammad Sodiq had made). Mostly, however, while in exile, Muhammad Sodiq tried to remain "below the radar"—writing on theological issues but avoiding journalists and media interviews in the hope that he could rebuild a relationship with the Uzbek government.

Muhammad Sodiq became a prolific writer in exile, spending much of his time reading and writing. From 1994 to 2000, he produced 60 percent of all his published work, including about 30 popular articles and some 25 books and pamphlets. These were mostly written in Uzbek, and some were translated into Russian. He was published mostly in Osh by the Islamic cultural center press (by the Kara Suu branch, which I have visited), which, frustratingly for researchers, prints neither place of publication nor year.

He is well read and actively seeks to read important contemporary works in many languages. He reads secular literature—mostly periodicals on politics, history, philosophy, and Oriental[26] studies—in their Russian or Arabic translations. And he has been known to comment on topics of current interest, such as voicing his objection to Samuel Huntington and the "clash of civilizations," adding his opinion that such a clash can occur only if politicians are in error; his knowledge of Huntington's work, however, was based solely on Arabic language discussions of it.

In discussions with Westerners as well as with Uzbek officials, he stresses the "peaceful nature of Islam, its natural tolerance," and its Judeo-Christian roots.

His political skills were also strengthened during this time, and he began to identify himself not so much as a theologian but as a politician with solid international authority. He knew that delegations from different countries would call on him, so he built a separate hall in his house, a European drawing room. He cultivated the protocol of diplomacy—how to behave with foreign politicians, journalists, researchers, and human rights activists, and how to converse with them.

He also used his time in exile to learn about life in Europe and America. He accepted as many invitations as possible and is said to have tried to tailor his presentations to the nature of the audience in order to leave a strong impression everywhere. Bakhtiyar Babadjanov listened to a video recording of Muhammad Sodiq's speech at an "Islam for peace" international conference in Egypt[27] in which the former *mufti* used very beautiful Arab phrases, speaking in the lustrous tones of an orator.

He presented a rather different image at conferences (primarily those in Russia) in which both secular experts and specialists in Islam participated. At such events Muhammad Sodiq demonstrated his mastery of more abstract analysis and rhetoric, which Bakhtiyar Babadjanov noted was a marked improvement on earlier presentations.

While in exile, Muhammad Sodiq had a lot of time to reflect on the totality of developments in years of his leadership as *mufti*, not just in Uzbekistan but also in neighboring Tajikistan, whose civil war continued for most of his time in exile. Muhammad Sodiq seems to have concluded that he made a mistake supporting the Islamists of Tajikistan (morally, and likely financially as well), instead of attempting to persuade them to use only peaceful means in the fight for their rights.

This conclusion would certainly be consistent with the positions that he has maintained since returning to Uzbekistan in 2000. While not seeking formal office, in an effort to enhance his status Muhammad Sodiq has now begun to refer to himself as Sheikh Muhammad Sodiq, a title he uses in all his publications. He returned ready to proceed with restraint and care, but not at the expense of his religious goals. Realistically, he must have held out little expectation of complete freedom of action. But he has also understood that his presence in Uzbekistan is itself a factor aiding in the integration of Muslims.

To paraphrase Muhammad Sodiq, he was ready to collaborate with all who were "not against Islam and Muslims," in his effort to gain and leverage political authority. This is a challenging task, because if he is going to maintain popular support as an independent religious figure he must hold the government at arm's length, but do it in a way that doesn't create the impression to those in power that he is their enemy.

Part of the reason for his changed behavior is that Muhammad Sodiq now seems to believe that Uzbek society is not ready to live solely according to the rule of Islam and that the development of religious consciousness will take far longer than some of the region's Islamic leaders believed would be the case in the late 1980s and early 1990s. Like many others, he seemed to have fallen victim to the sense of euphoria that anything was possible, when something as seemingly impossible as the collapse of the Soviet Union occurred. But now, having lived for many years in Arab countries in which Islam is much closer to the shared political core and having had the opportunity to read deeply in contemporary Arab social, geopolitical, and religious thought, he seems to have begun to appreciate just how different Central Asia is from countries in the Middle East. For all the values that Central Asian clerics and believers share with their coreligionists, local custom and practice still play an important role.

Muhammad Sodiq returned home more confident of his ability to influence the thinking of believers through his writings. His wide-ranging reading while in exile led him to explore new themes, such as the need for unity among Muslims. This is rather at odds with official state ideology, which holds that Islam in Uzbekistan is in some way uniquely Uzbek, formed by age-old local teachings, rituals, and practices.

But he shares with Uzbek authorities the conviction that it is unacceptable to use violence to achieve religious goals. He frequently says, seemingly with great sincerity, that violence and terrorism serve only to discredit Islam. The religion, he argued, has adequate appeal "to conquer the world without violence and weapons," and he seems to truly believe that in the distant future Islam will become the only religion in the world.

Muhammad Sodiq's desire to preserve his intellectual—or better yet his spiritual—freedom has led him to champion state causes on which he might otherwise be silent. For example, Muhammad Sodiq went on television on May 20, 2005, just days after the shootings in Andijan, to speak out against Akrom Yuldoshev, the founder of Akramiya, which is believed to have been involved in the Andijan unrest. Muhammad Sodiq strongly criticized Yuldoshev, saying: "Who is this Akrom? No one! He is illiterate in both religious and secular matters."

He has also been valuable in the fight against the radical ideology of Hizb ut-Tahrir, which Muhammad Sodiq honestly opposes, as it threatens the hierarchical and institution-based Islam with which he has been associated all his life, not to mention its ideological rejection of Hanafi Islam (and the remaining three schools of law). For their part, members of Hizb ut-Tahrir and Akramiya have gone on the attack against him. Hizb ut-Tahrir even wrote Muhammad Sodiq several letters, some published and others private, with accusations that he should have used his authority to "join the struggle against Karimov's regime."

Recognizing that Muhammad Sodiq would be a formidable political critic, given his continued authority among believers, the Uzbek government also blows warm and cold in its attitude toward its most prominent cleric, depending on the content of his message and what forums he is using for spreading it.

Muhammad Sodiq has also tried to maintain an international role for himself, seemingly free to speak and travel throughout the Arab world, making some carefully orchestrated trips to Europe and the United States, and attending events in other post-Soviet states. For example, Muhammad Sodiq hurried to Moscow to offer his services as a negotiator when a group of armed Chechens stormed the Nord-Ost Theater in October 2002. Although the hostage takers agreed to speak with him, he was unable to successfully negotiate with them.

While Muhammad Sodiq and his family seem to have something of a protected status, his supporters' safety is not guaranteed. This was demonstrated by the arrest of the popular sports journalist Khayrullo Khamidov in 2010 on charges of illegal religious activities. He was convicted even though Muhammad Sodiq pressed for his release.[28]

A regular critic of Uzbekistan's limited number of religious educational establishments, its declining numbers of mosques, and a state policy that is consciously designed to impede the spread of Islam, Muhammad Sodiq cooperates with the state when it suits his broader mission of bringing people back to the faith. He hopes to do this through a broadly based, large-scale movement for improved Islamic education of the masses. For this reason he publishes in the vernacular of ordinary Muslims in order to raise their level of religious education.

Unsurprisingly, Uzbek authorities do not like when Muhammad Sodiq criticizes government policies in interviews with the foreign press. But he appears relatively free to explore the themes that interest him in his Uzbek language websites, which put him in contact with a very focused audience, generally media-savvy young Uzbeks. The content of Muhammad Sodiq's sites is mild by comparison with radical Uzbek language sites or materials on YouTube. Much of the radical material is accessible to enterprising Uzbek Internet users, and YouTube is not blocked at all.

Islom.uz, the umbrella site that he uses, was initially sponsored by grants that Muhammad Sodiq received from the embassies of Kuwait and Saudi Arabia in Uzbekistan, as well as some financial help from Uzbek businessmen. The site has general religious materials (www.islom.uz); a discussion forum (www.forum.islom.uz); a site devoted to maintaining a Muslim way of daily life (www.muslimaat.uz); and news relating to Muslim believers (www.info.islom.uz); as well as other sub-sites.

Forum participants asked a wide variety of questions, such as: How can true Muslims "properly" run a business in a secular state? Is it appropriate to pay the *zakot* tax to mosques? Why does Ramadan start one day later in Central Asian states than in Arab countries? Is it allowed to stop fasting while traveling? Is it abnormal to marry a divorced woman, if you yourself have never been married?

The range of topics covered is very broad, and most of them were derived from the daily routine faced by Uzbek men. Meanwhile, young women, who often prefer to remain anonymous in open forums, also shared their household concerns, raising questions about the relationships within their families, or anxieties regarding their marriages. All comments are prescreened before posting.

Muhammad Sodiq's website rarely includes discussions on the nature of the relationship between religion and politics, except to offer positions that are supportive of Uzbek government policy. For example, several members of Hizb ut-Tahrir made it known that they had sent harsh open letters to Muhammad Sodiq's website. It is not clear whether he failed to reply because of cautiousness or fear, yet the letters have not appeared online.

In addition to raising public observance of Islam, Muhammad Sodiq would like to see religion become more independent of the state. One way he believes this could occur would be through the creation of an independent council of *ulama* in Uzbekistan, which he would like to chair. But such a council is unlikely ever to be created by the current Uzbek ruling elite, let alone a council similar to the one Muhammad Sodiq dreams of heading, which would include representation from throughout Central Asia.[29]

So it is likely that Muhammad Sodiq will have to content himself with the influence he continues to garner through his writings and his preaching, as well as from the works of students he has taught and influenced.[30] He still gives lessons in his house to a small group of trained clerics, many of whom were his former students. Muhammad Sodiq continues to hope that these people would be able to have a strong influence over the religious environment in the country.

MUHAMMAD SODIQ'S MAJOR WORKS: PRESSING FOR UNITY AND TOLERANCE[31]

Muhammad Sodiq is without question the most prolific theologian in Central Asia, and quite possibly in the entire former Soviet Union.[32] He writes primarily in Uzbek, and his writings are very popular among Uzbek-speaking Muslims. Some fifty thousand copies of his most recent book, *Religion Is Edification*, were distributed, and a second edition needed to be quickly planned. It is fair to note that many ordinary Uzbeks buy Muhammad Sodiq's books to display them to demonstrate that they are observant and learned Muslims, though those with little religious training often find the prose hard going.

His writings strive to raise the level of public consciousness about the teachings of Hanafi Islam and spread the message that Islam is a faith of peace. It does this in a way that reduces divisions within the community of believers.

In recent years he has included the following at the beginning of his books:

> Our motto: We aspire toward a true faith, toward a pure Islam, we desire to study the Quran and Sunna in order to follow them, and we want to spread the study of Islam. We want to follow the true *Mujahids*[33]—the blessed ancestors (*as-Salaf as-Salihun*); we want to spread toleration and brotherhood (of Muslims). We also want to eradicate religious illiteracy and to put a stop to our contradictions and splits, to purge our fanaticism, and our sinful affairs.

In keeping with Hanafi tradition, Muhammad Sodiq rejects the literal, "external" interpretation of Quranic verses and *hadith*, arguing instead for studying the historical context and the circumstances in which the particular verse was written or the *hadith* formulated. Thus, pretty much emulating the classical *tafsir* writers such as at-Tabari and al-Baydawi, Muhammad Sodiq follows the contemporary or "reformed" style of Muslim exegesis.

He argues that in the conditions of the contemporary world, and given the development of civilization, literal interpretation of the *ayat* will alienate youth from Islam and force Muslims to live in conditions akin to those encountered in the Middle Ages. At the same time, Muhammad Sodiq believes that the commentator should not only directly interpret a particular verse and extrapolate its meaning to fit the contemporary situation, but also carefully study the reasons behind the verse, the exact cause of why the verse was sent, and compare the historical circumstances of the verses.

This is how, for example, Muhammad Sodiq approaches the verses about jihad. He writes that in the circumstances of the times in which they were written, these verses were appropriate. The invocation of jihad in today's world, however, should be done not by individuals, he believes, but by the decision of a Council of *Ulama* of the entire Islamic world. By making this assertion, he denies legitimacy to all the jihadist groups that have been formed in Central Asia over the past two decades.

Hadiths and Life (Hadis va hayot)

In his work *Hadiths and Life*, Muhammad Sodiq addresses the question of relationships of Muslims with others of different confessions, or the status of Muslim communities in non-Islamic or secular governments.

For example, in interpreting the well-known *hadith* of the Prophet—"The Muslims who live among polytheists are alien to me"[34]—Muhammad Sodiq notes that this *hadith* was said in reference to the need for retribution for the death of a group of *ashabs* (companions of the Prophet) who died (at Hasam) during prayer. What is important to remember, he adds, is that Muslims have lived, and will continue to live, among members of different confessions, and they should look for ways to interact with them and learn from the many good examples of this interaction that are mentioned in the *Sunna*.

Muhammad Sodiq tries to explain to the reader that varying interpretations of Islamic law and differing ritual practices are quite natural, but because they exist he feels it is a mistake for Islamic leaders to engage directly in politics. For that reason he is against religious-based political parties and opposes groups such as Hizb ut-Tahrir and Akramiya.

Islam does not contradict some of the pillars of democracy as they are understood in the West, he says, but Islam offers a conception of democracy that is suited to Muslim ways of living. Islamic societies should be free to experiment with ideological and philosophical orientations of their own choosing.

Religion Is Edification (Din Nasihatdir)

The title of this book, published by a government-owned publishing house, is a quote from the Quran.[35] Here, too, the message is that Islam should be a force of peace and reconciliation among peoples, and the book is designed to use the Quran, *hadiths*, and other religious teachings to argue that Islamic militants are enemies of Islam.

As he writes early on in the book:

> It is not a secret that very abominable events, wars and conflicts are taking place throughout the world. And we know well that there are some aspects related to Muslims as well.... The Islamic world, an inseparable part of the whole world, has suffered most from these troubling world events. Energetic work is being done to stop conflicts, to correct past mistakes. The Islamic world condemns the mistakes of those who step outside religious boundaries—those who are too militaristic, those who set out with arms. But it is not enough for the Muslims to condemn these events. The calls have been made for Muslims to establish an internal dialogue, to do away with internal contradictions, and to find a correct solution to problems together.

Muhammad Sodiq notes that Muslims in the Central Asian countries have these same problems, adding that as many people as possible should participate in the process of reconciliation within the region. The book tries to explain the applicability to current circumstances of the mission of prophets, specifically those who were contemporaries of Muhammad, when the verses of the Quran were sent by Allah forbidding internal strife and polytheism.

He begins with a discussion on "Faithfulness to the Precepts of Allah." Muhammad Sodiq explains several *hadiths* that require believers to beware of spreading information that could be harmful to the unity of a community. He cautions that "enemies of Islam try to exploit contradictions and splits among Muslims," echoing the age-old boilerplate phobia of elusive external enemies, which tragically distracts attention from the fact that Muslims are their own worst enemy.

Muhammad Sodiq then offers four short chapters summarizing each of the first four caliphs' rule, arguing that divisions among Muslims in those years were often overcome thanks to decisive actions, many of them military. He also argues that the reason that the murders of two caliphs (Usman and Ali) occurred is that the "enemies of Islam" were able to triumph because Muslims had abandoned the covenants of Allah and the Prophet.

Muhammad Sodiq then considers the problem of Muslim apostates, those who have left the faith. He makes the argument that those who cause or even permit rifts within the community should also be considered apostate. This argument lays the foundation for his chapter on "Growing Problems and Internal Conspiracies (*fitna*) among Muslims," in which Muhammad Sodiq observes that the number of conspiracies and problems among Muslims has increased recently. He writes:

> The number of organizations, movements and parties, that include such religious terms as "Faith," "Islam," "Jihad," and "Grace" in their names has grown recently. The names and charters of these parties and movements are different, but the goal is the same—to obtain influence, using Islam as a cover.

These organizations claim to be introducing a "new Islam" and so weaken Islam and the authority of Islamic scholars. He quotes noted Arab theologian Muhammad Said Ramadan al-Buti:

> This is not the religion sent by Allah. This is a religion that comes from the heads and ideas of some people. This religion contradicts Islamic norms and Sharia.... Today we are witnesses to events in the Islamic world that are the result of these "new messengers [of Allah]." It was not always this way. They want their Islam to replace the Islam we knew before and the Islam that was sent to us by Allah.... They claim that their Islam is based on *fiqh*. But it is not so.... Killing Muslims, they claim, that acts of suicide in planes full of innocent people is a dictate of Sharia.

He then goes on to examine the situation in Central Asia, starting when Islam first came to the region, and including the contribution of famous local theologians such as al-Bukhari[36] and al-Termizi.[37] He then discusses the stresses religion experienced during the period of colonization and the irrevocable damage of the Soviet period. He contrasts this with the positive changes that have occurred with independence. He argues, though, that the return to religion was not without problems; there was a lack of educated theologians and excessive conservatism, especially in small communities. But worst of all, he contends, has been the damage done by the activities of foreign missionaries seeking to spread the idea that there is a "new Islam."

These missionaries have been able to take advantage of the "longing for Islam," of young people in particular. He puts the efforts of Hizb ut-Tahrir in this category, borrowing heavily from Arab sources that criticize the movement, noting that it is banned in much of the Muslim world. He also notes that it is granted "refuge" in Europe, operating freely from staff offices in London, and speculates that this may be because some in the West want to deepen splits within the Muslim community.

Muhammad Sodiq notes that Hizb ut-Tahrir claims to be alone among Muslims in calling for *davat*, roughly, evangelical Islam, though the group understands *davat* as political rather than religious propaganda. How, Muhammad Sodiq wonders, can it call for the spread of Islam without a solid understanding of the basic tenets of Islam?

To him there is no question that Hizb ut-Tahrir has "left the faith" because of its rejection of basic Quranic teachings.[38] He also accuses Hizb ut-Tahrir of excessive rationalism, of "excessive belief in [the members'] own intellect, rather than belief in Allah," and he complains that they exploit most Muslims' pervasive ignorance of Sharia by trying to convince them of the possibility of a unified Caliphate, in Central Asia, where conditions (set forth in Sharia) are essentially missing.

Muhammad Sodiq is especially angered by Hizb ut-Tahrir's promotion of jihad through martyrdom as *shahids*[39]:

> Hizb ut-Tahrir calls not to be afraid of death and to sacrifice oneself "on the path of Allah" by all possible means, including suicide. However, when it comes to them, they do their deeds undercover.... So, why don't they want to make their names known? Why do they want to stay alive, while they are prepared to send their ordinary members to death? Why do they call on their followers to conduct their propaganda openly, while they are in hiding? They say to their followers: "Go and kill yourself for Allah's sake! Then you will become *shahid*." So, why don't they want to do it themselves?

In the chapters "Who Is to Blame?" and "What Is to Be Done?" Muhammad Sodiq offers a kind of homage to the Russian intellectuals who posed those questions in the tendentious years before the Bolshevik Revolution.[40]

Muhammad Sodiq answers the first question, saying that he and all Muslims themselves are to blame and that local Muslims should think critically and carefully about what is offered to them as "the truth." He writes that societies must place great importance on cultivating and educating truly wise *ulama*. If societies (and presumably governments) ignore such people, then dangerous ideas may come to dominate:

> Only those *ulama* can become true examples for us, who have mastered the knowledge of Allah, who follow it, and themselves serve as an example of genuine faith and moderation. They can lead a society down the correct path and preserve its unity. And unity is a very important factor.... Therefore we should try to train such *ulama* whom people will follow and who will strictly adhere to their positions.... In a society where there are no such *ulama* or where they are inactive, various other foreign communities or parties will certainly appear. Moreover, we should study the state of religious affairs in the society and provide conditions for correct development.

The message would seem clear: If Uzbekistan's government ignores the opinion of someone as learned as Muhammad Sodiq, then ignorant and potentially politicized figures will come forward to speak for Islam.

He is trying to make a case for the gradual (and eventually the complete) embracing of Islam by Uzbek society, but he makes the argument for this in ways that do not countermand the goals of the Karimov government. One of the ways that he seeks to do this is by emphasizing that Islam can be spread based only on the receptivity of the population to learn about their faith. It cannot be forced on them; it must be spread peacefully, by those from within the society, those whose message should accurately reflect religious teachings. Otherwise, people will fall prey to propaganda.

In the final chapter, "Good News" (*Yaxshilik bashorati*), Muhammad Sodiq rather immodestly puts forth why he is an acceptable person to fulfill the responsibility of spreading Islam in Uzbekistan. He cites two reasons: his level of religious learning and the support that he enjoys among Muslims in Uzbekistan.

He writes of his interactions with believers since his return:

> Sometimes parents brought their children to be shown a true path. Sometimes Muslims addressed me with bureaucratic problems they could not resolve. Scholars, too, started coming to me.

And he notes the positive reception of his earlier writings:

> I heard especially many positive responses to my book *Hadiths and Life*. For many it was news. Some people who read this book declared that they were leaving parties, various groups. And although this book did not have a word on various groups and parties, it had the right influence on people, and we realized how strong people's quest for true knowledge is. And therefore, our "*ulama*" should speak of our religion in simple and accessible language.

Muhammad Sodiq then recounts that a fan called him at home to say that if his book had been read earlier, the 1999 Tashkent bombings would not have taken place. While this observation is offered as if in ironic jest, I suspect that Muhammad Sodiq truly believes that had he not been forced into exile, extremist groups might not have gained as much support. He claims, tangentially in support of this, that members of Hizb ut-Tahrir were given his book to read after they were arrested, and that they repented and came back to local Hanafi teachings.

In the conclusion of the book, Muhammad Sodiq argues that every Muslim should remain with Sunni *mazhab*, adding that "in studies of our religion we should follow the ideas of our blessed ancestors." Then, speaking of the advantages of local *murid* schools of the Hanafi tradition, he goes on to close with the following invocations:

- *Ulama* should be respected and followed.
- Special attention should be given to the upbringing of our children.
- Beware of membership of different groups and parties.
- Strengthen peaceful coexistence between people.
- Serve your motherland and people.

SUMMING UP MUHAMMAD SODIQ'S POLITICAL MESSAGE: ISLAMIC UNIFICATION

While Muhammad Sodiq notes that a Caliphate is the ideal for the Muslim world to strive for, he understands that it cannot realistically be restored now, because of the complete lack of unity in the Muslim world.

But at the same time, he believes that Muslims must preserve the image of a peaceful religion, strengthen traditional Islam, and unify around the idea of Sunni unity.

An adherent of contemporary Syrian theologian Muhammad Said Ramadan al-Buti,[41] whom he often cites, Muhammad Sodiq speaks against the division of Islam into political parties and movements, arguing that this contributes to the dispersion of Islam's intellectual and physical forces and interferes with real unification and rapprochement of Muslim states.

Muhammad Sodiq and al-Buti alike speak in favor of Muslims' unification for the sake of unification and rapprochement of the positions of Sunnis (the Shia are not mentioned at all). But he fears "that the conditions for a political union of Muslim countries are disappearing as the West finds new ways to colonize Muslims."

Bakhtiyar Babadjanov notes that Muhammad Sodiq's position, which he calls "conservative modernism," is remarkably similar to that of Sayyid Jamal ud-Din "al-Afghani." Babadjanov writes that Muhammad Sodiq's "conservative modernism" is embodied in his book *The Essence of Contradictions*, where he writes that there is no need "to change Islam and its religious traditions" in order to change and adapt to the realities of the modern world; it is only necessary to use the tool of *fatwa* more effectively.

Muhammad Sodiq notes that he has both read and agreed with al-Afghani's book *Refutation of Materialists*.[42] Like al-Afghani, Muhammad Sodiq believes that Muslims must not remain apart from technical progress. Instead, they must master technical knowledge, be more open in this sense toward the West while preserving their religion, values, and ways of life. Muhammad Sodiq argues that Muslims must increase their knowledge of religion and religious traditions. This is their first obligation, but they should also master the secular sciences. Only on this basis, Muhammad Sodiq believes, is there a chance to preserve and strengthen the Muslim community (*umma*) spiritually, politically, and ideologically.

Muhammad Sodiq, though, insists that he disagrees with al-Afghani in many ways, parting with him in terms of the latter's rejection of *Sunna*, which is at the core of Muhammad Sodiq's understanding of Islam. Muhammad Sodiq believes that al-Afghani was too enamored of Western political institutions. To a considerable degree, Muhammad Sodiq shares the opinion of Edward Said, whose book *Orientalism*[43] he read in an Arabic translation.

Along with many other members of the theological unification movement, Muhammad Sodiq is certain that if such unification occurs, Muslims' international and economic problems will find new sources for solution. Only then will Muslims be successful at resisting neocolonialism and the "pernicious influence of the West."

The drive for religious unification—often as a form of purification—has been a response to Western incursions in the Muslim world since the eighteenth century. This was the aim of the Wahhabi movement of Muhammad ibn Abd al-Wahhab, which became the state ideology of Saudi Arabia, or the ideological searches and activity of organizations that have emerged more recently, such as the Muslim Brotherhood. Most of these movements have asserted the need to move away from the *mazhabs*, the traditional schools of law, and embrace "pure" Islam, such as the Salafi ideal of returning to the practice as Islam as it was at the time of the Prophet. But this has generally led to splits between the Salafi or "purists" and adherents of the Islamic schools.

To try to counteract this trend and avoid schisms within Islam, a number of major inter-Islamic organizations (such as Rabita), Islamic educational centers (such as Al-Azhar in Egypt), and many prominent Muslim theologians over the past few decades argued that joint actions are necessary to overcome (or, as a last resort, to fully eliminate) the differences between the *mazhabs*. They argue that the four *mazhabs* are equally legitimate and that religious unification can occur in a way that the unity of Sunnism and adaptation to local conditions are both preserved.

For most of these people, the means to this end is through reforming religious education, to teach greater awareness of and tolerance toward different Islamic schools. Some of the funding for this effort in Central Asia has come from Islamic organizations in the Arab countries that are interested in funding Islamic revival in the post-Soviet states.

These ideas have found great appeal among a younger generation of clerics and advanced students of Islam, who have themselves studied at or had contact with the major Islamic educational and religious centers in Egypt, Saudi Arabia, or Libya. They include graduates of the Higher Islamic Institute and of the Tashkent State Institute of Oriental Studies. In turn, as is elaborated in a later chapter, they bring these ideas back into the curriculum of secular and religious institutions that offer instruction on religious themes, and into their work in various government institutions including the consultative boards of the State Committee on Religion, and the office of the adviser on religious affairs to the president of Uzbekistan.

Muhammad Sodiq has also been a strong and very effective advocate of nostrification,[44] which gives students from religious schools the ability to get jobs in the police, the judiciary, and the educational system, and has increased the number of advocates of an expanded role of religion in society.

These people have served as effective lobbyists for *fatwas* directed at the struggle against various local forms of Islam (customs and rituals that come from local practice but are not part of Sharia). At the same time, these same people openly attack the religious policy of the state as being in violation of traditional (local) Hanafi Islam.

Their numbers seem to be growing, suggesting that it is only a matter of time before the question of the political status of Islam as a form of official state religion is raised. These individuals are but one of a number of forces working toward de-secularization. Radical Islamists also support this goal, as do traditional Hanafi Muslims, those who are more interested in practicing the traditions of the faith than mastering the doctrinal teachings. So while Muhammad Sodiq seems to be realizing part of his dream, a return to Islam by the Uzbek people, the goal of unity within the country's community of believers seems as elusive as ever.

6

ISLAM
IN THE COMMUNITIES

THE FOUR COMMUNITIES

The next two chapters look at the survival and revival of Islam in Uzbekistan, through the use of interviews conducted by a group of Uzbek scholars[1] in 1992 and 1993 in a research project of my design. They offer a portrait of religious practice at the household and community level, and show how the survival of Islam in Uzbek communities was sufficient to support religious dynamism during the period of religious revival in the late 1980s and 1990s.

This chapter focuses on survival, and tries to capture the reasons why some people tried to preserve the teachings and practice of their faith, while others were either too frightened or too indifferent to do so. It examines the ways in which the teachings and practice of Islam survived and looks at why it was better preserved in some communities than in others, and how even within communities the population made very different decisions about whether to try to preserve the teachings and practice of their faith. The next chapter focuses on the relationship between how the degree of survival of Islam impacts the speed and way in which Islamic revival occurred.

Four communities were selected,[2] in Namangan, Ferghana, Samarkand, and Surkhandarya oblasts.[3] The sample was designed to reflect what we anticipated would be differing patterns of religious survival, with villages in Namangan and Ferghana chosen because the revival of Islam had begun earlier in the Ferghana Valley than elsewhere in the country.

The differences that were found between communities were rather predictable. The Islamic revival was proceeding most rapidly in the Ferghana Valley, in the Namangan region in particular, and knowledge of Islam was most extensive there as well. Islamic traditions, as well as a sense of religious continuity, was also characteristic of Baisun (Boysun), in Surkhandarya, which had been a part of the Emirate of Bukhara until the Russian Revolution and thus had never experienced Russian colonial rule.

The study overall provides evidence of much greater religious continuity than would have been expected from a reading of Soviet and Western literature on Islam in Soviet Central Asia. Religion was not dead, and in many places far from dormant. There were people in each of the communities who had received some religious education, albeit by teachers not sanctioned by Soviet authorities, so major life-cycle rites could be properly observed by those who sought someone to read prayers for them. And even those who lacked any religious education and had little interest in religious rituals still wanted to pursue some form of "Muslimness" in their lives. The study provides evidence for the argument that Uzbekistan's religious revival predated the Gorbachev era, but it leaves unresolved the question of whether Sharaf Rashidov's leadership of the Uzbek Communist Party or Moscow's growing indifference during the "stagnation" (*zastoy*) of the late Brezhnev years was the cause.

In each community, fifteen to twenty families were selected for interviews, with two or three generations of a given family participating whenever possible. The interviews were conducted in Uzbek by a trained sociologist from the village or from a nearby community. The interviews were taped with the permission of those interviewed, and the interviewees were not paid for participating in the study, although each was given a modest gift in keeping with the rules of hospitality. The Uzbek research team, of course, was compensated, and was able to keep a copy of the interviews to publish or use as it wished.[4]

Uzbekistan was going through a very unusual time during 1992 and early 1993, when these interviews were being conducted. As such, it was very easy to get people to talk about the role of religion in their lives, in the past and since independence, and how the role of religion was changing in their community. It was also not difficult to get permission to do such a study. The local government was informed of what we were doing, and in some cases these government officials asked to see the five or six questions that formed the core of our "conversation" with the interviewees. But that was really the only degree of formality that was required. The questions were innocuous; the researchers were known in the community; I had introduced myself; and Uzbekistan's leaders at the national and local level had more serious challenges to focus on.

Life in a Border Community: Baisun, Surkhandarya Oblast

Baisun district is the most remote interview site included in the study. Surkhandarya Oblast borders both Afghanistan and the Kurgan Tyube (now Khatlon) province of Tajikistan and what was known as Eastern Bukhara before the Russian Revolution; it had been ruled by the Emir of Bukhara and not by the Russian colonial authorities.[5]

Most people in and around Baisun remained loyal to the Emir, who was briefly lodged in the town of Baisun as he fled to Afghanistan in 1920. After the Emir's departure there was a good deal of local fighting to resist Bolshevik forces in the district around Baisun, one resident, born in 1906, recalls. He recounted the death of his father, Buri-Toksabo, a village elder and local representative of the Emir, who was rounded up and shot with other local elders during the civil war.

During the civil war years many prosperous families who had served the Emir fled to the mountains to avoid the Bolsheviks; eleven of the seventeen families in the sample say that their ancestors were among them. Most of these families had some ties to the Baisun region, but to this day the *mahallas* in Baisun are composed almost entirely of civil war refugees from Karshi (Qarshi), in Kashkadarya, and their descendants; many of these families suffered losses during the Stalinist repression.

The viciousness with which anti-religious policies were pursued by the Soviet authorities seems to have traumatized many who were religious or had an interest in continuing to practice Islam. Moreover, the region itself was always something of an outpost, so that while there might have been small madrasas in communities in the time of the Emir of Bukhara, people seeking advanced religious training left the region. Thus, Islam's presence was much more muted than what one found in the Ferghana Valley, or even a drive down the road toward the outskirts of Dushanbe.

Dushanbe (Tajikistan) is the nearest large city to Baisun, although after independence it became difficult, and then nearly impossible, to get there.[6] In 1924 the region was assigned to Tajikistan, which was then an autonomous republic of Uzbekistan; in 1929, when Tajikistan was granted status as a full union republic, this area remained in Uzbekistan.

Southern Surkhandarya is a mountainous region with degraded semi-arid pasturelands—only Karakalpakistan (Qoraqalpogiston) is more isolated in Uzbekistan—and its remoteness helped keep the traditional family structure of communities in the Baisun region relatively intact.

Baisun itself is a city of some forty thousand people; most people who work in the city are tied to the social service sector. What little industry exists is largely linked to processing food for the local population. The city is poor, the poorest we visited for this study; most homes lack any form of indoor plumbing, although there is a system of local wells and public bathhouses. The situation is even bleaker in the countryside around Baisun. The higher we traveled into the mountains, the worse life got, although all of the villages had electricity and access to television, the main source of information.

During the time that these interviews were taking place, Baisun's residents were glued to their TV sets, enthralled by "The Rich Also Cry," a Mexican soap opera. The contrast in lifestyles between Baisun and the soap opera was extremely sharp. One episode, which aired at roughly the time of the interviews, featured a simple housekeeper who was dying in an immaculate, well-equipped modern hospital room. By contrast, the hospital in Baisun lacked indoor plumbing and had shortages of even the most basic medical supplies. Disease was a familiar part of life in Baisun, where poor sanitation compounded the problems of poor diet and overpopulation. Villagers at the base of the mountains complained that the only public bathhouse in their village was often closed for months at a time, while those who lived in villages near the top of the mountain had to draw their drinking water from untreated mountain streams.

It takes more than two hours of driving (on dry roads) in an all-terrain vehicle to cover the ten miles from Baisun to the outskirts of the state farm that we chose for our study.[7] The state farm consisted of some eight thousand people living in eight villages, scattered over an area of nearly ten square kilometers. The principal economy of the farm is livestock breeding, of sheep and some dairy cows. There is also some very small-scale truck farming.

The people we studied at the state farm lived in five villages that were predominantly Uzbek and three that were predominantly Tajik. Although few people in the area could claim to be "pure" Tajik or "pure" Uzbek, people generally settled on one nationality or the other based on where their ancestors had come from and the language spoken at home. Most people who lived in these communities spoke both Uzbek and Tajik, but only the Tajiks were literate in Tajik. The Uzbeks and most of the Tajiks were literate in Uzbek.

Life in Rural Samarkand Oblast

The village of Turkipoen in the Katta Turk agricultural district of the Chelak Rayon of Samarkand Oblast was another interview site.[8] Life in the villages around Chelak is very different from that in the mountains of Surkhandarya or in the towns of the Ferghana Valley, and religion played a much smaller role in daily life in Chelak[9] before and during the Soviet period as well as in the present.[10]

This is despite the fact that the grave of Abu Abdullah Muhammad ibn Ismail ibn Ibrahim al-Bukhari al-Jufi, known as Khoja Ismail al-Bukhari, located in Kharang, is not far from Samarkand and from Turkipoen itself.[11] Shrines such as the one dedicated to Khoja Ismail gained importance after Soviet authorities sharply curtailed the number and role of public religious institutions, but it was far enough away to be of little consequence to those living in the community that was chosen for the study.

Turkipoen is about fifty kilometers northwest of the city of Samarkand. The area around Samarkand is dense with villages, but, unlike in the Ferghana Valley, the worlds of village and city do not mix easily in the Samarkand region.

This region is home to both Uzbeks and Tajiks, but Turkipoen itself is almost entirely an Uzbek settlement. Turkipoen is an old *kishlak* (village); one of those interviewed was able to name his "seven fathers,"[12] all of whom had lived in the same village. Most of the other respondents are from families who have lived in the environs of the *kishlak* as far back as anyone remembers, although a few of the families had fled there from regions farther north, nearer the Kazakh border, after the Soviets nationalized their property.

As in the villages in the Ferghana Valley, the *mahalla* remains a central focus of most people's lives. There are sixteen *mahallas* in Turkipoen. The economic life of the village, of course, has changed over time. Before the Revolution, the area was one of small farmers and absentee landlords. At the time of the interviews, the local collective farm, which employed most village residents, had yet to be privatized.

The residents of Turkipoen do not appear to feel comfortable going to Samarkand, finding it modern and alien. People speak of the city as if it were several hundred miles away, and a few of those interviewed seem never to have visited Samarkand at all. The respondents from Turkipoen seem more oriented toward the city of Bukhara, even though it is nearly three times as far from the village as is Samarkand. Even then, few respondents from Turkipoen travel to Bukhara with any frequency. All who mentioned the city seemed to feel at ease there and to visit it with a sense of awe, as if by visiting they were recapturing connections to an ever-more-distant Uzbek past. Unlike with Samarkand, an Uzbek peasant who goes to Bukhara feels somehow at home. This is probably because of the fact that while buildings of the old city of Bukhara remained intact, their splendor then still completely faded. In its narrow streets it was easy to remember the pre-revolutionary past, while the "new" city was a strictly and wholly separate Soviet one. Samarkand, by contrast, was a nineteenth-century Russian garrison town, with a large "new city" right up against the imposing ruins of Timur's rule and that of his descendants.

Kuva: Between Two Worlds

Two communities from the Ferghana Valley were included in the study. One sample comes from three villages in the Dehqonobod agricultural district in the Kuva (Quva) Rayon of Ferghana Oblast, the other from Tova in Namangan Oblast.[13] The villages are only thirty-odd kilometers from a Russian-influenced commercial and industrial center in the city of Ferghana and are the same distance from the old Uzbek market town of Margilan, an Eastern-style city on the outskirts of Ferghana that was a center for Uzbekistan's "second," or "black-market," economy. Local Soviet authorities, who themselves grew rich from the Margilan clan's control of Central Asian trade, turned a blind eye to commercial and other activities in the city. This is probably why Hakimjon qori's *hujra* located there was tolerated.

More than anywhere else in the study, the communities in the Ferghana Valley offered a story of continuity. Twenty of the twenty-eight interviewed in Kuva described faith and prayer as a lifelong central pillar of their lives; five of them admitted to having some sort of formal religious training, while the remaining fifteen received some religious instruction at home.

Tova: Near the Center of Islam's Renaissance

Nowhere is Uzbekistan's post-World War II population explosion more in evidence than in the Namangan region, one of the main centers of the Ferghana Valley's Islamic revival. In Namangan, the city and neighboring communities are all expanding to meet each other. Tova, a community of two thousand families and just over ten thousand people, was considered remote from Namangan two generations ago. Now it is a forty-minute drive from downtown Namangan in heavy traffic, and some members of the community go back and forth from Namangan to work or school daily, while the newest portions of the city are visible in the distance from the ridge on which Tova sits.

For all its proximity to Namangan, the *kishlak* of Tova is very much a self-contained community, itself containing several *mahallas*. The thirteen families chosen came from several different *mahallas* in the village.[14] What is most striking about the sample is how many of the respondents have parents or grandparents who were religious leaders in the village or in the broader Namangan region; six of the thirteen families had ancestors who could be so classified.[15]

Much like in Kuva, community life in Namangan and towns like Tova were dominated before the Revolution by their many local religious leaders. While life in Tova was dramatically transformed by the years of Soviet rule, if this sample is at all indicative of the larger community, respect for Islamic practices and values remained more a part of most people's lives here than they did outside of the Ferghana Valley. In fact, prior to

1990 there were three functioning mosques (little more than public prayer houses) in the village.

There had been a fourth mosque, which had been built by *basmachi* leader Abdu Malik; however, it became dysfunctional, as it was turned into a museum in 1975 in honor of the thirtieth anniversary of the victory over fascism. At the time of the survey, Abdu Malik's mosque still had not been returned to the control of the believers.

That fact seemed to serve as a constant reminder to the community that life had not yet changed completely. This may in part have been because Tova had been a center of *basmachi* resistance, albeit a minor one, the memory of which appears to linger; at least one of those interviewed (a teacher and the son of a *mahalla* chairman, born in 1946) noted with great pride that he was the grandson of a local *basmachi* leader.

In general, these interviews portray a community that markedly seems never to have been very alienated from its Islamic roots, which would help explain the speed and scope of the Islamic revival in this part of Uzbekistan. Even our atheist host boasted of being a *sayyid*; for proof, he produced long-hidden family documents, written in the first half of the nineteenth century by the Khan of Kokand, ruler of the region. And though mentioning that he had no religious education (as befitted his position), he noted that "although I am not a religious person, there are some *suras* and *ayats* which I think one must know."[16]

THE EARLY YEARS OF SOVIET RULE

Prior to Soviet rule, Islam was at the center of public life in every community included in the study. For example, in Kuva, several of the older people interviewed complained that the Islamic community of their youth no longer existed. A collective farm worker born in 1911 offers a vivid description of what life had once been like there:

> In the years of my youth there were a lot of mosques. Some of them were destroyed, and some were turned into stores. I remember well that we had our own large mosque here, where the elders used to go and pray. After praying, they sat an hour or two conversing, and then in the evening they would gather at someone's house. They would brew *kuknori* [ground, dry poppy pod] in

the teapot and sit up until late talking and chatting about this and that. There were especially a lot of people during *Hayit nomoz*.[17] Sometimes women also came and watched from afar as their husbands did the rituals. During *Qurbon hayit* [*Eid al-Adha*], people who had the means did sacrifices, killed livestock, and handed the pieces out to the people, especially to the poor. All of that was before.

A medical assistant in Kuva, born in 1959, noted that he was the son of a well-known *mullah* (from Ferghana Oblast), who was driven by religious faith to spend the years of World War II collecting and distributing aid to people who had been evacuated to Uzbekistan. Though he lacked formal religious education, the medical assistant now attends the local mosque each day.

Many still remember what life in Baisun and its surrounding villages was like before the Soviets, when Baisun was part of the Emirate of Bukhara, and the central role that religion played in the community. For example, a statistician born in the Baisun area in 1923 describes the past as it was recounted to him:

> There used to be a lot of mosques and madrasas. Usually every village had two or three of them. The whole community gathered here and prayed. As far as I know, before the Revolution there were as many as 500 mosques and madrasa in Baisun alone.... It is impossible to over-exaggerate the formative influence of the community and the mosques. This is the hearth of real moral education and enlightenment for people. There used to be a great many trained religious people, who had gotten very good religious training in Bukhara.... They [referring to specific noted clerics from the region] didn't even accept money, considering that it was their duty to lead the people. They were true learned active men, who could answer any questions the people put to them, because they knew all the books beautifully and could comment freely on any text.

A tractor driver, born in 1930 in a village near Baisun's state farm, recalls with pride the role his father, a *mullah*, played in his own community, and the sacrifices that it took the family for him to have gained a religious education:

> When my father was fifteen (around 1903), my grandfather gathered up all he had saved and took him to Bukhara,[18] to a madrasa. My father Ostan studied two years in a madrasa and got a higher religious education, receiving the title

of *mullah*, and then he returned to the village.... Our village was never too religious. Even so the role of religion in the life of the people was large. Just think, in this small a village there were four *mullahs*, which is a lot.... People respected him greatly. When he read the *suras* from the Quran, many people wept. The neighbors came to listen to him read. He had many books in the Arabic language, and in the Arabic alphabet. When the Bolsheviks came he buried them in the yard, where they are to this day. I don't know exactly where they are buried.

He went on to describe how in his village the population helped protect the clerics during the repression that followed:

Soviet anti-religious policies were practically a terror against the clergy and against the religious values of our people. The way it used to be was if you knew Arabic, even if you just knew the Arabic alphabet and had studied in the old schools, that meant that you were a potential enemy of the people, and if you were a *mullah* and you were literate in the Arabic script or you're a person connected to religion, then you were an enemy of the people and your place was in Siberia or in prison. Of the four *mullahs* of our village, three had to run away and lived in hiding in other parts right up until the 1940s. They would have been sent to prison but they weren't caught, because the population helped, and warned them about dangers. The old schools were destroyed and so were the *mullahs* with their knowledge, and so we lost our memory. Today there are very few people who can read our old books, the sources of our history.... This persecution only died down in the beginning of the 1940s. But then the war began.

His father sneaked back into the village in the 1940s but then was drafted into a forced labor brigade, finally returning home only in the 1950s to live out his life in the Baisun area.

As the retired statistician recalls, many community notables were not as fortunate:

A heavy fate also befell the educated people. How many educated people were destroyed, how many religious books and manuscripts were burned in the tundra? ... They came around at night to the homes of educated people and took them to the police and the KGB. Some of them were shot right there, and others were forced to Siberia. It resulted in government going into the hands of illiterate, pitiless people who have no souls. And how many of our fellow countrymen were forced to leave their homelands? Almost all of them were intelligent, business-like, entrepreneurial people. Up to about two mil-

> lion Uzbeks were forced to emigrate to Afghanistan, Pakistan, Saudi Arabia, and Turkey.... Things got so that we couldn't even express our sympathies to families when there were family deaths. There was an instance when the *mufti* of Baisun died. I was friendly with his son, but even so I was too afraid to go to him and express my sympathies, and all the same I was accused of religious sympathies.

There are similar accounts from the children of survivors in all of the villages that were studied. The last of a long line of *halal* butchers recalls the horror of these years and the role that local collaborators played in the destruction of the community's religious life:

> So in 1929 to 1933 many people, our *mullahs*, even if they were barely literate, were arrested and sent into exile, to the Caucasus or Siberia. Many of them died, along with their families and children. Not many were left who are still alive. Now some of them live in America and England and Afghanistan and Pakistan, for example. There are Uzbeks everywhere. They are the ones who left in 1929–1933. The rest went in 1936, when they rounded up the *mullahs* again, calling them Trotskyites, like Faizulla Khodjaev[19] and Akmal Ikramov[20] and the *mullahs* that remained in the villages. They called them all throwbacks and rounded them up and arrested them, even the barely literate ones. That was during Stalin. Of course at the time Stalin didn't say anything, didn't give concrete orders to arrest anyone [in] particular. Those people were in the villages, right? How was Stalin or anyone in Moscow, to know what kind of people lived in our villages? It was our people who did this.... The mosques and madrasa were built by good, intelligent, well-trained people. We had a mosque here in this village. There were also about twenty *mullahs* in the village.

The son of a *kulak* (affluent peasant) family from Kuva, born in 1927, describes how difficult it was for ordinary people who tried to maintain even a semblance of the practice of their faith:

> Many of the older generations claim that in the past villagers hid in the reeds or went up on the roofs of their houses, or hid in the cow barns to say the prayers, in spite of the extremely strict interdictions against it by the authorities.

The hardships that people experienced during the Stalinist repressions of the late 1920s and 1930s continued to have negative consequences for the next generations, either directly, or because of the fears that they internalized as a result. The Baisun *mullah*'s son (the retired tractor driver born in 1906) complains of the submissiveness that resulted:

> When the Red Bolsheviks came, they forbade religion. And what happened? Everyone was frightened. Until the beginning of the 1950s no one read the *namaz*, except some who read in secret. But many didn't read at all, for which they were praised. Yesterday they read the *namaz* and were Muslims, then they stopped reading the *namaz*, and so what were they? You know that by his nature man is a weak creature, like a ... what's that creature that changes its look according to the conditions? Ah, yes, a chameleon.

Given the economic deprivation that Baisun experienced in these years, it is not hard to understand why people went into survival mode. As the retired statistician (born in 1923) recalls:

> Those were very hard years. I remember in the beginning of the 1930s there was drought, and a lot of people died. When they started making *kolkhozes*... in those years there were 56 *kolkhozes* just in Baisun ... then things seemed to get a bit better. Some of the wealthier residents were exiled to Siberia as *kulaks*, and all of them were stripped of their livestock. Then they started to take the livestock away from the simple people, and to set up *kolkhoz* farms. Many people starved then. And those were very stern times. They used to put people in prison for pilfering a kilogram of barley or something. Now people steal by the ton, and there's nobody to ask about it.

People became too frightened to study religion. Religion went underground in this community during the decades of religious persecution, but it did not disappear. Several of the respondents born in the 1920s in Kuva made essentially the same complaint as a collective farm worker born in 1925:

> I dreamed of studying in a religious school. However, as you know, in our time they cut off the slightest possibility of acquiring religious knowledge. If any attempts to give young people a religious education cropped up anywhere, the people guilty of attempting this got punished very severely. We were kept in fear.

But some children in Kuva, especially those from well-known clerical families, managed to gain religious training, sometimes in childhood, sometimes in adulthood, even in the worst years. One woman born in 1915, who was descended from several generations of *otin buvis* [older female spiritual leaders],[21] began her formal religious education at ten and then married at fifteen. She said that she remembers well the years when "we had to read the prayers wherever we could, and sometimes we had to do the rituals and traditions in secret." She also felt that the sacrifice that clandestine worship entails was worth it, because "as you become religious, you cleanse your soul, your tongue, your household."

The pain of those years has remained with many of the respondents to this day. One woman, born in 1917, recalled how much she suffered after her father, a noted *mullah* from the Baisun area, fled to Turkmenistan. His abrupt departure did not spare the family; her mother was arrested in the 1930s, while she herself was hidden by relatives, married at thirteen, and became a war widow a decade later. She describes the desperate straits in which she found herself:

> What I had to survive then is impossible to describe. In order to feed my children, to give them an education, to rear them to be good people, I had to throw myself into fire and water. For nights on end, I had to sew so that I could sell the things at the bazaar and feed my children and myself. In the 1940s, I worked in an orphanage and in various workshops.

While things eased during World War II, in the last years of Stalin's life, state authorities again sought to limit the practice of Islam. One respondent, a retired driver born in 1928, recalls how in 1950 Turkipoen's remaining mosque, erected by a local believer, was torn down. It was now also forbidden to recite *namaz*, to fast during Ramadan, or to say *janaza* (a funeral prayer) over the dead. As the respondent recalls, the chance of being caught was real, and the sanctions considerable. Things were so bad that, "even when you asked *mullahs* questions, they would brush it aside."

An agronomist from Kuva, born in 1935, tells sadly about how his father (who had given him religious instruction) finally succumbed to pressure in these years, eventually ceasing to serve as a religious leader for his people:

> My father was a famous *mullah*. I remember people would come to him on holidays and in sorrow, asking him to say prayers, cleanse their souls, or to

recall a departed one with good words. My father was unable to refuse them. Afterwards he would be called into the proper organs [security forces] and worked over. Then it became a rule that on holidays and every Friday my father would hide from his fellow villagers. He would leave home early in the morning and go to Margilan or Ferghana.

THE KHRUSHCHEV AND BREZHNEV YEARS

Even when the memories of the terror receded somewhat, most people remained afraid to get religious education. When weighed against the potential costs to one's educational and career opportunities, spiritual needs appear to have come in a distant second.

As an engineer from the Baisun state farm who was born in 1923 put it:

> I spent 1970 to 1980 in school. In those years studying in religious schools was strictly forbidden. Of course we knew that people took lessons in the homes of certain *mullahs*. Personally I had no desire to study in a religious school, but my mother's father (my grandfather) often used to say to me, Grandson, there is a *mullah* (a relative of my grandfather), let me take you to him, a religious education won't get in your way in life. But I was afraid for some reason (and probably not just me, but also many of the kids my age). I was afraid that if the school teacher were to find out that I was studying in a religious school, I sensed that he would change his attitude toward me, and then good-bye to any gold medals for good grades. That is why I always refused my grandfather.

Others received religious education and then became too frightened to practice their religion. For example, a retired teacher born in the Baisun region in 1932 and who was a grandson of a *mullah* admitted how he abandoned his practice of Islam in the 1940s or 1950s:

> In my childhood I was taught to read the *mullahs*, and each time I say them I grow more convinced that the *namaz* gives strong discipline. It helps one to use and save time properly, and the most important thing, it accustoms one to cleanliness. Later, when the attack of militant atheism began and they began to persecute people who read the *namaz* and who kept other rituals and practices of a religious nature, I quit doing the *namaz*.

A minority were willing to get a religious education, even though this entailed considerable effort. For example, a teacher from the Baisun area born in 1957 recalls that:

> However, thanks to my father, I read the Quran (to be sure, without understanding the content of the texts) and the *hadiths*. Studying Arabic in courses I paid for at the university allowed me to come to understand the content of the religious texts.

There were no negative consequences of this, or the private religious instruction that he paid for at night while in Tashkent, and at the time of the interviews he was the local chairman of the National Democratic Party of Uzbekistan, the party initially organized as the successor to the Communist Party.

The same was true for a teacher from Kuva born in 1934, who served sixteen years as head of his *mahalla* and was its vice chairman at the time of the interview. He describes how he went off to Margilan in the 1950s to work with a local religious figure:

> Once when I was a student in the *technikum* [technical-training school] I read an article about religion and the Quran in a newspaper. I got interested. In order to find out the content, the sense of religion, I went to Mullah Khoshim, in the city of Margilan. He let me read the Quran and explained passages to me for 35 days. That was how I mastered the Quran, the *ayats*.

But those who sought to practice their religion often found that they were unable to cope with the difficulties that this created for them. One woman from Tova who was born in 1956 recounted how (two decades previously) when she was a child, the "godless ones" [atheists] who ran the local Soviet school had forced her to eat when it became known that she was fasting during Ramadan. She was the granddaughter of a noted Sufi leader who had served the Khan of Kokand's family and had hidden in Tova after the Bolshevik Revolution. While she married a man who had also been raised in a religious home (both of her husband's grandfathers had made *hajj* before the Revolution) and described her life as one "subordinate to the laws of Islam," she admits that from high school on she ceased to publicly practice her faith.

One of the most interesting accounts of how people secured religious education comes from Turkipoen, where there were no *hujra* schools during these years, despite the fact that the attitude toward religion became considerably more relaxed when Sharaf Rashidov, himself from the Samarkand area, whom some respondents called "Sharaf aka,"[22] was in power.[23] As a welder born in 1956 notes, it was during those years that "we became conscious of our Muslimness."

There was a *hujra* at the relatively nearby shrine of Khoja Ismail, but it took a stay at a nearby sanitorium for this local welder to become aware of its existence, so private were discussions of religion even in those years. As he describes:

> Then, when I was in the hospital with a certain teacher, it turned out he had some kind of connections to religion. He turned out to work in Khoja Ismail, that is, in the *sovkhoz* [state-owned farm] Paiyak. He was a *mullah*, it turns out. He was teaching in a mechanical institute, and the rest of the time he taught here. And he was a big *mullah* in his village. So when I was with him in the hospital, he got us interested.... "How long do you remain a young man?" he said, and added that it was time to learn about the necessary things. "Then if you get interested," he added, "you can study later yourself." He had books there. He read the Quran to us and some other things.... You know yourself how in Islam our weddings and our funerals are always with us at the necessary time. For example, it can happen that you go to a funeral and maybe there isn't a *mullah* there. How long can you wait for someone to come? If you know a bit of the religion, you can say the prayers yourself, and that makes things easier for you. It's Islam, after all, and you need to have that. I have learned how to read a bit out of the Quran, when you go to a grave. I am also trying to learn more. I know a few *ayats* so far, and I'm learning the *namaz* bit by bit. When I'm older, I'll read the *namaz*, too.

While this welder's religious education was minimal, it was obtained from the aforementioned *mullah*, who seems to have been using the facilities of a state-funded technical school at which he worked as the site of his "madrasa." The welder traveled to this school, where he completed a "course of studies," and returned to his village with a certificate proclaiming him to be both a master mechanic, and having the religious knowledge necessary to allow him to preside over funerals and daily prayer sessions. By doing so, the welder seems also to have been fulfilling a form of traditional family obligation, as his grandfather, whom he had never met, had been a *tabib*, or healer who used traditional medicine.

In the other instance, another welder, born in 1956, went with his mother[24] to a sanitorium[25] in Margilan that generally treated people from the Ferghana Valley (several hours' drive away from Turkipoen), and he encountered a very different lifestyle than he was used to in his community:

> In the Ferghana Valley, in Margilan near Kokand, I was in a sanitorium, and as soon as it got dark the young men and women would come to say prayers. We were embarrassed. They invited us to come, but we didn't. They were young, but they all had long skirts and boots on. They did the *namaz*. We were invited but we didn't go, we were embarrassed to admit that we didn't know anything. It's true, we know nothing. My mother, for example, was 63 before she knew the *shahada* [declaration of belief]. We were embarrassed that these young girls were going to do the *namaz*.

During her own sanitorium stay, the mother worked intensively with a woman from Namangan, and when she returned home she began the religious education of her grown sons:

> The young girls who lived with my mother, they also went to do *namaz*. Then a certain religious woman came from Namangan, who told my mother that she could teach her the *namaz* in 24 days. So my mother every day after dinner until midnight would study the *namaz*. Now my mother knows the five daily prayers entirely, and five times a day she says them. I also learned something, and after I got home I learned two or three *suras*. There was no one to teach me at home. My brother brought me a book from Margilan, and I taught myself from that book. Everything is written in the book, which *kalimas*[26] and which Quran passage must be said at funerals, and what to say during the *namaz*. Everything is written out, and that's what I learned from. For example, I can read one of the *suras* that they say at funerals and cemeteries [which he then recites to the interviewer]. So I have the book and keep studying, every course. Everyone should know the old alphabet, as much as possible. You have to do the five daily prayers and keep Ramadan.

The institution of *otins* was very well developed in the Uzbekistan in general, and in the Ferghana Valley in particular. The daughter of a noted religious figure in Kuva, born in 1927, was initially instructed at home by her father. In 1972, he pressed her to leave her work as a seamstress and become an *otin*:

This is how it was. My father came and said, enough sewing for everybody. How much of your own cotton batting have you wasted, when there weren't enough customers for batting for *khalats* (robes)? You have done a lot of good for people, and you know how to take on another person's sins. My father also said: "I want to ask you something, daughter. Do you read the prayers? Do you read the Quran?" I answered: "Yes." "When," he asked, "if you are laboring all the time?" My father concluded: "From today on, sit and study how to read the prayers. Bring back your talents, which I noticed in you before." A short time later I was studying with an *otin*. Day and night I memorized *suras* and *ayats*.

She has been training students ever since and has practiced healing as well. Spiritual healing has always been a feature of local religious practice, and for her a person without faith can never be completely healed:

... even ten *otins* can't help a sick man or woman, when what they need is a doctor. It doesn't take a doctor long to diagnose the disease and see that an operation is necessary. However, people need doctors, and religion also has its place for helping people. One must believe in religion, too. People often summon me to help. I come. A child is unwell, is crying. I sit next to him and say prayers with all my soul, the child calms down, goes to sleep. The next day the child is healthy. I could introduce a number of examples from Islam and the life of the prophet to convince you of the power of faith. I have read in books how in infancy the prophet nursed at the breast of another woman, when his own mother could not give him suck. There was a voice which announced that the milk was unhealthy. The prophet was operated on and was saved from death. There is another story, about Ibrahim and Adham. The dervish Adham loved Malika, the daughter of Ibrahim, a rich man. They wouldn't let Malika marry a poor dervish. When Malika died, she was buried. Adham came to the grave and wept bitterly, praying to Allah for her soul. God took pity on him and sent an angel to Malika. The angel gave her an injection in the veins, breathed life into her, and she returned to life. The dervish came once again to the cemetery and heard the voice of his beloved Malika coming from the grave. He opened the grave, where he found Malika alive, and she told him about how she had been given an injection. I am telling you this story to show that medicine has inherited this from religion, this ability to return life to people through injections.[27]

But such people were exceptional. A retired teacher from Tova, born in 1925, recalls the late Soviet years:

People used to be afraid of everything. Even believers had to do their prayers timorously. When I was working in the rural council the rayon administrators demanded that we keep people out of the cemetery, that we didn't give them an opportunity to do religious rituals. And they used to put activists just outside the prayer rooms in the various mosques and cemeteries at the time of the Friday prayers. Thank God, even that didn't allow them to destroy our religious values.

GORBACHEV'S ANTI-CORRUPTION CAMPAIGN

While being in Samarkand Oblast was a real advantage during the Rashidov years, for much the same reason it became a definite disadvantage after his death, when the Communist Party leadership decided to "clean up" the Uzbek Communist Party and began its efforts in Rashidov's home region.

During the anti-corruption campaigns of the mid-1980s, officials in the Samarkand region came under particular scrutiny. With religious practices being identified as encouraging corruption (to fund expensive ritual celebrations) even in a small village like Turkipoen, local party and state officials felt constrained from attending the funerals of their close relatives, because their presence was sure to be noted and reported by a security official, or even just by someone eager to please the new men in power.

Worshippers were detained for praying at the shrine at Khoja Ismail, even though this shrine was formally under the control of SADUM, making it a site where worship was permissible.

Worst of all from the point of view of the community and in Turkipoen, it became much more difficult to provide deceased relatives with a proper religious funeral. As a retired chauffeur born in 1926 complained, when Imonjon Usmankhojaev[28] was in power:

> ... if someone died, they didn't even permit celebration of the prayers on the third day after death (*khudoya*),[29] and people were afraid to go to say *fatiha*[30].... It destroyed a lot of people.

A teacher from Kuva, born in 1936, complains that Islam has consistently been treated far worse than Christianity under Soviet rule:

> I can't help comparing Russia and Uzbekistan when the talk comes around to religion. I mean really, why did our administrators in the republic totally destroy all the mosques? I happened to be in some big Russian village. I counted, there were seven old churches there. But in many of our villages they destroyed all the old mosques.

He was not the only person to hold such views. A retired military reservist in Turkipoen, born in 1926, came away from his years of military service both supportive of Uzbekistan's Islamic revival and highly anti-Russian:

> ... we need that sort of knowledge, we need the mosques. Because we mustn't forget our religion, forget Islam. These are our traditions.... Now people are saying that we were slaves of Russia for seventy years, and that's right. Our scientists were always smarter than Russian scientists, so they were all killed. The poets were, too, and the people who established power in Uzbekistan, like Faizulla Khodjaev, and Akmal Ikramov, they were destroyed.

But still there were those who were angriest at Gorbachev for letting the Soviet Union fall apart. A journalist from Baisun (born in 1936) lamented that:

> ... thoughtful and reasoned decisions by an administrator can bear good fruits, and the opposite, too, thoughtless and hurried decisions can bring only bad.... When M. S. Gorbachev was in power, his hasty thoughtless decisions led to the collapse of the USSR, to interethnic clashes and bloodshed. Because economic ties have been broken and productivity has collapsed, the populations in all the former republics are suffering enormous deprivations. Did our society need *perestroika*, or at least that kind of *perestroika*? Probably not. All we got from *perestroika* was that we became independent, that's all.

"MUSLIMNESS"

In a fortuitous addition to the questionnaire, residents in Kuva were asked to comment on their understanding of what constitutes "*musulmonchilik*" (Muslimness)[31] and to define what role religion should be accorded in the community. Every one of those interviewed stressed the importance of Islam and "Muslimness" in the community, and even the communists among those surveyed still saw "Muslimness" as the definer of a person's basic moral values. The interviews provide a window on the personal nature of each respondent's effort to define "Muslimness."

Although there was some variety as to how people explained "Muslimness," the director of the Ferghana Institute of Sociology,[32] born in 1961, explained it as follows:

> I understand "Muslimness" to mean the strict observance of religious rituals, and most especially doing the *namaz*. "Muslimness" means, more than anything, humanity, truthfulness, being of good conscience. To live in accord with "Muslimness" means to live without deceit, not to be envious, not to covet another's goods, to feed one's family by one's own honest labor, to orient yourself in rearing your children to these principles.

Although this same question did not appear in the other surveys, in every community in which interviews were done, respondents on their own frequently offered some version of what "Muslimness" or being a Muslim meant to them.

A mechanic born in Tova in 1950, and one of two brothers interviewed who descended from generations of *mullahs* on their mother's side, notes that, while he is not a religious person, "as a Muslim I am obligated to know the basic rules and requirements."

For a retired *kolkhoz* worker born in 1926 in Turkipoen, "Muslimness" seems to be his own sense of wonderment during a trip to Bukhara where he found a young man who could pray for him at a "holy place" encountered by chance in Bukhara:

> One year I was in Bukhara... it seems there is a *technikum* there. A young fellow in a *chopon* [traditional robe/coat] ran up to me, like my own son, greeted me; he asked us what we were doing there. I said that my wife and I were strolling and looking around. Then I asked him what he was doing, and he said that they were studying. Then I asked, and it turned out that there is a holy place there, could he say a prayer for us? He asked the watchman and they opened the gates, letting me and the wife in. I walked around the grave and kissed it, while the young man said a prayer.

His son, a welder born in 1956 who studied Islam in Margilan in the 1970s, elaborates on the point. For him, proper burial lies at the core of religious belief and religious obligation:

> Every Muslim, when he dies, regardless of who he is, king or pauper, is buried after the Quran is read. Nobody says, look, this one was the president and that one was just a worker or something. Before they kept Ramadan and said the *namaz*, and then it was all forbidden. The people who forbid those things, now when they die, they are also being buried with Quran readings. It's not right otherwise.

A similar answer is offered by an engineer, born in 1961, also from Turkipoen, who had received some rudimentary religious training at home:

> ... we are all Uzbeks, so it wouldn't hurt us to know a few *ayats* from the Quran. When you are frightened, you should say the *kalimas*. Or when you're at the graveyard, you should know something from the Quran. I myself have read at the cemetery three times. I read everywhere, in different ways, depending on the situation. My father taught me how to do this when I was little, in the evenings and after school. I'm not sorry now. If I go anywhere, I never have to blush for my ignorance. I can read the prayers myself.

The answer of a collective farm worker born in Kuva in 1946 is also representative. Although he never received formal instruction, the man says with pride that "no one can accuse me of not praying," asserting his Muslimness in that fashion.

A bookkeeper from Tova who was born in 1957 sees "Muslimness" as defining morality:

> It is impossible to deny the positive role of religion in the life of the *mahalla*. But religious figures and elders must set people on the correct path, must propagate Muslim morality.

An agronomist, born in 1935 and the son of a *mullah* from Kuva, echoes this sentiment:

> I suppose this "Muslimness" means faithfulness to one's religion, to Islam. To exhibit "Muslimness" means not to covet another's goods and in general to be a moral person.

Morality is at the core for most people, and frequenting the mosque or praying does not compensate for immoral behavior. As a *mahalla* elder born in Kuva in 1912 notes:

First, "Muslimness," or behaving like a Muslim, means to be honest, to follow the proper course. Second, if you pray and yet at the same time slander someone else, that doesn't mean you are a Muslim. That's why I repeat that to behave like a Muslim means to be honest, not to slander and to follow your conscience.

For some, the moral values of "Muslimness" could coexist perfectly well with their work as communists.

A man, born in 1935, the son of a *mullah* and at the time the head agronomist on the Kuva collective farm, said:

> I think that many of the communists' principles coincide with religion. Myself, I always respected and observed the Muslim principles, kept the religious holidays, and I can also read prayers.

For at least one person interviewed, a retired electrician from Kuva born in 1924, "Muslimness" was the prospect of immortality:

> I have eighteen grandchildren, many of them are school age. Since I also had a religious education, I have tried to give them love and respect for the teachings of our Prophet [Muhammad]. Because religion is primarily purity and honesty and respect for work, only pure, honest, hardworking people can enter paradise.

One of the points of disagreement among those interviewed was the relationship of "Muslimness" to nationalism, and the relationship between faith and patriotism. This potential tension lies at the center of many of Uzbekistan's efforts to regulate religion in the last twenty years.

For some, commitment to Islam is a form of supranational loyalty. To quote a resident of Kuva born in the mid-1930s (to a household repressed for being *kulaks*):

> ... "Muslimness" as our fathers and grandfathers taught us, does not permit nationalism, and means to act as peacemakers. Our grandfathers shared their bread and fruit, and we too should be that sort of Muslim. It is a mistake to define "Muslimness" by the prayers and other religious rituals.

He goes on to express seeming displeasure at the intrusion of politics into the mosque, saying:

> Praise Allah! I pray often, but I do not always observe the rituals in their full strictness, including the *namaz*. When I am in the prayer house, for example, I pray asking for the strengthening of freedom and independence of Uzbekistan.

Similar sentiments are expressed by a medical assistant born in Tova in 1939, the son of a *mullah*:

> ["Muslimness" is] first of all dedication to one's own land, one's own people, love and respect for people. Second, it is honesty and truthfulness. It is very difficult for me to find the words with which to characterize "Muslimness" ... Musliminess does not permit insulting people of other nationalities. Muslimness cannot include nationalism, either. Our grandfathers and fathers were against this, after all. A Muslim is not just a person who knows the *namaz* and keeps other rituals. A Muslim in my understanding is a person who is developed in all regards.

As we will see in the next chapter, the state was effectively obligated to restore religion to the communities, to allow Uzbeks to build mosques and religious schools, and to gain religious training. Religion had to be restored to the community, but it also had to be kept in check, so as not to threaten the state. How to do this is a question that is highly debated within Uzbekistan, and there is no consensus on where the divides should be.

7

ISLAMIC REVIVAL IN THE
UZBEK COMMUNITIES

As early as late 1992, when the survey was done, it was already possible to see real divisions within Uzbek communities as to what the appropriate government policy toward religion should be and what role Islam should ideally play in Uzbekistan. In this period, Uzbek government policy toward religion was not yet well defined. Local communities were filling the void left by the collapse of Soviet power and the new independent government's lack of capacity to enforce its preferences on recalcitrant populations.

For this reason, it was possible for people to speak freely and, where desired, quite critically about what was going on, and many showed no reticence in doing so. While everyone thought that it was a good thing that mosques and madrasas were being built, some were concerned about how much money was being spent on buildings rather than on necessary social services. There was also a lot of disagreement over how to balance religious norms with the needs of modern education and training. The question of education for women and their role in society was especially contentious. Finally, there was a lot of disagreement over how actively the state should regulate religious affairs. While all this was going on, people were mindful of the ongoing civil war in neighboring Tajikistan and feared that it could be a harbinger of things to come in Uzbekistan as well as have a direct impact on conditions in their own country.

THE RETURN OF RELIGION

In all four communities, our respondents talked about the dramatic changes that had occurred in the daily lives of their communities as a result of the change in policy toward religion over the past few years. The greatest changes had come since independence, roughly a year earlier. Mosques and madrasas were being built or repaired and reopened, usually with money collected in the community. Local officials previously charged with monitoring and if necessary prohibiting religious practice in their communities were now frequently heading up these fund-raising drives.

Some respondents were euphoric from the opportunity granted them to openly study and practice their faith. A sweets-maker from Baisun, who was born in 1936 and whose ancestors included clerics, began his interview with a recitation from the Quran, and then continues:

> Ever since I was a child, I wanted to get both a secular and a religious education. Probably that was the result of the influence of my ancestors. My father was a pretty well-educated man, and my ancestors were famous *mullahs* on both my father's and my mother's side.... I regret only one thing. At one time my father had a great many good books, which were stolen or taken away by the authorities and burned. If only these books were here now! I would devote the rest of my life to the study of those books. Now I read everything that I can get my hands on, but mostly I read the Quran and *hadiths* in the evening in the mosque... Now I sit here and I think that in those years no one could even have dreamed that a time would come when it would be possible to go to mosque freely, to read the Quran, and to get a religious education. The changes occurring today are like a dream for us. Praise Allah that religion has come back to us, our traditions and values, that mosques are opening again, that everyone who wants to can get a religious education in Bukhara, Tashkent, Samarkand, Namangan. This is all thanks to the fact that Allah gave us freedom, and we have become independent of the atheists.

Many spoke about how the return of religion was a part of Uzbekistan's embracing its historical past. For many it was a fitting accompaniment to independence and a cornerstone to build upon in developing a new national ideology.

An engineer-mechanic from Tova, born in 1950, and whose maternal line included a number of famous clerics, notes that Uzbekistan's history has always centered around its mosques and madrasas, and how "great people" like Alisher Navoi,[1] Fizuli,[2] and Khoja Ahmad Yasawi were all "true Muslims," who were honored by preserving and treasuring old mosques and by building worthy new ones.

As one would expect, the religious revival was proceeding most rapidly in the two towns in the Ferghana Valley. By 1992, Tova was no longer too dissimilar from rural communities in other Muslim countries; there were 20 mosques or prayer houses, all but three newly opened, that served as the center of the community's social life.

Almost all of these mosques and prayer houses had been built through public contribution, in the form of *hashar*[3] or the collection of *xayr-sadiqa* (charity, donations) by the elders of the *mahalla*. Vast sums of money were raised, an average of six hundred thousand rubles per mosque (at a time when the average salary was under three thousand rubles per month), at a time of growing economic hardship and uncertainty.

One resident of Tova (born in 1956) notes with pride that "today both young and old go to the mosque to say *namaz*, and although many people do not pray five times each day, everyone tries not to miss the morning *namaz*."

The situation was much the same in Kuva, where strong support for the revival came from within the community of believers themselves. Many sought to live their lives within the confines of the teachings of Islam and not just offer public manifestations of observance. As one devout local resident (born in 1927) puts it:

> It is a proper thing that they are building mosques. Not for weddings or ceremonies, but rather for people's souls, for correcting people's errors, and making their lives easier. A man goes to the mosque cleansed, and he prays. Praise Allah, the All-merciful and Most Generous, the Great. A man prays there and cleanses his soul, thinks about another world, about the eternal world.

The elder of one of the *mahallas* visited, who was born in 1912, described the process of erecting a mosque in his neighborhood. It began as the result of pressure exerted by a young religious activist who came to the village:

> Once a young fellow by the name of Ibrahim came to our village from Ferghana, and asked, have you begun to build mosques? I answered, no, we haven't. So he said, don't waste time, if the *raykom* [*rayon komitet*, or district committee of the Communist Party] won't help, if the chairman won't agree,

then find me, I'll do something, but for now take this 100 rubles. That's how construction began here.... [Then] the villagers came to me and said, we need a mosque, and we all agreed that people will help as they can. They began to gather money. One man gave 25 rubles, another 50 rubles, another a thousand. The *kolkhoz* gave a car and a cart. All of the villagers helped in the construction of the mosque. One was a watchman, another made food, a third group did the construction, a fourth group carted the building materials here from all over.... Without a doubt the mosque has a great and positive influence on the whole of our life, particularly a moral and formative influence. While services are going on in the mosque, a lot of attention is paid to questions of raising the young, how to achieve a good environment in the family, resolve conflicts, and wish success on labor initiatives.

Three years after Ibrahim's visit, various respondents described the mosques as full to overflowing on Fridays and on holidays, so much so that one of the respondents, a teacher born in 1936 who described himself as trained in the "old school," complained how difficult it was to teach on Fridays:

... it has become common that on Fridays many students skip classes or don't come at all, because they are going to Friday prayers in the mosque. And the community once again collects and distributes food to the poor on religious holy days.

The pensioners of the community are described as passing their time going from mosque to mosque at prayer times, while separate groups of men and women gather in the evening near the mosques to learn to read Arabic and recite prayers. Many young men have taken to wearing full beards, while *hijab* dress among young women (the modest clothing prescribed by Sharia) is described as no longer uncommon, and increasing in popularity. In other words, the face and faith of the community are changing.

The re-Islamicization of Turkipoen proceeded far more slowly than in the communities of the Ferghana Valley; the discussions suggest that this was also true of the Samarkand region more generally.

Virtually all of those interviewed spoke very positively of the return of religious institutions to the village. Several respondents mentioned that they and various members of their family were all learning how to read the Quran or to recite *namaz*. Those interviewed also talk about how it has become common for people to gather on Fridays and holidays to pray together, in crowds where people under thirty are in the overwhelming majority. This enthusiasm of the young for worship augurs well, they said, for the future of Islam in the community.

In Turkipoen, only five or six of the sixteen *mahallas* in the village were said to have their own mosques, and there was a shortage of *mullahs*. The shortage was so bad that a worker in the local "House of Culture" (born in 1956) who had sparse religious training in the 1980s mentioned that sometimes he was called upon to lead people in prayer. But by his account he could do little beyond saying the *kalima* by himself:

> I can say the *kalima* myself, I memorized it. Every person who considers himself a Muslim, no matter what the circumstances, whatever circles he finds himself in, there may be no *mullah*, and so a person has to do this for himself. So I can say the *kalima* [the interviewer reports that he then does].

The situation in Turkipoen varied a great deal from *mahalla* to *mahalla*. In Tashkuva, in addition to a mosque, there was a religious school, which was organized by the son-in-law of the local *mullah* who taught the boys, while his wife provided some religious instruction for the girls. Several respondents referred positively to the work of the school, which was organized at the initiative of the head of the *mahalla*. The residents of this *mahalla* built what was said to be quite a beautiful new mosque in 1989 and 1990, raising the necessary money within the community.

In many other *mahallas*, the residents had been far less enthusiastic about raising the money and donating the labor necessary to build new mosques or repair older, abandoned ones. In Turkipoen and some of its environs, public funds seem to have gone toward the construction of mosques, a practice of questionable legality. This required aggressive lobbying by local mullahs, a *mahalla* leadership being firmly behind the task, and the cooperation of the next highest level of government when public funds were being diverted. In this area, the initiative of *mullahs* alone was often insufficient to get mosques built. A retired chauffeur and lifelong believer (born in 1928) complained that this is precisely why his community did not yet have a mosque:

> In the villages the people are asking the regional *hokimiyats* [governments] to build things. Maybe in other places they listen to people, I don't know, but here it's two years already that people want to build a mosque, but I don't

know, they say there are no funds. See, the contributions all go to the city, and they are building there. Where the share of the regions is going to, I don't know.... In the Chelek zone, they were supposed to build two mosques, for instance, but neither of them is built. One of them they wanted to build here, not far from here, but as one of the *mullahs* said, he said to build next to the cemetery, but the people didn't agree. They said there had to be water for the building to be good. That's how it's stayed, the *mullah* is pulling one way, and the people pull another, and then the people stopped working on it. They wanted to build the second mosque in a place called Kapa, over towards Mitan, but it's also not built. But if the government will start building, the people will take the rest on themselves. Even if it's done as *hashar*, there has to be one religious type to supervise construction. Or the elders even say that it's the young, not uniting. But if the young are asked to, they give money. There needs to be a man who can spend that money on construction. That's *hashar*, as I understand it. The people give money for a mosque.

The retired *kolkhoz* worker (born in 1933) has a similar story from his *mahalla* where incompetent organizational efforts seem to have thwarted the project from the outset:

They collected money here to build a mosque. The old mosque is still standing, and they still haven't built the new one. This year the new building committee is going around right now, organizing the construction of the new mosque. Just organizing it. They still have gotten the money. The last time people gave 200 rubles or 500 rubles, whatever they could. The roof of the mosque wasn't finished, just the sheathing. There was no floor, and now they've done the floor. The mosque isn't very good, that's why they want to make a new one. The new committee wants a place where people will always be, so there will be a *mullah* and so that young will come, too, to study.

In contrast with the state of projects in the village of Turkipoen, the activities of believers around the shrine of Khoja Ismail al-Bukhari seem to have increased tremendously since the change of official policy toward Islam. A retired collective farm worker described the scene there a few days previously, when he had gone to pray at the shrine as part of his Ramadan observance and came back in awe:

Yesterday they read such a prayer at Khoja Ismail's shrine that you can't even retell it in words. People even came from Bukhara and from Samarkand region. What a gathering there was! ... The All-High who created us has poured down rain for a whole month. It seems He heard the prayers, people saying, O God, you have given us your rain as you wished, but now the peasants are late with the planting, so please stop your rain, and give us your warmth. That was the prayer of all the *mullahs* at the shrine of Khoja Ismail. So now what do you think, after Ramadan, March 24, and today's the 29th, how much has the weather changed? They say, don't take gold, take a prayer, that a prayer isn't gold. What can you say about a prayer? Here, this shows it, it's been five or six days already since the weather improved.

At the time of the interviews there was a Quran school and at least one madrasa at the site, which drew pupils and students from surrounding villages, including some from the Chelek *mahalla* at Turkipoen. And some of the instruction, at least in the period under study, seems to have been taught by radical Islamists, because its female students were described as wearing modern-day *paranjas*.[4] The retired chauffeur described his encounter with one such student, who impressed him with her level of knowledge:

> [One] day when I was riding the bus, there were four girls on the bus, from Khoja Ismail. All you could see were their eyes, their faces were covered with cloth. I asked one of them, why are you dressed like that? She said that she was studying in the Khoja Ismail mosque. I think that it was plain from how they talk that they learn well in both kinds of schools [state and religious].

Not everyone in the community was comfortable with the work being done at Khoja Ismail. A factory worker who was born in 1923 and who had spent a good part of his adult life working in Siberia complains of the rote nature of the religious education and observance being taught at Khoja Ismail.

> Children from all over are studying in Khoja Ismail. They study, but they don't know the language. They memorize the prayers, and if you ask them to read something, they just read what they memorized, and that's all. If you ask them to translate or to explain the sense, they don't know it. They don't understand what they are reading or saying. They say memorized prayers and put a *chalma* on their head and walk around like *mullahs*.

This respondent displayed the greatest anger toward Islam of anyone interviewed in the village. Although his own brother is a *mullah*, he himself is more typically a "Soviet Man," arguing that Uzbeks would be better served in independence if they were to continue to learn Russian rather than Arabic, and asserting that there is nothing "natural" about the relationship between the Uzbeks and Islam. In fact he describes the role that religious leaders play as corrupt:

> Once I read a history book. It seems that we, the Central Asian people, prayed to Buddha and to fire in the past. When the Arabs attacked us, they killed a lot of our people and then forced us to go into their religion, into Islam. Anyone who refused had his head cut off or was killed. Then they brought in their own people from there, from Arabia, and called them *ishans*, leaving them here to control the others. They gave orders that whoever didn't accept the Muslim religion was to have his head cut off. They said to the *ishans*, we are putting our faith in you, stay here. You won't have to work. People will bring tribute, some of money, some of livestock, and you will get part of the wheat harvest. And once a year, the *ishans* went around the villages, collecting what they could. They went from house to house. Those who were able gave money; those who were not gave a goat, or a ram. It's still like that; they give men, or a man's robe. If a child gets sick or something, they call in the *mullah*, ask him to say a prayer. If the *mullah* is an alcoholic, a drinker, he mumbles something that God alone knows what it is, and then asks for something, takes it, and sticks it in his pocket, and leaves.

He goes on to argue that because the Uzbeks were converted to Islam by conquest, they are free to reject the faith, especially as he sees little to commend the religion in the example that the believers provide, claiming that most people turn to Islam for personal profit:

> On the one hand, religion teaches people so that they won't go on the wrong paths, so they won't steal, so they work and don't covet other people's things, so that they earn their own way. They have talked about this for ages. And they don't pay any attention to what they themselves are teaching. They teach it, but don't obey it themselves. So if there's fifteen or twenty thefts in one village, right after Ramadan the thefts will start again, and at celebrations people will take their affairs out on each other, barking like dogs. I have heard how people look and keep silent. In general they themselves are godless people, the ones who keep *Ruza*[5] and say the prayers. Some of them are middlemen at the bazaar. They buy a bad cow or a pregnant cow and then fool simple people, making two or three thousand rubles on the deal. What point is there in them keeping Ramadan, wheeler-dealers like that? There's an awful lot like that now. And drunkards, lying around on the streets half naked. They keep *Ruza* and think that they are saints. You have to believe in the religion, too.

The argument he is making is shared by only a small minority in the sample we selected. Most respondents saw Islam as the only real source of morality in society, the only way to reverse the growing social decay of the late Soviet years, when alcohol and drug addiction had become common among unemployed youths, and divorce and child abandonment were no longer alien to Uzbek culture. Several of those interviewed claimed that the presence of the mosques was now changing public behavior. This is especially true in the cities of the Ferghana Valley, but some in Baisun echoed this viewpoint. To quote a collective farmer from Tova who was born in 1931:

> The role of religion in the life of the *mahalla* is significant. Religion has brought a lot of people to order. Young people who come to the mosque have quit smoking and drinking. Religion and the mosque make for better relations between people, stimulate charity, and bring out the good, honesty in people.

Almost the identical sentiment was expressed by a Tova state farm worker who was born in 1943 and reported that he had prayed all his life:

> I must say that the resurrection of religious values, the reappearance of the mosques, and the return of people, especially the young, to religion is having a noticeably positive effect, lowering crime and the number of legal infractions in our village.

A collective farm worker (born in 1925) from Tova put it even more strongly:

> Allah be praised, the times have changed. The fact that life has gotten worse, that there are many criminals, thieves, and speculators, is connected with the fact that people ceased to fear God, and many people became atheists. It is impossible to live without Allah, without praying to Him daily. Or if one lives that way, it is as animals live. But a man must live with faith in Allah.

The *mahallas* in the villages throughout the Baisun district, also generally conservative, all united behind the task of building mosques and madrasas. A big mosque has been built in Baisun itself, while lesser mosques or prayer houses are being put up in every *mahalla* and village, no matter how small.

But many of these people seem to have changed their values so quickly that there is an inevitable sense of the impermanence of the shift. A high school teacher from Baisun who was born in 1932 explains his rapid shift from Marxist principles to religion and his hopes from going from "doom" to "spiritual perfection."

> Since my youth was passed in those times when there was no place for religion in our lives, and the ideology of Marxism-Leninism ruled everywhere, I looked at religious education and everything connected to it negatively. However, only now, after many decades, I came to understand that we were all led into error and that in general it was that ideology which led us all to catastrophe, to doom. It is only now that I am beginning to realize the riches, the spiritual and moral fodder of which we were deprived. Now I read the Quran with enormous interest, and the *hadiths* and other holy texts, and I am becoming convinced that there is nothing in them which would prevent the moral and spiritual perfection of a man. Quite the opposite, they promote the development of better qualities in a man.

THE RIGHT ISLAM?

While at the surface level everyone spoke positively about the return of religion to public life, when pressed it became clear that many people had real concerns about what kinds of changes this would likely bring. Some feared that the advantages of living in a modern secular state would be lost, while others expressed concern that a new strata, the clerics, had been empowered, with little popular control over the values they sought to spread, or recourse to object to their authority.

In all the communities studied, the preparation of *mullahs* was very uneven (as was true of Uzbekistan as a whole in those years). Graduates of the two legal madrasas, in Bukhara and Tashkent, were able to staff only a fraction of the new mosques and madrasas that were being organized. In addition to clerics coming from Bukhara and Tashkent madrasas, many other *mullahs* were educated in various *hujra* schools that were forming in the Ferghana Valley; others received training in Tajikistan, and many were simply self-taught.

Still, despite such a dramatic difference in the religious education level of new *mullahs*, most of those surveyed were willing to accept the authority of the clerics serving the community and raised little concern over their competence. This is especially true of many of the farmers. The views of the Tova collective farmer who was born in 1925 are representative of this group:

> It is only now that I am old that I have learned to read the *namaz*. Thank God, there are good *mullahs* in the village. If we don't understand something, they explain it to us. Now, God grant our president health, there are all the necessary conditions for keeping the rites. Earlier almost no one could make a pilgrimage to Mecca. Now look, in the past few years how many people just from our region have touched the holy earth in Mecca and Medina? Although I was not able to get a religious education, I have been trying to rear my children and grandchildren with a sense of respect and love for the holy book, for God.

But who is a good *mullah*? What a local villager considers as a good *mullah* need not coincide with the criteria of Uzbekistan's religious authorities, or those of their government. Both are concerned that the "wrong" Islam is being taught by people who lack the proper understanding of Islam. For the villager, this mostly means people without a classical Hanafi religious education; for the government, it often means people who are too radical or politicized.

A number of people in the survey expressed concern about the competence of the clerics who were serving their community, fearing the consequences for those who followed their advice, both in heaven and on earth. This was of particular concern in Baisun, which was absorbing Uzbek refugees from Tajikistan, creating a sense of immediacy to concerns of Islam as a source of politicizing populations.

In the words of a tractor driver born in 1930, the son of a *mullah*:

> Now there's not a single *mullah* with a specialized religious education. Of course people do the job of a *mullah*, but how well? All of the *mullahs* now are self-taught, or even worse, are self-appointed charlatans. They don't know religious teachings well, don't know the Quran, *kadisoia*,[6] the laws of Sharia, or the precise and correct way to perform rituals and rites, and so they bring down large sins on the shoulders of simple people, and on their own. They are going to have to answer for this to God.

A retired high school director in Tuzar, Baisun (born in 1927) from a family with two *mullahs* on his father's side, who married the daughter of a local party official, is far more concerned with answers that may have to be rendered here on earth. He expresses great concern over the low level of preparation of the clerics in Baisun and argues that the state must be aggressive in its surveillance of Islamic education or suffer for its abdication of responsibility:

> I am absolutely convinced that there is not a single *mullah* in Boysun who is fluent in Arabic or who is able to explain or comment on a simple text. And that sort of studying with poorly educated *mullahs* I regard as destructive of young souls, and a complete deception. Greed, the desire to get rich, is what drives these people, who often have no idea whatsoever about Arabic. I look at this as a fraud, and in the end it will lead to having the young people lose interest in high school, and they will become the same sort of poorly educated people, just as illiterate as their teachers and *mullahs*. All of this too should be under the control of the *rayon* and oblast authorities and the minister of education. Otherwise the consequences will be bad.

Another Baisun teacher, who was born in 1957 and also has some religious education himself, shares this view entirely, warning that the goal of many of these *mullahs* is to destroy the state and introduce a religious regime in its place:

> I think that either the Baisun authorities or the regional *hokimiyats* must establish control over the activities of the mosques, although I am not against religious education. In fact, the opposite is true. There is nothing bad in the Quran or the Hadiths (you have no doubt read the Hadiths of Imam al-Bukhari or Imam al-Termizi), and there is nothing amiss there. But everything depends upon the hands it falls into, who is teaching and how. I mean, look how our Bolsheviks and communists distorted the teachings of Marx. They destroyed everything that was positive, all the best that there was in Marx's theories. The same thing is happening with religious education. In the mosques, there are *mutavals*[7] and *hatibs*, whom I cannot call educated people. These are very ordinary people, the sort who become fanatics, indeed uncivilized ones. Unfortunately religion today is in the hands of spiritually and morally impoverished, backward people. They are not capable of doing anything positive for society, because they are too narrow in their views, and they don't understand much even about religion. That's why control is necessary.... Today we don't know what is going on in the madrasas and mosques, and we don't know what the youth are being taught. I think that we should make an active effort to get into these processes. I also think that in addition to religious training, the mosques should also introduce other disciplines, such

as mathematics. Otherwise, it will simply be too late and we will run into very serious problems. For example, I spoke with some young *mullahs* who had studied in Namangan. You know, they have a completely different mood. They are extremely decisive. Their goal is to make a revolution, to overthrow the present powers and set up their own regime. But the authorities don't seem to notice.

There were similar concerns expressed in the other communities as well. A teacher from Kuva (born in 1954) complains that young people are not getting good advice from either secular or religious leaders and bemoans the fact that now, in its first days of independence when Uzbekistan needs wise and all-seeing figures, "there are no Avicennas or Ulugbeks among us." A fellow teacher, born in 1936, with some religious education himself, talks very explicitly about the dangers of turning over the religious education of the younger generation to the *mullahs*, trained clandestinely during the years of Soviet rule, who are now putting themselves forward as competent to the task:

> ... the *karnay*[8] is being sounded too early, because the wedding hasn't yet taken place. We are playing the music a bit early. I mean the religious schools. After all, one has to lay the fundament first, accumulate building materials. Otherwise, once you've begun, and attracted the young and started teaching without first teaching your teachers, and getting the proper material and technological resources, they can destroy a lot of human souls.[9]

Others in Kuva express concern that "servants of the cult" might use their positions as spiritual leaders for their own material advantage. Several of the older residents felt that the spirituality of the community was already being undermined by the ostentation of current religious practices, shows of wealth that were to the personal advantage of the clerics but of no benefit to the community of believers and were diminishing public piety. The spiritual healer and *otin* (born in 1927) was unequivocally of this opinion:

> We ought to change our attitude [toward] funerals and weddings, for example. Cast away all this excess. In fact, a neighbor woman died. The relatives decided that they must bake 6,000 wafer breads. I wondered what the point of so much expense was. One thousand would have been enough. After all, it is said in the religion about funerals that things should be given to people, but it doesn't say how much. I think that it would be absolutely adequate if the

> Muslims were to come, drink a cup of broth, eat a piece of bread, and that's enough. But no, I've been before and sometimes now, too. People come, and they bring bread, nuts, pilaf, and they have to be sent home with bags of bread and things for show. Who needs this? The dead person? Isn't it enough that people came and remembered the soul of the dead person, prayed? Even the Russians say, "Stretch out your toes according to your clothes."

Even in Kuva, in the heart of the Ferghana Valley, there was concern that Islamic institutions and Islamic rituals were being introduced into the community too fully and too suddenly. Because of peer pressure, people were doing things with consequences that they little understood. To quote a teacher (born in 1936) who complained about the surge of mosque building:

> It's like the people are stampeding into it. In hard times like these, they drop everything, leave everything topsy-turvy, and go help build mosques. The young particularly take part. Peasants too often leave work. What I mean is, work time is wasted on the mosques.

Once a *mahalla* committee got behind the idea of building a local mosque, community residents who refused to take part risked ostracism. To defy the *mahalla* committee was to defy communal will, which such close-knit communities simply do not tolerate. Always a powerful institution, the *mahalla* committee, and especially the elders who sit on it, grew even more powerful with the decline of Soviet rule.[10] In towns like Kuva, in addition to invoking state authority, the *mahalla* chairman could represent the interests of religious authorities.

The *mahalla* elder from Kuva (born in 1912) makes this point very explicitly:

> I told my countrymen from the very beginning that those families who do not take part in this undertaking which is pleasing to God would in the future find no material or moral support from the *mahalla*, whether they were marrying someone or burying him.

Indeed, at the time that these interviews were being conducted, there was serious discussion about whether the *hashar* contributions for mosque building should become a form of obligatory taxation on enterprises, rather than voluntary contributions from individuals. This was true even in Baisun, and not just in the towns and villages of the Ferghana Valley.

The retired high school teacher from Tuzar, Baisun, complains that a neighboring village is already requiring such contributions, and he criticizes the regional government for allowing the situation to continue:

> I consider it incorrect that mosques and madrasas are being built at the expense of the public. Things have gone so far that in one village the elders demanded a kind of tribute from the people, demanding that every family set aside a certain sum of money for building a mosque. Of course the people will give the money, because our people are timid and simple. I am absolutely against that way of building mosques. I am also against buildings mosques on every corner. Earlier, three or four years ago, there were mosques in Denau and Termez, and the old people who could do so went to them for Friday prayers. Now here in Baisun, each *mahalla* as a rule has its own mosque. I think that the administration of the region, the oblast, and the republic should do something to bring order to this.

A Russian literature teacher from Baisun who was born in 1955 complained about his community's misplaced priorities and argues that in the long run it will cost the community dearly to emphasize the construction of mosques instead of schools and other social outlets:

> I don't really understand or approve of what is going on around this building of mosques. Now everyone has run over to this side, somebody giving a thousand rubles or two thousand for building. In my opinion we have gone far beyond any limit in this. There are small villages and settlements where four or five mosques are going up. Almost my entire conscious life has been spent in high school, and I don't recall that even a single person has ever come up and offered so much as ten rubles to build or repair a school. Many of the schools are collapsing, and a lot of them are in catastrophic condition. And what can one say about the schools in far-out villages? They literally are falling apart there! Why shouldn't people think about the high schools, too? After all, it's their children who are studying there. Aren't they sorry for their own children at least, who often have to study in cold rooms where there is no glass in the windows? But they put thousands into the mosques. If the high schools got one percent of these funds they wouldn't be in such a pitiable state. That's the attitude of parents toward the general education schools. I can't help put out the following, namely, that now some of the parents won't let their children go to school but send them to study with uneducated *mullahs*. What are they thinking about? Are they even thinking about the fate or future of their

children? I don't know. How are these children going to find their place in life later, what are they going to do? I don't understand.

While all can see that the number of mosques has grown by leaps and bounds, the community has not really grown more moral and even its piety can be called into question. For example, the daughter of a *kolkhoz* member (born in 1940) from Kuva expressed concern about what she sees as a reduced commitment to Islam in her community. She considers the commitment weaker now that people are free to practice Islam than it was in the past, when harsh restraints were placed on believers:

> Although they were hard years, I remember them with pleasure. People lived amicably and had deep respect for one another. In those years we were taught good Muslim rules. The religion is just and wise... In the past, the authorities forbade religion, but all the same the religious teachers and *mullahs* insisted and taught the people: Don't steal, don't covet another's goods, don't deceive. ... They opened the road to religion in independent Uzbekistan, but still thievery flourishes, as do lies and deceit.

RELIGION AND THE SCHOOLS

At the time that the interviews were being conducted, Uzbekistan was in the process of introducing its first major set of curriculum reforms, which included experimenting with substituting courses on the history of religion and religion and ethics for the Soviet-era courses on scientific atheism.

Many saw this as a good thing. For example, a teacher from Kuva (born in 1936) talks very positively about the role of the local school (the name of which had just been changed to honor the Uzbek poet Khamza, after decades of being called KIM, the Russian initials for "Communist International of Youth") in preparing people for family life "in the old way," that is, in accordance with traditional Muslim values:

> In our school, assistant director Odiljon Makhmudov teaches history of religion to the tenth and eleventh classes. At the moment, he is drawing up a proposal for the authorities about the necessity to introduce into schools a course analogous to what in the old times was performed in rich families by

a nanny [*oqsoch*]. They taught the boys and girls the wisdoms of family life, from the point of view of morality, tradition, and customs.

Although President Islam Karimov and Uzbekistan's education authorities intended state instruction about Islam as a way to keep people from attending clerically sponsored religious schools (as one respondent had pointed out in Namangan), some of the people in Kuva saw state instruction about Islam as a way to prepare students for advanced religious education. This was the view expressed by another teacher and former *mahalla* head (born in 1934):

> Perhaps it would make more sense to introduce a course on the religion of Islam and the question of faith into the general schools. After the seventh or eighth class, students who have expressed interest and ability in questions of faith could enter the madrasa and devote their further study and lives to religion.
>
> Graduates of madrasas strive to get jobs teaching courses on the history of religion and on ethics precisely because they want to attract students in these schools to get further religious training, or at least to becoming observant Muslims.

The question of whether young people should forgo or limit state education in order to get religious education was a very contentious one in all of the communities studied. In Turkipoen, where a course on "Ethics and Psychology of Family Life" had already been introduced to teach about religion, public opinion seems to have been firmly on putting restrictions on religious education. Respondents spoke of how such religious education must remain in its "proper place." A high school math teacher (born in 1960) makes this point quite explicitly:

> I approve of building these religious schools, but now the education of today's youth is of great importance for the state. The young are our future, and if they are sent straight to religious school, that would be wrong. All right, let every student choose, let those who want go to religious school. Let whoever wants work, or learn how to read the old script or learn the religious rituals. But they shouldn't study political and economic questions in the religious schools, questions of governmental significance. It is extremely important for the government that there be general education schools. It is these schools

which provide the main directions for life. For example, state subsidies should be limited, and you should be able to open only one religious school per region.

Similar opinions were voiced in the Baisun region, where a teacher in a state orphanage (born in 1952) goes so far as to claim that there is a deliberate plot on the part of those who run the Quran schools to leave state schools, and those who study in both kinds of schools are neglecting their state-sponsored education. He, too, favors the teaching about religion, including an introduction to the Quran, in state schools as the solution:

> But there is one danger which can't be ruled out. Using the freedom they have been given, some people are trying to use things in their own selfish interests. Self-taught *mullahs* have appeared who have absolutely no religious training or permission. These people gather the young in their own homes and try to teach them and to beat into their heads a negative attitude toward the general education schools. It's no secret that because of their influence, for example, during the Friday *namaz* many young people leave their work and go to the mosque or to these *mullahs*. In our school at the orphanage, there is one student who used to get excellent marks in almost all his subjects. Recently, though, he has somehow grown cold to study. When you speak to him, it turns out that one of these self-educated *mullahs* has talked him into quitting school and going to the religious school instead. It's possible to find lots of examples like this. In order to get an idea about religion, about the prophets and so on, one doesn't have to quit high school. That's why a special course has been introduced into the schools, where beginning in the second grade teachers who have had a special training course teach the history of religion and read the Quran.

A high school teacher (born in 1937), at Darbent, Baisun, also complains that students who are studying Islam with *mullahs* have become indifferent to their secular studies:

> There is a doctor working in our hospital, called Mansurov. He is from a religious family. One of his sons is in the ninth grade, where I am class leader. In seventh and eighth grade, the boy did very well in his studies, got all the assignments done and was in general a very able student. But then this year he was sent to a *mullah* during the summer vacation. School started in September, and it was as if they had snatched him away and substituted another boy.

In order to find out what had happened, I went to his house and spoke to his mother. She thinks that after her son went to the *mullah*, he lost interest in high school. That is what I would say in answer [to] your question; to say that what *mullahs* teach these children may be incorrect, rather they may divert them from the correct road.

Several noted that children were returning to state schools, the initial enthusiasm for religious education having waned somewhat. As the director of the Ferghana Sociology Institute (born in 1961) noted about his community and environs:

A year or two ago, a fair number of girls and boys began to go for lessons at the homes of the *mullahs* and *qoris* [those who have memorized the Quran]. Now that wave has crested, and children are returning to the general education schools.

He thought that it was a good thing that the "wave has crested," because "you can't force children to go study in the madrasa" and besides, to do so is "going to cut into their ability to learn about natural science," which he sees as critical to Uzbekistan's survival as an independent state.

A teacher born in 1954 to a religious family in Tova also noted that instruction about religion in state schools was helping to get students to return to the state schools:

... the positive work which was begun and is being conducted by the Ministry of Education to a certain extent is undermining the basis of religion. For example, they introduced a course on old Uzbek orthography in all the high schools. Now it is no longer necessary to go to the mosque or madrasa or to the *mullah* in order to read the Quran or the *hadiths*. It is possible to get that same knowledge and preparation in high school as well. It is also a good thing that the ministry has introduced a special school course on the history of religion. All of this helps the youth who were going to the mosque to come back to the schools now.

But the values that young Uzbeks are getting will be strongly shaped by the people who teach them. Here, too, the study shows that at least the first group of teachers trained in pedagogical institutes, especially those in the Ferghana Valley, got a heavy dose of training in religion to impart to their future pupils.

A humanities student from Tova, born in 1972 and studying at the Namangan Pedagogical Institute, noted that he spent a fair amount of his time learning about his Islamic past:

> ... [my] greatest dream has been to get a higher education. They are teaching us old Uzbek and Arabic in the university simultaneously. I think that if one does not know religion, then one cannot understand one's own history, one's origins. A person who is trying to become a teacher must know Islam, its teachings and canons. We must use the Quran and the study of Islam in raising children. I myself, for example, am taking extra lessons about Islam and Islamic history in the university, from one of the instructors. In general, I want to study Islam more deeply and more seriously.... Since we are Uzbeks and Muslims, we must know our religion well, know its history. When we study the history of the religion, we are in many ways studying the history of our state.

But he adds: "Religion must keep to itself, while the government keeps to itself." Yet many did not share this view, wanting the government to be a moral arbiter and seeing teaching religious values in the schools as one sure way to achieve this. As the retired sweets-maker from Baisun lamented:

> I think that in the high schools today, there should be more lessons about theology, about the Quran, and the history of the Muslim religion. Then as the number of religious schools and madrasas grows, completely separate education for girls and boys should be introduced. That is one of the basic demands of Islam and Sharia. Because what goes on today between boys and girls is beyond description—we never had this sort of immorality and shamelessness. Television makes this worse, too, where every day, especially from Moscow, they show shameless pictures of naked men and women, as if we didn't have anything else to be doing. I think that an end should be put to this, since this contradicts Sharia and all the demands of Islam.

THE WOMEN'S QUESTION

In many communities, the revival of Islam has led to a reexamination of the role of women in public life. It showed how many people, especially in the older generation, resented Soviet policies designed to create equal opportunities for women, as well as the concerns of women who were frightened that the reintroduction of Islam would lead to diminished opportunities for them and their daughters.

In the samples in the Ferghana Valley, few respondents were willing to champion the cause of women's economic or political rights. Most of those who were interviewed volunteered that a woman's primary place was in her home; only a handful argued for the complete segregation of women from public life. One of these, an *otin* from Kuva (born in 1927), described an adulterous woman as having been "justly" cemented alive into the wall of a well, while another *otin*, born in 1923, said that young brides who committed suicide because they couldn't endure their marriages did so because they lacked faith and "patience."

In Tova, some respondents complained that Islamic activists were trying to get women to adopt Islamic norms of dress, and several objected to strong pressure by Islamic activists to have women "age twelve and older not show their faces to men."[11] Social pressure was sufficiently strong that in 1992 some Namangan Oblast schools agreed to the requests of Islamic activists to segregate male and female students in the state-funded secondary schools, a measure that lasted only a short time. Most of those interviewed believed that this decision was misguided, but others, such as a collective farmer (born in 1925), saw the move as positive, because:

> ... a woman's main concern is her family, children and husband... Women are not put on earth to be administrators. As a rule, such women have bad families and bad children... It would be good if all girls got religious education. It is only then that they would understand their place in the family and would take up the rearing of children.

The "women's question" came up far more frequently in Baisun than it did anywhere else, a likely reflection of the isolation of the community. Many in Baisun understood the destruction of traditional family life to be the root cause of most of the social and moral problems in the community.

Female integration had not progressed very far in Baisun. Apart from a few high school teachers, there were almost no women in positions of responsibility (even junior positions) in the Baisun region. Even in Baisun itself, the only women who wore European dress were Russians. Even today most marriages in Baisun are arranged, and the few couples who make their own plans are still careful to gain the approval of their parents.

Women do go to school and frequently even seek advanced training, but they generally do so only if they can find a place in a technical school close to home.

For all of these constraints on female participation in public life, many respondents still felt that women had been given too much freedom and that the role permitted them under Soviet rule was a threat to the morality of the community. This view was clearly expressed by those representing the older generation, such as the male retiree (born in 1906) who said:

> I don't like how women behave today. The way they behave isn't in the Sharia or in Islam. Look at them, how many of them are dressed like unbelievers. The Sharia says that a woman should stay at home, serve her husband, and occupy herself with the household and the rearing of children. Here, though, it comes out the opposite. A lot of husbands sit home, and their wives stroll around the streets and the bazaar. It's true, isn't it? So that's why we have so many ruined women, poorly raised children, thieves, and criminals. Girls today know neither shame nor conscience. They do whatever they want to. We have so many ruined women now, whom nobody will take for a wife.

Tempting as it might be to explain such views as what was to be expected for a respondent who had been born in 1906 and raised in the world of the Emir of Bukhara, upon a closer investigation it becomes clear that such views were not generational. The view of another respondent (a teacher, born in 1932) on the role and education of women was virtually identical. The commentary he offered was lengthy and reflected a lot of consideration of the issue:

> Until very recently, I was in favor of that [boys and girls studying together]. In fact, we teachers used to insist that at every desk there had to be a girl and boy. It is only now that we have begun to understand that from the viewpoint not only of Sharia, but also simply of Eastern culture, morality, and code of behavior, it is not permitted that boys and girls should study together. After all, in the old days, before the revolution, schools were divided, and as a rule women taught in the girls' schools. Everything that we see in the schools today is the result of the artificial transplanting of the demands of European and Russian culture and their system of education, although even in Russia before the revolution there were female gymnasiums and other schools.... East and West have always been different, and are different both in culture of behavior, and in clothing, and in etiquette, and in the system of education. I think that the lost values should be brought back. If we are teaching boys and girls

separately, giving them good knowledge in the spheres of various sciences, then at the same time we will give true religious education this way as well, and both they and society will benefit from it.... Understand, we are living some sort of artificial, made-up life. Look how many women use artificial food to feed their infants. This is absurd, because a number of good qualities are passed to children through the milk of the mother. In general, women have changed a great deal. There have appeared a great many unnaturally coarse, unpleasant women among them. Many of them have forgotten their primary duty, to rear children, because nature provides women with the best qualities of the nurturer. However, Soviet and European standards break our women. All of them are on the streets now, while the house and the children are left unsupervised. After all, even sitting at home one can do a great job—nurture a good person. Let's take Navoi again. The fact that he became a great poet and a government figure, he owed primarily to his mother. I could offer as many similar examples as you might want. It used to be among us that the grandmothers gathered their daughters and the neighbor girls about them to teach them wisdom—how to sew, how to prepare food, how to dress, how to rear children, and a great many other things. Now every married woman tries to work—just life and necessity force her to do so. The government and the state must understand for once and for all that the primary pre-designation for women is to rear children, and so they must create the circumstances to allow her to do only that, not thinking about a crust of bread, about clothes, or other things. It would be good if good traditions were to take root, if grandmothers and elderly women gathered the young girls about them and taught them not just Quran and the *hadiths*, but also the things that they will need further on in life.

Almost identical views are expressed by another teacher, born in the same year (1932) but living in another village of the same state farm:

If you approach it from the historical position, then we all know that boys and girls used to study separately, because the Most High, when He created all that lives, divided them into men and women, with natures, particularities, and physical and mental capacities suited for each. These differences have always existed and look as though they always will. As far as I recall, joint education was introduced here in 1941. They said then that this was the American system, and that it was very pragmatic and effective, because it allowed schools to get good results for low cost. However, this system has proven not to be suited to us. Our school has gotten worse, and many of the girls' characteristics have passed to the boys, and vice versa. Sometimes in the cities now you can't even figure out sometimes whether you are looking at a girl or a boy. And I also think that having boys and girls study together absolutely goes against our morality, traditions, etiquette, and Muslim culture, Eastern traditions of education in the family and the *mahalla*. So I am in favor of separate education in the schools for boys and girls.

And yet another teacher, in a third village of the state farm, born in 1957, during the Khrushchev years, also wants women's role to again be circumscribed:

> The first and most important of women's concerns is the rearing of children. In the course of 70 years, a lot of women at least lost their authority in the family and the *mahalla*, while some are amoral, lost women, who have forgotten about everything on earth, and who are trying by any means possible to get a position of some sort. This has had a bad effect not only on the rearing of their own children, but on the rearing of their grandchildren as well.

To be sure, even in Baisun, some of the women in the sample find such ideas to be disturbing. A teacher who was born in 1956 and has five children of her own said that she would like women to be more fully integrated into society but feared that exactly the opposite would happen:

> Of course, for the time being, women do not occupy their fitting role in the family, in the *mahalla*, or in society. I would like it if the woman's role were to grow. Because look what is happening, now there are very few women in high positions, meaning that there just isn't equality between men and women.... If religious education is going to spread, the number of women's religious schools is going to grow, which will lead to women being forced to work mostly in the family and in rearing children, and women won't take part in public life. In principle, if a man can provide for his family's material needs entirely by himself, then the woman might not work, if she doesn't wish to, because raising children and taking care of a family is also a big and complex job. But we are far away from that state of affairs. The situation is forcing women to work, because otherwise it is practically impossible to feed a family.

There were other respondents who shared her views, such as the journalist (born in 1936) who lamented the collapse of the Soviet Union and believes that the growing role of Islam will mean fewer and fewer avenues open to women. But he saw little opportunity for influencing the community view:

If the role of religion in society grows stronger, and its influence in all spheres, I think that the role of women in the society, in the *mahalla* and in society as a whole will not have any serious meaning, but rather the opposite, will become less. We have already spoken about how among a part of the population, especially among those who visit the mosque regularly, there has appeared a mood to separate boys and girls at studies.

Overall, the respondents in Turkipoen were most concerned with the negative consequences that the revival of Islam might have for women. A handwriting teacher at the local primary school (born in 1960) who was on maternity leave when she was interviewed offered the most serious objections to the way that the religious revival in her community was taking place. In her opinion, Islam is a faith of individual choice. She believes that Islam is able to make concessions to modernity and that modern society should not be reshaped to reflect the values of particular believers. She is especially explicit about this as it pertains to a woman's role in the community:

Religion has a particular role in an independent country. Because every person can believe, and can pray in the religion that he wants, and as he wishes.... What we modern young girls, those of us who have education, need from that religion, for example, is that there is no possibility to return them to past times. Because if the girls are told, wear a *paranja*, they can't do it. And if they say that they shouldn't go out on the street, or go to the old mosque and study there, they can't do that.

The Islam that she is encountering in her community in Turkipoen does not threaten her. However, she expresses support for what the local *mullahs* are doing:

That's why the *mullahs* and religious people in society have to have large meetings with the young, and talk with them. They must give the young modern education, how to live well, how to follow the true paths, not be bad, and then they have to explain how we should be charitable to one another, and be modern, and never steal, or smoke too much or hang around the streets, and that girls and boys shouldn't have fights. They should tell us how to avoid all of that, that's the sort of advice that they should give for educating the young. That would be very good.

RELIGION AND THE STATE: WHAT SHOULD THE RELATIONSHIP BE?

The people surveyed all understood the religious revival as something granted them by the state. A collective farmer from Tova, born in 1925, expressed the sentiments of many when he said:

> Praise be to God, and thanks be to our president, that thanks to his proper policies, many people have begun to turn to Allah.

Or a war veteran, born in 1926, from Turkipoen:

> Now things are very good. Islam Karimov has chosen the right path, may he live and be healthy. They have given permission to everybody, to *mullahs*, religious people.... After independence, people have begun to pay more attention to religion and have put religion on the level it should be on. People have begun to say the Friday prayers, and people have begun to learn how to live in a clean-fleshed way, to live well and cleanly. That's why we need religion.

But there is concern that religious activists are being too critical of the government. Fears about this were expressed in all the communities studied, with many commenting that inappropriate activities by religious activists could threaten the gains made for all. This is especially the case in Namangan, where in fact religious activists were pressing hard to expand their gains. Although support for a secular state was weakest in Namangan, there was also concern that things were being pushed too far.

A female bookkeeper from a religious family in Tova (born in 1957) complains that the leaders of some of the mosques and madrasas are openly critical of the president and government policy more generally, which she finds quite disturbing. She sees the role of religion to support the efforts of the government:

> The influence of the religion organizations is this—the mosques and madrasas must show themselves primarily in the formation of good moral qualities in people, in respectful, good-hearted attitudes of respect for one another. They should support the efforts of our president and should help our village to flourish.

Another respondent from Tova, a chauffeur (born in 1945), believes that by challenging state authorities, religious leaders are imperiling what they have already achieved:

> I am not against religion or the mosques, but I can say straight-out that some of the religious activists have forgotten their own past, have lost a sense of measure. In that regard I would like to tell the following story: Once upon a time, there was a poor man. After a while he grew wealthy and became the wealthiest man in that place. When he did, the man hung his old shoes at the entrance to his house. People began to remonstrate, asking why such a rich fellow had not tossed out his ragged old shoes. The man replied, "Every day when I come in or out of my house, I see my old shoes and I remember the days when I was poor." But some of our religious activists have forgotten that just a few years ago it was impossible even to dream about this sort of freedom....

A retired teacher (born in 1925), also from Tova, offers a similar caution:

> Thanks be to the government for giving religion freedom. But this has to be valued. Freedom, after all, doesn't mean the ability to do everything that your soul desires. Especially in our oblast, the *ishans* and religious figures have begun to take too much upon themselves, have begun to interfere in everything. Their main job, after all, is to educate the young, to teach them intelligence and wisdom. So that's what they should be doing.

Most of the respondents in the sample seem pretty comfortable with the current balance of religious freedom and state supervision of it. To quote a welder from Turkipoen (born 1956) who received religious training in the Brezhnev era:

> Religion has its own place in independent Uzbekistan. People have acknowledged their religion, their Muslimness, they have returned to Islam. Earlier people didn't take time off during *Qurbon hayit* and *Ruza hayit*, and now these are state holidays. Muslims need this now, of course.

Others comment on how good it is that there are now religious programs on television, and in this regard a technician from Turkipoen (born in 1961) notes with concern the disappearance of Mufti Muhammad Sodiq Muhammad Yusuf from television. Muhammad Sodiq's clash with Karimov in February 1992 had gone largely unreported:

> Our main *mullah* goes on television every third day to explain the *ayats* to people and to read. Now he has disappeared, the last couple of months. The role of religion is to unite people, to preach human values, to respect one another, to be charitable. These values mustn't be lost, it is necessary to help, using religion. Otherwise our Uzbeks will lose their charity.

A few people offered somewhat cynical judgments that Uzbek authorities had embraced a public role for Islam in order to get foreign assistance from the Muslim world. A factory worker and farmer, born in 1923,[12] speculated that such a strategy would likely be successful:

> In our Central Asia, in Arabia, Turkey, Pakistan, Afghanistan, Iran, Indonesia, in the Muslim countries they thought that we had left Islam, which they didn't much like, so probably they will like it that we have come back to religion, in the hope that they will support us, from the Muslim side, help a Muslim people. Probably they will help.

Some argued that a carefully elaborated state policy toward religion could serve to get the population to set limits on religion for themselves. What made people nervous, though, was the possibility of not having a shared understanding of appropriate limits between the government and the population. Knowing what was happening in Tajikistan and the violence that occurred in the Ferghana Valley in 1989 and 1990 made some people nervous. An agronomist from Kuva who was born in 1935 and was the son of a *mullah* expressed these fears quite explicitly:

> Religion has been given the freedom to develop, and people are inspired. We see that on holidays and on days of mourning, all people are united, together. In such moments, religion helps people. I am convinced that if barriers had not been put before Islam, and the religion were open to people, there would not have been the bloody events of Osh, Ferghana, and the Tashlak region.

TAJIKISTAN'S CIVIL WAR

The proximity of the civil war in Tajikistan was of real concern to the respondents in this sample, especially the residents of Baisun region, who feared that the war could have both direct and indirect impacts on their villages.

Although mountain Tajiks and mountain Uzbeks had always lived in close proximity, during the 1920s and 1930s many people fled their homes or were forcibly evacuated by the Soviet authorities. This brought more Uzbeks to Kurgan Tyube and many Tajiks to Surkhandarya. Scholars write about the keen ethnic rivalry between the Tajiks and Uzbeks, but I saw no immediate evidence of it in Baisun and its environs, nor is there much evidence of it in the interviews themselves. The Tajiks and Uzbeks whom I met were welcome in each other's homes and attended each other's family gatherings. The two groups intermarried as well, although the property exchanges involved in marriage created powerful economic incentives to remain entirely within one's own community.

At the same time, virtually all of the respondents in Baisun feared the arrival of refugees from Tajikistan; a wave of Uzbek refugees might spark a spontaneous and violent deportation of local Tajiks by the Uzbeks of Surkhandarya, while the arrival of Tajik refugees would simply put an additional burden on a population already stretched too thin.

The community of Baisun was not dissimilar to Kurgan Tyube across the border in Tajikistan, save that the ethnic balance between Tajiks and Uzbeks is reversed. Both regions were part of Eastern Bukhara before the revolution. Although most residents felt that Islam played a larger role in communities in Tajikistan than in Baisun, they believed that Islamic activists could mobilize further support and eventually politicize communities like those in the Baisun region.

Many in Baisun believed that the civil war in Tajikistan was largely the product of religious groups usurping functions that more properly belong to the state. A tractor driver, born in 1956, offered the following observation:

> Independence depends upon every man, here's a simple example, what large rights were given to religion in Tajikistan? And how many innocent children and people perished in Tajikistan? In my opinion, nothing good comes of giving large rights to religion.

By October 1992, a steady stream of refugees was coming through the villages of Surkhandarya, each refugee an eyewitness to some horrible act of intra-communal violence. An elderly man (born in 1906) who spent much of his time around the mosque repeats some of the stories he had been told:

> People say that it's all the fault of the Wahhabis. They've caught a lot of them and killed them. They say, too, that there's not many people left in Kurgan Tyube. They tell stories of how on the streets and everywhere in the irrigation ditches there are piles of corpses. And no one can give them a human burial. … Right now, for example, Russian troops in Kurgan Tyube are guarding the important points and the reservoir. If God forbid they should blow up the reservoir, then Termez, Kum Kurgan, Jarkurgan [towns in Surkhandarya Oblast] would all be flooded. But then there's complete lack of discipline in the army, and no one's in charge. People kill other people, and nobody asks a thing about it. It's hard even to understand who is killing whom and why. The most terrible thing is that Muslims are killing Muslims. They say a *palvan*[13] [he is referring to Sanjak Safarov,[14] the leader of the National Front Army] has turned up in Dushanbe, that he was let out of prison, he got together an army of 40,000 men and is killing everybody, not sparing old or young or women or children. They say he is selling Tajik girls to the Afghans and getting guns in exchange. Who is going to put an end to this? Our land is blessed. You won't find land like it in America or Russia or Turkey. Just you have to work hard at it, without stopping. And it should be that there's peace between people, so Muslims aren't killing Muslims. You see yourself how everyday there are refugees coming to Baisun and to Uzbekistan. Everybody in Baisun who has relatives or friends has taken in children and wives…. I don't see any army that's defending anyone. People who know say that the people who ran away from Tajikistan over to here were put in cars and sent back to there. What are those poor people to do, where should they go?

Concern was expressed by some of the respondents that Uzbekistan's government was not drawing the proper lessons from what was happening in Tajikistan. As a Baisun teacher (born in 1957) complained, bad government and religious fanatics are a potentially deadly mix, and Uzbekistan already has the former in the locality and the latter as a risk:

> Have the events in Tajikistan really taught us nothing? It really looks as though they haven't. Today the *hokimiyat* is attracting sycophantic, poorly educated people, but what we need is people with modern education, who are able to think, to rethink in a new way the processes which are going on in society, including in the mosques and madrasa. Otherwise, the regime of today will meet the same fate as did the communist regime…. If the religious schools will provide true knowledge from the Quran and the *hadiths*, I am convinced that there will be no theft, no bribe-taking, and prostitution and things like that will stop, and mutual love and respect between people will grow stronger. However, the problem is that we don't believe in God or in the present gov-

ernment. Society will not be the loser if religion grows stronger. But we must draw the conclusions from the events in Tajikistan. In other words, we have to do everything so that religious fanatics don't come to power.... It is very important to note the hands into which power is falling in religious society. If badly educated fanatics are getting power, then that will bring only evil. If we are striving towards becoming a civilized state, then those who control the mosques and madrasas and those who are directly in charge of the religious groups, the *sayyids* and the *ishans*, must be highly educated, cultivated people. Otherwise this will cause society a lot of harm.

The high school teacher from Darbent, Baisun (born in 1937) expresses many of the same sentiments. But he then goes on to warn that Uzbekistan will be unable to preserve its independence if its government falls into the hands of Islamic "extremists." In his opinion, Russia would not tolerate this:

In general, though, religion causes more harm than good to upbringing. Whether we take, for example, the Ferghana events, the Osh events, or the war in Tajikistan, I am convinced that the major guilt lies with the religious activists. If that's wrong, if religion is so authoritative, then why can't it stop the bloodshed in Tajikistan? And what's going to happen there anyway? Famine has already started.... I would very much like our state to be as it was in the past, and that the neighboring republics should be quiet. We must do all that we can so that we don't have nationalism here. The religious activists are putting a lot of effort into fanning nationalism, especially in Tajikistan and Ferghana, are insulting the Russians, Tartars, and other nationalities. I don't think that they have done anything bad to us. In general I think that this sort of nationalist sprout must be lopped off. If we submit to the pressure of the religious activists, then we will begin to drive out the Russians and others. Do you think that Russia will stand on the sidelines and watch? Hardly.

In many ways, the residents of Baisun were the most pessimistic of those in any of the four communities. In most of the rest of the republic, independence was still a novelty and something in which respondents did not yet fully believe. By contrast, the residents of Baisun were nearly close enough to hear the artillery in their neighbor republic, and thus certainly close enough to the swelling civil war to be able to imagine what such guns might sound like in their own region. In Baisun, the risks of independence were already clearly visible just over the border, while everywhere else the risks to the stability of their community were largely left to individuals to imagine.

8

"MANAGING ISLAM"
SINCE INDEPENDENCE

Like all post-Soviet states, Uzbekistan confronts the challenge of creating politically loyal citizens. True to their Soviet upbringing, Uzbek leaders have turned to ideological indoctrination, rather than political participation, as the foundation for building national unity and political loyalty.

Like many others in Central Asia, Uzbekistan's rulers believe that ideology is the glue that promotes political and social stability. As such, they have applied a great deal of energy, and in some cases resources, to try to cast a new nationally oriented ideology for the Uzbek people. It is based heavily on the idea that Uzbek nationhood—and even Uzbek statehood—is centuries old, the latter dating to the time of Timur.[1] The validity of the ethno-historical basis of this argument is less important than the vigor and consistency with which it is presented.[2]

The historic approach taken to building political loyalty has meant that the Uzbek government is forced to return Islam, at least in some form, to public life, thus giving the Karimov government the same challenge that confronted earlier rulers—namely, that of allowing Islam to occupy a public role while having to figure out how to regulate it.

Religious leaders are also trying to define the role of religion in Uzbek society. But unlike the government, most are seeking to enhance the role of religion in the state, and some want to make religion the yardstick by which state actions are judged. For this reason, the Uzbek state is fearful of using religious leaders to spread its message, but at the same time it realizes that securing public loyalty will be impossible without a measured use of religious leaders. Many clerics are clearly well respected by the population, and for that reason, they are potentially powerful messengers for state ideology.

So the Uzbek leadership is always trying to identify sympathetic clerics, ones who the government believes will espouse a message fully supportive of the state. This would be a message that draws on Hanafi traditions that have long been popular in Central Asia, traditions that are generally associated with religious tolerance and with the need of Muslim believers to obey leaders who come from outside of their own religious traditions, as long as those leaders respect Islam.

And the government still maintains close supervision of religious institutions and over religious believers. Muslim institutions are subject to many of the same kinds of control as during the Soviet period. The Spiritual Administration of the Muslims of Uzbekistan (UMU) is responsible to the State Committee on Religion, and this committee is subordinated to the Council of Ministers and the president.

Over time the freedom of action of this organization has been restricted, and this has reduced its authority among clerics and in many cases believers as well. UMU's monopoly over the licensing of mosques, religious schools, and clerics is a less total means of control than it was in the Soviet period, given the more public role of religion and the relative looseness of state control. But UMU's financial power is much greater than earlier, and the opportunities for raising funds directly from the community are enhanced.

The practice of religion is also regulated by the government. Although the laws governing religious practice are more liberal than the legislation that applied during the Soviet period, the limitations on religious practice have increased over time. The Uzbek government has the toughest laws on religious extremism in the region, and it has subjected those charged with breaking these laws to the harshest punishment.

The Uzbek government was the first country in the region to broaden the definition of "extremist" organizations to include Hizb ut-Tahrir (the only group on the list with a mass following), the Nurchi (Gulen) movement, *Tablighi Jamaat*, Akramiya, *Hizb Nusra* (Party of Victory—an offshoot of HT), *Musulmon biradarlari* (Muslim Brotherhood), *Adolat*, *Islom lashkarlari*, *Islom uygonish partiyasi* (Islamic Revival Party), *Uzbekiston mujohidinlar uyushmasi* (Mujahideen Union of Uzbekistan), *Taaba*, and the

Turkestan Liberation Movement. The Islamic Movement of Uzbekistan and its various splinter groups—the East Turkestan Islamic Movement (ETIM), the Islamic Movement of Central Asia (IMCA), and the Islamic Jihad Union (IJU)[3]—are also banned.

But even with the strong political controls that have been introduced, there is a lot of competition in the "marketplace" of ideas in Uzbekistan—in schools, in private settings, and in sanctioned and non–state-sanctioned media—over who will speak for Islam. There is competition between those who are seeking to propagate traditional Hanafi ideas and those with a more radical Salafi or neo-Salafi orientation. While the state has managed to dominate the process, Uzbek leaders have been forced to constantly make adjustments to try to maintain control over the development of religious trends in the country. The results are not really satisfying to the government, religious authorities, or the population itself.

THE CREATION OF A NATIONAL IDEOLOGY

The Uzbek government sought to inculcate political loyalty among its citizens by embracing a combination of nationalism and Islam as the spiritual-ideological glue that could hold society together. Using the idea of "Our Islam," the government tried to define the new state ideology as the antithesis to what had been done in communist times when, as Islam Karimov described in his speech, "Moscow in its cruelty" used its repressive economic and social policies to "destroy the Uzbek people as [a] historical nation, its culture and sacred religion of Islam."[4]

By advancing both Islamic (*islomiy*) and nationalistic (*millatchilik*) slogans, the government hoped that the notion of "our Uzbek" Islam would build on religious identities to create an overarching national identity that would be more powerful than regional or local ties. To this end, much like its Soviet predecessors, the new Uzbek government repackaged history as nationalistic propaganda, hoping that the unified version of history in general and Islam in particular would provide the desired control over the population.

The emphasis of nation building has been to focus on the central role of the Uzbek ethnic community in the history of the land, using the Uzbek language as the dominant language of instruction. Classical "Uzbek" (more accurately, Persian and Chagatai)[5] literature banned during the Soviet period because of its religious motives now became central to the culture and literature curriculum. Uzbek history was completely rewritten to stress the age-old presence of the Uzbek or proto-Uzbek people, as well as the major role played by Islam in their history.

But there has been a deeply rooted reluctance to allow the religious elite to define the role that Islam has played. The political elite quickly appreciated that the clerical establishment could become strong political competitors. The extant tape of Islam Karimov meeting with local leaders in Namangan during the 1991 presidential election campaign gives a sense of just how fragile secular rule was at that time, at least in the Ferghana Valley. The tape shows a very non–secular-looking crowd jammed into a small space and seemingly hostile to Karimov. His behavior after the presidential elections, when he targeted virtually all unorthodox Islamic clerics by jailing them or driving them out of the country, suggests that he took careful measure of his opponents and credited them with posing a potentially successful challenge.

He also quickly came to appreciate the dynamism and charisma of his own supposedly loyal Islamic elite, those tied to the Spiritual Administration of the Muslims of Uzbekistan, with Uzbek authorities moving in 1992 and 1993 to remove such independent figures as Mufti Muhammad Sodiq Muhammad Yusuf, who were able to use the power of their religious learning to counter the interpretations of religion provided by the government.

The effort to use religious elements in fashioning a national ideology was hampered by the fact that the state officials responsible for devising the religious component of the national ideology often themselves had a limited understanding of Islam and so made inappropriate choices as to who would be responsible for articulating the religious component of the ideology.

Government initiatives sought to use religion in a variety of ways to serve the creation of a new national ideology. These components included the publication of religious literature, making active use of television to allow religious leaders with "positive" values to reach out to the population and commemorating the lives of historic Hanafi religious figures from Uzbekistan while simultaneously showing the trials of religious activists who opposed the state's message.

The goal was to do battle against the ideas of those who preached a politicized form of Islam ("Wahhabis")—by reemphasizing the importance of "Our [Uzbek] Islam." Numerous slogans, *fatwas*, and articles were devoted to the theme of asserting patriotism through defeating terrorism: "Let's protect our religion!" (*Uz dinimizni himoya qilamiz!*), "Let's protect our religion from all enemies!" (*Dinimizni yot kuchlardan saqlaylik!*), "We shall never give up our sacred religion!" (*Biz muqaddas dinimizni hech kimga bermaymiz!*).[6]

While Uzbek leaders have found it relatively easy to choose which historical rulers to draw attention to, beginning with Timur and then following the line of dynastic descendants through to the Russian invasions in the nineteenth century, they have encountered more difficulty choosing which religious figures to honor.

The government sought to give the "appropriate" interpretation to the lives of prominent religious figures of the past, explaining their legacies in ways that emphasized national values over religious ones. In Soviet style, they planned celebrations of various religious leaders of the past, such as Imam al-Bukhari, Imam al-Maturidi,[7] Baha ud-Din Naqshaband, Khoja Ahror, and Abd al-Khaliq Ghijduvani. For each of these men, commemorations were held in universities, public schools, and academic research institutions, and in some cases there were larger public celebrations.

The jubilee of Khoja Ahror in 2004 caused controversy. Khoja Ahror is a Sufi theologian well-regarded throughout most of the Muslim world, and the Uzbek state is very proud of the country's historic role in developing Sufism. So the Cabinet of Ministers decided to hold an international conference in his memory. Bakhtiyar Babadjanov reports, though, that after the Presidential Council received a detailed memo on Khoja Ahror's activities and his "political credo," which included religious justification for when the brotherhood should engage in politics, the jubilee celebrations were scaled back to a small conference for local scholars.[8]

The challenge is one of figuring out what message to send to the population. For example, Bakhtiyar Babadjanov writes that there was a lot of confusion over whether to mark the centennial of the Andijan uprising of 1898. Initial plans for public celebration were abandoned because of concern that the public would fasten on Dukchi Ishan's desire to restore a "righteous" Islamic state rather than see him simply as a fighter for national independence.

The state has maintained tight formal and informal controls over the media, in an effort to support its ideological goals, and broadcasting about religion is designed to try to reinforce the legitimacy of Hanafi interpretations of Islam, including its rich Sufi heritage. The emphasis of Sufism in particular is an attempt to neutralize Salafi and other forms of radical Islamic teachings that emphasize the Quran and *hadiths* as the sole legitimate form of religious teachings.

As part of this project we[9] followed some of the broadcasting on three national radio stations around Ramadan in 2006, generally broadcast and even rebroadcast before the fast began each day. Radio ORIAT Dono-FM 106.5 MHz is a national broadcaster that offers programming only in Uzbek. During the month of Ramadan, religious-oriented broadcasting was offered twice a day[10] and contained religious enlightenment (*diniy marifati*) programs, including *Ramazon fonusi* (Lighthouse of Ramadan) and *Kongil hilvati* (Paradise of the Soul), as well as readings from the Quran, Muslim legends, and Sufi tales. The target audience for the program is between the ages of 25 and 40.

Radio ZAMIN-FM 105.4 MHz, another national broadcaster, offered the program *Tazarru* (Confession), which features readings of *suras* from the Quran. The program sought to deliver a message of repentance that emphasized Islam's rejection of violence. This program was hosted by Afzal Rafikov, a well-known Uzbek singer.

Radio Navruz-FM 88.4 MHz offered a program on religion called *Holislik* (Fairness), with former Mufti Muhammad Sodiq Muhammad Yusuf as host. Throughout the year national radio hosts religious programs often offering opportunities for audience participation, with questions selected to give listeners "straight answers" on religious issues. There are similar live programs in several provincial centers, including a very popular program in Urgench that has discussions of Sufi poetry.

Competition for time is greater on the country's national television stations. Throughout most of the past decade, 45 minutes of religious programming has been broadcast twice a week, most of it straightforward Hanafi proselytizing, advising people to follow the norms of Islam, with additional broadcasting during religious holidays and the month of Ramadan.[11] Some of the programming is prepared by ZIYO studio, which is part of Tashkent Islamic University. More "folksy" programming relating to the role of Islam in daily life is broadcast on local television stations, but since the mid-2000s the government in Tashkent has restricted the amount of airtime that can be devoted to religious broadcasting by regional television.

Some of this broadcasting has been used to try to get people to abandon lavish weddings, funerals, and celebrations of circumcision (*sunnat toy*). In addition to an inordinate drain on family budgets and a seeming motivation for seeking bribes or not paying taxes (the new economy's modern version of the Soviet-era complaint), many prominent clerics object to such practices as diminishing the spiritual content of these life-cycle events.[12]

While the Uzbek government has brought in people with formal Islamic training to advise the State Council on Religion, much of the literature seeking to proselytize the new national ideology was prepared by Soviet-era intellectuals with little grounding in either traditional Hanafi Islam or local Sufi teachings. What they wound up turning out were historical exposés or other publications for a popular audience that read a lot more like Soviet-era anti-religious propaganda than the writings of religious leaders designed to convey to an interested reader the spirituality of the Quran or of *hadiths*. Religion went from bad to good, but the messages in these works generally conveyed none of the power of religious faith to its audience.

While the government is able to dominate the population's access to information, its control is not all-encompassing. In urban areas in particular, many Uzbeks have access to cable television, which includes independent sources of news both in Russian[13] and in Turkish. Physical access to the Internet is better in cities and large towns, and it is quite good in Tashkent.[14] While filters are in place to prevent access to Uzbek language opposition sites, ingenious users are able to access them through proxy servers, find reprints on unblocked sites, or find almost anything on YouTube that is not blocked.[15]

The government has also found it difficult to control most clerics who have decided to create their own religious materials, generally on audiocassettes. Distributing such materials was perfectly legal for more than a decade, but now they must be distributed through the Spiritual Administration of Muslims of Uzbekistan, the only organization legally entitled to import or print religious materials and media with religious content. However, in Tashkent at least, it is possible to find unsanctioned religious materials for sale, and it is hard to believe that clerics have much trouble distributing any materials they produce within their own communities, given the many informal settings in which they meet their co-religionists. This is particularly true of things that are not state-sanctioned but are similar in content to materials that are.

It is impossible to know how successful Uzbek authorities have been in creating a sense of national loyalty that combines a sense of ethno-religious loyalty. The government seems to have succeeded in reinforcing an ethnic identity based around the idea of Uzbek statehood, which need not be synonymous with support for the president or the current government.

The population does not seem prepared to grant the government the right to define the nature of the Islamic identity that is linked with "Uzbekness," seeming far more comfortable leaving that to the clerics who regulate and help define communal and national religious life.

At the same time though, most Uzbeks seem willing to grant the state the right to regulate religious affairs, viewing that as a legitimate government prerogative. After independence, many ordinary Uzbeks initially hungered to learn more about Islam, but over time many decided that they were more comfortable with a loose practice of religious traditions than with the imposition of a rigid moral code that they feared would come if Islamic clerics came into positions of political or public dominance. People wanted the freedom to practice Islam, but most seemed to want it on their own terms.

Given this evolution in popular sentiment, especially among the older generation, the state was able to maintain a large degree of public support when it started closing unregistered mosques and religious schools by the mid- to late 1990s, without evoking strong popular resistance. But the state was never able to determine the content of religious doctrine, or even strongly influence it, even after Abduvali qori disappeared and Muhammad Sodiq Muhammad Yusuf went into exile. Nor was the state able to modify the public behavior of those who enthusiastically embraced public displays of religious devotion, such as wearing pious religious attire, securing prominent imams to preside over weddings, or making pilgrimage to local holy sites (the government never sought to eliminate pilgrimages to Saudi Arabia, although it did assert more control over who received the slots awarded to Uzbekistan).

LEGISLATING RELIGIOUS BEHAVIOR IN UZBEKISTAN

The constitution of Uzbekistan, adopted on December 8, 1992, provides for freedom of conscience and grants everyone the right to profess or not to profess any religion. It also makes the compulsory imposition of religion a crime (Article 31). Moreover, it asserts that religious organizations and associations will be separate from the state, and it guarantees that the state will not interfere in the activity of religious organizations.[16]

These constitutional guarantees, though, could give someone the wrong impression. Uzbekistan is a peculiar kind of secular state. It is a state in which the government exerts a great deal of supervision over the religious practices of its citizenry and is willing to apply the full power of the law to those who do not take the legal restrictions seriously.

While it is conventional wisdom among Western human rights groups and democracy advocates that the threats posed by radical Islamic groups in Uzbekistan are mostly the product of Uzbekistan's harsh anti-religious policies,[17] radical Islamic groups have posed some threat to secular authorities since the early 1990s. These threats are detailed in the next chapter.

Political instability in the Ferghana Valley, coupled with the civil war in neighboring Tajikistan, which was separated from Uzbekistan in the early 1990s by hundreds of miles of porous and unguarded borders, shaped Karimov's decision to take a hard stand toward religion, as well as to close, and at times even mine,[18] Uzbekistan's borders with neighboring states.

Initially Karimov proceeded quite tentatively in his campaign against radical Islamic activists, taking great pains to present himself as a practicing Muslim. In January 1992 Karimov had insisted on swearing his oath of presidential office with his hand on the Quran; soon after, he gave interviews in which he spoke of having become a believer who now ate only halal meat. He also said that, as a firm advocate of religious education for children, he planned to return nationalized property to Islamic institutions.[19] In fact, many important religious sites were handed over to the UMU.

In late 1992, after Emomali Rahmon came to power in Tajikistan and the fighting there started to wind down, Karimov felt that the direct threat to security in his country had abated enough that he should start to try to control the threat posed by radical Muslim groups. Muhammad Sodiq was removed as *mufti* in favor of a more predictable and loyal figure, Mukhtarkhon Abdullaev.[20]

Abdullaev was appointed in an attempt to oust supporters of Muhammad Sodiq from positions of responsibility and to move against radical Islamic groups in the Namangan area such as *Islom lashkarlari*, including removing clerics with even distant ties to them or to the Islamic Movement of Uzbekistan or its fighters. However, Abdullaev lacked the authority to do this, and so civil rather than clerical authorities went after radical clerics, threatening them to change their behavior or face government retaliation.[21] Uzbek authorities also forcibly broke up militant Islamic groups in the Namangan area.

The most prominent leaders of these, Tohir Yuldoshev[22] and Juma Namangani, had gone to Tajikistan to fight with their Islamic colleagues, and their Islamic Movement of Uzbekistan sought to establish an Islamic government in Uzbekistan through the use of violence if necessary. The movement, based in Tajikistan through 1998[23] and then in Afghanistan, never posed a direct threat to the survival of the secular Uzbek state. But it had a definite appeal to the disaffected youth of the country, especially those living in the Ferghana Valley, and was a source of potential destabilization of Uzbekistan.

The existence of such a threat played a direct role in leading to the introduction of the Law on Freedom of Conscience and Religious Organizations, adopted on May 1, 1998. This highly restrictive law was modified most recently in 2005, when fines for repeated violations of the law on religious activity were raised to between 200 and 300 times the minimum monthly wage (at judicial discretion). Registration of religious groups is difficult; minors are prohibited from participating in religious organizations; private instruction in religion is banned. Only clerics are permitted to publicly wear "religious" clothing, and distribution of unsanctioned religious materials is illegal. The latter two prohibitions are enforced only sporadically, but most aspects of the law are closely enforced, and human rights groups estimate that there are several thousand prisoners of conscience. The 1998 law also significantly complicated the procedure of registering religious organizations, which led to a 40 percent drop in the number of registered religious organizations in the country in the first five years after its adoption.[24] Registered religious organizations were also barred from receiving funds from foreign charities.

The law is also supported through the provisions of Uzbekistan's Criminal and Administrative codes, which have also been amended. Several articles of the Criminal Code have been used to try to control the development of religion in Uzbekistan, including Article 159, on "attempting to overthrow the constitutional order." The article has been interpreted quite broadly to include any calls to create an Islamic state, or to distribute literature containing such a call, even if the change of the constitutional order is proposed to be done peacefully.[25]

Article 216-2 criminalizes any religious activities organized or carried out by an unregistered religious group, and Article 229-2 of the Criminal Code criminalizes any religious instruction by persons lacking special religious degrees, instruction without a permit from the central department responsible for regulation of religious organizations, and/or individual instruction. Article 244-1 of the Criminal Code, added in 1998, in particular criminalizes "publishing, storing and distributing materials containing ideas of religious extremism and fundamentalism." This provision also fails to distinguish between materials advocating the use of violence and those that call for expanding religion's role solely through peaceful means. In addition, only the central headquarters of officially registered groups are allowed to publish religious literature. Any violation of these conditions entails administrative or criminal prosecution. Article 244-2, added in 1999, covers membership in religious extremist and fundamentalist organizations, and Article 246 labels as contraband all materials advertising religious extremism and fundamentalism. Since the adoption of these laws, controls have become so much tighter that even scholars sent abroad on official exchanges are likely to have their Arabic or Persian language research materials seized upon returning home. These scholars can be charged with violations of the Criminal Code (though fortunately they rarely are).

Article 184-1 of the Administrative Code is designed to supplement the 1998 Law on Freedom of Conscience and Religious Organizations and prescribes punishment for wearing "religious clothes" in public by persons who are not religious ministers. Articles 240 and 241 of the Administrative Code also contain a ban on "unsanctioned religious activities."[26]

With these laws and regulations in place, the Uzbek authorities were able to react quickly on February 16, 1999, when six bombs exploded outside various Uzbek government buildings in Tashkent, killing thirteen people and injuring 120. President Islam Karimov, who believed himself the target of these attacks, escaped unharmed. The Uzbek government blamed the violence on IMU terrorists and on Hizb ut-Tahrir,[27] and some individuals were accused of having allegiance to both organizations.[28] For that reason, many outside observers questioned Uzbek government claims that the perpetrators of the incident were in fact from Hizb ut-Tahrir. For many in the Uzbek security establishment, loss of full control was seen as tantamount to having no control.

The bombings led to a major shift in government policies toward Islam. The unanticipated nature of the explosions left the government frightened that further attacks were imminent, and it moved quickly to insert security officials in many of the most popular mosques. Seemingly disloyal clerics were pushed from their posts, and numerous members of Hizb ut-Tahrir and other fringe Islamic groups were arrested.[29]

Meanwhile, the government continued to publicly emphasize its devotion to "true" Islam, that which opposes violence and preaches peace. In a speech delivered to Parliament shortly after the explosions, Islam Karimov began with the words, "Allah is in our souls, in our hearts" (*Alloh bizning qalbimizda, yuragimizda*).

The day after this speech, Karimov appointed the well-known theologian Abdulaziz Mansurov[30] as his adviser on religious affairs. Negotiations between Uzbek authorities and members of Muhammad Sodiq's family also began in the months following the bombings to help arrange terms for his return home, to create more support among devout Muslims for the government's struggle against terrorism and extremism.

Within a few months of the explosions, the government also began to offer amnesty to those who had fled the country to join the Islamic opposition in Tajikistan or in Afghanistan. At least several hundred people returned under this program, most of whom were able to remain at liberty.[31] Among other things this made it easier for the Uzbek authorities to learn about and better monitor the activities of the Islamic Movement of Uzbekistan.

The anti-religious legislation was most consistently applied against individuals charged with membership in Islamic schismatic groups, such as Hizb ut-Tahrir and Akramiya, and in rounding up suspected members of the IMU or other Islamic jihadist groups after bombings in Tashkent and Bukhara in March 2004[32] and later that summer against the U.S. and Israeli embassies.[33] Uzbek authorities claimed that the bombings were organized by the followers of Obidkhon qori, and the Tashkent cleric was forced to flee southern Kazakhstan, where he had been living, for exile in Europe after Uzbek authorities pressured their Kazakh counterparts.

Modifications to the administrative and criminal codes in 2005 and 2006 imposed lengthier prison terms for those who organize meetings of an unregistered religious group and raised the fines for those who participate in such groups. In recent years, the definition of what constitutes religious and political extremism seems to have broadened as well. An increasing number of groups fall into this category, including terrorist groups formed by the splitting off from Islamic Jihad Union and the Islamic Movement of Uzbekistan, and those like the "Nurchi" group (followers of Said Nursi),[34] which had previously been operating relatively freely in Uzbekistan but whose members began to be arrested in 2009 and 2010.[35]

DUALITY IN EVERYDAY LIFE

Despite the state authorities' painstaking attempts to maintain constant surveillance and tight control over the Uzbek population's religious expression, the individual perceptions of "Muslimness" and the local practice of Islam still are not fully shaped by official Islamic discourse promoted by the state. While conforming to the state vision of the role and import of religion in Uzbekistan on the normative level, individuals also develop their own understanding of their Muslim identity on a daily basis by participating in local social practices and life-cycle rituals. A large part of Uzbekistan's population appear to view their religious identity as multilayered, with the national, state-approved definition of Islam and Hanafi tradition as its centerpiece, but which may be at odds with other values formed as the result of personal experience. Most individuals seem to find ways to create a congruent value system out of potentially conflicting interpretations of religion.

Although the collapse of the Soviet Union rekindled popular interest in Islam and reintroduced religion into public life, the majority of Uzbeks, and certainly the majority of those born under Soviet rule, still lack formal religious education. For these Uzbeks, participation in life-cycle communal rituals is still the primary way in which their identity as Muslims is developed.

In *Islam in Post-Soviet Uzbekistan: The Morality of Experience*, Johan Rasanayagam offers a compelling argument on the centrality of social and communal practices for the formation of one's Muslim identity. These practices, such as the participation in the communal festivities—*nikoh toys*, *sunnat toys, jinazs*—enable regular Uzbeks to express their Muslim identity by letting them feel like full-fledged, active members of the community.

Each *mahalla* unit is defined partly in relation to the nearest mosque. Similarly, a *mahalla* committee may include individuals recognized for their piety and knowledge of Islam, and there is an implicit association between *mahalla* and religion, as the proper observance of a particular ritual makes the role of the community indispensable. For example, the household must seek the advice of the *oq soqoli*, the *mahalla*'s elder (literally "white beard"), on the proper conduct of festivities, and he frequently guides the family on the ritual aspects of the ceremony, as well as supervises the implementation of numerous logistical details, advises who should be included in the guest list, and even determines the quantity of food to be prepared for the feast. To put it simply, a *mahalla* is perceived by regular Uzbeks as something more than a simple residential subunit—instead, a *mahalla* serves as a moral community of sorts.[36]

Because a *mahalla* serves as a nominal yardstick of one's Muslimness, enactments of spirituality acquire greater value if recognized and approved by the community. Rasanayagam's study included a series of interviews with residents of different *mahallas*. Their responses aptly illustrated the centrality of the social factor for the validation of one's religious identity. *Mahalla* residents often complained of "the villagers' [inability] to live fully according to Islam,"[37] since they could no longer arrange lavish wedding feasts—that would include more guests—because of people's declining incomes. This quote clearly demonstrates that for many Uzbeks, "Muslimness" is not just about one's fulfillment of religious precepts, but to a great degree it is about the level of one's participation in the social framework.

Communal participation is critical for all social groups. Even those who were self-proclaimed diehard atheists or secular intellectuals during the Soviet era currently participate in religious festivities that are part of the *mahalla*'s activities. Participation in religious events has a social component, and participating in funeral prayers is imperative for every member of the community in order to be viewed as a moral individual.

As stated in *Islam in Post-Soviet Uzbekistan*, "a modern or contemporary believer (*sovremennyi chelovek*) looks to Islam for inspiration in answering his questions about virtuous conduct in society."[38] This quote aptly captures the intrinsic connection between Muslim identity in Uzbekistan, that it is the source of defining righteous behavior for individuals and for the community, which serves as the moral compass that reinforces the relationship of the individual to Islam, and the community, which tends to act as a moral compass that links the first two elements together.

The social mechanism of the *mahalla* also plays a second role—that of public legitimization of state discourse. The relationship between the *mahalla* and the state vividly illustrates how the state uses local social and religious traditions to promote a nationalist agenda.

Historically, a *mahalla* acted as an independent local organ of self-governance, administering basic social services, overseeing economic development and the distribution of land resources, and supervising the enactment of major religious rituals.[39] Administration of the *mahalla* was vested in the hands of a small committee, usually comprising several learned and well-respected elders, a *mullah*, and an *oq soqoli* who officiated at the ceremonies and acted as the nominal head of the community. Although the collectivization of agricultural production during the Soviet era stripped *mahallas* of some of their prerogatives and responsibilities, they continued to exist, albeit in an altered form. With the disintegration of the Soviet Union, the importance of the *mahalla* has come back to the fore. Although *mahallas* were declared to be nominally independent, the actual independence of these institutes of local governance is viewed by many as compromised: Several members of the *mahalla* committee staff receive small state salaries, which in turn obliges the *mahalla* to take on some of the regional government's responsibilities and necessitates close cooperation with state law enforcement agencies.

Because a *mahalla* exemplifies such qualities as respect for elders and commitment to the communal good, it comes as no surprise that *mahalla* is viewed by Karimov as an extension or microcosm of the Uzbek state, with Karimov as the *oq soqoli* of this big national "family." One of Karimov's most famous sayings—"From a strong state to a strong society"—clearly underscores the idea that a *mahalla* is viewed as a social instrument to naturalize the current government's rule.[40]

The members of the committee are responsible for the distribution of services that were previously handled by the state government. These services include tax and utility payments collection, maintenance of registers of eligible conscripts, distribution of child support, and welfare payments.[41] More importantly, *mahallas* are expected to act as "the eyes and ears of the government,"[42] leading some to complain that they are a mechanism of social control.

Despite the government's interest in the *mahalla* serving as a means of promoting "good" and rooting out "bad" Islam, the *mahalla* does not simply act as an extension of government ideology, leaving enough room for individuals to form their own understanding of religion. Uzbeks shape their communal activities and ways of religious self-expression by their personal drives and local practices. Thus, for instance, *mahalla* imams who may disapprove of certain state views on religion, such as the state support of pilgrimages to holy shrines and tombs of the righteous (*avliyos*) due to their historically pagan roots, need not compromise their religious views just to conform to state ideology. By taking cues from the government and assisting the state on such fronts as the condemnation of radical Islam, they manage to provide subtle resistance on others. Although local imams' ability to openly vilify and condemn such state-endorsed local practices as *ziyorat* is somewhat limited, the majority still manage to deliver sermons denouncing such traditions and preaching a more mainstream version of Hanafi Islam, while adhering to the government-set regulations on all other fronts.

Rasanayagam recounts an *aqiqa toy* (celebration in honor of the birth of a child) that he attended while in Uzbekistan. He recollects how amazed he was to observe the absolutely genuine emotional reaction of regular

Uzbeks while listening to the preacher's sermon. With tears in their eyes, they were avidly internalizing his moral lessons.

EDUCATING THE NEXT GENERATION OF MUSLIMS

Uzbek authorities, like their Soviet predecessors, have viewed control of the education system as providing them with the best opportunity for shaping the political outlook of the next generation, including the "proper" attitude toward Islam. To this end, from the early 1990s elementary and middle schools introduced mandatory instruction in "enlightenment and spirituality" (*marifat va manaviyat*), which replaced Soviet-era training in "scientific-atheism."

But as we saw in the communities discussed in the previous chapter, parents, rather than central government officials, began to exert a strong influence on local school administrations. As a result, in many areas imams were brought in to provide the instruction, turning many of the classes into little more than instruction in the faith.

In general there have been efforts to introduce changes in the curriculum to correspond to changes in religious policy. It did not take long for the central authorities to become concerned that they were losing control. In 1997 through 1998, Royiq Bahadirov,[43] President Karimov's adviser on religious affairs, worked on a number of decrees to make sure that the instruction about religion (in primary schools, in particular) would be exclusively secular in nature.

But the changes in curriculum have done little to address what appears to be the return of tradition, including much greater religious observance, in rural Uzbekistan. Bakhtiyar Babadjanov made a series of trips to schools throughout the Ferghana Valley from 2002 to 2006 and repeatedly heard complaints from teachers in state schools that only half of the students would attend class on Fridays.[44] This was particularly true of students in grades five through ten, an age families considered suitable to go to weekly prayers at the mosque. In a number of rural schools, teachers also complained that up to 80 percent of the young women attended school in *hijab*. These girls typically dropped out of school after about eight years of primary education, because when they reached the age of fourteen, their parents would arrange marriages for them. These underage marriages[45] have become more common in recent years, even in Tashkent.

In addition to the influence of families, the values of the teachers can be a source of introducing religious values to children from secular homes who attend state schools. It has remained perfectly legal to invite clerics to teach in the schools, assuming that they are graduates of the Higher Islamic Institute, or any of the Islamic colleges run by UMU that are described below. Graduates of religious education institutions are entitled to fill the same jobs as graduates of secular schools, that is, they can hold any state jobs for which their degrees qualify them.

It is inevitable that teachers with clerical backgrounds seek to convey the religious material that they are teaching in a way that calls students to spiritual observance. Local officials who were devout believers also sought to introduce religious education in the schools. I had the opportunity to meet with the *viloyat* (region, oblast) official charged with supervising religious affairs in Ferghana in April 2005.

I was surprised to learn that he had studied at Al-Azhar in Cairo. Rather than being focused on spreading a secular-based ideology, he seemed more concerned about making sure that the youth got the "right" exposure to religion. He took his own religious inspiration, he explained, from Muhammad Sodiq Muhammad Yusuf, and he presented us with a gift of some of the former *mufti*'s writings.

He told me about the new "history of the world's religions" programs, and explained that in Ferghana *viloyat*, at least, local imams provided most of the instruction and that these religious leaders were also being called upon to organize a variety of after-school activities in local schools.

Devout students studying in secular institutions are also a source of introducing religion in the schools. Bakhtiyar Babadjanov reports colleagues at Tashkent Islamic University and Tashkent State Institute of Oriental Studies have complained of the strong effect that even one devout student had produced, recounting how "from day one, he practiced *davat*." As a result of this missionary work, the professor noticed that the attitude toward Islam steadily changed in the classroom. Some of the girls even started to wear the *hijab*.[46]

Uzbek foreign policy has also had a decided impact on the way teaching about Islam has evolved in the state education system. Often government officials have not been fully aware of just how much the government's outreach to the countries of the Middle East has influenced the curriculum that has developed and how it is taught.

From the early 1990s, numerous philanthropic foundations from Arab countries sent religious textbooks to academic institutions throughout Uzbekistan, which brought in literature from the other three *mazhabs* and materials that were Salafist in orientation. Even after restrictions on importing religious books, this literature continues to find its way into Uzbekistan through legal and not so legal means. Few supervisory personnel actually read or are able to read the textbooks that are being taught in the universities.[47]

As a result, advanced students with good Arabic language skills have been able to gain exposure to Salafi literature in a completely legal fashion. Salafi religious texts are found in a number of secular institutions, not just in madrasas.

Bakhtiyar Babadjanov writes that the curriculum of the Department of Religion and Islam Studies in Tashkent State Institute of Oriental Studies and the Department of Islamic Studies at Tashkent's State Pedagogical University (named after Nizami) all include works by authors from the Arab world who are generally considered to be supportive of the ideas of the Muslim Brotherhood or other Salafist or radical Islamist authors.

When it was initially opened in the early 1990s, the department lacked secular specialists able to serve as professors. Instead, they brought in young graduates of madrasas and other religious institutions, ranging from graduates of *hujras* to alumni of early educational exchange programs in Saudi Arabia. The teaching methods of such faculty were based on *davat*. Many of the early textbooks used were Salafi or fundamentalist in orientation, something that was not hard to get past state curricular review boards. Classes on Arabic language were also often taught by former imams, owing to the shortage of people with Arabic language skills willing to work at state salaries. The educational approach of such teachers strongly influenced the first graduates of the department, who themselves became missionaries of Salafi ideas. Babadjanov went so far as to complain that in the early days of the institute, he was about the only one with a secular background in teaching, a statement that might have been something of an exaggeration. But it is much easier to accept Babadjanov's contention that the young Salafi educators found a receptive audience among the recent secondary school graduates.

Babadjanov also argues that the Nizami Pedagogical University served as something of a magnet for students from religious families, as much by accident as by design, because it is easier to gain admission there than to Tashkent State University. Nearly 70 percent of the students there come from the provinces, where teaching is considered a prestigious career option. Rural youth are also much more likely to come from religious families, and even those that are not from religious families have spent most of their lives living in close proximity with people who are devout. In fact, Babadjanov argues that an overwhelming majority of students in the universities of the Ferghana Valley come from religious families and usually have a basic religious education. He also claims that a significant number of professors at Kokand and Andijan State universities (regardless of department) openly practice Islam (for example, pray regularly, observe Ramadan, and dress according to Muslim norms).

Similarly, Babadjanov reports that Salafist literature is taught in the humanities departments of several provincial universities and even in the higher grades in some secondary schools. In addition, some of this material is taught in courses at several secular higher secondary institutions throughout Uzbekistan.[48]

However, it is far too early to draw dramatic conclusions from the fact that so-called fundamentalist literature is available to students in Uzbekistan's public education system. As anyone who has taught students in any school system knows, it is one thing to make books available, or even assign them; it is quite another thing for students to read them, let alone be transformed by what they read. But the fact remains that despite efforts of the Uzbek government to the contrary, students in Uzbekistan are able to access some of the most radical ideas circulating in the Islamic world, and they are able to do this without having to engage in any sort of clandestine activity.

Tashkent Islamic University[49]

One of the ways that the Uzbek government hoped to solve its cadre problem for teaching religion in state schools was through the creation of the

Tashkent Islamic University. TIU was designed to be a secular alternative to the Higher Islamic Institute. It was created as the result of an April 7, 1999, presidential decree calling for the establishment of a "secular education institution that prepares specialists in Islamic studies and Islamic law." It has not really served that purpose.

The two senior Uzbek officials who were the architects of TIU, Hamidulla Karomatov[50] and Zuhriddin Husniddinov,[51] had little understanding of how a Western-style educational system operates.[52] And while TIU is not the only Uzbek higher educational institution to be found wanting, official fears about the spread of Islamic radicalism are so great that the authorities decided in 2006 to substantially reorganize the institution. However, Bakhtiyar Babadjanov, who has been a part-time faculty member at the university, does not believe that these new measures will be sufficient to transform the university and make it able to serve its original goals.

Students, in his opinion, were taught to understand religion not as a component of the secular state, but as the main source of positive values in the governance and in the historical heritage of the nation. Rather than creating an intellectual atmosphere in which there was a discussion of religious scripture, teachers often urged the students to treat them as consecrated texts.

Compounding the problem is the selection bias on the part of the students chosen for admission. Babadjanov notes that more than half of all students entering the university come from religious backgrounds or are practicing Muslims and that about a third of the faculty appears to be religious themselves, but their number includes several Al-Azhar graduates as well as others who were trained in the Arab world. Furthermore, Babadjanov observes, as students go through the program they tend to become more religious.

Babadjanov also cites problems of an organizational nature. At the time of its creation, TIU failed to establish a division between departments teaching secular subjects and those teaching religious subjects. Instead, both were staffed by faculty who had a background in teaching in religious institutions or were graduates of madrasas. The administration of the institution is said to have provided very little supervision of the content of the lectures and seminars. As a result, he says, the content and style of instruction is said to have frequently been far closer to preaching than to secular higher educational instruction. The end result, in Babadjanov's opinion, is badly trained quasi-imams, lacking the rigor or religious education and unable to teach in religious institutions but unfit to teach religion to students using a secular approach.

In the first years, the readings that students were assigned relied heavily on works by Salafi authors instead of the region's own Hanafi authors, and students had very limited exposure to writings by Western theologians or materials on comparative religion. In addition, the institute's library was poorly equipped. With the exception of Arabic language sources, much of which came as gifts from foreign Islamic charitable institutions, most secondary literature had been bought during the Soviet period.

The Uzbek Security Council was sufficiently concerned that it ordered a complete overhaul of the institution in May 2006, putting it under the leadership of Shuhrat Yovkochev,[53] who had been appointed President Karimov's adviser on religious issues in October 2005. Yovkochev was likely chosen for the job because of his research specialty on the challenge of reformation in Islam, a topic that he has continued to write on since his appointment.[54]

Yovkochev quickly started replacing imams and Al-Azhar graduates with secular-oriented faculty recruited from other Uzbek universities and promoted them to administrative positions in the university. He also revamped the curriculum in the Department of Islamic Studies and added a new Department of Religious Studies, whose courses are modeled after those at the University of Washington in Seattle, where Uzbek specialists on religion have held fellowships through a U.S. government-funded exchange program.

He encourages professors to use interactive methods of teaching, to screen relevant movies, speak openly about issues of women in Islam, and to conduct seminars and discussion groups about the reformers in Islam. All of this is part of an effort to restrain missionary work within the school. In general the intent is to depoliticize discussion on religion, so that observance becomes a question of individual choice rather than acceding to group pressure.

A good example is the campaign to get women who were wearing full *hijab* (and some were even all in black, in the Iranian style) to dress in traditional Turkish scarves. The intent was to get them to substitute ethno-religious dress for what most observers saw as religious garb that was intended to make a political statement.[55] Admissions standards have also changed, with an explicit effort now being made to identify pious students and to redirect them to the religious institutions, to madrasas, or to the Higher Islamic Institute under the Muslim Spiritual Administration of Uzbekistan.

In recent years the university has also developed a website, www.tiu.uz, geared to a mostly undergraduate student audience and aimed to increase religious awareness. The design of the website leaves much to be desired. It is less user-friendly than the site maintained by UMU (www.muslim.uz), and both of these sites lack the skill and imagination that Muhammad Sodiq's staff has put into the ones that it maintains (www.islam.uz and www.islom.uz).

Even today, TIU remains something of a victim of the situation it was designed to eradicate, in that the Uzbek government still lacks sufficient secular specialists in Islamic studies to oversee and participate in the project. Regardless, it is not in any way preordained that teachers of religion who are themselves devout will pose a threat to the state's ideological goals, even if their doctrinal beliefs are radical by Hanafi standards.

Education Sponsored by the Muslim Spiritual Administration of Uzbekistan

The Spiritual Administration of Muslims of Uzbekistan serves as a partner of the state in teaching the country's youth about Islam, through its Department of Education.[56] The department, organized in 1992, has overall responsibility for UMU's Imam Bukhari Institute and ten specialized secondary schools or colleges, as they are known in Uzbekistan. The department is responsible for the selection of applicants to institutions for Islamic education throughout the country and provides textbooks[57] to institutions for religious education. UMU's Department of Education also provides assistance to Tashkent Islamic University and, on request, the Ministry of Education.

Uzbekistan's leading religious institution remains the Imam Bukhari Islamic Institute in Tashkent, which now has roughly two hundred students enrolled at any given time. In 1998 it was officially registered by the Ministry of Justice and received accreditation by the Board of Religion in the Committee of Ministers of the Republic of Uzbekistan as an institution of higher education.

The institute has two departments—the Department of the Foundations of Religion and the Department of the Law and History of Islam—and three chairs: the Chair of Religious Sciences, the Chair of Social Sciences and Humanities, and the Chair of Foreign Languages. There is also a Women's Group that trains female teachers for the special religious secondary schools for women. Because it seeks to maintain its state accreditation, the institute also offers courses on secular subjects, including the history of Uzbekistan, philosophy, Uzbek culture and history, economics, history, and foreign languages in addition to its full religious curriculum, which includes courses on the history of Islam, readings of the Quran, *fiqh*, and Arabic language study.

The Mir-i Arab Islamic Secondary Special School in Bukhara, the only Soviet-era Islamic secondary school, has also increased the size of its student body and has expanded its curriculum. It, too, was re-registered by the Ministry of Justice of the Republic of Uzbekistan in 1998 and certified by the State Committee on Religious Affairs. More than seven hundred students (aged 15 through 35) completed the school's three-year program of study during Uzbekistan's first decade of independence. It remains the foremost Islamic secondary school in the country.

In 1992 UMU opened the Juybori Kalon Islamic Special Secondary School for Girls[58] in Bukhara. The school specializes in the training of teachers of Arabic and ethics. The curriculum includes courses on the history of religion, foundations of Islam, the Quran, *fiqh*, *hadith*, *tafsir*, the history of Uzbekistan, ideas of national independence, basics of a spiritual life, foreign languages, literature, chemistry, and other disciplines.

In the late 1990s, in conjunction with the decision by Uzbek authorities to crack down on non–state-regulated religious education, the decision was made to allow UMU to operate a total of a dozen secondary schools, and all privately run religious high schools were ordered closed. The secondary schools run by UMU were all registered or re-registered in 1998 and are expected to meet Uzbek government standards for secondary education.

Secondary schools run by UMU in Tashkent include the Kukaldosh Islamic Secondary Special School (originally known as the Madrasa of Darveshkhon when it was founded in the sixteenth century), and the Khadichai Kubro[59] Islamic Special Secondary School for Girls, located in the building of the Ahmadjon Qori Mosque. Both offer a range of secular subjects similar to that of state schools as well as instruction in the Quran, *hadiths*, and an introduction to *fiqh*. In 2002 and 2003 there were 179 and 114 students enrolled in these schools, respectively.

In addition, there is the Imam al-Bukhari Islamic Secondary School, named for Muhammad ibn Ismail, born in 810 AD in the city of Bukhara. It was built in the Pay-Arik District of Samarkand and is licensed as a *hadith* center, with some 90 students enrolled at any given time.

The Khoja Bukhari Islamic Secondary Special School is named for Said Ahmad Vali Kulakduz Khoja al-Bukhari, one of Naqshaband's close relatives and a leading disciple, who came to Kitab, the city in Kashkadarya Oblast where the school is located, to the popularize Naqshabandiya *tariqa*. Founded in 1992, it is one of Uzbekistan's largest religious high schools, with an average enrollment of some five hundred students.

The UMU administers two high schools in the Ferghana Valley. The Mullah Okhund Kyrgyz Islamic Secondary Special School in Namangan was established in 1991. It is named for Mullah Okhun, a religious leader who was born in Namangan in 1850 and also received recognition as an agronomist in cotton and silkworm cultivation. The Sayyid Muhyiddin Makhdum Islamic Secondary Special School, named for Hazrat Sayyid Muhyiddin Makhdum, was established in 1992 in Jalabek (in the Oltinkul district of Andijan Oblast) at local initiative.

UMU also operates the Imam Fakhr al-Din al-Razi Islamic Secondary Special School in the city of Urgench, in Khorazm Oblast, which has a library of some 3,500 books collected in the region, as well as the Muhammad ibn Ahmad al-Biruni[60] Islamic Secondary Special School, located in the Muhammad Imam Ishan Mosque in Nukus, the capital of the Karakalpak Autonomous Republic of Uzbekistan.

These institutions all charge fees for instruction, although stipends are made available to worthy students. The fees charged, though, do not cover the costs of running any of these madrasas.

UMU's Funding

The Spiritual Administration of Muslims of Uzbekistan maintains its vast education network largely from its own financial resources, receiving a maximum of 20 percent of its budget from the State Committee on Religious Affairs.[61] This funding is intended to defer the salary costs of the al-Bukhari Higher Islamic Institute, and this funding is closely monitored.

The bulk of the funding that UMU receives comes from contributions from the more than two thousand legally registered mosques, which have been increasingly monitored since 1999, and funds are supposed to be deposited in accounts with the national bank. But the government has little opportunity to supervise the actual collection of funds and is dependent on the records kept by the mosques and religious institutions.

UMU sets quarterly targets of funds to be raised by each mosque (and deposited with the Muslim Board) and the imams of mosques that frequently fail to meet their targets are generally dismissed. UMU returns a portion of the money by paying the salaries of the imams; most, however, still need to supplement their income through other earnings, either through teaching at a religious institution or in the case of more prominent clerics, by leading religious tours or helping community members make business contacts in the Middle East.

Imams collect fees received for leading the celebration of life-cycle rites for families in their communities such as wedding ceremonies, funeral rituals, or circumcisions, and part of these fees are supposed to be shared with the Muslim Board, the appropriate breakdown being determined by the imam involved. Despite the fact that Uzbekistan does not permit the mosques to offer after-school or "Sunday-school–style instruction" (the latter term is one the Uzbeks themselves use), many mosques have some form of unsanctioned study groups run by their clerics. The imams and *mullahs* who teach at these schools are paid by the students who study with them, sometimes in cash, sometimes in kind.

The mosques collect the bulk of their money during major religious feasts such as Ramadan, when most people who attend services give charity. A large mosque in Tashkent may pick up $10,000 a day in donations on major holidays. Money is also collected at the main Friday service. Funds are donated anonymously in a specially marked box and at the end of every Friday or holiday service, the box is opened by a special committee headed by the *imam-hatib* of the mosque. He then is supposed to bring this money to a branch of the state bank for deposit in the account of the Muslim Board. Mosques often run small gift shops to sell religious books, amulets, and small gifts such as women's scarves from the Holy Land.

Both before and after independence, people donated goods, jewelry, rugs, dishes, livestock, and food to the mosque. The proceeds from the sale of these items are to be used at the discretion of the imam and never are recorded anywhere as income. In wealthier *mahallas*, this can be a considerable sum. Since 2001, imams have been required to list the income obtained from such gifts in their official financial ledgers, but this is very hard to monitor.

The leaders of mosques can also appeal to the community for assistance—*hashar*—to meet particular tasks, such as asking for the donation of construction materials or labor to repair or build a mosque. When such a building project is required, the heads of mosques often look for "corporate" sponsors, an enterprise located in the *mahalla* that can donate goods in kind. In the early years of independence, vast cauldrons were put on the street to collect money for such projects. In fact, the cost of reopening the large Juma Mosque was apparently raised over a few days by collections put in such a cauldron on the main street in Namangan, although now such behavior would clearly be frowned upon.

One other big change in the last several years (introduced after the Tashkent bombings of 1999) is that mosques are now required by the state to pay a tax of 20 to 30 percent of all the money raised, with the percentage due varying by region. The highest percent is found in the Ferghana Valley. Tax collectors have access to the mosque's official financial records, but the imams also press the believers among them to do their duty to the faith before they do it to the state. UMU is exempt from this requirement as it has pledged the upkeep of a number of orphanages, schools, and hospitals. But it is not clear how much money it actually transfers in the form of charitable donations, and the *mufti* himself is said to make all the decisions about how much money will be donated, and where.

The Muslim Board also earns money through its publishing house, Mouvarranahr, which prints various brochures, journals, and religious calendars. UMU also is responsible for the import and distribution of foreign religious literature. Any publications of the Muslim Board must be cleared by the State Council on Religious Affairs. The degree of control has varied substantially over time and is partly dependent on who chairs the State Council on Religious Affairs. State controls have toughened considerably since early 1999, though this does not seem to diminish the popular appeal of such publications.

UMU has had responsibility for arranging for Uzbek pilgrims on *hajj*, including choosing who would be awarded the spots allocated for Uzbeks. While the Saudis paid for the cost of transporting Uzbek (and other Central Asian) pilgrims in the early years, a great deal of money changed hands in order to get one of the spaces.[62] Some of this money went to UMU directly to pay for the cost of refurbishing mosques and madrasas, and some made its way into the hands of friends of friends of those serving on UMU's *hajj* committee, who might facilitate the process. In recent years Uzbek pilgrims have had to pay for transport to Saudi Arabia, but in return for arranging the pilgrimage the Muslim Board is able to keep five percent of the fees collected. While demand to go on *hajj* has dropped, not everyone who wants to go passes successfully through the screening process (to get a spot one must be considered by the Muslim Board as not at risk of becoming an extremist), and so some Uzbeks continue to go on *hajj* by purchasing spots on Kyrgyzstan's quota and quietly leaving the country through Kyrgyzstan.

TRYING TO HOLD THE FOREIGN ISLAMIC WORLD AT BAY

One of the challenges that the Uzbek government has tried to deal with is maintaining good relations with its various foreign Muslim partners such as Turkey and Saudi Arabia, while simultaneously managing the country's religious revival in ways that reinforce the state's ideological message.

In the first few years of independence, foreign governments and foreign missionaries were largely free to influence the development of Islam in Uzbekistan, providing of course that they were willing to spend money to achieve their ends. The one exception was the Islamic Republic of Iran, because Tashkent viewed the Shia theocratic elite in charge in Tehran as offering something of a triple threat—Iranian (and so pro-Tajik rather than pro-Uzbek), radical Muslims, and Shia besides.[63]

The Muslim Board of Uzbekistan was able to receive monetary and in-kind gifts from foreign governments until after the Tashkent bombings in early 1999. Bakhtiyar Babadjanov claims that prior to this it was routine for foreign embassies based in Tashkent to make or transfer cash donations, sometimes as high as $100,000, directly to UMU, for the construction or repair of mosques and madrasas.[64]

In the first half of the 1990s in particular, even brief access to foreign currency was a way to get rich, given the different black market rates in the trading of foreign currency. Those who had access to this money were able to further enrich their mosques and madrasas—and possibly, if they wished, themselves and their family members—while the gifts became construction materials and construction contracts.

During these years there were frequent rumors that some of this money went astray, not only during Muhammad Sodiq's administration, but also during that of his successor Mukhtarkhon Abdullaev. Abdullaev was favored by President Karimov because his Naqshabandiya roots gave him entree in the proper moderate Islamic circles in Turkey. This was especially important during the presidency of Turgut Ozal, who was a strong advocate, aiding the Central Asian countries in the name of Turkish unity and whose inner circle was closely tied to the Naqshabandiya order.[65]

Abdullaev made a number of trips to Turkey, including with President Karimov. During his term in office Abdullaev was included in trips to Turkey, where he secured funding, the rebuilding of Baha ud-Din Naqshaband's mausoleum, found outside of Bukhara as well as the complex of buildings surrounding it,[66] where presumably opportunities for earning money (for himself as well as for the Muslim Board) presented themselves. Over time, Uzbek authorities grew much more concerned with the kinds of religious influences that were coming from Turkey and sought to reduce contacts with Turkish religious circles. Initially, as David Abramson notes in his study on foreign religious education of Central Asians, Uzbek authorities were quite willing to have students accept scholarships for study in Turkey, Pakistan, and Saudi Arabia, but over time the Muslim Board has been required to take firm control of the process, in an effort to limit foreign study to those already enrolled in Uzbek madrasas. Abramson says some Uzbeks do manage to make their own way to study abroad, especially in Egypt.[67]

According to Abramson, Uzbek authorities recalled all their students enrolled through official channels in Turkey in 1997, allegedly because the Turks had allowed Uzbek opposition figure Muhammad Solih (head of *Erk partiyasi*) to operate freely there. Then Uzbek authorities became increasingly concerned over the rise of Islamist groups in Turkey, which is precisely how they interpreted the increasing popularity of the Welfare Party (then renamed the Virtue, and now the Justice and Development Party,[68] reorganizing itself after each legal ban) even before it took power in November 2002.

In 2000 Uzbek authorities closed all the Gulen schools, named for the Turkish theologian Fethullah Gulen.[69] Graduates of these schools and several hundred supporters of the Gulen began being arrested by Uzbek authorities in 2008, charged with membership in an extremist organization.

After the Tashkent bombings, the *Tablighi* movement from Pakistan was also banned from any missionary work in the country, and its schools were closed as well.[70]

While Uzbekistan has generally maintained good relations with the various Arab nations, as already noted, over time much stricter controls have been imposed over the money flows coming into religious organizations from that part of the world.

In the early days of independence, a small community of Uzbeks living in Saudi Arabia (those who were maintaining Central Asian *waqf* holdings at the time of the revolution, joined by *basmachis* or other religious migrants right after it), said to be a few thousand people, served as a source of helping fund the restoration of mosques and madrasas in their native regions. Many of these people were traders, and they also developed business interests in these areas, mostly small- and medium-size enterprises. In general, relations between the Saudi-based Uzbeks and the Karimov regime became much more strained after the bombings in Tashkent in February 1999.

New restrictions have also been placed on study in Egypt, the product of tougher measures on both the Uzbek and the Egyptian side. Like the Uzbeks, the Egyptians want more control over who is studying in their country, trying to avoid importing "radicals" from abroad. In addition, very few Uzbeks have the necessary Arabic language skills to successfully handle normal study at Al-Azhar.

Taken collectively, all of these restrictions—on study abroad; on access to religious education at home; on registration of clerics, mosques, and madrasas; on funding for religious institutions in general; on strong state supervision of the content of education and media—as well as the risk of strict punishment for any who fail to observe the laws that govern religious activity have helped shape the nature of Uzbekistan's religious revival. But even taken collectively, they have not made Uzbekistan's religious establishment a handmaiden of the state, nor have they substantially modified the nature of Islam in Uzbekistan.

9

THE RISE OF RADICAL ISLAM
IN UZBEKISTAN

At the end of the 1960s and the beginning of the 1970s, the post-World War II generation began reaching maturity, and they included a number of interesting religious figures. While some, such as Muhammad Sodiq Muhammad Yusuf, came from noted religious families, others, like Rahmatulla-alloma and Abduvali qori, came to the forefront without any particular family recommendation to open their doors. Most of these men were considered "radical" by their elders because they took issue with the political pacifism of the Stalin and Khrushchev-era clerics. Most saw the roots of this radicalism in the way that Hanafi Islam had evolved in Central Asia under colonial (that is, infidel) rule. While the teachings of these men eventually served as a source of inspiration for the Uzbek jihads of the 1990s, in the preceding decades, Soviet security officers were content to simply monitor the activities of these "radicals," believing that they posed no immediate political threat.

The new generation of Islamic leaders was keenly aware of their opportunity to spread the faith—an opportunity initially provided by the growing weakness of Soviet authorities, the seeming diffidence of local security forces charged with supervising religious affairs, and later by the even more tenuous hold on power by the newly independent Uzbekistan government.

These people had been relatively quiet during the years of the Soviet occupation in Afghanistan, when there was a real expectation in the West that Soviet power in Central Asia could be brought down if Islamist ideas were imported from Afghanistan into the region of Soviet Muslims.[1] Islamic leaders in the Soviet Union were well aware of unrest just beyond the Soviet borders, as tens of thousands passed through military service and hundreds if not thousands of Central Asians served as technical experts there. Many of the technical experts had contacts with Tajik, Uzbek, and Kyrgyz co-nationals in Afghanistan. Materials relating to the situation in Afghanistan found their way into the hands of interested recipients in Central Asia and throughout the Soviet Union.

The unsuccessful war in Afghanistan helped bring about the decline and collapse of Communist Party rule in the USSR, and it fed into the growing disaffection of Soviet youth. But it had only tangential impact on the growing religious revival in Central Asia until the beginning of the Tajik Civil War in 1992.

The younger generation of Islamist clerics, like Rahmatulla-alloma, Abduvali qori Mirzaev, and Obidkhon qori Nazarov—radicals who would later provide the ideological guideposts for the generation of jihadist fighters such as Tohir Yuldoshev and Juma Namangani—believed that the reintroduction of Islam was a process that could not proceed at a faster pace than society's capacity to absorb the message. This was an important point in common with Muhammadjon Hindustani. While these Islamic radicals disagreed with Hindustani's sense of the message to be conveyed, they also recognized important differences between Afghanistan and Central Asia. Central Asians were far better educated and far more secular than their Afghan counterparts; education was universal, and religious institutions had all but disappeared from public life. So the focus of Central Asia's small group of Islamists was on spreading the faith and creating some sort of public presence (albeit in smaller cities and communities in which the ethnic Russian presence was very small) to attract young people to the study of Islam and instill in them a missionary spirit.

The radicals, though, did not accept the need to revere the teachings of the older generation of *taqlidchis*. They rejected the notion that their interpretations of the Quran and the *hadiths* needed to be largely shaped by Hanafi teachings and the *fatwas* of Central Asian theologians over the centuries. Though always insisting that they remained true to the Hanafi school of law, the young radicals held the Quran and the *hadiths* as the core of the faith, deserving of being elevated above any later writings. They argued that this gave Islam the strength and flexibility necessary to remain a vital faith as human conditions changed.

These arguments were often over seemingly small things, but at stake was the respect for authority implicit in the Hanafi tradition. If this respect for authority was rejected, senior clerics would lose the ability to shape the practice of the faith. Even more important, the government would lose its traditional tool for maintaining control over religious authorities.

To outside observers, the early fights between Hindustani and Rahmatulla-alloma might seem inconsequential, but at the core of Rahmatulla-alloma's argument was his effort to focus attention on what was important in Islam, its central teachings. To make this point in a sermon that was offered during a celebration of *sunnat toy*, he took issue with the common practice of people asking *mullahs* to read a *dua* for the sick in hopes of curing them. The *mullahs* generally were happy to oblige and almost always received a monetary token of appreciation. Rahmatulla-alloma is reported to have said, "It is easier to go to a drugstore and buy aspirin or any other medical drug to get cured," a declaration that raised Hindustani's ire to the point that he traveled to Andijan in the summer of 1980 and organized a meeting with Rahmatulla-alloma, Abduvali qori, and Hakimjon qori, as well as other clerics from throughout the Ferghana Valley. Like most of Hindustani's activities, this would have gone on with the awareness of local security officials, who presumably had a way to learn about the content of the proceedings.

For Hindustani, any attempt at "modernism" was a rejection of the tenets of the faith. Radicals like Rahmatulla-alloma and Abduvali qori believed that just the opposite was true, that to deny the centrality of the Quran and the *hadiths* was to strip the faith of its real meaning and its dynamism. Their position was strongly influenced by the writings of theologians from the contemporary Arab world, at least as far as they were able to piece together their arguments through the books and pamphlets that made their way to Tashkent in the 1970s.

Hindustani worried about the prospect of a doctrinal split within Islam between the older generation and new innovators, the *Mujaddidiys*. He was also troubled by the political dimension of their theology, their implicit assumption that "true Islam" and Sharia could be implemented only in an Islamic state. For Hindustani and many of his generation who had lived under Stalin's reign, the greatest fear was associated with the annihilation of the faith, which they believed remained an ever-present risk under Soviet rule.

For Hindustani and many other Hanafi clerics, the focus was on maximizing adaptation toward highly unfavorable conditions, with the goal of preservation of religion; in this case, ensuring the transmission of knowledge while not irritating the atheist government.[2]

Shaped in part by the greater degree of openness in society, the postwar generation of theologians was initially guided by the sentiments of their elders. But as they grew older, they came to doubt the political acumen of the Stalin-era Hanafi clerics and grew more secure in their own political judgments, which in turn gave them greater freedom to experiment with new and seemingly more contemporary theological ideas.

Until the very end of Soviet rule, the Islamic radicals did not seek to directly challenge Soviet authorities. Men like Rahmatulla-alloma and Abduvali qori recognized that the majority of believers were quite content with the Hanafi traditions that shaped traditional religious practices. As a result, they confined their attention to trying to train a new generation of clerics who would be prepared to bring the fight to the community of believers, and in this fashion within a generation or two the nature of the religious community might be transformed. Only then would it make sense to engage directly with the atheistic rulers whose writ extended over Central Asia.

While Soviet security officials, at some levels at least, undoubtedly knew of the existence of the *hujras* and radical study circles run by these clerics, they did not feel the need to stop their activities, believing that monitoring them was sufficient protection for the regime, and that the activities wouldn't unnecessarily rile up the population. Retired KGB officials in 2003 through 2006 admitted that most of these circles included agents or informers, and there have been repeated rumors that Abduvali qori himself played that role for a certain period at least.

But everything changed as Soviet rule began to crumble in the early 1990s, in 1990 and 1991 in particular. Some of these radical Muslims must have looked around and realized that they were living in the midst of a political vacuum. This was truer of the cities of the Ferghana Valley than of Tashkent. And, like Lenin before them (an example that had been hammered into their heads since childhood), they decided that an attempt to seize power should be made at the very time when the population was becoming ideologically prepared to live in the new religious order that was being established.

So Abduvali qori and a group of like-minded clerics in Namangan set about trying to introduce Islamic law (either de jure or de facto depending upon the circumstances) in the communities in which they lived, hoping that this would serve as an important first step toward Sharia's gaining status at the national level. By now Hindustani was dead (he died in 1989), and the leading Hanafi figure was Mufti Muhammad Sodiq, who himself had a complex political agenda.

The most serious miscalculation that the Islamic radicals made was to underestimate the speed with which a strong secular authority could be reestablished. Frightened by what he witnessed in Namangan during the December 1991 presidential campaign, Islam Karimov made it an early priority to strengthen the presidency in order to isolate and defeat the Islamic radicals that he encountered during his trips to the Ferghana Valley and to stamp out as well those active in Tashkent before they grew too powerful.

Karimov was thwarted in part by the shifting landscape outside of Uzbekistan. Most of the clerics proved relatively easy to defeat—some, like Obidkhon qori, fled, others were jailed, and Abduvali qori just plain vanished. But the civil war in neighboring Tajikistan proved a magnet for some of their followers, such as Tohir Yuldoshev and Juma Namangani, the future leaders of the Islamic Movement of Uzbekistan, who wanted to wage war in the name of Islam. As described in the next chapter, the battlefield in Tajikistan became the precursor for joining the global terrorist struggle through Afghanistan. Through the present day, small groups of jihadists trained and based in Afghanistan continue to pose a threat to peace and stability in Uzbekistan and throughout the Central Asian region.

HINDUSTANI VERSUS THE YOUNG RADICALS

Hindustani is frequently depicted in Central Asian scholarship as the figure who played one of the most critical roles in laying the groundwork for the post-Soviet Islamic revival in Central Asia. His teachings are responsible for spreading and restoring faith among the disillusioned Soviet Central Asian population, and—even more important—inspiring young scholars of Islam, who later took Hindustani's teaching in different ways. One of Hindustani's students who deserves a special mention (for his major contribution to the development of Salafism and the dissemination of Salafist ideas in Central Asia) is Hakimjon qori of Margilan.

Hakimjon qori is generally viewed as a rather controversial figure whose theological views fluctuated greatly over his lifetime. After a period of intensive study under Hindustani, Hakimjon qori left his mentor as a result of a disagreement over the fundamental approach to Islam. While Hindustani maintained that he threw Hakimjon qori out, the latter claimed that he left of his own accord because he rejected Hindustani's conformist tendencies. "Mullah Muhammadjon is like a poplar in the field," Hakimjon qori is reported to have said. "He blows in the direction of the wind." But while too radical for Hindustani, by the late 1970s Hakimjon qori also began to seem to be too theoretical in his orientation and opposed to any direct confrontation with Soviet authorities. Frightened over potential retribution from the Soviet authorities for bringing up radical disciples and fomenting seditious Salafi ideas, Hakimjon qori reversed direction and began to oppose his "Wahhabi" followers.

This seems to have been the major reason that Rahmatulla-alloma and Abduvali qori, two "new generation" clerics who first studied with Hindustani and later with Hakimjon qori, distanced themselves from their teacher and established their own *hujras*. Both men seem to have been especially influenced by Abd Al-Wahhab's *at-Tawhid*, Sayyid Qutb's *Fi Zilalil Quron*, and Maududi's writings, which they became acquainted with as participants in an "underground" study group run by Egyptian exchange students in Tashkent in the late 1970s.[3] They had read some of these texts while studying with Hakimjon qori; later, after participating in these study circles, they came to interpret the texts differently. As a student of Rahmatulla-alloma later reflected about *at-Tawhid*:

> Allah aided Ibn Abd al-Wahhab in his work because Wahhab set before himself the task that God wished: to cleanse Islam by any means necessary of intolerable innovations and the domination of unbelievers.[4]

For Hakimjon qori, the point of contention was not the need to cleanse Islam, but the injunction to do so "by any means necessary." Although Hakimjon qori was willing to advocate the use of force in principle, he shared Hindustani's view that force should not be used against Soviet authorities. While the Soviet state might deem Islam its enemy, Islamic clerics could not risk labeling as their enemies the Soviet state or those who served it.

Hindustani's own words offer the best introduction to the ideology of the fundamentalists who opposed him. We find this in two outlets: first, a series of debates among Hindustani, Abduvali qori, and Rahmatulla-alloma that took place in 1980 (audiocassettes of the debates were obtained and preserved by Bakhtiyar Babadjanov). The other is Hindustani's "Letters in response to those who are introducing inadmissible innovations into religion," in which he is answering "unknown" critics. His letters were likely written in stages from 1984 to 1989.

Much of the fight between Hindustani and the young radicals was about what constituted innovation. For Hindustani, Hanafi Islam offered innovation by prompting religious thinkers to incorporate new ideas through the lens of past teachings, rather than by discarding those teachings and relying solely on the Quran and the *hadiths*.

Hindustani viewed his young critics as dangerous, terming them "Wahhabis." He spoke of the "alien quality" of the teachings of those "who have lost the true path" and who made themselves the enemies of Islam by threatening to divide the community of believers and who thus should be considered an enemy of Islam.

He feared the impact that "Wahhabi" demands and proposals would have on the local Islamic way of life and Hanafi daily customs, which they complained were in direct violation of the "true" way to perform the rituals as prescribed by the early Arabic texts they had been reading. Hindustani strongly opposed changing the ritual surrounding the offering of prayer among local Hanafi Muslims.[5]

Hindustani was also sharply critical of attempts by some to label certain popular customs and rituals "un-Islamic" or "heretical." These included the recitation of certain *ayats* from the Quran at funerals and for healing sick people—or even animals; the widespread practice among believers of worshipping "saints," treating their gravesites as shrines or holy places; and the local practice of accepting payment for recitation of the Quran.

It may be difficult for a Western audience to understand the importance of these two objections, for with each proposed innovation the radicals were, as Hindustani rightly accused them, of potentially introducing enormous rifts within the community. Prayer in mosques is very much a communal activity, and any deviation from accepted practice—be it the placement of hands or the recitation of a previously silent devotion—would be very jarring to all of those assembled and a glaring break with tradition. The same is true of changing the prayers always invoked at funerals. In both cases the intent is the same: to argue that what has been traditionally practiced is flawed and impure.

The Soviet invasion of Afghanistan was another area of disagreement, for even though the war in no way served as a rallying point for Central Asia's Islamic radicals, they definitely sympathized with the *mujahideen* cause. Hindustani's position was quite different and was characteristic of that of the Hanafi clerics more generally.

> You praise the Afghan *mujahids*, believing that they are waging a true jihad. But their jihad is the destruction of Muslim mosques, the murder of those who pray, the confiscation of people's property, the murder of women and children. Is this truly jihad? This is nothing other than the destruction of holy places and the annihilation of sacred things. In particular, an ancient robe of Allah's Prophet was preserved in Kandahar—may Allah bless and preserve it! And they burned it! Is this really holy jihad? No, not by any means! Why did they not accept Najibullah's peace proposals? Indeed, in the Quran it is written: "But if they incline toward peace, make peace with them." [Quran, 8:61] That is, in this *ayat* addressed to [the Prophet] Muhammad, it is said that if the unbelievers are inclined toward peace, then you should work for peace. So, even if you claim that those who live in Afghanistan are unfaithful, the [above-mentioned] command remains unchanged!"[6]

For Hindustani, and even those more radical among the older generation, like Hakimjon qori, the war in Afghanistan, though troubling, could not rise to the level of a personal grievance as it had no direct impact on their lives or those of believers in the Soviet Union. Even the younger generation of fundamentalists saw it as a further argument for jihad, at some remote time in the future. But the argument that it engendered left Hindustani very angry, because the young radicals had accused him of being a collaborator. For someone who had been incarcerated in the Stalin-era prison camps, this was a difficult charge to bear, and he fought back hard:

> It is a shame that you do not know our biography; if you knew, you would be more discriminating and just. In my life, I have been deprived of my freedom three times on the charge that I was inciting the people against the Soviet government. The first time I was sentenced to a year in prison, the second time to three years, and the third time—to 25 years. I suffered such deprivations for this anti-government activity! And yet you call on me to take up the jihad. You admonish me, as if I were lost in ignorance. But I have searched for 25 years to find knowledge. How long have you studied to call me ignorant? Shame on you and on those who taught you![7]

For Hindustani, both emotion and dogma were at issue. He rejected the young radicals' understanding of jihad; he believed that armed struggle was excluded except when physical survival was threatened. He chastised his young critics for extolling Dukchi Ishan, whose attempt at jihad in Andijan in 1898 led to the execution of all of its organizers and the exile of countless innocent followers and their families.

In his rebuke, Hindustani asserted that his critics lacked the proper understanding of jihad, which first demands that the believer deliver himself from ignorance:

> Do you know how many parts the jihad for the faith consists of? If one part is the jihad against unbelievers on the field of battle, then another is to cleanse oneself of evil thoughts and deliver oneself from ignorance. The Lord Prophet of Allah called this second part jihad-i Akbar, the greatest jihad. I, praise be to Allah, have also waged the "jihad of the tongue," and for this have been deprived of my freedom many times. And I have also imparted [religious] knowledge to so many people, delivering them from ignorance and turning them away from evil behavior.[8]

ABDUVALI QORI AND THE ANDIJAN RADICALS

Rahmatulla-alloma and Abduvali qori, the students of both Hindustani and Hakimjon qori, argued that Islam would not be preserved in Central Asia unless proponents of the faith were more aggressive. Rather than pursuing only clandestine activities, they sought new supporters by printing and distributing religious literature, which they would conceal under the book covers of Communist Party propaganda.[9] They also advocated a return to the external demeanor of the religiously devout—*hijab* for women; long hair, beards, and no ties for men—even if this made them stick out in secular schools.

By the mid-1980s, it was no longer courting immediate arrest to advocate such practices. And by the late 1980s, the legalization of cooperative-based trade associations and small private enterprises provided Islamic groups with ways of funding their activities.

Radical Islamic groups were strongest in Andijan and Namangan. In Andijan, it centered on Abduvali qori, whose supporters managed to secure control of a formerly desecrated mosque in 1990, along with an adjoining warehouse that was blocking access to it. Abduvali qori preached in the mosque through part of 1994. I visited the mosque twice, in 1992 and 1993, and missed meeting Abduvali qori, as he was out of the country, although I did get to visit at length with his deputy on both occasions.[10]

During his period as the imam of the mosque, he recorded some 87 audio cassettes with his lectures (*maruzas*) that include commentaries on the Quran and several *hadiths*.[11] Some of these "lessons" have been posted on Salafi-supported websites (although with considerable editing to make Abduvali qori appear more in line with a classic Salafi interpretation). Collections of his sermons have also been published in book and audio form in Central Asia and are sold clandestinely in Uzbekistan and openly in Kazakhstan and Kyrgyzstan. Finally, in 2002, a shortened version of these "lessons" was issued on a CD by his son, Abdulquddus ibn Abduvali qori. Bakhtiyar Babadjanov reports that all of these projects were probably underwritten by the Uzbeks in Saudi Arabia.

Abduvali's *tafsir* drew heavily on the interpretation of the Quran offered by Sayyid Qutb, and he referred to it as *Fi Zilalil az-Zilal*—a play on the title of Sayyid Qutb's commentary. Sayyid Qutb's commentary translates as "In the Shadow of the Quran," while Abduvali titled his work[12] "In the Shadow of the Shadow." According to Babadjanov, Abduvali qori uses his commentary to try to make a compelling case for theocratic rule, as opposed to secular government. Abduvali's lectures were not published in book form until more than a decade after his presumed death,[13] and were intended to provoke a debate on just what form of government Uzbekistan should have.

To make this point, Babadjanov provides sections from the commentary of the second *sura*, al-Baqara, in which Abduvali qori describes the nature of "divine power," according to which Uzbekistan's Muslims should live, and criticizes those who opt for secular rule.

From the commentary to *ayat* 61[14]:

> ... there are ... many "scholars" among us preferring to take the path of infidels instead of the prepared path of Allah. There are also those who instead of following the directions of Allah, call into the "great future."[15]

And Abduvali qori makes the point even more explicitly in his commentary to *ayat* 85[16]:

> ... there are other important directions of Allah that demand the Laws established by Him to be realized in all spheres of Muslims' lives ... and what is now realized of Allah's laws? Nothing! What rights do we Muslims have? No rights! Why are we being told that Islam must only be in our homes and in mosques? Why shouldn't Islam be in political spheres? Why is the state separated from Islam and Muslims?

He tries to goad his audience to action in his commentary to *ayat* 89,[17] when he likens their weakness to a loss of freedom:

> We Muslims have also left the path and Allah's commands, have forgotten the Quran. That is why we are very weak and Jews are ruling us. Other infidels are also ruling us. We are losing our faith and our freedom. If we cannot realize all directions of the Quran in our life in the nearest future, even monkeys will laugh at our situation.

There is frequent complaint about being "ruled by Jews" in much of the radical Islamic literature emanating from Uzbekistan in the 1990s, and rumors spread that Islam Karimov himself was Jewish [which he is not]. There are similar sentiments expressed in Abduvali qori's commentary to *ayat* 91[18]:

> Even now there are people among us that are like Jews. If we tell them that we should follow the Quran or some *hadiths*, then these people, who call themselves Muslims, reply that they follow the religion they received from their fathers and grandfathers.... How are they following their fathers and

grandfathers? They say that, supposedly, we make Islam our religion, but will follow a secular path of development. So, is this what our fathers and grandfathers said? So, did our fathers and grandfathers follow Western models of public and political systems? Or did our fathers and grandfathers sell our faith to Jews? Or did they let their women on the streets without *hijabs*?

And an explicit condemnation of secular rule from *ayat* 107[19]:

> Those who say that instead of the Great Quran and Sharia they chose different "imported" paths and [political] systems and say that "we will follow the path of secular development,"[20] those people, instead of believing in one Allah, believe in oppressors and trouble-makers...

But according to Bakhtiyar Babadjanov, even the radical Islamists like Abduvali qori and those advocating Islamic rule in Namangan envisioned the governance of Uzbekistan in terms of highly centralized power, thus echoing the historically popular idea that Uzbekistan must be ruled by a strong leader, a *podishoh* (king). He argues that the Uzbek Islamists understood that power on earth and in heaven belongs to Allah and that the representative of divine authority on this earth (a caliph) is an exponent of Allah's will and must rule strictly according to his laws.[21] In this way Babadjanov argues that the radical Islamist conception of the "ideal ruler as Allah's deputy" shared much in common with the centuries-old Hanafi understanding of a "Just *Podishoh*."

While absent from the Uzbek political scene for more than fifteen years, Abduvali qori has assumed something approaching iconic status for Uzbekistan's jihadists. Videos of his sermons were used in many of the Islamic Movement of Uzbekistan recruiting films made in Afghanistan and are on Jihadist websites, including Islam Nuri (www.islamnuri.com), as well as on YouTube.[22]

OBIDKHON QORI (NAZAROV), THE "FATHER" OF RADICAL ISLAM IN TASHKENT

Many of Abduvali's views were shared by his pupil and most prominent disciple, Obidkhon qori, who led the Tukhtaboy Vacha Mosque in the old city of Tashkent from 1990 to 1991 until he fled Uzbekistan in 1998. During 1992 and 1993, I was able to interview Obidkhon qori on three separate occasions.[23]

Obidkhon qori was born in 1958 to an observant family in Namangan.[24] Upon graduating from middle school in 1975, he served in the Soviet army in Saransk.[25] After the military service, he worked for some time at a repair plant in Namangan. He took correspondence courses and graduated from a commercial financial college, and then studied a year and a half at Abduvali qori's *hujra*. In 1984, he entered the Higher Islamic Institute in Tashkent. During his final years there, Obidkhon qori worked at the Tilla Sheikh Mosque as an imam's assistant. He bought a house in the old city of Tashkent and began to develop a reputation among Tashkent's religious activists, for the quality of his Quranic recitations.

Obidkhon qori was among the leaders of the demonstrations against Shamsuddin Bobokhonov in March 1989, and as a reward for these efforts Muhammad Sodiq appointed him the *imam-hatib* of the Tukhtaboy Vacha Mosque, which was badly in need of restoration at the time.[26] Obidkhon qori eagerly accepted the offer[27] and raised money from those living and working around the mosque and its complex in the old city for the rebuilding. He gained popularity and authority because of his bold sermons which voiced widely shared complaints against the government. He also spoke frequently of the need to honor Islam and Sharia norms. He was the last in Tashkent (and most elsewhere) to openly criticize the government in 1993 and 1994, when the government began to arrest clerics who were considered to hold radical views. In contrast to Muhammad Sodiq, who always took pleasure in the regal trappings of religious authority, such as embossed robes and fine head gear,[28] Obidkhon qori's personal style was quiet and modest. This style obviously helped him withstand arrest in these years, despite his large number of students and seemingly radical views. Helpful, too, was the fact that Obidkhon qori had sided with those who had sought to oust Muhammad Sodiq as *mufti* in 1992, putting him (at least temporarily) in the camp of Abdurashid Bahromov, the imam of Tilla Sheikh Mosque and the future *mufti* (appointed in 1995).

For a while the opposition (Bobokhonov-Bahromov group) seems to have toyed with the idea of putting forward Obidkhon qori as its choice for *mufti*, mistakenly viewing him as malleable and hoping that his roots in Namangan would make him acceptable to many in the Ferghana Valley. Bakhtiyar Babadjanov reports that Obidkhon qori strongly opposed this move, saying: "If you elect me *mufti*, you will push me into a gorge" (*Agar meni saylasangiz, meni jarga itargan bulasiz*), thus demonstrating his acute awareness of the balance of power in Uzbekistan's clerical and political arenas, and his own political skills.

Obidkhon qori's main priority in this period was to get Uzbek authorities to grant religion and Sharia law a defined and protected role in Uzbekistan's evolving political system. Both he and Abduvali qori sought to engage Uzbek authorities in these discussions. Obidkhon qori believed that the ultimate goal of all Muslims of the country should be complete realization (or restoration) of Sharia norms; the process, however, had to occur gradually, first at home, then in society, and finally enshrined in law.

He encouraged the formation of *jamoas* of five to ten people who would study the Quran and the basics of Sharia together for a few years, based on a course of study devised by Obidkhon qori.[29] This would equip them to reintroduce Islamic norms in their families and be involved in *davat* and recruiting new members, and eventually lead *jamoas* of their own.

According to Babadjanov, Obidkhon qori began talking about the need for *jamoas* in 1991, employing the traditional way that radical Islamic groups (and all different kinds of underground organizations) built and trained a membership. A few years later, he wrote a pamphlet, "*Jamoalarga yigilish musulmonlarga vojibdir*" (To gather/unite in communities is obligatory for Muslims).[30] In this essay, the author cites the *hadith* in regard to the early history of a Muslim community.

This pamphlet offers a Sharia-based defense of *jamoas* claiming, according to Babadjanov, that it was in such gatherings or communities that the first Muslims discussed their problems and formulated questions for the Prophet, resulting in the *Sunna* and providing the basis for the establishment of Islamic law. So by analogy, the author argues, in Uzbekistan, where most young people do not know the majority teachings of Islam or follow its law, Muslims should unite into *jamoas* and study Sharia under the guidance of those with more expertise in order "once again to bring Islam back into families and into the society." The author also carefully hints that the revival of Islam "in houses, at bazaars, on the streets, in public relations" would create conditions where Muslims "would have the happiness of praying in a mosque together with a *podishoh*" in what one may presume is a state in which Islam has been restored to its proper place.

Ruhiddin Fahriddinov, a former imam of the Samarkand Darvaza Mosque in the old city of Tashkent, became Obidkhon qori's deputy for work with the *jamoas*, and by 1993, *jamoas* had been organized beyond city limits into several communities in the Tashkent Oblast.[31] Ruhiddin was said to have also made the *jamoa* movement financially solvent by recruiting members who were merchants or traders and encouraging donations that formed the basis of a small trade to pay the movement's expenses associated with the purchase and reproduction of educational materials. By 1995, there seemed to have been sufficient funds for the movement to buy some apartments where members could live or hold meetings. It is unclear whether *jamoa* members had any interest in or training for undertaking violent actions against the state before Obidkhon qori and Ruhiddin Fahriddinov fled the country, a charge that Uzbek authorities subsequently levied against them. Members also got some training in martial arts, something that was common to most of the radical Islamic groups (and many other Uzbek youth at the time).

Obidkhon qori used his Friday noontime sermons as a platform for public education, making the case that Sharia should outweigh public norms of behavior. His message was often tailored to a particular audience. He urged businessmen to give *zakot* to the mosque and to legalize their commercial deals in the mosques rather than with public notaries, making the mosque the guarantor that the agreed conditions would be followed.[32] Obidkhon qori was also willing to collect *zakot* from the income of organized crime groups active in the old city, as long as they entered the mosque with the proper reverence.

According to local rumor, Obidkhon qori apparently publicly dismissed one local boss who asked Obidkhon qori to refrain from criticizing illegal trading as in violation of Islam. In response, Obidkhon qori retorted that no one should enter a mosque without an ablution (*tahorat*) and with a cigarette in his mouth, and then recounted the story the next week in his sermon, saying:

> I am not afraid of them [criminals], I only fear Allah. And I urge them to fear Allah as well.... What can they do to me? Beat me up or kill me. But they can't beat or kill Allah, can they?

For Obidkhon qori, fulfilling his responsibility of *davat* by bringing criminals to Islam superseded any responsibility to help secular authorities enforce their laws. While some communal elders seem to have been uncomfortable with Obidkhon qori's willingness to take alms for the mosque from almost anyone,[33] others were pleased that these sinners were returning to the mosque. For Obidkhon qori's purposes, though, businessmen on either side of the law were much the same, and both were obliged to pay *zakot*. He is reported to have said:

> ... if you are concealing payments from the state, you are concealing it from a state that we cannot accept as an example of divine governance. However, if you are concealing the *zakot*, you are hiding it from Allah. And you cannot hide anything from Him....

It was quite another thing, though, in Obidkhon qori's opinion for the state to abuse the law to attack innocent people. That is precisely what he argued was frequently done in the mid-1990s, when narcotics were sometimes planted on radical religious leaders, who were then arrested.[34] That tactic sufficed for authorities until the late 1990s, when the adoption of the new Law on Religion and changes in the criminal code provided legal grounds for stopping the activities of the radical religious leaders.

Obidkhon qori was one of the first to protest these fabrications organized by investigative organs of the Ministry of Internal Affairs and openly spoke about these cases in his Tilla Sheikh Mosque. Obidkhon qori even granted interviews to foreign journalists—something unheard of and very dangerous. An excerpt of a September 1995[35] interview survives as it was used in an IMU recruiting film "*Ular*" (Them).[36]

Obidkhon qori:

> *Bismilloh* [in the name of Allah] ... All this accusation of possessing drugs is, of course, unjust. On the contrary, we became witnesses to very frightening events.[37] I find it appropriate to mention this one comparison, even if some people might not like it much. Even in the former Soviet Union, we did not witness these things and only saw them after the Independence. Once again,

we see persecution of religious leaders, jailing, people disappearing, and so forth. We have not seen such things in the last 40–50 years of that world-famous Communist empire of the Soviet Union. But the government of Uzbekistan started a fight against common Muslims under pretense of fighting against religious extremism and fundamentalism. We express our negative attitude towards these events, and, at least, simply preserve our faith.

Obidkhon qori's public stance greatly increased his popularity, bringing into his mosque more people, especially younger Uzbeks, including many who had little interest in religion but who wanted to hear his take on the pressing social and political issues of the day. As most voices became silent on such issues, Obidkhon qori took on the issues with greater frequency, arguing that the state and its leaders could only gain moral standing by enhancing the role of Islam. As one former parishioner described him, Obidkhon qori was a "brave man who could openly express his critical attitude towards any actions of the regime."[38] For those who flocked to hear him, this was much more important than his stature as a theologian.[39]

RADICAL ISLAM IN NAMANGAN

In the late 1980s, Islamic institutions began increasing rapidly in the Ferghana Valley. By late 1991, Abdujabar Abduvahitov writes, the number of mosques and madrasas in Namangan had exceeded the pre-revolutionary number of 360 mosques and two madrasas, and he notes that hundreds of young men and women were getting advanced Islamic training in semi-clandestine madrasas.[40]

In Namangan, more than anywhere else in Uzbekistan, Islamic radicals threatened the continuation of secular rule by forming Islamic militia groups such as *Adolat* and *Islom lashkarlari*. In 1991, they even tried to press for Namangan to become either the center or at least an outpost of an Islamic state (*islomiy davlat*).

Adolat

Adolat[41] was formed in 1988 on the model of the Soviet *druzhinniki* (a nominally voluntary public order squad) to help protect Namangan merchants and traders from local racketeers.[42] By 1990 the group had come under the strong influence of Tohir Yuldoshev,[43] and by 1991 it had transformed itself into *Islom adolati* (Justice of Islam), or the *Islom lashkarlari* (also known as the *Islom militsiyasi*, or Police of Islam). By then all money collected was going to support the upkeep of the fighters, and toward religious training for them and others.[44]

Members of *Islom adolati* were asked to take an oath (*qasam*) or make a *bayonot* (statement): "… to promote by any means possible the establishment of the Sharia order in Namangan and then in the whole Uzbekistan."[45]

Their functions changed, too, going way beyond the kind of client-oriented protection with which they began. Patrols, composed primarily of young people, took responsibility for guarding the bazaars, catching petty thieves and punishing them by lashing. They also pressed merchants to close their stalls and go to the mosque for noontime prayers. Other patrols forced the closure of shops selling alcoholic beverages, as well as discothèques where people indulged in Western-style dancing or alcohol. They sometimes even turned up at weddings to press the celebrating families to stop dispensing alcoholic beverages. Despite lacking legal standing, they effectively functioned as an Islamic moral guard defending Sharia. Eventually some 2,000 members of *Islom adolati* accepted Tohir Yuldoshev's authority,[46] while Abduvahitov claims a membership of some 8,000, at the time of the group's dissolution in 1992.

Early efforts in 1990 and 1991 by local authorities to end *Adolat* groups' self-proclaimed writ fell flat. For example, in the Namangan region, prosecutor Chori Juraev opened 32 criminal cases against members of *Islom adolati* for murder, petty theft, assault, invasion of privacy, and other crimes. But the local security forces were too frightened to investigate. This was not surprising, as members of *Islom adolati* laid siege to the building of the prosecutor's office and confiscated case files as well as the weapons of the security force housed within the building. Then the prosecutor general was grabbed and beaten and was forced to apologize in front of the crowd and resign. As a crowd chanted *takbir*, saying "*Allahu akbar*," the case files were taken from the building by *Islom adolati* demonstrators and burned in the yard of the prosecutor's office.[47]

This success spurred members of *Islom adolati* into organizing what they called *yurishs* (from the Uzbek term *yurish*,[48] which was used to describe medieval military expeditions), including rallies in front of the city mayor's office. Given that throughout the last half of 1991 in particular it was becoming increasingly unclear who in fact held power anywhere in the USSR—the communists in Moscow, or the newly turned former communists in Tashkent—it was not terribly surprising that local authorities allowed power to slowly seep away to what had effectively become an armed Islamic opposition.

As Babadjanov points out in his interview notes, the members of *Islom adolati* did not call themselves *mujahideen* or describe their actions in terms of jihad. Initially their names were more of secular origin—*Faollar* (activists) or *Guruhlar* (groups). But by the end of 1991, several paramilitary groups started to call themselves *Islom lashkarlari*, reflecting their claim to be a "parallel power" in the city.

One of the things that kept secular authorities from losing complete control was the fact that there was no single preeminent religious figure accepted by all as their leader. Muhammad Sodiq was undoubtedly a power, but he was required to work with local leaders and sought to maintain control over the religious situation in Namangan through his various close associates. These included most prominently Umarkhon domla,[49] the *qadi* in Namangan, who among other things provided the personal security force for Muhammad Sodiq, some 20 men, all said to have had black belts in karate. His appointment as *qadi* by Muhammad Sodiq was said to have been in recognition of the key role that Umarkhon domla had carved out for himself.

"Who's Who" in Namangan: Umarkhon domla

Umarkhon domla was a characteristically Namangani kind of religious figure, with very little secular education but with extensive religious training. This included four years of religious instruction in a *hujra* school run by his relatives in Namangan; a period of study with Hakimjon qori in Margilan, where he was reputed to have been one of the top students; and then two years (1980–1982) of study with Zokirjon domla in Tashkent, a well-known Hanafi theologian who also served as a teacher for Obidkhon qori.[50] But despite his broad religious education, Umarkhon domla failed to gain admission to the Mir-i Arab Madrasa in Bukhara because he reportedly could not pass the (secular) subjects of dictation and history. The failing grade in history, though, may have been a reflection of his theocratic worldview that the only history that matters is sacral, and that it can be preserved only in oral form.

Without formal madrasa training, Umarkhon domla was forced to earn his living in the secular world, eventually enjoying success as a baker, with his own profitable bakery, until 1986[51] when he became imam of a mosque in Namangan. But alongside his bakery, Umarkhon domla ran a *hujra* school, providing young children and adolescents with basic instruction in Hanafi Islam.

Umarkhon domla's closest followers called him "*Sher*" (lion, or brave one), because of a bold but unsuccessful campaign in 1986 to get the first secretary of the regional Communist Party to return the former main mosque of Namangan city (then used as a winery) to the Spiritual Administration of the Muslims of Central Asia and Kazakhstan.

Beginning in 1990, he organized a debating club in his mosque. Each Saturday the club held a forum in which his radical Hanafi supporters debated religious questions with youths termed "Wahhabis." He began organizing training in karate and kung fu for young men studying in his mosque in case the arguments turned nasty later outside. Those who attended these meetings maintain that Tohir Yuldoshev was a frequent participant and that he often took Umarkhon domla's part in the argument.

The real relationship between the two men is under question. Umarkhon and his defenders obviously have reason to cast it in as negative a light as possible, but some in Namangan argue that Umarkhon domla had a strong influence on the evolution of *Adolat* from its early incarnation as a self-defense group into *Islom adolati*, when it became an instrument for delivering justice as well. In the latter period, Umarkhon domla is even said to have even written some of the verdicts based on Sharia that were pinned to the bodies of those who received punishment. In fact, at least one of the regular participants in these Saturday meetings maintains that the very idea of pressing for the establishment of an Islamic state came to Tohir Yuldoshev from Umarkhon domla at one of these sessions.

Umarkhon domla maintains that he always viewed Tohir Yuldoshev as having "excessive ambition and love of authority" and that he wrote these verdicts only at Tohir Yuldoshev's insistence.[52]

Umarkhon domla was arrested in November 1993 and charged with abuse of office. He was convicted and imprisoned until November 2002.[53] He now is formally employed as a farmhand but in reality is very much a gentleman-farmer/cleric, with followers and students working his land. He still seems to enjoy a great deal of respect from devout Hanafi Muslims in the Namangan region. Ironically, Umarkhon domla served in the same prison as Abdulahad Barnaev, the Wahhabi leader, and upon his release the former commented that only in prison did the two come to understand that the split between them had worked against the interests of Islam.

Abduraufkhon Gafurov

Abdurauf Gafurov was another important actor in the religious life of Namangan and was a close associate of Muhammad Sodiq, serving as the formal representative of SADUM in Namangan during much of this period. The two began working together in 1986. Gafurov was born in 1947 in Namangan, grew up in an observant family, and got training in trade and finance, a potentially lucrative sector even in Soviet times. He was director of the oblast wood shop and wood storage facility, enabling him to "help out" enterprises throughout the oblast to meet state quotas; had they depended upon their state allocations of wood, the quotas would have gone unmet.

Gafurov, who until 1985 also served as a member of the Soviet executive committee in Namangan, was generally regarded as one of Namangan's "underground" millionaires when the Soviet Union collapsed and was said to be a close associate and supporter of Shukrullo Mirsaidov.[54] Gafurov was also on good terms with Burgutali Rafikov, then *hokim* (regional governor) of Namangan, and he used his various ties to build a local light industry empire in the late 1980s and early 1990s, owning furniture, textile, and candy factories.

Using his own funds,[55] he paid for the construction of a huge mosque in the Namangan suburb of Nurobod, said to cost twice the annual budget of Namangan Oblast. The mosque was opened by Islam Karimov in December 1991, during the same visit that Karimov appeared in the "captured" regional government committee building described below.

Babadjanov reports that Karimov's address at the Nurobod Mosque was designed to reassure local entrepreneurs that his government would not renationalize the private property that they had accumulated as the Soviet regime was collapsing. For the business community in the Ferghana Valley, protection of property was the key question in deciding to whom to throw their support. They had to decide whether to trust the old Communist Party as represented by Karimov, Muhammad Sodiq, and the SADUM crowd, or Abduvali qori, who had a lot of support in the business community of Andijan but who had preached sermons saying that the Bolsheviks stole their egalitarian ideas from the teachings of Islam.[56]

Gafurov had built a "light-industry empire" through his contacts, and his financial skills were an important acquisition for SADUM.[57] In 1989, he was named *qadi* of the Ferghana Valley (which included all three oblasts), where he served as SADUM's chief financial officer in the region, monitoring all the financial donations received by the local mosques. He also supervised the *hajj* process for the region, sending on the names of those chosen to go from all nominations and collecting all fees. It was hoped that he might be able to use the office to create a greater sense of unity among the competing clerics. Little came of his efforts, however, as he was on good terms with Hanafi clerics but was also rumored to be helping, through middlemen, to fund a substantial part of the cost of Tohir Yuldoshev's *Islom adolati* patrols.

Abdulahad Barnaev

Abdulahad Barnaev, the imam of the Gumbaz Mosque from the time of its opening to his arrest in 1993, was another leading figure in Namangan. Abdulahad was born in 1959 in Namangan, and was described by his high school classmates as physically weak and beaten up a lot when he tried to assert himself. According to his sister,[58] Abdulahad turned to his grandfather to teach him about Islam in his search for comfort. After his army service, he worked in a local automotive repair shop, remaining there for seven years until 1985, when he went to Andijan to study with Abduvali qori. After two years in Andijan, he returned home to open his own *hujra* school, which received financial support from Abduvali qori.

In 1988 he and his students, some armed, were successful in occupying and gaining control of the Gumbaz mosque in Namangan. They refused to turn over the mosque to the jurisdiction of SADUM and physically barred supporters of Umarkhon domla from taking control of the property. The central location of this mosque also afforded physical control of much of downtown Namangan and was used as a gathering point before the major demonstrations in downtown Namangan. But it is not clear whether Abduhakim (Hakimjon) Sattimov and Tohir Yuldoshev either formally supported Abdulahad or were formally supported by him.

Abdulahad and his supporters were directly involved in the large demonstration in front of the Namangan Regional Communist Party Committee building in 1990, demanding that the city legalize the wearing of *hijab* and forbid the employment of women. Abdulahad has always maintained that Sattimov and Yuldoshev bore sole responsibility for the seizure of the Regional Communist Party Committee building in Namangan in December 1991.[59]

One argument in support of this is that although Abdulahad lost control of the Gumbaz mosque (which was given to the Uzbek religious administration) shortly after Abduvali qori disappeared in 1995, he was not arrested until 1997. When he was arrested, he was sentenced to seventeen years in prison and served two years. Sufficiently scarred from this experience, he lives quietly in Namangan and runs a candy shop.[60]

At least some local informants argue that the lack of direct engagement between Abdulahad and the youth mobilized by Tohir Yuldoshev and Sattimov was a question of perception rather than reality. This version claims that Abduvali qori urged Abdulahad to preserve the seeming independence of the Gumbaz Mosque and Madrasa so that the large basements in the building that they occupied before 1989 (when they moved completely into the former winery) could be used for paramilitary training of youth. It is possible that the facilities were used for the training of the first group of "*Tavba*," the paramilitary arm of the Uzbek branch of the Islamic Renaissance Party. Eventually, the Uzbek branch of the IRP came under the direction of Abdulla Utaev, another former student of Abduvali qori. Their activities were largely centered in Tashkent.

Dovudkhon Ortikov

Dovudkhon Ortikov is another very prominent cleric of Namangan. Though it is debated as to whether he was born in 1929 or 1931, he was the only leading cleric in that city who remembered the Stalin era. A Sufi of the Qadiriya order, he claimed descent from Affak Khoja (who lived in Kashgar in the seventeenth century). He is the grandson of Mavlon Khan-tura, and the son of Ishan Khan-tura.[61] His uncle, Abdulboki Khan-tura, served as his lifelong teacher.

He led the Aziz Khoja Eshon Mosque and Madrasa, which was reopened in 1990, funded mostly by neighbors who were living on former *waqf* lands that had once belonged to the mosque and madrasa. (The neighbors were pressed into funding the mosque because of vague threats that the lands could be seized by radical clerics.) An ardent anti-communist, Dovudkhon used his Friday sermons to plead for Islam's return to the center of local society. His mosque and madrasa were meeting places for all young Muslims, regardless of their religious focus. In fact, when I visited him there in 1992, a group of young *Islom adolati* supporters, including quite probably Juma Namangani, were sitting in one of the outer rooms, and during at least one Friday service Tohir Yuldoshev was invited to come forward and sit with the elders and authoritative *ulama* of Namangan.

Just how close Dovudkhon was to those who seized the regional headquarters is a topic of conjecture. A frail old man at the time the book was written, arrested and released numerous times in the early 1990s,[62] he was enigmatic about his role during those years. Claiming that it was partly the product of the times, he said to Bakhtiyar Babadjanov nearly fifteen years after the events in question:

> Then we were all fighting roosters. We tried to finally remove Communists from everywhere, as we thought that the time of Islam had arrived. But I did not understand anything, although clever people warned me that all our rash steps and actions would end badly.

But when interviewed in 2003 and 2004, Dovudkhon still was willing to cautiously talk about the need for Islam to play more of a political role in Uzbekistan. Answering a question as to whether Sufism should be occupied with political activity and concern itself generally with worldly matters, he said, "Sufis are obligated to be concerned with Sharia law and press for Sharia to be the law of the country." But he added that he has learned that this can be done only by working with rulers and pointing them on the way to the Sharia, much like Khoja Ahror, "who was advisor to many *podishohs*, and even Timur listened to him." (In fact, Timur died in 1405, before Khoja Ahror was born.)

THE NAMANGAN MEETING

The "who's who" of Namangan religious politics becomes important for two reasons: because Islamic groups came closest to seizing power in Namangan, and because they failed to do so.

A lot of what we know about what was going on in Namangan in late 1991 and the role of various actors (Muhammad Sodiq, Umarkhon domla, Dovudkhon, Tohir Yuldoshev, and his young soldiers) centers around the seizure of the regional committee building in Namangan that had been occupied by Tohir Yuldoshev's soldiers (the *Islom lashkarlari*). While under occupation, this building was the site of an election meeting with President Karimov on December 19, 1991. In addition to the film (and transcript) of Karimov's meeting there, we have interviews with eyewitnesses to the event.

This meeting, as well as Karimov's December 1991 visit to Namangan, is worth studying in depth in order to understand the evolution of Karimov's policies toward Islam and the different forces that acted upon him.

While some claimed that Karimov's antipathy to Islamic radicals was a result of their having humbled him in Namangan, it is more likely that Karimov came away from Namangan with a new appreciation of the strength of those committed to radical Islamic causes.

Committed to staying in office and preserving Uzbekistan's sovereignty, Karimov used his speech at the meeting to characterize himself as supportive of Islam, promising to be sworn in as president on the Quran (which he was) and to allow his presidency to be blessed with prayers. In response to demands from the crowd that an Islamic republic be created in Uzbekistan, he responded that this would depend on what was decided by the country's elected officials (the reference here is clearly to parliamentarians who would be elected after the current parliament was disbanded).

While it is beyond improbable that Karimov would have assented to the establishment of an Islamic republic in Uzbekistan, his statement allowed him to gauge the seriousness with which the request was viewed by those at the gathering.

Muhammad Sodiq is said to have warned other clerics (in a meeting that included Umarkhon domla and Obidkhon qori) that he feared that Tohir Yuldoshev would go too far at the meeting and could lead to the Islamic establishment's being discredited before the authorities. In Namangan just before the meeting, he is said to have warned his colleagues to stay away:

> ... I am telling you that we are still weak, but they [the secular authorities] are still strong and tomorrow they can break your horns. So be careful. Understand that right now our main task is to learn to be more skillful, in order to be able to return Islam to its true home. Forceful actions on your part can discredit us, making [the authorities] afraid of us. Islam must be introduced quietly.[63]

I learned about this meeting of clerics from an account by Rahimjon Akramov,[64] who then served as the provincial monitor on religious questions.

While Umarkhon domla and Muhammad Sodiq seem to have been silenced by Akramov's arrival, Obidkhon qori broke the silence by saying that "I think that we shouldn't be afraid to show them our strength."

This was sufficient for Akramov to pick up the thread of the preceding conversation, and he then asked Muhammad Sodiq directly, "Do you think that it is right for you [meaning the religious elite, and not just Muhammad Sodiq] to interfere in politics at a time when the country is going through difficult times?"

Everyone apparently turned to Muhammad Sodiq in anticipation of his answer, and he said, "No, it's better to refrain from politics." But Akramov maintains that the startled look on everyone's faces was proof enough for him that Muhammad Sodiq had reversed his earlier position. Regardless, Muhammad Sodiq did not attend the meeting with Karimov, as he clearly believed that to do so would undermine his position and by doing so end all prospect of unity within Uzbekistan's Muslim leadership.

Young fighters from *Islom adolati*, having already taken over the city mayor's office (the old regional Communist Party headquarters), gathered a crowd in the square outside the building and the young fighters filled the building's inner courtyard. They invited Uzbekistan's president to hear their demands.

When Karimov entered the courtyard, he was greeted with chants of "Allahu akbar."[65] Throughout the meeting, Tohir Yuldoshev comported himself as if he and not Karimov was in charge, a slight Karimov undoubtedly never forgot. When Karimov tried to take the microphone to address the people, Yuldoshev sought to shove him away and yelled for the benefit of the crowd: "No! I am the master here yet! You will speak here, but only when I let you. As for now, you keep silent and listen," while the *Islom adolati* fighters started to chant *takbir* so loudly to drown out Karimov that many people covered their ears.

Then, after some general phrases, Karimov was presented with the demands, which Tohir Yuldoshev read aloud. These demands were written on a single scrap of paper and then passed to the front from back rows where religious leaders of the city were sitting. The demands included the following points: to declare Uzbekistan an Islamic state; to dissolve the parliament; to nominate a Muslim leader as a presidential candidate;[66] to transfer the seized building to the rally participants to establish a "Sharia center" and to use it as an office for the "Islamic party"; and to disallow men to work in medical centers where women give birth.[67]

Yuldoshev, though, then effectively lost control of the meeting to senior community leaders (one presumes many were elders from Namangan's leading *mahalla*) representing city residents who had been gathering outside (some twenty thousand by this time), and they, too, had a list of demands for Uzbekistan's president. When Yuldoshev initially refused to accept their list, the community leaders threatened to hold their own rally. They were not mollified by Yuldoshev's response that an Islamic state and Sharia should be introduced first, and that then their problems would solve themselves. They said, "Tohirjon, these demands that you announced are your demands. And now we demand ours to be read."[68] Yuldoshev consulted with religious leaders and immediately read the demands of city residents, which were of an exclusively economic nature, such as increasing salaries and stabilizing food prices.

Islam Karimov must have been taking in the local drama playing out around him, and that made it easier for him to deliver his address, which focused on economic problems that had become acute since the collapse of the USSR. As for the political and religious demands, Karimov declared that he could not decide those issues by himself and that any change needed to be done according to accepted political rules, including, if necessary, a country-wide referendum. The content of the speech satisfied enough of those gathered, and the rally broke up soon afterward. The Uzbek president emerging unscathed but determined to ensure that he never faced a similar situation.

Once the December presidential elections were completed, the government moved against *Adolat* and its various offshoots. In relatively quick order, Karimov's government reasserted control over Namangan, although small public protests continued for a while.

Upon Karimov's return to Tashkent, however, a list of 71 local activists was circulated, and nineteen who were alleged to be members of the Islamic Renaissance Party were arrested in a crackdown that was now broadened to any groups that might be considered Islamic "extremists." In June 1992, a second Islamic defense group in Namangan, the *Islom lashkarlari*, was banned, and a Congress of Muslim Intelligentsia was forbidden to hold an organizing session, because of the group's alleged ties with the IRP.[69]

For all this pressure, however, when I traveled to the area in March 1992, the Islamic revivalists whom I interviewed described their situation as stable, although of course they were highly critical of Karimov's government. When I interviewed these same leaders in May and August 1992, they were far more positive about the local situation in the Ferghana Valley, largely because they now perceived themselves as having the support of Mufti Muhammad Sodiq. They believed that SADUM provided them with a new and strong umbrella under which their proselytizing could continue.

Throughout 1992 and most of 1993, the government's campaign against Islamic activists intensified. Several key activists were arrested, although the spiritual leaders of the main revivalist mosques managed to avoid arrest by scrupulously maintaining a politically neutral public posture. Given the support that the religious leaders in the Ferghana Valley commanded, Karimov was somewhat more tentative in his treatment of Islamic activists than he was of secular democrats, but by 1994 and 1995 he felt confident enough to begin arresting most of the prominent radical Muslim leaders left in the country.[70]

In a kind of spiral, the government continued to keep pressure on those identified as religious activists throughout the mid- and late 1990s, as well as broadening the definition of what constitutes extremism. As jihadist groups crossing into Uzbekistan from Tajikistan and Afghanistan became bolder, radical Islamic groups did not have difficulty recruiting new members.

As the next chapter details, the radical Islamic groups did not disappear. Some disbanded, and some were reconstituted in neighboring Tajikistan, where they took the name of the Islamic Movement of Uzbekistan. Many sympathizers of the radical clerics' agenda were content to remain outside of any organized movements but still supported the idea that Islam must return to its "proper" place, as a legal and not just a moral beacon of independent Uzbekistan.

10

THE ISLAMIC MOVEMENT OF UZBEKISTAN
IN TAJIKISTAN AND AFGHANISTAN

This chapter looks at the role of the Islamic Movement of Uzbekistan prior to the U.S.-led military operation in Afghanistan. While Uzbekistan's radical Islamists were unable to coalesce into a sustainable political movement in the Ferghana Valley, they did achieve this aim once they fled to Tajikistan, recruiting fighters from Uzbekistan to fight alongside their Muslim brethren in the Islamic Renaissance Party. Through their participation in the Tajik Civil War, leaders of the IMU, as they began to call themselves, were able to deepen their contacts with global Islamist forces and gained access to elite strata in Muslim countries supporting the IRP cause.

The IMU built its strongest ties with Islamist groups in Afghanistan, and through them with Pakistani groups. It also made contacts in Turkey and Iran. In Saudi Arabia, it was able to take advantage of the small Uzbek expatriate community as an additional point of contact.[1] When the IRP agreed to participate in Tajikistan's National Reconciliation Agreement in 1997, the IMU began to focus more on turning itself into a jihadist group targeting Uzbekistan as its first priority in order to end President Islam Karimov's rule and replace it with an Islamic order.

From 1998 on, the IMU was an increasingly inconvenient guest in Tajikistan, where it was relatively easy to receive the small but steady stream of recruits who were coming, sometimes with families, to live and train in its camps. Some of these recruits had received minimal training while still in Uzbekistan. Once in the Tajik camps, they were given more systematic paramilitary preparation, as well as religious instruction.

After a string of IMU operations in Uzbekistan in 1999, and in the Batken area of Kyrgyzstan in 1999 and 2000, the IMU fled to Afghanistan. There, the IMU made common cause with the Taliban,[2] and largely through them with al-Qaeda (separately, they had some access to al-Qaeda through Uzbeks living in Saudi Arabia). This was partly because Afghanistan's Northern Alliance, which had a Tajik majority and included many ethnic Uzbeks, was now more closely tied to the governments in Central Asia and Russia and would no longer permit the IMU to live in alliance-controlled territories.

The behavior of the IMU in Afghanistan, and their alliance with the Taliban and financial support from al-Qaeda, raises the question of whether the leaders of the IMU were committed jihadists, or simply pro-Islamic soldiers of fortune. Uzbek critics of Juma Namangani and Tohir Yuldoshev have long maintained that both men saw their "Islamic revolutionary principles" as a path to financial gain. In Yuldoshev's case there was also the seeming lust for political power.

The alliance with al-Qaeda brought a great deal more money to the IMU's leaders. While in Afghanistan, the IMU set up more elaborate camps. The IMU leadership also became more aggressive in recruiting potential fighters from Uzbekistan, as they seem to have been paid money for each new recruit they brought to the camps. Competition over the control of this money deepened tensions between Yuldoshev and Namangani, as well as between their various subordinates. While some IMU fighters returned home during amnesties offered by Uzbek authorities, and others fled after September 11 when a U.S.-led invasion of Afghanistan seemed imminent, most remained in Afghanistan and fought against the NATO forces. By the time the Karzai government took power in 2004, Juma Namangani, the IMU's military leader, was dead and the IMU had lost its organizational integrity. With this, the first phase of jihadist struggle in Uzbekistan effectively came to an end.

This chapter draws extensively on primary source material from both documents (including notebooks from IMU training camps) and video recordings made by the IMU that were collected in Uzbekistan, as well as by Western sources in Afghanistan.[3] It also draws on my interviews in the Ferghana Valley over the past twenty years, including with several former IMU fighters who returned to Uzbekistan under the framework of the government-sponsored amnesty program.

THE CIVIL WAR IN TAJIKISTAN AND THE RISE OF THE IMU

Many Islamists in the Ferghana Valley felt that their faith obliged them to join the Tajik fighters. And their motivation only increased from late 1992 through 1997, when the IRP had already been defeated and its leadership was in hiding, and those who supported its cause effectively became guerrilla fighters.

Uzbekistan's Islamists clearly sympathized with the IRP, whose battle they saw as a form of jihad. Uzbekistan's Islamists saw something of a romance in violence, a product of the overwhelming sense of anarchy that surrounded the collapse of the Soviet Union, empowering people to dream about goals that had previously seemed not merely improbable but impossible.

The views held by the leadership of the IRP, who fought in the Tajik Civil War as part of a unified Islamic group (known as the United Tajik Opposition), were in fact more nuanced than their Uzbek colleagues often appreciated. The IRP was fighting for the right to have the legal status of a political party, with the appropriate legal protections that this status would confer. It was also fighting to gain a role in government (particularly in the social and educational sector) and to use this leverage to help bring the population to a greater awareness of Islam.

For Muhammad Sodiq Muhammad Yusuf, though, the question of whom to support among the Tajik Islamists, and how to provide that support, was never simple. As *mufti*, he was a member of Uzbekistan's establishment, a position he believed was both in his interest and that of Uzbekistan's Muslim community for him to retain. At the same time, he seems to have had strong ties to the IRP. That is not surprising, given his friendship with the IRP's Akbar Turajonzoda, with whom he had studied, as well as his sincere conviction that a victory by the Tajik Islamists would serve as an important precedent for Uzbekistan, prodding the country's much stronger secular leadership into some sort of power sharing relationship with "moderate" Islamists such as himself.

Eyewitnesses in Namangan told Bakhtiyar Babadjanov that Muhammad Sodiq organized the collection of money, food, and other durables to be sent to "the aid of the Tajik brother Muslims," through the auspices of Umarkhon domla. At least one person, Rahimjon Akramov, who served in the local administration during these years, maintains that guns were included in these shipments.

This allegation, of course, cannot be substantiated, nor can the account of Saifullo Dalilov[4] verify these rumors. He maintains that Muhammad Sodiq visited Turajonzoda while Dalilov was held captive by Tajik opposition members and secured his release.

Although it is likely that Muhammad Sodiq maintained ties with Turajonzoda during Tajikistan's civil war and probably even aided the IRP cause surreptitiously, there is absolutely no evidence suggesting that Muhammad Sodiq ever supported Tohir Yuldoshev or the IMU. In fact, all the evidence points to the opposite conclusion, that the former *mufti*, proud of his extensive theological training, always viewed the largely self-taught Yuldoshev as a religious charlatan.[5]

It is hard to know how many hundreds or thousands of youths went to Tajikistan to fight with the IMU in the mid-1990s. It seems certain that it was fewer than ten thousand, but as many as five thousand at some point may have gone off to fight with the IMU or in one of the other "jihadist" fronts in the region.

After Tajikistan, the most popular place for young fighters to go was Chechnya, where a full-fledged war was waged from 1994 to 1996. The Chechen cause quickly became the rallying cry for recruiting fighters to a global jihad. The Jordanian fighter Khattab[6] came to help organize in the North Caucasus and traveled among the IMU to get its members to join in the fight as well. It appears that a few hundred members of the IMU fought in Chechnya in the late 1900s, although in the one firsthand account I received from a former IMU member, most were largely press-ganged into it, as their true battle, he said, was with their own local authorities.

In the mid-1990s, the appeal of global jihad was really quite limited in Central Asia. Even today, it would likely be difficult to recruit fighters for causes that had no direct applicability to changing the conditions of their own lives or those of their families.

This was also true of much of the IMU leadership. Tohir Yuldoshev seems to have always viewed the situation in Tajikistan as little more than a training ground to prepare the forces that would be necessary to take power in Uzbekistan. He took on responsibility for their ideological preparation. For that reason it is rather ironic that after his camps were bombed by NATO's International Security Assistance Force (ISAF), he was swept up into the global jihad in Afghanistan and seems to have had little or any role in preparing the small groups of fighters that have crossed into Central Asia since the beginning of the ISAF operation.

By contrast, Juma Namangani, a former paratrooper who served in Afghanistan, was the real fighter of these two Uzbek IMU leaders. He seems to have focused on whatever battlefield life presented, going to Tajikistan to help those whose cause he sympathized with, and, after the truce in Tajikistan was announced, keeping the dream of jihad alive by operating out of Kunduz from 1996. He attracted the Taliban's attention in 1998, when they took control of the Kunduz region, and he wound up dying to defend the Taliban.[7]

When the war in Tajikistan began petering out, both Juma Namangani and Tohir Yuldoshev faced the problem of raising money to fund their militant activities. One of the former IMU members we met recalls meetings with Abdukadir Margiloniy in 1995 or 1996. Margiloniy was from a Margilan family that lived in Saudi Arabia throughout the Soviet period and collected money from Uzbek entrepreneurs living in Saudi Arabia[8] to make a "holy war" at home. It is hard to know just how wealthy these people were, and how much support they actually sent, but in the early to mid-1990s very small amounts of hard currency went very far toward the purchase of weapons, ammunition, and means of transport.

There have long been accounts of Juma Namangani in particular having provided protection for the drug trade from Afghanistan across Tajikistan and from there through Central Asia and on to Russia and Europe, and using the money collected to fund his operations.

In addition, Namangani is said to have traveled to Saudi Arabia, and Yuldoshev spent much of his time in Pakistan, where he was able to dispatch a few of his fighters at least for training. I have in my possession[9] a copy of an October 7, 1996, letter (in Arabic) to the Peshawar madrasa al-Haqqani, with the seal of the Uzbekistan Mujahideen Center and signed by Tohir Yuldoshev, sending four people (one from Uzbekistan and three from Dagestan) to Pakistan to study. It was apparently very difficult to get assigned to madrasa study. One of the former IMU fighters complained that he was refused permission to study in Peshawar;[10] the explanation he was offered was that he was to remain a fighter instead.

Turkey was also a leading transit point through which guns, money, and human traffic flowed to the IMU. We know about some of the meetings because Uzbek intelligence was tailing prominent members of the IMU, including Tohir Yuldoshev. In those years, Yuldoshev also tried to recruit support from Muhammad Solih (head of *Erk*) and Abdurahim Pulat (head of *Birlik*). After long denying it, both now admit that these meetings took place, and both claim that they refused Yuldoshev's offer of the post of prime minister in his future government.[11] These meetings seem surreal when viewed from an outsider's prism, as it is hard to believe that either Solih or Pulat believed Yuldoshev had any serious likelihood of ousting Karimov. Maybe they didn't but saw this as a way to demonstrate that they were not too secular to be religious donors. It is entirely possible that some of the same Turkish sources aiding the IMU gave money to *Erk* and *Birlik*, using the logic that any group seeking to undermine the Karimov regime was their friend.

THE IMU PREPARES ITS FIGHTERS[12]

The IMU appears to have operated some small training facilities in Uzbekistan in the mid-1990s and larger camps in Tajikistan, and also to have tried to recruit people through circulating materials explaining the IMU's mission of jihad.

There appear to have been "Ten Lessons on Jihad." In total we were able to find two types of handwritten documents, a computer printout, and two audiotapes containing only four of the "lessons" (starting approximately from the middle of the second lesson). The text came into Bakhtiyar Babadjanov's possession in 2000 or 2001,[13] but it appears to have been written much earlier, prior to 1997,[14] given the reference to IRP leaders in Afghanistan. It is very likely that the materials in this text are the "teacher's notes" for those providing instruction on jihad to the individuals who took notes in the notebooks referred to above.

The materials in the lessons that Babadjanov and I have in our possession are extremely primitive in their content and are written in a style that imitates the structure of authentic religious literature—a tenet, followed by the commentary. In reality, however, the author had limited religious education, having virtually no knowledge of classical Islamic writings on jihad. The materials are definitely Uzbek in origin, given how much local knowledge is displayed. They also contain stylistic and grammatical errors.[15]

It is Babadjanov's belief that Juma Namangani was the author of these "lessons on jihad" or at least recorded them on the tapes, as many people for whom Babadjanov played the tapes while doing research in the Ferghana Valley said they recognized the voice on the tape as Namangani's.[16] It is equally plausible to me that Tohir Yuldoshev was the author or one of the authors, given the pretense of religious learning in the style of presentation. In videocassettes of sermons recorded in Afghanistan, Yuldoshev liked displaying himself as a learned cleric. Yuldoshev is probably not the reader on the tapes, as his voice is easily recognizable from the Afghan videocassettes. It is also not possible that Abduvali qori or Obidkhon qori was the author or the reader. Their voices are easily recognizable, and the content of the lectures is far too primitive to be associated with either of them.

The content of the "lessons" is similar to that in the IMU materials collected from the abandoned camps in Afghanistan after the ISAF invasion, making me more comfortable with the conclusion that these lessons were produced by those associated with the IMU.

The text views the mission of *davat* in an essentially politicized way, that in returning to Islam, the Uzbeks at the same time need to return religion to the state level, hence the call to jihad. The message is for ordinary Uzbeks, simple villagers, those who are "distant from the luxurious life and the parasitism, and [whose] hearts demand justice," and who are "only formally" Muslims. They must be taught the spirit of "pure Islam." Those who refuse to do this, the text says, risk being destroyed, along with all "temporary allies" like Christians or Jews, who, after the victory of the *mujahideen*, would be destroyed.

The lessons were designed to attract potential fighters to their cause, promising that they would appear as "champions of justice" when the time came to take revolutionary actions against the government. The lessons talk about the use of expanded propaganda and actions (that could later be denied) such as explosions at power stations, factories, and other targets that would damage the economy and increase popular dissatisfaction with the government, which would then be overthrown and replaced by Islamic law.

In later videocassettes made in the Afghan camps, IMU leaders would try to depict themselves as Hanafi Muslims (albeit purer than most who are prominent Hanafi clerics in Uzbekistan). In these lessons, they present themselves as something more akin to Salafis. The author of the text says:

> Everything must be based only on the Quran and the *hadiths*. If everything is not explained by the Quran and the *hadiths* then many will be lost and they can make many errors.

There is little guidance on which *suras* or *hadiths* should be read or how they should be interpreted. The enemy, though, is clearly defined. It is the government of Uzbekistan and its president (Islam Karimov). The author or authors maintain that it is a government of Jews and special forces, including the presidential guard, the organs of state security, and of the Ministry of Internal Affairs. The goal of jihad is to eliminate this regime and to replace it with a government that honors Islam. The description offered of how this government will serve Islam is presented in a simplistic, if not incoherent fashion:

> At the head of every affair is its goal. Commentary: The sole goal for Muslims is that Allah be pleased with them. This means fulfilling all of the commandments of Allah, to fight to make the word of Allah higher than everything that comes to pass that Islam dictates, to bring Allah's commandments to life throughout the world.
>
> An idea. Any commandment other than the commandments of Allah is oppression regardless of its form. We will fight until this oppression disappears entirely, even until "judgment day."
>
> Slogan. It is necessary to build a political and military system so that it never changes, never enters into agreement with the unfaithful, having refused their [the unfaithful's] political system, their culture, and to remove them from all positions of responsibility and to establish only Islamic order. This is our slogan. That is "La ilaha illa Allah, Muhammad Rasullallah."[17] Commentary: There can be no exception! Not even television, radio, the bazaar, even churches. Even if everything becomes expensive. The slogan must be realized no matter what. All foreign connections will be broken and are constructed only in an Islamic fashion. Will there be a bank? Only if it is established according to Islamic order. In an Islamic state there will be no Ministry of Foreign Affairs. Everything will be liquidated.

Similar outlines of the vision of the Islamic government appear in IMU materials found in Afghanistan, although those materials are slightly less sophisticated in their presentation. This text is striking in its immaturity and seems written by someone who has no idea what a government does or how it is organized and simply wants to use Islamic-sounding phrases to depict some kind of abstract but ideal state:

> In the country there must be one (leading) Emir, also in every city. There must be an Emir for every ten or even five people. They must be selected by a concrete group which can also replace them. The Emir cannot name the lesser Emirs in the cities that are subservient to him. Commentary: We cannot, for example, choose the Emir for a group of ten people. That is not wise. Since we, after all, do not know all the members of that group of 10, we do not know how the relationships among themselves and among others, that kind of imposition of power can again give rise to a system of unfaithful, to dictatorship, and then the collegial group will disperse....
>
> ... The supreme Emirs (*Akh-i akhid*) they unite in order to be firm on the path to the Almighty Allah, and for achieving the goals, the ideas and the slogans. Commentaries. The qualities of Allah's messenger are an example to us. That is, if you are on this path you must sacrifice yourself. City, region, oblast, all must join together so as to be on this path to the last breath. Every Emir will have his own council. The Emir from every oblast can come to us, or send his representative.

The description of what qualities are necessary for a leader are not well thought out. The author vacillates as to what they should be, although it is clear that a conventional religious education is not necessary:

CONDITIONS FOR THE ELECTION OF AN EMIR

1. You need to have both religious and secular education. Commentary: One must not be just a *qori* or *sheikh ul-Islam*, or enough to have education from an institute. That is when knowing about religion, he must not be without knowledge about others in the world, and having secular knowledge he must not forget about faith. There are, for example, clerics who can be told that Muslims are being tormented all around, but they will answer that nothing particular is going on. They do not know or understand events, and when you talk to them about jihad, they know absolutely nothing about it. May Allah have mercy on them, who has known about

the affairs of this world and acknowledged Allah, that is he who has fulfilled the commandments of Allah in this world. Many clerics, if you ask them for a *fatwa*, they will give it based on circumstances in the time of the Islamic Caliphate. Others, who are in the state of the unfaithful, will call Muslims to go to the mosque based on the *hadiths* of Allah's messenger who said, that he is prepared to burn down the houses of those who do not go to mosque. This is a product of their ignorance.

2. The Emir must be in Islam for no fewer than ten years, and serve Islam with correct understandings. Commentary. The term can be less, five to seven years, but the person must lead his life according to all Islamic laws, and he must be subjected to tests after he enters Islam. He must grow every day.... For example, Abduvali qori grew every day and he came to knowledge of questions of jihad....

3. He [the Emir] must be about 30–40 years old....

4. Sharia also has other means of testing people. Tests based on these methods must be set up. For example, we acknowledge as a genuinely faithful person Muhammad Sodiq Muhammad Yusuf, but if he meets with any good cleric and has learned discussions with him, he can prove the weakness of Muhammad Sodiq Muhammad Yusuf's knowledge, his adherence to [Hanafi] *mazhab*, etc. In this way, his knowledge is tested by the genuine knowledge [of another person]. After all, the Messenger of Allah, peace to Him, said "If someone is happy when Muslims are being pressed, then he is a hypocrite."

5. The Emir is not chosen for any set length of time, and if there is a need he can be replaced. And if there is no need he can be left in place and not changed.

There was little awareness of what a government should do or how its executive branch should be organized, and the functions that are outlined in the document on the qualifications of the Emir are much more strongly influenced by the experience of Soviet rule than of any Islamic state:

> The three people who are subordinated to the main Emir have great responsibility.
>
> - The deputy who is in charge of propaganda. At the beginning, this person sends Taliban (followers) to other countries. Commentary: This is then in order to learn all necessary religious knowledge and secular sciences.... He

observes also how in the country scientific workers are taught, how they work... what they do so they familiarize themselves with Sharia...

- It is necessary that the clerics of our state be respected people.... Commentary: These clerics cannot be kept separate from affairs. However, in the business of propaganda if one cleric makes some kind of decision on a concrete question, another cleric should not contradict him. Arguments on petty questions are not permitted. These questions must only be discussed in councils and decided from the point of view of Islamic laws, and if the clerics do not remind everybody about the religion of Allah then we will in no way be distinguishable from simple hooligans.

- Another is the political instructor. He must first of all construct precise and regular printing business. He must publish every week a newspaper and pamphlets.... If Tashkent is closed to printing, then this must be done in Samarkand, and if all of Uzbekistan is closed, it must be set up in Kazakhstan. Or it is possible to find an organization that is unhappy with the government. For example, to pass pamphlets off to the BBC, and they will read it every day on the radio. This propaganda must not reveal its weak sides. That is, we must not reveal our true intentions or else we will be frightening to the enemy...

- The Deputy [Emir] responsible for supply. The collection of goods must be organized from whether feasible: from the rich, from businessmen and even from simple workers. Commentary: There is a group engaged in terror [from those who are targeted and do not give voluntarily]...

- Furthermore, we have to open the road to trades, wherever they are, because they require travel to other countries. Besides being useful, you can use them to establish connections. For example, in Pakistan and Turkey there are things that we need that we do not have. There are poisons there that, with just a simple swipe on a wall, can kill people who enter the house. In these foreign countries these things are sold in the bazaars.

LIFE IN THE IMU CAMPS

The Notebooks

In the course of my research, I have gained access to notebooks and copies of notebooks containing "lessons" on jihad written by students in IMU training camps that cover the period of the mid-1990s through 2001. I also have films made by the IMU during this same period. Some of these notebooks came to me indirectly from the Uzbek authorities and were most likely taken from IMU members during arrests and searches.[18] Others were authenticated copies taken from abandoned IMU camps in Afghanistan by people traveling with ISAF forces. There is no real difference between the materials that came through the Uzbek authorities and those that were taken out of Afghanistan by American citizens. As a result, I have absolutely no reason to believe that the Uzbek materials were forged by the Uzbek authorities. Moreover, I have handled all of the Uzbek materials myself, and they look, feel, and literally smell, authentic.

The earliest materials come from a collection of notebooks, and photographs of some of the contents appeared in the *Foreign Policy* magazine in 2003.[19] I have seven notebooks—all from the period 1993 to 1995—and they contain the notes from about a dozen different students who were, judging by the dialects used, from the Andijan, Namangan, Khiva, and Tashkent regions.

The students received paramilitary training, akin to what was taught in Soviet pre-military preparation courses or to new conscripts, including the use of firearms—in some cases Soviet-made weapons, in other cases Egyptian-made weapons. Appropriately, some of the instructors were Russian speakers and others appear to be Arabic speakers. "Students" were also taught how to make simple bombs, with very precise instructions and from materials readily at hand. The contents of some of the notebooks overlap, suggesting that the students (though from different parts of the country judging by their written dialects) either studied together or the "teachers" traveled around.

Some of the preparatory work seems to have been done in Uzbekistan, likely as an offshoot of some of the radical[20] Islamic study circles in the Namangan region, but the bulk of it was most likely done in Tajikistan and eventually at the IMU camps in Afghanistan. It is not clear whether the "students" went to firing ranges while in Uzbekistan, but the films from the IMU camp in Tajikistan show firing ranges and weapons training, and accounts from our interviews make mention of small numbers of IMU "soldiers" getting specialized training at camps in Pakistan as well (in the mid- and late 1990s)

The content of the notebooks suggests that the students were given very rudimentary religious instruction, and learned little Arabic. Some of the students did write a few words in Arabic, but references to the Quranic excerpts are in Uzbek, suggesting that the instructors read them out loud to the students in Arabic and then offered Uzbek language interpretation. The former IMU members whom we interviewed offered conflicting views of the importance of prayer in the daily life of those living in the IMU camps. Bahrom,[21] from Margilan, who joined the IMU at age seventeen[22] and fought with Juma Namangani in Tajikistan, mentioned that a great deal of time was spent in praying or reciting the Quran and that the rites of Islam (such as prohibitions on smoking and drinking) were strictly observed. Those who were with Tohir Yuldoshev in Afghanistan, meanwhile, talked about a much more casual attitude toward prayer and observance—except for the prayer meetings at which Yuldoshev offered his sermons, where attendance was obligatory.

Those leading the lessons also do not appear to have much religious preparation, and Bakhtiyar Babadjanov maintains that the interpretation of jihad that is offered in these texts differs substantially from classical Hanafi and Shafi Islam that were taught in the region.[23] There seems to have been considerable variation in the content of religious studies in the different camps, as the notebooks offered varying descriptions of the basic tenets and rituals of Islam.

Students were also given some background on the type of warfare that they were being prepared for, a "war without rules" to quote one of the notebooks,[24] "as they [the students] have no state and no atom bomb." This same notebook goes on to discuss the four justifications of this kind of war. The first is the dogmatic obligations of such a war, because of their faith of Islam, to make Allah pleased, to eradicate oppression against Muslims, and to establish the rule of Islam in perpetuity. The second aspect is political, to make people understand the politics of Islam and that the politics of Islam embody the politics of life. The third is economic, to learn how to deprive the enemy of his income, and to prevent the unbelievers from exercising economic power over Muslims.

One of the examples of an "economic military action" was "to destroy all raw materials that are being exported from the country by unbelievers. Including fruit, or to poison one or two cases of fruit. When this is discovered… those who transport things … will be warned once or twice, and then everything will be confiscated from them." During this period, much of the fresh fruit sold in Russian markets came from Uzbekistan, and this served as a major source of income for those with small private plots.[25]

Fourth and finally, one must learn how to fight the enemy militarily and to know the enemy's weakness and strike him there. But the notebook stressed, "It doesn't pay to organize explosions in those regions where people think well of the Muslims and the *mujahideen*." The same student notes that "the Emir," their leader, must be competent in all four areas, "as was the Prophet of Allah, to teach his comrades."

There is no way to know from this text if the commanders actually had worked through any sort of systematic plan of attack. The military strategy outlined was that of guerrilla attacks, much like those during the civil war in the early 1920s: "We will liberate and defend the mountains, that is, the mountains close to the cities." But the expectation was that the cities themselves would be hard to capture.

There is a real brutality about the mission they set for themselves. From the same notebook: "All representatives of enemy nationalities [Jews and Russians, as earlier elaborated] who occupy senior posts in the government will be killed." But at the beginning at least, "ordinary Muslims, even if they work in the government should not be disturbed." The goal instead should be to teach them their faith.

Although there is very little mention of Israel and nothing about the Palestinian cause, the lessons contain a strong anti-Semitic tone. This suggests much more of a local agenda than strong commitment to any kind of global jihadist cause, although the text offers justification from the Quran for the premise "that Jews are cursed by God is demonstrated by *ayat* 14 of *sura al-Hashr*."[26]

Camps in Tajikistan and Afghanistan

After Uzbek authorities increased their surveillance of religious activists, most of the IMU training began to take place in Tajikistan. The presence of camps there was known to both Tajik and Uzbek officials, but because the camps were in areas that were effectively outside of the control of the Rahmon government, in the mountains north of Garm and in the Tavildara region in the middle of the country, very little could be done to liquidate them during this period. One camp was just outside Ordjonikidzeobod,[27] roughly an hour's drive from Dushanbe. There also seem to have been some smaller camps, more like "hideouts," in the Gorno-Badakhshan region.

My knowledge of conditions in these camps comes from several films that were done in the period 1998 to 2001, filmed at the Studio Jundulla, which was first situated at the camp at Tavildara and then in northern Afghanistan, as well as from discussions with people who lived in the camps. The films seemed designed to meet three purposes: to help recruit new fighters, to offer accountability to funders, and to maintain the level of ideological preparation of the fighters. A lot has been written about how drug trafficking accounted for much of the IMU's money,[28] and while Juma Namangani and his fighters definitely received "tribute" for safeguarding shipments of drugs and other kinds of illegal transport, other kinds of money also were received. Some of it likely came from the same sources as those supporting the UTO, but, most important, money was received from Uzbeks in Saudi Arabia, in particular from Abdukadir Margiloniy.

How wide a distribution these films got is unclear. Some could be bought illegally with effort in Uzbekistan, and presumably with even less effort in the neighboring states, although nobody I met in the movement had joined because of having seen the films. All said that they had not viewed any of the films until they were in the camps. I also do not know how many different films were produced. Footage of the film studio, which appears in some of the films themselves (those accounting for funds to donors), shows a rather substantial library of videotapes.

The materials designed to recruit fighters sought to show the fun life that the *mujahideen* lived, dividing their time among religious study, military training, and sports, all while enjoying a healthy diet. The films were designed to make Central Asian young men feel good about joining the IMU, and lyrics that explained the goals of jihad were matched with catchy tunes.

The Tajik camps were mostly in abandoned Soviet-era *kurorts*, nominally resorts for relaxation, or a sanitorium for "restoration of health" where people took medicinal baths or other "cures." The facilities were simple: cabins or rooms more like dormitories than anything a Westerner would consider a hotel, with minimal recreation facilities, such as volleyball courts or Ping-

Pong tables. Not everyone was based in these camps; those preparing for military operations were sometimes bivouacked separately.

One bit of the film was particularly chilling, as it showed young boys, one of whom did not appear to be even ten years old, learning to shoot semi-automatic weapons against the background of someone singing, "The Triumphal March of the *Mujahideen* of the IMU":

> We will return here, we will destroy every tyrant and pharaoh, we will get back all that belongs to us, and destroy all enemies. Soon we will begin a battle with them. We will destroy that tyrant and we will take back all that was taken from us and for sure we will destroy our enemies. For sure we will destroy them. For sure we will destroy them. Those places where there is no justice of God we soon will liberate. Into this world full of sin and vice we will bring pure Islam [*pok islom*] soon we will enter into battle with them. We will destroy the tyrant pharoah. We will liberate lost land and for sure we will destroy them. The Armies of Islam cannot be defeated. We bow down only to him and with his name we go into battle. Soon we will take revenge on our enemies. Soon we will enter into battle with them. We shall destroy the tyrant pharaoh. We will return all of our lost freedoms and for sure we will destroy the enemies. We will enter into battle with terrible force. We will liberate lost justice and all those who have departed from the faith we will drown in the rivers. Soon we will enter into battle with them. But first we will destroy the tyrant pharaoh. We will return our lost freedoms, and for sure we will destroy the enemies.

When the IMU moved its camps to Afghanistan, the amount of money available to it increased substantially. IMU members lived in their own camps, with families living separate from single fighters. Tohir Yuldoshev is shown in the film in quarters that were very comfortable (especially by local standards), but the former fighters we interviewed complained of how harsh the living conditions were for ordinary families; people lived in communal rooms or apartments, and food was rationed very tightly—save when sponsors made inspection tours, some of which were sparked by the IMU members' complaints against Yuldoshev and how he was spending IMU funds.

A lot of money was spent on propaganda. The "studio" and print shop in Afghanistan had technical equipment worth millions of dollars (as shown in the films), while the films from Tajikistan featured much more rudimentary equipment. In both cases, those responsible for putting together the films had at least a good amateur knowledge of how this was done: The material was arranged with deliberation, obviously using storyboards, and the dubbing or titles always matched the original sound track. Radio programs also were made.[29]

THE IMU'S VIEW OF ITSELF

Not so unlike their Soviet predecessors, IMU leaders loved producing enormous amounts of propaganda materials. As IMU members fled their camps in Afghanistan to escape NATO bombs, these materials were left behind, and their content argues for the authenticity of the materials collected in Uzbekistan. The Afghan materials make it very easy to reconstruct the goals of the movement.

What follows are the lyrics to the opening tune of the movie "The Call," produced at the IMU studios in Afghanistan in 2000:

> The Islamic Movement of Uzbekistan is a movement of Sunni Muslims, that consists of representatives of various nationalities that use all their might in fight for establishment of the laws of Almighty Allah—Islamic Sharia—here on earth. Our goals are to bring people from worshipping men and other kinds of idols to worshipping the Only Creator Allah, to convey to the present and future generations the true faith, initiated by the greatest prophet Muhammad (peace be with him!), the faith we received from our fathers and grandfathers. Our activities are guided by Islamic Sharia of Hanafi interpretation.
>
> The goals of the Islamic Movement of Uzbekistan cannot be other than the goals of true *khalifas*. We believe that in present times of technological progress it remains of utmost importance to bring Islamic Sharia to people, to take people out of the darkness and into the light. The Movement has been actively working in this direction for many years.

The "call" in the movie's title refers to the call to jihad, and the film goes on to offer a history of Russian colonization and Soviet rule in Uzbekistan. According to the film, this history of colonization and oppression provided the constant incentive for jihad and local rebellion—from the Andijan uprising of 1898 to the resistance to the Bolsheviks in the 1920s, from the period of collectivization until the present, when the Uzbek people were urged to rise up and support the IMU under Tohir Yuldoshev's leadership to oppose the godless regime of Islam Karimov. The movie even went so far as to make a direct link between the resistance in the early 1920s and that of Yuldoshev's organization, by showing him meeting with some of the descendants of the last Emir of Bukhara, who were living in Afghanistan.

By comparison to the goals of the IRP—to gain legal recognition and a formal role in the governing of Tajikistan—those of the IMU were much more fantastic if considered in the context of the Central Asian political realities of the day. Unlike the IRP, the IMU leadership sought to take power in the name of Islam and to rule themselves through the application of Sharia. The following comes from the IMU journal no. 1, May 29, 1999:[30]

THE IMU'S VIEWS OF THE SITUATION IN UZBEKISTAN

The movement holds that the Uzbek people prefer Islamic thought and the people have defended their Islam in the most difficult moments of history, and this people has a long Islamic history. The rule of the Russians has ended on this territory. But instead of returning to an Islamic way of life, power in this territory has been seized by a band of departers from the faith. They have begun to battle against Islam. They have even succeeded in this more than the Bolsheviks did, destroying even more Muslims, they have thrown *ulama* in prison. They pursued and killed them. They particularly pursue young Muslims. They have closed all of Allah's mosques and even forbid the name of Allah to be pronounced. If before they served the interests of the communists. Now they serve the interests of Israel and of Jewish America.

And it is our right to defend the faith and their suppression of the Sharia and oppression of Muslims gives us the right to fight against these hypocritical forces. And nevertheless we do not lose hope that all of these problems can be resolved peacefully if our conditions are fulfilled.

The solution of the problems in our view could be the following:

1. The president must resign immediately and over the next six months the country must be ruled by an independent temporary government, and during this time the following things must be done

    a. All believers must be freed and particularly young believers.

    b. To return to the country all *ulama* who have emigrated and all who have emigrated for political reasons.

c. To call a higher gathering of *ulama* they will appoint worthy people to the government who are capable of establishing Sharia laws for the government, to conduct foreign and domestic policy.

d. From among these who have been selected by the council of *ulama* the people can choose the leadership of the country and of the organ of the higher council (*oily shuro*).

2. After the renewal of the state structure, all of the innocent and those who have been put in prison must be freed, and those who oppressed them must be found and turned over to the organs of the Sharia laws.

3. All agreements of the present government are annulled and foreign agreements and policies will be built on the basis of Sharia, mutual benefit and equality. Uzbekistan will never be in friendly relations with governments which are enemies of Islam and Muslims, with those who take away this land where our people live and with those who help these governments with these black deeds. Since every inimical act against any Muslim is an inimical act against all Muslims and we are obligated to follow the *Hadith* of the prophet. The relations of Muslims to one another are like the relations of various parts of the body, one to another. If even one of them is sick, the others react to this with a raised temperature.

The IMU considers that there still is time to fulfill all of these demands without bloodshed. However, all the barbarian policies of this present government and the persecution of Muslims contradicts the peaceful path, and may in the future provoke the same kind of explosions that happened not long ago in Tashkent. For this reason, the IMU calls on the present government to consider the possibility of accepting the offered steps and to announce its decision. After all there is a limit to the patience of Muslims. These tyrants will soon understand what they are heading for.

Signed
The leadership of the IMU

For Tohir Yuldoshev, the fight against the Uzbek government was a personal contest between himself and the Uzbek president, whom he believed was unfit to rule, being both an orphan and an atheist.

Take the following speech by Yuldoshev, in response to a speech of Karimov from 2000 in which the Uzbek leader criticized the IMU:

Karimop[31] says that he is the father of the people of Uzbekistan. He particularly stresses that the youth are his children. O you, cursed by God! You are no father to us. Our origin is well known. We were born as Muslims. We have none among us like your prostitute mother. [Here some cried "Takbir!" and all of the listeners began to shout "Allahu akbar! La ilaha illa Allah…"]

This is a reference to the fact that Karimov was an orphan and spent part of his childhood in an orphanage:

And he Karimov calls all of us his people. No we are not your people. You are a Jew and not from us. You are a son of those who opened the gates to the unfaithful. You have no right to call the young your children, since your origin is unknown. You are an atheist and do not have the right to call Muslims your children. You are looking for gold and money, and even if you are from this people, you have sold it. You have no right to say you are from this people. They call you *Yurtbashi* [father of the homeland]. No, you are a calamity that has come down on the head of this country. You are an atheist who for his own benefit has thrown hundreds of thousands of Muslims in prison. You are the one who continues the business of the pharaohs. You have spilled the tears of hundreds of thousands of children, hundreds of thousands of mothers. You are not the father of the nation. You do all of your acts for your own benefit, and to please your *kibla* [the direction to Mecca] Israel. But we do not rely on any international organization. Our sole support is Allah, whom we revere.

WHY DID PEOPLE JOIN THE IMU?

It is hard to know what impact this propaganda had in getting people to join the IMU. Restrictive policies in Uzbekistan, impeding the practice of unsanctioned forms of Islam, rather than the appeal of the IMU per se seem to have played a much greater role in explaining why people joined the movement.

In March 2005, I had the opportunity to interview six former members of the IMU. These men had returned to Uzbekistan through a government amnesty program. All of their addresses were known to the government, and presumably they remained under some sort of surveillance by the Uzbek authorities.

These interviews were conducted in their homes, with family members and Bakhtiyar Babadjanov in attendance.[32] The questions did not have to be submitted to anyone. The interviews were taped with permission, but to the best of my knowledge were not shared with anyone in the government. All six former IMU members had already been back in Uzbekistan for several years at the time of our meetings, and all had returned to some sort of normalcy in their lives (one was a physical education teacher and all the rest were involved in small businesses of some sort generally owned by relatives). All of the men lived either around Kokand or Namangan. Taken as a group, their reminiscences spanned the period of 1994 to 2001. These interviews are interesting because they provided an opportunity to verify many of the things seen on the films that I had obtained from the camps. Obviously, all chose to come home, rather than remain as part of the global jihad.

The people that I met had joined the IMU for a variety of reasons. One person, who really seemed broken from his experiences, had joined because of the money that he had been promised as a fighter, but he wound up as a sentry in the camp for families in Afghanistan. He, like everyone else I interviewed, was part of an unsanctioned religious study group or movement, and he complained that there was virtually no religious instruction for adults in his camp, although everyone gathered to hear Tohir Yuldushev preach or to watch movies of him preaching. In fact several were part of a group that was reminiscent of *Ahl-i Quran*, a study group that was devoted to teaching people to read the Quran in Uzbek. The group was using Alauddin Mansur's translation of the Quran that first appeared in *Sharq Yulduzi* (Stars of the East) in 1990 and 1991.[33]

An auto mechanic from the Margilan area, the nephew of the founder of the local "*Ahl-i Quran*"-like group, joined the IMU at age seventeen in 1994. He offered the following observation about the reasons that young Uzbeks joined the movement:

> It all depends. For example, some people met *davatchis* [those engaged in summoning others to the faith] in prison, with those who were arrested. Many sincerely believe that if you do jihad, you will go to heaven. So, everyone thought that jihad is going on in Tajikistan, and it was said in *hujras* that if you get there, that would be jihad. And many people got deceived that way. There were many who were looking for fortune and money. I met those people. It turns out, they were promised five thousand dollars per month, including for every member of their families. So, they came with their families up to eight

people. They thought that if they go through three months of mandatory training, they would already make fifteen thousand dollars per person and then they would manage to escape someplace.

The mechanic, who was in the Tavildara camps with Juma Namangani, talked about how lessons in religion were a key part of the camp experience, some four or five hours a day of religious instruction in addition to the paramilitary training.

A local physical education teacher (he taught Uzbek folk wrestling) was about thirty years old when he left Uzbekistan. As one of those committed to studying the Quran in Uzbek, he explained why he was devoted to this version of Islam:

> A: So, you know, our Prophet Muhammad—peace be with him—was Arab. Naturally, he read in Arabic. He read everything in Arabic. The Quran and the prayer. But he was Arab, while we are Uzbek. And if an Uzbek translation of the Quran is published, we read it in Uzbek and we understand exactly what Allah had said and what we address him with. And if we read the prayer in Uzbek, it is even better.
>
> Q: And so your initiative or your innovation, was it perceived negatively by others?
>
> A: Yes, negatively. Generally, those who were against us were middle-aged and old people from our *mahalla*. We did not read the *namaz* as they did. Then, police spoke out against us. In particularly, our local policeman.
>
> Q: He did not try to understand you?
>
> A: Right. They called us Wahhabis. But we did not come out on the street and never said we were Wahhabis or that we belonged to Hizb. So, what was our fault in reading the Quran as published by the state?
>
> Q: But how many times did you read your prayers?
>
> A: As it is prescribed, five times. But we only read the prescribed [*farz*[34]] part of the prayer. This *farz* is Allah's command. While we do not read the part prescribed in *Sunna* because the Quran says nothing about it.
>
> Q: So, you based it on the Quran?

A: Yes, exclusively on the Quran.

Q: Well, what about commands of the *hadiths*?

A: We do not recognize the *hadiths*. *Hadiths* are human creations.

Q: Can you be called *Ahl-i Quran*?

A: Of course! After all, those who read the Quran are *Ahl-i Quran*! And what do those who read the *hadiths* win? That's a book written by some man. While at this point, the Quran is not known neither in Uzbekistan, nor in Arabic countries, or anywhere else in the world. Maybe I can't explain it all now, but my teacher can explain it all. The Arabs themselves do not know the meaning of the Quran.

He viewed going to Tajikistan as *hijra*, moving from where his religion was suppressed to where he believed he could freely practice his faith. Like some of the others, he made it seem like he was inveigled into fighting when he got to Tajikistan, but he admitted to being a deputy commander for three years with Juma and then three years with Mirzo Ziyoev.[35]

It is interesting to note that even in the mid-1990s, the Uzbeks that we met viewed leaving Uzbekistan for Tajikistan as exile, so firmly were the two already seen as different countries (even with the breakup of the Soviet Union being less than a decade old).

One of the IMU films produced in Afghanistan, "Them," describes the essence of the idea of exile, with a video clip from a speech by Abduvali qori from April 1992 devoted to this very theme. The "them" in the title is the Uzbek government of Islam Karimov, and the film is devoted to showing how the regime broke with the faithful.[36] The need for the true believers to find the strength to defy and break with those who do not accept the values of Islam is the meaning of exile explored by Abduvali qori in this speech. But by using it in the film, the IMU is making the case for a different kind of exile: leaving the country to join their cause.

> There is a *hadith* of our Prophet, may Allah bless and greet him. Islam began with exile (*gariba*) and will return to it. That is, Islam will return to condition of exodus as it began. Those in exile have paradise waiting for them. Who are exiles? Exiles are the sort of people who live among drunkenness, vice, prostitution, the violence of the Mafia and think always about how in such condi-

tions to preserve their faith, think constantly about what actions correspond to *Sunna* and what are the inadmissible novelties. They think, "What should I do so that Allah will be at peace with me?" These are people who try to make their life correspond to *Sunna*, but living among all of this vice and drunkenness they are exiles, and no matter how much these exiles say to those around them, "Hey brothers, let's return to the path of truth," no one understands them. Who are the exiles? They are those who try to put their family or wife on the path of truth, on the path of the Sharia following the model of the life of the prophet. But they are not understood, and people say to them "you are lagging behind the times" and his children say to him that "papa, you have nothing to talk about except the end of the world." That person is an exile in his own family. Who is an exile? It is the one who is always worried about how to constantly follow real, pure Islam when his parents say to him, "Are you our son or not? Why do you never have fun, like all young people? Why do you not go to the *toy* [ceremony, celebration], and drink for fun with your friends? Why do you not want to have fun while you are young? Why do you refuse the pleasures of youth? What has happened that you have grown a beard and begun to speak only about Islam?" Women now are exiles too, who like the wives of the prophet, and the wives of the Askhab, who try to preserve their purity, to refrain from sin, who try to conceal the parts of the body, to wear *hijab* and for that they are laughed at. Who following the demands of their faith and feeling responsibility before Allah try to raise their children properly on the path of Islam. Those women who from early youth have tried to see that Allah was pleased with them in order to be like our true Muslim women. But for all of this they became the objects of ridicule for those who are spoiled, who are prostitutes. These kinds of women are true exiles. The exile is he who has lived his whole life among ignorant, unfaithful people, among hypocrisy and vice. And once having heard the call to Islam, he decides firmly to fulfill the demands of Islam, to devote his whole life to Islam. But for this he hears from his old friends "What has happened to you? You used to be a normal person. Look who you have come to resemble. Literally, it is just like you are mad, *majnun* [madman]." Then that person answered, "Oh, if only if you could try just a little bit of that satisfaction that I feel." But they answer him, "What kind of pleasure is that? If you walk around as if you are nuts?" That person is an exile. That person wants only the best for you, and if he is not understood, and people laugh at him, then he is an exile. Among these exiles there is one who has achieved *Sunna*. He understands the commandments of Allah correctly. He correctly understands the Hadiths of our prophets. And may Allah bless and greet him. And when he calls the *ulama* to follow the *Sunna* properly they understand his goal perfectly well, they understand that he is correct. But these *ulama* do not want to lose their false authority and when he calls them to stand on the path of truth they slander him and despise him. That man among scholars is very much an exile. Dear brothers, all errors and nastiness in which these people are living will disappear in a single second. Until truth appears they will live on, and when truth comes towards them, Allah will assist the truth.

Tohir Yuldoshev was also eager to make the link from Abduvali to himself, in order to give himself more credibility as a spiritual leader. The films make clear that he sought to embrace that role, despite the fact that Yuldoshev had limited religious education and could not in any way be considered to be a theologian of the Abduvali caliber.

The IMU leadership went to great lengths to deny that IMU fighters were being offered money. Yuldoshev railed about this in a speech included in "Them."

> They say that we used religion for the sake of our own interests. No, it is you who concealed your goals through religion! We are here because we want religion to rule over everything! [The voices of listeners: "Allah the great!"] They are those who sell their religion and accuse us of using religion to cover our goals. No!! We have taken this path to make religion dominant in our souls and then in the whole world! *Mushrikams* [those who believe in many gods][37] and those faithless, *kafirs*,[38] claim we came here to earn dollars. We are here to find paradise (in the future world).[39] We are here hoping our God will be content with us. And our salary cannot be measured with dollars! Never will anybody sell a part of his/her body, even for a lot of money.
>
> For example, you are told "give me your eyes. I will give you a million dollars for your eyes." Will you give your eyes away? Hey, you nuts! We are ready to sacrifice our lives for these $700,[40] which you are talking about.[41] The regime of this disloyal Karimov claims that we get $700 a month. Could anybody sacrifice his life for $700? No!! We won't turn off this road until we are in paradise. [Voices of the listeners: "*Insha Allah*! (God Willing)"]
>
> We will continue on this path because we took this road responding to the call of theologians, on the basis of Islam theology, on the basis of our concepts, and on the basis of our belief. We did not choose this way blindfolded! These disloyal men say we are left homeless and hungry! No! Among us there are those who are rich and satisfied like Musab ibn Umar. When he went along the streets of Mecca, all women whom he cast a glance immediately fell in love with him. And after he walked down a street, there would be a pleasant smell left for several days because he wore so much perfume. There were dozens of his slaves and servants around him. But then he got to know the true belief. The day he was killed in a Budre battle by the mountain Uhud,[42] he could not

find himself enough cloth to make a *kafan*[43] for him. When people covered his head, his legs were seen. But if they covered his legs, his head was seen. So he was buried with his head being covered with his own clothes.[44] We have people like Musab ibn Umar among us.

They sacrificed all their property on their way to Allah. Oh, no! You faithless, remember we are not looking for dollars. We here are not looking for Russian rubles. We are not thinking how to take away the power from a faithless figure. We chose this way and devoted all our life to it because it is the way to which the Prophet, his faithful caliphs and companions devoted their lives.

Everyone we met said he had been promised some sort of payment to be given to him or to be sent to his family, although all maintained (truthfully or not) that they had never seen any of this money. All, though, were adamant that the IMU was receiving money for each fighter who was part of the movement. One person talked about how each fighter was worth $10,000 to $15,000 from the Arab sponsors. This figure seems rather fantastic. Another told us about how the IMU was receiving $200 (presumably per month) for support of each fighter's family and was offering unrealistically high estimates to their sponsors of how many families there were. When the sponsors tried to verify the numbers, sometime around 1999, the IMU arranged for an entire village to cross the border to Tajikistan (using chartered local Uzbek buses). They got the buses because they paid a community elder and a school director a considerable sum of money to populate the camp with children for the new madrasa that was being organized. It apparently took several days for the Uzbek authorities to notice the missing village (close to 500 people in total). There were about 150 or 160 families living in Afghanistan, most having come from Tajikistan together.

The Oath They Took

As the interviews demonstrated, whatever reasons people may have had for joining, it was obvious that they relatively quickly found themselves subordinated to a strictly disciplined organization, thus shattering any romantic illusions fighters may have held prior to joining the IMU.

The film "Them"[45] shows Tohir Yuldoshev swearing in a new group of *mujahideen* and preaching after they swear their loyalty. I have two versions of the oath that the IMU fighters swore:[46]

> I, *Mujahid* ... I subordinate myself to Allah, his messenger, and I obligate myself to fulfill their commandments. I swear before Allah to fulfill all of the orders and commands of the Emir of the IMU.
>
> On this path of Allah and his messenger, I swear to fulfill all orders on the path of jihad, for the sake of Allah, I am ready to endure all hardship and deprivation, difficulties and pain on the path of jihad. I swear to complete jihad on the path of Allah and his messenger to serve jihad with all my property and my life. I swear to fulfill all of the orders of the commanders who are named by the Emir of the IMU, Muhammad Tohir. If on this path of jihad I commit treachery, cowardice and am frightened by hardships, I agree to endure punishment following the commandments of the Sharia.

During the swearing-in of his fighters, Tohir Yuldoshev used (at least in this instance) the first *sura*:

> Brothers, our oath of faith is very important. We make the promise. We bow down only to you, Allah. That is, we will be satisfied only with your power and we do not agree to be under anyone's power except yours. We are only for realizing in life your Sharia and your power. On this path we will not ask for anything from the atheists and hypocrites. For the Lord of the World promises to help the one who fights for his religion. You will help the faith of Allah, Allah will help you and make you strong and unyielding. And if Allah will help you, then no one can defeat you. He promised that in his Quran. Thus, my brothers, all the promises, predictions, and foretellings in the *ayats* must be understood correctly. "We bow down to you and ask for help."
>
> —*Sura* al-Fatiha 1:5[47]

We bow down to Him, we pray to Him, we are his slaves. But this is not to Karimov, not to Bill Clinton, not to Putin only to Him, to our Allah. And we will not ask for help from people, from God's creatures, only of You. We must make our oath understanding all of this well, because we will be asked about this oath on the day of judgment. The one who has been helped by our Lord, the messenger Muhammad, in the first days of his life as a prophet was alone. And ten years after his call only 70 people were worthy of taking Islam, and even when he moved from Mecca to Medina the Emperor there, Kisa, sent three soldiers to capture Muhammad in order to punish him. He did not send an army after him, but only three soldiers (*bogatyrs*) because he considered the *umma* to be weak. But the Lord proved to be the victor. The Lord of the World will always be the victor. Only one thing is demanded of us, to be faithful to our oath. In the Quran it is said that Muslims keep their oaths that they have given to the Lord, and on this path they became *shahids*. Brothers, I return again to this *ayat*, we bow down to you and ask for help; this is an oath between the Lord and his slaves, and we must follow this oath. May the almighty Allah help us to follow this oath.

[Listeners cry, "Allahu akbar!"] And the main reason why Jews and Christians do not value the 1.5 billion Muslims is because the Muslims themselves are not faithful to their oath to Allah. After all the unfaithful Christians and Jews have no fear of Muslims, even if they are in the majority in millions. But they fear those Muslims who go among the mountains almost barefoot, with old rifles, chased from their land, since Muslims like that cannot be bought because those kinds of Muslims are the true slaves of Allah (*abd Allah*). But those Muslims who consider themselves to be good Muslims but who sit it out in warmth and in good houses they are slaves of money (that is *abd al-derkham*), slaves of hypocrisy (*abd ar-riya*) and slaves of the dollar (*abd al-dollar*). They can be bought for dollars. So brothers let us be faithful to our oath.

One of the points made by each of the former IMU members interviewed was how difficult it was to leave the movement after joining. Some said that it was because neither Juma Namangani nor Tohir Yuldoshev wanted to lose the money that they were collecting for each fighter, but there also must have been a real fear that any fighters who went back to Uzbekistan would provide information on who was with the IMU and where they were training. I also heard accounts of the IMU shooting deserting fighters, and then blaming their deaths on the Uzbek authorities, in what the IMU claimed were failed guerrilla attacks.

Several former fighters repeated versions of this story.[48] The most detailed account came from the mechanic:

Q: We have heard from those we interviewed before you that 17 of your own militants had been shot. Do you know anything about that?

A: Yes. They were shot, but first, they were allowed to come back here [to Uzbekistan].

Q: What do you mean—first they were allowed to come back?

A: They were permitted to leave, and then were shot. Juma gave them permission to leave in front of everybody, but then sent Yuldoshev and had them shot unarmed.

And then he said those guys were shot by agents of the Uzbek police.

Dying for the IMU

Although suicide missions did not become commonplace until the IMU was joined with al-Qaeda after September 11, the IMU always entreated its followers to strive to become a *shahid*. Even in these early notebooks, the IMU recruits were being prepared to die for their cause. The same notebook continues: "If a person is completely dedicated, he is able to fasten explosives to his own body and to blow himself up along with his enemies...."

The former IMU members that I met also clearly stated that martyrdom was presented to the young recruits as their reward should they lose their lives while fighting for the movement's cause. As the mechanic explained:

Q: So, how was the term "jihad" explained to you during your religion lessons?

A: Actually, they were doing it very well, they could get into a man's soul. First, they cited *ayats* from the Quran. After all, we are Muslims and believe in God, and therefore, believe in the Quran. But Arabs distorted the Quran. And that was what we were presented. For example, this was the order—a call for Sharia, then Jihad and murder. Really, the *ayats* about Jihad begin with the *Baqara sura*.[49]

Q: That's right. It is also in *al-Anfal sura*.[50]

A: So, you should follow that. That's how it was explained to us. And we believe that one should live according to the Quran. And then they were telling us about heaven and hell. And we imagined it as the truth. And we understood and believed that if we die that way, we will go to heaven.

Q: So, they were explaining heaven to you? You took notes at those lessons, didn't you?

A: Yes, we took notes. As for heaven, they told us what is written in the Quran. It was enough for us. But we were told that the only and the easiest way to heaven is Jihad.

Q: Did they tell you that there, in heaven, you will be married to 72 heavenly black-eyed *houris* [virgins],[51] or something like that?

A: Yes, we were told that even before your soul leaves your body, those *houris* will immediately carry you into heaven.

The IMU journal no. 2, dated July 5, 1999, offers its readers a description of the qualities of the *shahid*.[52]

> Our prophet said that the Shahid has 8 superior qualities.
>
> 1. With the first drop of blood all of his sins will be forgiven.
>
> 2. He will see with his own eyes his place in paradise.
>
> 3. He shall be dressed in the clothing of true faith.
>
> 4. He will be married to 72 black-eyed *houris*.
>
> 5. He will escape torment.
>
> 6. He will be calm on the great day of judgment.
>
> 7. On his head will be placed a crown—just one of its stones will be more valuable than all of the riches of earth.
>
> 8. He will have the right to intercede for 70 members of his family.
>
> This Hadith is found in the writings of Imam al-Termezi.

Though fighters were sent on missions that might result in their death, it was generally hoped that they would return alive, given how few fighters were attached to the movement. However, once the IMU moved to Afghanistan and began receiving funds from the al-Qaeda network, the IMU began to inculcate its fighters to aspire to become *shahids*.

One film, "Shahid Abu Dujon," done in late 2000 or early 2001, was devoted to this theme, and recalls the last days and death of a young fighter recently arrived from Bukhara who stepped on a land mine near the camp and died from the horrific injuries that resulted. The film claims that he is the first *shahid* from Uzbekistan (a dubious claim in itself as several IMU fighters died as a result of actions in Tashkent in 1999, and others died in prison).

While the film was made sometime later, the decision to film his death was obviously made within the first hour or so of his being wounded, as the movie contains films of his awaiting surgery, of the surgery itself (which includes people dipping their fingers into his wounds to be blessed by the martyr's blood). What is most chilling about this film was the cold calculation of the decision to spontaneously decide to film someone dying in order to make a martyr of him.

The film's storyline is that Abu Dujon knew he was going to become a *shahid*. It includes discussions of those who knew him describing the spiritual state that he was in for the several days before his death, that he had presentiments of the angels waiting for him.

The real Abu Dujon, however, was very different from the way he was portrayed. One of the former members of the IMU, the sentry, lived with him in the camp featured in the film and described him as no different from the others there. He was, according to this acquaintance, a lonely man who missed his wife, someone with no presentiments of his death or of an upcoming spiritual reward:

> But it was an accident. I don't think he was feeling anything. He stepped on that mine by accident. If it was me, the same would have been said about me in that video of yours.

THE END OF THE IMU

It is very hard to get a sense of how important the IMU ever was in the al-Qaeda operation. In 2000 and 2001, more money began to flow into the IMU in Afghanistan. But rather than creating a unified fighting force, this money increased the tension that was already present in the organization.

While my intent here is not to provide a comprehensive history of the organization, it is important to note that the IMU never took the step beyond stating its mission—taking power in the name of Islam—to being able to realize it.

It appears that the IMU leadership in general, and of Tohir Yuldoshev in particular, mostly confined themselves to virulent rhetoric and threats. The real acts of terror were generally carried out by fringe groups within the IMU or by lower-level commanders who either acted on their own authority or in contradiction to commands they had received.

For example, the interviews strongly argue (based on accounts of people with little or no prior contact with one another) that it was Khattab's "Chechen" group that was responsible for the attacks made in Tashkent in February 1999, and they may well have been planned without the prior knowledge of either Juma Namangani or Tohir Yuldoshev. Ironically, in the aftermath of these bombings, the crackdown against anyone remotely suspected of ties to Muslim militants led to an increase in IMU membership.

Similarly, neither Juma Namangani nor Tohir Yuldoshev seems to have made the decision to take the group of Japanese geologists[53] held captive by IMU supporters in summer 1999 in Batken, a mountainous and remote region just over the Kyrgyz-Tajik border. That incident led to the IMU's ouster from Tajikistan and its move to Afghanistan, in addition to bolstering the IMU's role in the international jihadist movement. Abduvali Yuldoshev (a deputy of Juma Namangani's) was said to be responsible for the hostage-taking operation. For his unsanctioned efforts, Abduvali Yuldoshev (no relation to Tohir) appears to have been assassinated on Juma Namangani's orders.

These independent actions were launched at least in part because Juma Namangani seems to have lacked sufficient funding to maintain his troops. The former fighters that were interviewed noted that Juma and Tohir Yuldoshev fought most of the time that the two men maintained camps in Afghanistan, and that the cause of their squabbling was largely over who would control the money that they were receiving from al-Qaeda. Juma unsuccessfully pressed for access to it, as he was responsible for managing the military operations. But Tohir Yuldoshev claimed that he had to maintain exclusive control in order to successfully discharge his overall organizational responsibilities. Tohir Yuldoshev also served as the spiritual leader of the movement, subordinate to Mullah Omar.

Mullah Omar had given Tohir Yuldoshev the title of "Mulk al-Emir," and put him in charge of the IMU's property with responsibility for its security, while Juma Namangani was "Emir al-Muminim," and was put in charge of an army of upward of 45,000 people. In this role, he was always in the front lines. He wound up dying in Afghanistan in November 2001, while Tohir Yuldoshev survived until 2009, when he, too, was killed in battle.[54] But from the start of the U.S.-led ISAF operation, even the fantasy that the IMU would someday take power in Uzbekistan could no longer be preserved.

11

THE POST-9/11 WORLD

The U.S.-led "war on terror" in general and the International Security Assistance Force operation in Afghanistan in particular hardened the resolve of the Uzbek government that religious life in the country had to be closely regulated by the government. While the chief security concern of the state has related to Islamic groups, Christian groups (and particularly evangelical sects)[1] have found it more difficult to operate as well, in part because Uzbek authorities want to secure a "special role" for Islam, as part of a strategy of maintaining rapport with the country's Islamic leaders.

The NATO bombing of the Islamic Movement of Uzbekistan camps in Afghanistan lulled Uzbek authorities into a false sense of security, leading them to believe that they could manage the risk of external threats posed by Islamist extremist groups. The IMU was crushed, at least for the short term, by the bombing campaign in Afghanistan. Juma Namangani was killed, and while Tohir Yuldoshev sought to preserve the IMU, he did so by linking it even more closely with al-Qaeda and a global jihadist agenda, a mission for which financial resources were more readily available. This left many of the surviving fighters unhappy, because they had joined the movement with the hope of sparking a successful jihadist movement in Uzbekistan (even if they had to work harder to raise funds to do so), while having little interest in spreading the jihadist message globally. They went on to form the Islamic Jihad Union as an alternative to the IMU.

With the external threat diminished, Uzbek authorities became more focused than ever to identify and prosecute those they considered to be extremists, radicals, or susceptible to radical ideas. In an atmosphere of enhanced external security, continuing tight control of their national borders seemed to them the way to ensure domestic stability.

Bombings in Kyrgyzstan in 2002 and 2003[2] and stories of incursions into Tajikistan fostered Uzbek fears, proving that Islamic terrorist elements had not only escaped destruction but were still finding ways to enter the country and were even able to gain safe haven from the population. These concerns were seemingly justified by suicide bombings in Tashkent and Bukhara in 2004, the first manifestation of *shahids* on Uzbek soil. Moreover, the fact that some of the *shahids*, or at least their supporters, came from the circles around Obidkhon qori (Nazarov), who, ostensibly, had been "holed up" just across the border in southern Kazakhstan, strengthened Uzbek isolationist tendencies and the conviction that the security services of neighboring states were incompetent. For a few years, Uzbek security officials had been trying to convince their Kazakh colleagues, with little success, that "terror cells" were hiding in the south of their country.

It was against such a background that Uzbek authorities sought to deal with the demonstrations organized by supporters of Akrom Yuldoshev, the so-called Akramiya movement, who had been quietly protesting under the watchful eye of local security officers for nearly two months before the violence in Andijan in May 2005. But the attack on the armory and the prison break that followed reinforced the biases of Uzbek security services, "demonstrating" convincingly to them that religious radicals would make common cause with terrorists.

That the Uzbek authorities overreacted when they sought to break up the demonstrations is something that even those in positions of authority in Tashkent would privately agree to. Where there is real unanimity in Tashkent is in the anger over the way Western authorities reacted (and from the Uzbek point of view, overreacted) to the crackdown that followed. Uzbeks, and for that matter their Central Asian, Russian, and Chinese colleagues, could not understand why those who seized the square in Andijan were not considered terrorists. Instead, the United States and the European Union sought to emphasize the excessive civilian loss of life, and not the events that led to its occurrence.

Once again the Uzbek authorities turned inward, as well as back to former friends, such as Russia, by rejoining the Collective Security Treaty

Organization, which they had dropped out of in 1999. But Uzbek authorities' drive to turn the country into a more competent security state once again was at odds with many of the realities of early twenty-first-century statehood.

While there are still no demonstrable domestic effects of the globalization of communications, the very fact that it exists creates potent new threats for Uzbek authorities to address. For example, Uzbek authorities may have found a way to eliminate Abduvali qori physically, but every day those who are interested may download his sermons from YouTube. That is possible even in Uzbekistan, where some of the Islamist websites that feature his work can be accessed only through proxy servers, given the filters that authorities put on Internet servers in the country.

Of even more immediate concern to Uzbek authorities is their inability to reduce security risks emanating from beyond their borders. In spring and summer 2010, the security of the Uzbek regime was placed at risk by Kyrgyz unhappiness with President Kurmanbek Bakiev. The interethnic violence in southern Kyrgyzstan after his ouster created a massive potential refugee problem. Uzbek security is also placed at risk by the seeming instability of President Emomali Rahmon's rule in neighboring Tajikistan, and of course by fears that ISAF forces will pull out of Afghanistan before peace is secured.

The biggest concerns are those relating to what happens after Islam Karimov's rule ends. Most in the country, no matter how unhappy they might be, don't believe this will be because he is overthrown (something that nonetheless remains a possibility). But inevitably he must depart from office, if not voluntarily, then when nature takes its course. At that time the political institutions that he has put in place will be tested, including the current balance between religion and secular rule.

ISLAMIST-INSPIRED VIOLENCE IN UZBEKISTAN

The U.S.-led bombing campaign in Afghanistan created disarray in the ranks of the IMU in Afghanistan, particularly after the death of Juma Namangani in late fall 2001.[3] David Witter's brief but well-documented history of the IMU and IJU since the ISAF campaign details the difficulties

Tohir Yuldoshev had in regrouping the Uzbek fighters under his command. In part, Witter believes this was because of Yuldoshev's fund-raising problems, because sustaining his movement appears to have been of secondary concern for those funding al-Qaeda and other jihadist groups once the war on terrorism began.[4] Eventually funding was found, and Yuldoshev and his supporters relocated to South Waziristan.

There is relatively little evidence of direct IMU activity in Uzbekistan in the first years of the ISAF campaign. While the IMU was blamed for bombings in Kyrgyzstan in 2002 and 2003, it does not appear that either attack was part of a concerted or integrated plan to attack either Kyrgyz, or more importantly, for present purposes, Uzbek authorities. The 2002 attack, in the Oberon Bazaar, may well have been caused by local criminal elements that were conveniently labeled as IMU.[5]

The more serious threat to Uzbek security in these years was posed by the Islamic Jihad Union. The IJU was organized by IMU fighters who rejected the global focus of the IMU. These men, led by Najmiddin Jalolov, also known as Abu Yahya,[6] believed that the primary aim of Uzbek jihadists should be to sponsor military actions that would undermine the rule of Uzbek President Islam Karimov.

It is hard to know how actively the IMU recruited in Uzbekistan during the first years after the ISAF operations began, although Uzbek authorities maintain[7] that a small but steady stream of young people was traveling to Pakistan and Afghanistan to try to join them. The IJU, though, was quite obviously engaged in recruiting and training both men and women to commit terrorist acts. At least some of the training was being conducted on Uzbek soil, and some in neighboring Kazakhstan.

In late March of 2004, bombs exploded in Bukhara, apparently a training exercise gone wrong. The bombing was followed a day later by explosions in Tashkent, including a deadly attack at the Chorsu Bazaar, one of the main shopping areas. Although police and other security officers seem to have been the target, this attack in particular was designed to terrify the ordinary population.[8] Those involved in the spring and summer 2004 attacks seem to have had only the most rudimentary training, supporting the notion that these were local cells organized around trainers who had come back to Uzbekistan to recruit. There is no evidence to suggest that terror camps were organized in Uzbekistan.

The incidents killed 47 people and were the first suicide bombing attacks in Central Asia and the first use of female fighters as well.[9] The government accused the IMU and Hizb ut-Tahrir of the attacks.[10] There is no real question that these attacks were launched by people who intended to become *shahids*. Letters to relatives announcing this intent were found in searches of the homes of those whose bodies were found at the scene of the Chorsu bombing.[11] The March 2004 bombings did not attract a great deal of international attention because they occurred almost immediately after terrorist attacks on the Moscow metro system and on commuter trains in Madrid.[12]

While it may have been more convenient for Uzbek authorities to blame the attacks on others—providing the grounds for rounding up hundreds more alleged members of Hizb ut-Tahrir—it seems very likely that the IJU carried out these bombings. They quickly took public responsibility for them, in an effort to recruit more members to what they hoped would appear to be a successful organization.[13]

On July 30, 2004, simultaneous explosions occurred in Tashkent outside of the U.S. and Israeli embassies and the headquarters of the Uzbek chief prosecutor. There were many fewer fatalities in these attacks—four Uzbek law enforcement personnel, in addition to the three suicide bombers. The IJU immediately claimed responsibility for the attack, which seems to have been designed to punish Uzbek authorities for prosecuting IJU members over the March–April bombings. A number of the fifteen people arrested and put on trial in July 2004 had previously been identified as having ties to the IJU.[14] The IJU again claimed responsibility on various Islamic websites and indicated that the attacks were committed in support of IJU's Palestinian, Iraqi, and Afghan brothers in the global insurgency,[15] which is one of the reasons that the Israeli and U.S. embassies were targeted.

One of the mysteries still surrounding the 2004 violence in Uzbekistan was the role played by Islamist groups training in Kazakhstan, and whether such groups had any ties to Obidkhon qori, who had been living seemingly quietly in southern Kazakhstan for roughly a decade since fleeing Uzbekistan.

Uzbek authorities had long maintained that various terrorist groups were training in Shymkent Oblast, just across the border from Tashkent and Jizzakh Oblasts. In fact, these claims were even made at international conferences at which I was present; however, the Kazakhs vehemently denied such claims. After the July 2004 bombings, Uzbek authorities presented evidence[16] that was convincing enough that Kazakh authorities put out an arrest warrant for Obidkhon qori and for some of those closely associated with him. Obidkhon qori, who fled to Europe and received political asylum, had not disclosed his exact location, and has always denied these allegations.[17]

At issue is whether the *jamoa* or *jamoa islomi* (community of Islam) is related to or derived from the study circles that Obidkhon qori formed when he lived and worked in Uzbekistan. Obidkhon qori's watchword was that "to gather/unite in communities is obligatory for Muslims."

Uzbekistan's security services had been claiming since 1995 that his *jamoa* had secret stores of weapons including homemade explosives, which were "revealed" through the use of hidden cameras on various television broadcasts. Bakhtiyar Babadjanov sought to verify this allegation by interviewing some relatively low-ranking former members of the *jamoas*. They maintained that the *jamoa*'s warriors had only martial arts training, and nothing more. Babadjanov believes that the men that he interviewed may have been fearful of admitting anything more, and he personally believes that some *jamoas* began military preparation in 1998 and 1999, possibly with the intent of organizing a series of explosions in Tashkent.[18]

Obidkhon qori denies that his communities have any link to terrorism. Uzbek authorities claim a prior relationship between Ruhiddin Fahriddinov, who was sentenced in 2006 for his alleged role in the 1999 bombings and Obidkhon qori. Furthermore, they argue that Fahriddinov's network was used to fund terrorist training.[19] They claim that Fahriddinov was tied to the 1999 bombings, which in turn, by association, implicated Obidkhon qori. Given the success of Obidkhon qori's asylum case in 2006, it seems clear that European Union officials do not accept those claims.[20]

In general, there is no certainty about the relationship between the various Islamic groups and major radical clerics in the Ferghana Valley. We will probably never know with any certainty whether Obidkhon qori had ties to armed jihadist groups. There is also a question of whether any of these fighters had ties to Abdulquddus Mirzaev, Abduvali qori's son, who is rumored to have lived in Saudi Arabia, is said to have been a frequent visitor to Afghanistan, and who certainly made his life's work the propagation of his father's teachings.[21]

Uzbek authorities' expectations of the clerics are simple: anyone—including religious leaders—who has reason to suspect that an individual has ties to a terrorist organization is supposed to immediately notify the authorities. If they don't notify the authorities, they are presumed to be sympathetic to jihadist ideologies themselves. This puts Islamic clerics in an impossible situation. They have spiritual obligations to tend to those who come to them, to guide them to the "true path." This does not by definition mean that clerics who attract such followers are sympathetic to their ideologies; of course, neither does it preclude the opposite.

This means that for the Uzbek authorities, someone like Obidkhon qori will always remain under suspicion for holding the same jihadist convictions as his followers in southern Kazakhstan who were found guilty of involvement in the bombings in Uzbekistan in spring and summer 2004. The same questions were raised in 2006 when Imam Muhammed Rafik Kamalov of Kara Suu was caught up and killed in a sting operation.[22]

THE ANDIJAN UPRISING OPENS A NEW ERA

The use of deadly force to break up a demonstration of thousands of largely unarmed demonstrators in Andijan on May 13, 2005, leaving hundreds dead, will remain the dominant image that most people in the West have of the Uzbek government well into the future.

I don't want to engage in the ongoing debate over whether Akrom Yuldoshev was a benevolent businessman who liked to write religious history and run a prayer circle with other local businessmen who aided his community, or whether he was a dangerous schismatic whose religious writings were designed to encourage his followers to make jihad.[23]

What is clear is that Akrom Yuldoshev was a very minor figure in the development of Islam in Uzbekistan, a schismatic and self-trained religious thinker. His followers were relatively few in number with no real prospect of spreading his ideas to distant parts of Uzbekistan, let alone other parts of the region.

But the government of Uzbekistan reacted very fiercely to him, not because of the religious threat that he posed, but because of the amount of violence around the prison break and the siege of downtown Andijan that followed. Uzbek authorities were already on tenterhooks, and that explains part of their overreaction.

Only two months previously, after weeks of demonstrations, angry Kyrgyz from southern Kyrgyzstan who were protesting the results of Kyrgyzstan's parliamentary elections marched north and were able to force the resignation of Kyrgyz President Askar Akaev. Fears that the same thing might happen in Uzbekistan seemed real when those attacking the armory and prison went to the main square of Andijan holding police officers and firefighters hostages.

Karimov even went to Andijan to try to appraise the situation personally. However, he did not leave the airport, and his orders to "take care of the situation" produced the debacle of incompetence for which he must bear responsibility. Negotiations got nowhere, because both the government and demonstrators were reported to have been inflexible. The threat of force yielded no results, and the demonstrators could find little they could agree on with the government.

Most of those protesting in the square seemed to have little to do with the imprisoned members of the Akramiya movement, although their female family members seem to have made up the center core. And it seems clear from the various eyewitness accounts that have emerged[24] that the focus of the demonstration quickly switched to complaints about Uzbek government policies, including calls for President Karimov's resignation.

Not prone to taking chances and unwilling to risk that the demonstrators would increase in numbers overnight and thus pose a more significant threat to the regime, Uzbek authorities decided that the demonstrations had to be broken up before dark. While the Uzbek government likely exaggerated the risk to their regime posed by the protesters in Andijan, they reacted with extreme force.

From that time on, Uzbek authorities in Tashkent have been more concerned about the potential of risks to Uzbek state security originating from the other side of the border. Certainly during the early years of President Bakiev's rule, Uzbek authorities sought to extend their writ over the Kyrgyz border. They did this by trying to persuade southern Kyrgyzstan's security officials to arrest people whom Tashkent viewed as putting Uzbek's security at risk. They often did so by arguing that these same alleged "felons" posed a threat to Kyrgyz security as well. Now, however, with the resignation of Akaev, the Uzbek authorities lost their leverage on the Kyrgyz and began to feel more insecure.

When persuasion failed, Uzbek authorities occasionally went so far as to kidnap suspected felons who were sighted on Kyrgyz territory.[25] In fact, when I went to complain to Kyrgyz authorities that security officers had dragged two of my colleagues (both Uzbek citizens) out of the *chaikana* (tea house) where we were sitting, I was asked, "Were they tossed into the back seat or thrown into the trunk?" When I answered "the back seat," the officer said, "Then it was our Kyrgyz that did it and not the Uzbek authorities."[26] Tossing people into the trunk facilitated border crossings without paperwork. Both of my colleagues, who were apparently mistaken for members of Hizb ut-Tahrir, were quickly released.

The Uzbeks also successfully pressured the new Kyrgyz government to toughen legislation against extremism by introducing further restrictions on the activities of Hizb ut-Tahrir, whose members were operating openly in much of Kyrgyzstan's south. In May 2006, a band of insurgents that was subsequently linked to the IMU attacked a Tajik-Kyrgyz border outpost, killing two border guards in the process. After the Kyrgyz National Security Service captured the gunmen, they found a book, *Faith Brochure*, by Muhammad Rafik Kamalov, with the author's phone number on the cover. Kamalov was a prominent imam of the Kara Suu's mosque (in southern Kyrgyzstan) and brother of Sodikjon qori Kamalludin (Kamalov), the Gorbachev-era *mufti* of Kyrgyzstan.[27] The family was composed of ethnic Uzbeks and citizens of Kyrgyzstan.

After initially interrogating Kamalov in May, the Kyrgyz security forces released him. But on August 6, 2006, Kamalov was shot dead in his car outside of Osh, along with two members of the IMU who were in the car.[28] According to official Kyrgyz government sources, Kamalov and his passengers refused to stop when ordered and, in addition, opened fire on the police patrol—who responded in kind. Kamalov's funeral drew thousands of mourners, and he was proclaimed a *shahid* by prominent religious clerics in the region.

Kamalov's supporters in Kyrgyzstan maintain that the two other victims just happened to be with the cleric, who in their opinion was diligent in his pastoral duties and worked with young people who held radical views to try to persuade them to follow the correct and peaceful path of Hanafi Islam. Bakhtiyar Babadjanov takes some issue with this characterization, noting that Kamalov was a student of Hindustani from 1983 to 1985, then attended the Mir-i Arab Mosque in Bukhara, and finally, studied in the same faculty as Muhammad Sodiq Muhammad Yusuf in Libya. According to Babadjanov, Kamalov deeply respected Hindustani, but criticized his teacher's "excessive conservatism and caution" as well as his inability to imagine that "this whole infidel system will disintegrate." As such, Kamalov became a sharp critic of the current government policy of separation of state and mosque.[29]

Uzbek security forces are likely more than a match for the jihadist groups currently receiving training in Afghanistan. All of the Uzbek border posts with Tajikistan and Kyrgyzstan have been upgraded since the Andijan events in 2005, and there has been an effort to improve the capacity of Uzbekistan's internal security forces as well.

The Uzbek jihadist groups have also continued to reinvent themselves. Tohir Yuldoshev and his forces remained much more closely linked to events in the South Waziristan region near the Afghanistan-Pakistan border than with developments within Uzbekistan proper. Although he preferred the role of theologian and became a popular speaker at local mosques in Waziristan, Yuldoshev spent at least a portion of his last years as a fighter, and after being rumored to have been killed on several occasions, he finally succumbed to wounds in August 2009.[30]

After Yuldoshev was confirmed dead, an interview with him was released in which he made mention of meeting Osama bin Laden and the impact bin Laden had in convincing Yuldoshev to commit his life to the cause of jihad.[31] There has been jockeying for Yuldoshev's position among the top IMU commanders,[32] with Usman Odil[33] seemingly taking charge, at least for now. None of the current figures has anything like the kind of "name recognition" that Yuldoshev enjoyed with Uzbek youths.

In 2009 and 2010, some of the Tajik commanders who joined the IMU after the Tajik civil war returned to Tajikistan with their troops to try to recreate a power base in the Tavildara region.[34] Subsequent skirmishes with

Tajik government forces created a serious scare for Tajikistan's president, Emomali Rahmon, who did manage to push back the insurgents. The fighting, though, left many wary of the long-term viability of Rahmon's regime and created concerns in Tashkent that the risks to Uzbekistan might be increasing. This was further brought home by an attack on local police in Khujand (near the Uzbek border) in September 2010 that was blamed on Tajik jihadists.[35]

The IJU has been more active on Uzbek territory than other regional jihadist groups. In late May 2009, insurgents crossed from Kyrgyzstan and attacked a border post near Andijan. The IJU claimed responsibility for the attack, which did not presage further violence on that border.[36] In July 2009, Anvar qori Tursunov, a prominent Tashkent cleric, survived a stabbing attack, only days after the deputy head of a leading madrasa in Tashkent was killed. The reasons for these attacks are unclear; they are possibly linked to business dealings gone bad, or possibly because the men were being punished for facilitating the prosecution of those accused of religious extremism.[37]

The IJU seems to continue to enjoy a recruiting advantage within Uzbekistan. It, too, has developed something of a global reach, since three alleged IJU members were arrested in a terror plot uncovered in Germany in 2007.[38] The need for international funding likely drives both Uzbek jihadist groups to try to broaden their membership and their theater of operations. The IJU website, www.sodiqlar.com, is also designed to appeal to an Uzbek audience; when we accessed the site in March 2011, it featured articles on the death of Abdulhakim qori. Like the IMU, the IJU tries to demonstrate its links to important Uzbek theologians to create a sense of continuity with its calls for jihad and the struggle for religious purity in Uzbekistan in the past. They, too, pay tribute to Uzbek *shahids* and try to provide the potential Uzbek jihadist with access to the proper reading to prepare him to take on this role.

The IMU website furqon.com, "The Standard," continues to try to target an Uzbek readership and provides a historical context for the current struggles of the IMU, with pieces on the history of the movement, links to the writings and videos of the sermons of Abduvali qori and Tohir Yuldoshev (Tohir Furuq, as he preferred to be called). The site has gained sophistication over the years; there are now blog entries and downloads for

MP3 players. The content is updated regularly. The theme of martyrdom is emphasized, with portraits of Uzbek *shahids*. The accounts of the *shahid* lives, though, make it apparent just how far from Uzbekistan the IMU's battlefields have been, in that most of the people died fighting in Afghanistan or Pakistan.

In the last several years, the Uzbek government's goal to control young people's access to information has become impossible to achieve. As a test case, in 2008, I sent a young assistant out shopping in Tashkent, looking for books and videotapes that were banned in a 2006 decree. My assistant was able to find numerous titles freely available in state-owned (or at least closely monitored) stores. Now with the expansion of the Internet, even works that are difficult to find in stores can often be found online.

These IMU and IJU sites are blocked in Uzbekistan, and the IJU in particular has changed its hosting sites to try to evade being blocked by others as well. Uzbek authorities also try to keep track of, and block, other potentially seditious sites, such as Obidkhon qori's www.islomovozi.com.

However, Uzbek authorities are unable to block the content on YouTube, unless they decide to simply cut off access to YouTube entirely, which they have been reluctant to do because the site is primarily a venue for people watching and posting entirely nonpolitical content. It is also a valuable channel for conveying "good material" about Islam, and Uzbek media-savvy clerics of all theological persuasions have been making increasing use of it. While millions of Uzbeks don't use YouTube, tens of thousands do, with people posting and reposting video recordings of Abduvali qori and Tohir Yuldoshev. When postings are taken down, new ones go up.[39] Efforts by the Uzbek government to get Internet cafés to take the passport information of users does not seem to have dampened Internet use, and it is not clear that Internet café owners are being strongly pressured to do this. Moreover, although Uzbek authorities probably have the capacity to monitor home use of the Internet through the various licensed providers, it would not be easy to implement. So for now at least the government is hoping that the filtering done by providers is sufficient.

The biggest challenge to date for Uzbek authorities to control the web was during the interethnic riots in Osh in June 2010. Uzbek human rights groups posted graphic videos of Uzbeks who were being killed by Kyrgyz, and there was serious concern that the Uzbek population on Uzbekistan's side of the border would be riled up and try to cross over into Kyrgyzstan in defense of Uzbek honor.[40]

The clashes caused several hundred thousand ethnic Uzbeks who were Kyrgyz citizens to flee their homes in Kyrgyzstan. Some took refuge with relatives, but many fled toward the border. The Uzbek government made the unprecedented decision to allow women, children, elderly men, and wounded ethnic Uzbek males from Kyrgyzstan to get temporary refuge in Uzbekistan.[41] The decision by Uzbek authorities to not let in most males was to keep families from permanently migrating to Uzbekistan as most would not stay without their head of household. Uzbek authorities have always viewed the Uzbek population from Kyrgyzstan with some suspicion, because they have lived under a political and economic system that was quite different from that of Uzbekistan for the last twenty years, and some of the Uzbeks who fled from Andijan to Kyrgyzstan were among those who were forced to take refuge in Uzbekistan in June 2010.

There is also concern that the Uzbeks of Kyrgyzstan are more radical Muslims than those in Uzbekistan's part of the Ferghana Valley. Hizb ut-Tahrir has operated very openly there, certainly by comparison to the other Central Asian countries. In addition, a number of prominent Uzbek clerics teaching and preaching in Osh and its environs are at minimum Hanafi "free thinkers," and many Uzbeks would see them as adherents of Salafi traditions. The two Kamalov brothers were the most prominent examples. Since the mid-1990s, Uzbek authorities have worked hard to limit contacts between these neighboring and often interrelated populations.

Until the June 2010 violence, there was little evidence that the Uzbeks of Kyrgyzstan had any particular interest in joining jihadist groups. IMU members seem to have been able to arrange refuge in Batken during the 1999 and 2000 attacks because they bribed Kyrgyz security officials. There are no accounts that I have ever found about Uzbeks in Kyrgyzstan harboring terrorists, or of Uzbek commanders in the IMU or IJU who were from Kyrgyzstan.

By contrast, since June 2010 there has been a great deal of speculation about the number of young Uzbeks who have fled Kyrgyzstan to join the IMU or IJU in Afghanistan and Pakistan. Uzbek sources claim that they are in the thousands, but a few hundred is likely a conservative estimate. During and just after the violence in June, Uzbek clerics, including Muhammad Sodiq Muhammad Yusuf,[42] and even Obidkhon qori writing from exile,[43] urged people to mourn the dead but not to confuse the deplorable violence with Islam. Uzbekistan's spiritual leaders on all sides of the political spectrum sought to counsel their followers that such behavior violates the precepts of Islam.

While the new jihadist recruits might be the source of fighters who will someday attack either the Kyrgyz government or the Uzbek government, more frightening still is the specter that the violence in Osh foretells interethnic fighting of the future.

Twenty years after independence, some things seem to have come full circle. The last years of the USSR were marked by ethnic unrest, first on the Uzbek side of the Ferghana Valley in 1989 and then in Osh on a larger scale in 1990. The fighting in Osh almost twenty years later to the day reminded everyone of the speed and virulence with which long-dormant ethnic tensions could spill over. More people died in a three-day period in southern Kyrgyzstan than have been killed in jihadist-inspired violence in the five countries of Central Asia over a twenty-year period.[44]

What most alarms people in the region, leaders and ordinary citizens alike, is that Osh might be a forewarning of what could lie ahead as the region's various strongmen continue to age and begin to falter. While it is granted that incursions by jihadists trained abroad or attacks from homegrown jihadist groups may play a role in further destabilizing the situation, it has been a long time since I have heard any serious discussion that this could be a trigger to provoke regime change or civil war in Uzbekistan.

ISLAM AND THE STATE IN UZBEKISTAN TODAY

At the same time, one of the fallacies still held by all the Central Asian governments is that Islam can be successfully regulated by the state, and Uzbek authorities have made their commitment to this premise a cornerstone of their state-building policy. It is their conviction that Uzbekistan will not remain a secular state unless religion is under the firm control of government authorities, who define nationalism to emphasize what is "acceptable" in Islam and exclude what is dangerous.

The re-emergence of Islam in Uzbekistan has not led to a uniformity of thinking among the country's community of believers. Though Islam has returned to public life in Uzbekistan, it has also been transformed by a process of simultaneous re-emergence, rebirth, and reinvention. All three are important, and all three had an interactive effect, creating political and social realities. These realities will be difficult to rapidly transform and are difficult for state or even religious actors to fully manage.

In many ways, Islam was like a long-dormant bulb in much of Central Asia, flowering quite abundantly when conditions became supportive of it. When policies toward Islam changed in the last years of Soviet rule, it turned out that seventy-plus years of Communist Party rule had not destroyed the fundaments of Islam in Uzbekistan. There were a lot of competent clerics in the region—not hundreds or thousands, to be sure, though at least several dozen. In any case, there were sufficient numbers to train those necessary for staffing the mosques and madrasas that were being formed to meet popular demand. Uzbek clerics were accepted as peers by Sufi clerics in the dominant centers of Islamic learning in the Arab world. They also were able to travel abroad, expanding their own contacts and making the ties necessary for a new generation to study in the madrasas of the Arab world, and of course in Turkey, where Turks both secular and religious were eager to welcome their Central Asian "brothers."

For all the discussion of the restrictions that Uzbek authorities have introduced on the unsanctioned practice of Islam and other religions, it is clear that there is an extraordinary difference in the relationship between Islam and the state in Uzbekistan since independence than what was the case during all but the first few years of Soviet rule.

Islam occupies a well-defined and honored public role. There is not freedom of religion in the Western understanding of it. Those who accept the definition of Islam that is offered by Uzbekistan's Muslim Spiritual Administration and those who preach in the mosques that they register and the schools that they sponsor are free to live lives that are fully in conformity with their faith, even to make pilgrimage to Mecca. They are able to do so openly, and they are considered fully respectable citizens who can compete for any public or private job for which they may qualify, with no expectation of encountering discrimination on religious grounds. This is a dramatic difference from the Soviet period, when formal religious training was almost impossible to obtain or pursue openly, mosques were numbered in the dozens and not in the thousands, and public worship put people at risk of being scrutinized by security officials.

Many restrictions obviously remain—belonging to an unsanctioned religious group is potentially quite risky—but these restrictions do not touch most ordinary Uzbeks, who become really aware of them only if a neighbor or a family member falls afoul of the Uzbek authorities. Most Uzbek citizens are content with the degree of religious expression that they have. They likely see themselves as living in a country that respects Islam and most probably believe the regime's claims as to the terrorist threat posed by extremist groups.

Some probably are dubious about claims that Hizb ut-Tahrir is a terrorist organization. Thousands of Uzbeks have ties to this group, so ordinary citizens may have had contact with one or two members and most likely did not see them as posing a terrorist threat. Yet Uzbeks are generally not comfortable with "differentness" or with religious expressions that are distinct from the mainstream views. For this reason, many Uzbeks get upset when Salafi Muslims come and worship in their mosques, because they use different hand gestures in prayers than Hanafi Muslims and speak parts of prayers that Hanafi Muslims recite silently.

Rather than concern themselves about such matters, in a world in which terrorist bombings have occurred in the United States and in Europe, it is much easier for people to accept that there are "bad seeds" among the Uzbek population, as in Russia and elsewhere, and that the state should punish them.

Despite internal religious polemics, for most Uzbeks it is far more important that Islam has "returned to its proper place." Islam's holy days are state holidays. Uzbeks can seek advice from an imam or a Sufi sheikh when needed, ask them to pray for the success of a business, the recovery of a relative, or for anything else that concerns them for that matter. Weddings, funerals, and circumcision ceremonies can all be performed in accordance with religious rights. Ramadan is openly observed by anyone who wishes it, and the end of each day's fast is an occasion of prayer and social gathering. State efforts to restrict the amount of money spent on religious rituals are far more likely to evoke heated arguments in communities than the news that strangers who want to practice their faith "in ways alien to our ancestors" are being subjected to arrest and ill treatment by the government.

THE MANY "ISLAMS" OF UZBEKISTAN

Despite the fact that the state has tried to popularize the idea that Uzbek nationalism and Islam are somehow conjoined in Uzbekistan, there is certainly not a single Islam being practiced in the country. This was true in the past, and it is true today. This is partly because of the clumsiness with which state authorities have designed their message, a result of their difficulty in controlling sources of alternatives to this message. But it is also a product of the nature of Islam as a religion. Simply put, Islam is a faith that has been marked by competing schools of interpretation, sharp differences on what role to assign the core text, and whether or not the faith accepts hierarchies.

For this reason, state institutions responsible for formulating and delivering the state's ideological messages have invariably come to reflect the divisions within the Uzbek religious community, almost to the same degree that these divisions are reflected in the mosques and religious schools themselves.

That said, traditional Hanafi Islam as interpreted by the official Spiritual Administration of Uzbekistan does dominate. Ironically, though, the state's inability to introduce Islamic uniformity is probably helping sustain Uzbekistan as a secular state. The diversity of views and variety of interests among religious leaders is inhibiting their ability to engage in collective action.

If they had such a capacity, they would use it to press more state recognition of Islam's tenets in the country's educational system and in social legislation. Moreover, if unified, they would likely get much of what they asked for. The government of Uzbekistan could not move to discipline mainstream Islamic clerics in the way that it has moved against schismatic elements within Islam such as Hizb ut-Tahrir or Akramiya, or those who have used violence in the name of Islam.

In Uzbekistan, the return to Islam is a more homegrown affair. Even those with Salafi training argue that their teachings and practices are in keeping with the true spirit of local Hanafi Islam and see their struggle as simply the modern reflection of the battle within Islam. However, they often have trouble convincing those who have long considered themselves believers that this "purified" version of Islam is preferable to what had been practiced for most of the twentieth century (and for many by their ancestors back as far as there is transmitted memory).

There are many causes for the return to traditionalism, and many different settings and ways in which traditional values are re-emerging. There is nostalgia for the past on the part of the white-collar, seemingly secularized, population. Some observance of religion or at least religious rituals seems a good way to demonstrate to one's milieu, and to oneself, a kind of cultural homogeneity, an effort to bond with earlier generations before Russian and Soviet rule when religious values set legal and social norms. This has taken a variety of forms, but it generally relies heavily on individual choice, either to select what part of religious doctrine and ritual one will accept as part of one's life, or in some cases to actually decide on a largely personally generated form of doctrinal interpretation.

For many, the return to tradition is simply the substitution of one moral compass for another. This is the case in many rural areas, and even in the "old city" quarters, where mosques and madrasas serve as major points of social organization. In these places the return of traditionalism is part of an attempt to fill the moral, and even more importantly, the economic vacuum that was left after the collapse of the Soviet Union. In many of these areas there was always some fusion of Soviet values with religious teachings, as the social welfare component of socialist ideology could be said to reinforce the commitment to social justice in Islam.

Economic losses, especially in rural areas, led to a re-emphasis of traditional cultural values. State-run collective farms, for instance, were legally reorganized as communally owned collectives. This increased the role of community elders and that of religious figures, who (now as public figures) also joined the ranks of "elders" serving in *mahalla* committees, regardless of their age.

Clerics who reaffirmed the old ways of practice found it easy to exercise authority. But this also is how Salafi ideas are able to spread, when young clerics from respected families return to their communities and proselytize new, more purified versions of the faith as a path to exit the corrupted environments in which they believe they are living. This message can have great power in the parts of the country (frequently rural areas) where sons lack the opportunities that their fathers routinely had in the Soviet era, and where the quality of social services more generally is viewed to be in decline.

The lack of uniformity in Islam is also the result of easier access to religious education. Today access is by no means as easy as it was in the early 1990s, and the content is more regulated. But over the past fifteen years or so, the "elitist" status of religious education has largely been lost. There are so many more state-sanctioned places where Islam is being taught that the state has had difficulty keeping track of the content. Even when the state is aware of the curriculum, those charged with supervision often lack the background to correctly evaluate whether the curriculum is being taught in a way that reinforces state aims. Similarly, while Western-style "Sunday school" religious instruction is banned, Uzbek authorities tend to ignore unsanctioned religious instruction, especially when it is presumed to be traditional Hanafi teachings in content and is offered in a way that does not draw public attention.

Consequently, believers in Uzbekistan come in many forms. Many in the older generation want the practice of Islamic customs and rituals to remain unchanged. People who grew up after Soviet rule are more inclined to see Islam as one form of connection to a wider world, and as they learn about the differences, they can be naturally attracted to Salafi or more schismatic forms of the faith. Of course, there are also people in both the older and younger generations who have little interest in Islam in any but its most symbolic role, and who prefer the old Soviet secular or modern globally secular ways.

Whether Uzbekistan will remain a secular state depends upon whether this generation—and more importantly, subsequent generations—works out the balance between religion and nationalism. For now most young people seem to be either nationalists or supportive of the sanctioned version of Islam, but with time the Uzbek state is likely to lose even more control of how religious values are transmitted.

Uzbekistan is a multilayered society of different regional identities and religious beliefs. Many practicing Muslims turn to religion to find salvation from desperate living conditions, and the state-endorsed version of Islam is not the only one people may encounter. Some prefer to listen to non-state and anti-state actors who define Islam in a way that distances their faith from the increasingly unpopular state.

In a context of deteriorating economic conditions and declining personal opportunities, young people may well be attracted to those with more radical views than those advanced by the state. Government control over mass media, which encompasses not only the press and television, but also the Internet, limits the sources of information available to young people, especially those who live in rural areas. Therefore, this group, the majority of all young people, is potentially susceptible to the ideas that neo-Islamists are spreading with the label of a "better life" that all Uzbeks, regardless of age, are still desperately seeking.

The Uzbek regime is not ignorant of this development and has sought to develop policies that restrain "unsupervised" practices by reintroducing the organized version of Islam. This is a risky strategy, however, because the government must do it in a way that does not increase the discontent of religious believers, especially those in the Ferghana Valley.

In this environment of relative religious tolerance, at least in comparison to most of the years under Soviet rule, ordinary Muslims have begun to use a religious yardstick to consider issues in their everyday lives, including economic, political, social, and even personal affairs. A small minority has begun to think about the social and political rules set down by the state as infringements on Sharia's norms, and come to consider secular forms of government as an obstacle to the embodiment of "fair Islamic governance."

The government's choice to use Islam as part of the national ideology means that the government will be further judged by its protection of the constitutional guarantees provided for religious believers. While advocates of Hizb ut-Tahrir or Akramiya have been labeled by civil authorities as violators of Uzbek law because of their commitment to introduce a theocracy, Uzbek Salafi and neo-Salafi clerics are operating fully within the bounds of the law. Because of that, most will be able to continue to seek to popularize their values.

As Uzbekistan participates in a globalized society, its population will continue to be exposed to a variety of developments in the larger Muslim community. At the same time, a new generation of clerics can be expected to once again try to introduce new ideas as well as bring their own considerations to Uzbekistan's long-standing Hanafi traditions.

MARTHA BRILL OLCOTT

WILL UZBEKISTAN EMBRACE THE "SUFI WAY"?

There is also still the question of what role Sufism will play in Uzbekistan's future. In many places, the legalization of religion has brought the return of Sufism. Now again, sites associated with the history of prominent Sufis can be openly venerated. This angers many Hanafi theologians who view Sufi practices as a smacking of paganism and believe that they degrade the centrality of the Quran and other subjects of religious learning. But from the point of view of the regime, it poses no political risk, keeps people happy, and even brings in support from the "right kind" of Turkish religious groups.

It is difficult to predict what will happen with the current revival of Sufism. Uzbek authorities are betting that it will continue much as it has developed over the past twenty-odd years. Prominent Sufis such as Ibrahim Hazrat, an *ishan* in Kokand, have large followings and many *murids*, but he has been content with training his students and disciples to focus on the spiritual mediation of problems that originate in their social or material realms, and to avoid political discussions.

There is nothing to stop subsequent Sufi leaders from making the transition to a political agenda, and the history of the region makes clear that the step would be a logical one. The tradition of Sufi learning at the theological level may also be restored, and if so Sufism will probably develop a spiritual vitality in the region and attract Uzbek intellectuals to it.

This doesn't seem to be likely yet for several reasons. For the most part, it is hard for intellectuals to identify with the most popular Sufi sheikhs in Uzbekistan partly because the sheikhs tend to seek a broad mass following. It has been observed on a smaller scale, however, through looking at the growing following of Ibrahim Hazrat, that prominent businesspeople in his own region tout his spiritual powers and others from the elite or with elite ambitions are drawn to him as well. If this were to happen at the national level, Sufism could become far more influential in shaping the development of Islam in Uzbekistan than it has over the past twenty years.

Still, this does not seem terribly likely in the near term. The current dominance of Salafi-style fundamentalism in recent decades emphasizes a return to purity on the foundation of the Quran rather than through later interpretative works that form the basis of Sufi teachings and practice.

President Karimov had initially sought to emphasize Uzbekistan's central place in the development of Sufism in Hanafi Islam as a way of bringing in moderate Islamic forces from Turkey in particular to help shape the evolution of Uzbek Islam. But even in Turkey itself, Sufism is forced to compete with other strains of Islam, and it no longer dominates political space in that country either, with Turkey's current leadership coming from a more Salafist-style religious tradition.

At the same time, the usurpation of the government's linkage among Sufism, Islam, and Uzbek nationalism during the early years of Uzbek statehood may make it difficult for intellectuals to identify Sufism as any sort of "independent" religious thought. But all this could change over time. The direction that Sufism will select for itself will depend on the behavior of the second and maybe third generations of Sufi leaders, and on the composition of its membership.

Should the secular intelligentsia become more attracted to Sufism and seek membership in the Sufi brotherhoods in Uzbekistan, the nature of the Sufi revival would rapidly change. This could lead to the politicization of such groups, especially if the political and economic ambitions of the intelligentsia are not being met. Sufi movements have played this role in Uzbek history, especially in the Timurid and post-Timurid periods that President Karimov is so fond of recalling. The biographies of those medieval figures provide role models as leaders who went into politics in order to make Sharia the sole law in the life of the state.

Though religious both in origin and primary motivation, Sufi orders have at various points in history transformed themselves into primarily political movements when their drive for reform led them to clash with or target political authorities as obstacles for their spiritual mission. Their hierarchical organizational structure is also well-suited for political engagement.

The current generation of Sufi leaders still remembers the restrictions placed on the practice of the Sufi way by state authorities. Quite possibly with this in mind (with the exception of those heated days during the waning of Soviet power), they have preferred to focus on the revitalization of largely dormant Sufi orders and to emphasize their traditional rituals. The next generation may choose to be bolder, in a political sense of the word.

Much will likely depend upon whether there is a general consensus that the basic social and economic needs of the population are being met. But it will also depend on whether the current distance between Sufis and other kinds of fundamentalists is maintained, either by government policies designed to keep the two separate and competitive or by the internal dynamism of Islam's own development in Uzbekistan.

Sufism is not an absolute "barrier to terrorism," as the Sufis close to Karimov used to maintain. Sufi leaders are likely to search for a basis for their political activity in the history of their brotherhood, and as they do they will find conflicting legacies. Sufism could become a vehicle for the radicalization of Hanafi groups, and it does not preclude cooperation between Sufi and Hanafi groups. As the history of the early 1990s showed, all three elements are capable of cooperating, especially if they are pushed in that direction by government policies antithetical to all Islamic communities in the region.

The potential for unification will be determined by the nature of the training of the next two generations of Sufi leaders, and especially those of Naqshabandiya groups of Uzbekistan, which have the greatest potential for political action.

This could well lead to politicization under the banner of the restoration of the Sharia as state law. And this in turn could lead to the unification of interests with the representatives of political Islam, both for the Sufis and for the conservatives, who for a time can forget about their hostility to Sufism in general.

But none of this is inevitable. There is also the possibility that Sufism could serve as a counterbalance to radical Islam. Regardless of the way the Sufi scenario will play out, efforts by the state (not to mention outside actors) to try to openly use Sufism are likely to backfire, especially if they encouraged the creation of a uniform viewpoint among clerics.

So far, Sufism poses little threat of destabilizing the secular ideology of the state. But everything depends on the policy of the state. Right now, it is not Sufis, but neo-Islamists, who have penetrated secular state structures. They are today's safeguard. But circumstances could make the second and third generation of Sufi leaders into tomorrow's enemies.

SOME FINAL THOUGHTS

For virtually the entire history of independent Uzbekistan, there has been speculation as to how long the regime can maintain itself in power and whether angry Islamists will help bring about its demise. Much of this discussion is a continuation of the dominant threads in Western commentary about Central Asia during the Soviet period, when the suppression of religion was seen as a potential spark to popular unrest against Soviet rule.

Now the argument is made in a slightly new form. Uzbek government policies toward religion, and especially the suppression of unsanctioned religious groups, are seen as possibly hastening the end of the Karimov regime, or a potential source of civil war when Islam Karimov departs from the scene.

While there is good reason to believe that Karimov will not give up power voluntarily, there is some chance that he will assume a role much like that of Lee Kwan Yew in Singapore and steer the succession process himself. This, of course, assumes that President Karimov survives until his term ends in late 2014, a likely decision point. It is difficult to predict what the post-Karimov period will look like. It is even harder to engage in the writing of alternative history, which is what the Uzbek president's critics are de facto doing, by arguing that the potential politicization of Islam in Uzbekistan is the result of repressive policies toward religion that have been pursued since the mid-1990s.

There is no question that Uzbekistan has a repressive political system. The heavy hand of the government is applied to regulate many features of social life as well as virtually all aspects of political life. While the Soviet-era apparatus of censorship has been dismantled, Uzbek media are closely managed. The formation of any sort of nongovernmental organization requires governmental approval, which is not automatic, even for the most nonpolitical of groups.

It is hard to know how much of the micromanagement that has occurred is a product of Uzbek culture, a legacy of the Soviet system, or the reflection of Karimov's personal preference. Undoubtedly all three play a role. But what is most important is that this effort of micromanaging is also applied in the area of religion.

One can speculate on how the relationship between religion and politics might have evolved had Uzbekistan developed a democratic political system or even a less autocratic political system, and whether the practice of Islam in Uzbekistan would have evolved differently as well. Obviously it is impossible to know. Speculation does not imply even tacit support for Uzbekistan's political choices. It is simply a useful analytic exercise as one contemplates what might lie ahead in a post-Karimov world.

It is important to remember that the politicization of Islam is occurring in well-developed democracies and relatively affluent societies such as the United States, the United Kingdom, Germany, and France. Islamic jihadist groups have been able to recruit successfully in every one of these countries.

Two lines of argument are offered for why the repressive nature of Uzbekistan's regime has served as a source of radicalizing Islam in Uzbekistan. The first is related to Uzbekistan's restrictive economic policies, which it is argued have hampered the development of free markets, thereby increasing poverty, which in turn serves as a recruiting ground for Islamic radicals. The second is that the persecution of innocent people who are simply pursuing their faith has attracted others to religion, both because of their example and because religious activists have recruited people while in prison.

It is worth exploring each of these propositions separately. Does poverty lead to the politicization of religion? It is often argued that membership in radical religious groups increases when there are no secular alternatives and when the secular authorities are morally corrupt. The social science literature on this is contradictory. Economic dissatisfaction appears to play a major role in the overthrow of autocratic regimes. But as demonstrations throughout the Middle East in spring 2011 have attested, this dissatisfaction need not lead to the politicization of religion as the trigger for the ouster of a secular ruler, even in Muslim-majority countries. Nowhere in the Middle East, even in Egypt with its long tradition of religious groups in opposition, has freedom of religion been the mobilizing factor.

The link between poverty and the politicization of religion is also unclear. The politicization of Islam in Western democracies indicates that economic deprivation need not be the only defining factor for radicalization. In fact, politicization of Islam in the West appears to be, to a large extent, a response to a sense of relative deprivation on the part of those who join radical Islamic movements. The sense of deprivation is often both economic and spiritual, and many of the radical Islamic groups are objecting to the supposed moral decadence of the West and inappropriate policies (either domestic or international) of a particular Western government.

Moreover, even if there is a causal relationship between poverty and the rise of religious radicalism, an Uzbek government that supported economic reform need not have found itself immune from the spread of radical Islam. Economic reform would still have produced "economic haves" and "economic have-nots," with the latter likely being as relatively dissatisfied as unemployed Uzbek youths are today. It is also unclear whether there would have been more job creation under the conditions of economic reform, and certainly it is likely that a large underclass would have continued to exist, as in virtually all other post-Soviet states. This does not mean that I am a supporter of the Uzbek government's go-slow economic reform strategy in the name of defending stability and social protection.

Similarly, Uzbek policies toward religion may not have created a more politicized atmosphere than would have been the case had the government pursued a more liberal strategy. Persecution does seem to have helped Hizb ut-Tahrir to increase its membership, at least insofar as it has been able to use the Uzbek prisons to recruit new members. In fact, it has been so successful there that Uzbek authorities have been willing to let Hanafi clerics hold services and effectively proselytize in the prisons as well, viewing this as part of the rehabilitation process.

It is harder to know whether the persecution of members of unsanctioned religious groups has increased their respective appeal. It is not just Uzbek authorities who are opposing them, but the Hanafi clerics also try to steer their flock against them. This is true of Hizb ut-Tahrir, Akramiya, and other fringe groups that have sought to practice an Islam that is solely based on the Quran, particularly if these groups advocate the use of an Uzbek-language Quran instead of the Arabic original. The latter is a kind of dual anathema, rejecting Hanafi teaching as well as the exclusive use of Arabic in Quranic reading and study.

All of these groups implicitly reject the leading social role of Hanafi clerics and so threaten their power base. Salafists, or Hanafi purists with classical religious education, pose a more difficult challenge for traditional pro-establishment Hanafi clerics. Salafist groups represent the contemporary version of a tension that has been present in religious circles in the region for generations. It is much like the challenge posed by Sufis who practice something resembling "folk Islam." The Hanafi-dominated religious establishment may not like them, but they represent the challenge that is part of normal religious discourse that must be dealt with accordingly.

For its part, the Uzbek government has not viewed these kinds of squabbles—between Salafists, Hanafi purists, Sufis, and Hanafi traditionalists—as posing a major political threat. The government does try to limit the debate over Salafi teachings versus Hanafi teachings as something of an academic dispute, and it certainly favors the Hanafi position, which is seen as more in line with the secular values that the Uzbek state seeks to promote.

Again, though I am not defending Uzbek policies here, it is also not clear how Islam would have evolved had Uzbekistan's political system been less autocratic. It is possible that its evolution would have been quite similar to what occurred, with Hanafi Islam dominating even in a more competitive religious environment in which dissonant sects were able to freely exist.

But those pressing for moderate Hanafi Islam would likely have had a more difficult task. In a democratic Uzbekistan, it is quite possible that Uzbekistan's Muslim Spiritual Administration would either never have been formed or have been transformed into a self-replicating council of *ulama*, and the state might have gone entirely out of the business of registering clerics and religious institutions. There is nothing in Sunni Islam that dictates a hierarchical structure; in fact, Sunni teachings eschew religious ranks. The Muslim Spiritual Administration was largely an invention of the Russian colonial authorities, but it has proved convenient to successive political regimes. Only the Tajiks phased out the institution as a side feature of national reconciliation, and until recently Tajik Islam was managed by a council of *ulama* whose membership was determined by leading Tajik Hanafi clerics.

Left unconstrained by an ecclesiastical structure that favored traditional Hanafi Islam and absent a national government using its instruments of power to achieve it, Islam in Uzbekistan might be even more politicized than it is today. Had the state not sought to moderate religious affairs, it is possible that mainstream Islam in Uzbekistan would have developed in a more radical way.

Many of Uzbekistan's religious leaders, and especially the younger generation who have received religious training in the last twenty years, are eager to be part of global Islamic discourse. This discourse has been far more critical of secular values than the debates that Uzbek authorities have tried to structure in their efforts to make the practice of Islam in Uzbekistan mirror some sort of "traditional" Hanafi ideal.

This foray into alternative history should demonstrate how difficult it is to predict the ways in which Islam will develop in Uzbekistan, or in any country for that matter, where religion has been an inexorable part of tradition and culture and has long influenced relationships between state and society. It should also make us a bit more humble about believing that our policy preferences can govern how these relationships evolve. Even if the United States and the EU had found effective levers for influencing Uzbek political policies, it is very difficult to predict what changes in Uzbek society would have occurred as a result, and if the United States and EU would have liked what emerged in the course of a twenty-year period any more than we do the current political situation.

Had Uzbekistan introduced a participatory democracy in the first years after the revolution, it is possible that the country would have evolved into a secular democracy, but that outcome was in no way guaranteed. At that time, especially in rural areas, religious leaders may have had more influence than secular elites, although they lacked the political experience. Today it would be even more difficult to predict whether democratic reforms would lead to a further entrenchment of secular values. Elites and masses alike are more traditionally oriented than they were twenty years ago, and the social role of religious leaders is better established.

Uzbekistan was a secular society at the time of independence, and the idea that the state has the right to monitor or provide guidelines by which religious authorities must be bound is deeply entrenched. From the mid-nineteenth century on, religious authorities were formally subordinated to state power. And for hundreds of years before that, certainly from the time of Timur onward, though the sovereign may have ruled in the name of Islam, he was in all possible practical ways above the sway of Islamic law.

At the same time, in some areas back as far as the eighth and ninth centuries (European settlers and some Asian deportees aside), Islamic traditions shaped the cultural and social values of the population of Uzbekistan.

Levels of religious learning varied dramatically, but that notwithstanding, people thought of themselves as Muslims. And until the middle of the nineteenth century, they were legally Muslims as well, and in that Sharia was the only source of jurisprudence.

Since independence, Islam and Islamic traditions have reclaimed a public role. Islamic clerics are once again publicly recognized authority figures, if not universally recognized as such. Secularized elites tend to still view them with suspicion and seek—for want of a better word—a more "Western" cultural and developmental model, although many are more comfortable with the Asian variants.

Many of the most "Westernized" Uzbeks live outside of the country. This is especially true of those who were educated in Europe, the United States, or Asia. Even those with degrees from Russian universities may choose not to come home. Those who have made their careers within the country and have lived there for the past two decades are well aware of the reassertion of tradition that has occurred both in rural areas and among urban youths with strong religious education. And it is those who have lived in the country who will choose Uzbekistan's next president, whether Karimov's successor is selected by Karimov himself, his inner circle, by representatives of Uzbekistan's leading families, or by crowds in the street.

Whoever this person is and however the person is chosen, he will have to seek legitimation from the population he is governing. Hopefully he will do so through democratic means. But regardless of how this legitimation is attempted, it is sure to involve embracing the special role of Islam in Uzbekistan's history. To achieve this end, the next president of Uzbekistan will need to be viewed as an acceptable figure by a significant portion of the country's religious leaders: to be viewed as a "just" ruler, a person who respects religion even if not devout himself, as Uzbekistan's Hanafi traditions are claimed to demand.

The new leader will also have to retain the support of the country's secular elite, those who hold positions of responsibility, as well as those who have remained in Uzbekistan waiting "by the gates" in second-tier positions to have a chance for advancement after Karimov's departure. However strong Karimov has been, there remain political and economic stakeholders of importance. Many of these people are interested in furthering economic and political reforms, and they do not believe that these reforms will occur if there is a capitulation of too much power to religious authorities or if Islam becomes the defining pillar of Uzbek nationalism.

What this means is that Uzbek authorities are likely to continue their efforts at a balancing act between asserting that Islam is an inexorable part of Uzbek nationalism and working to keep religious authorities from so dominating the moral plane that state power must be partly ceded to them. Fear that religious authorities will become a dominant political force is likely to still serve as a brake on democratic political reform. This in turn will further distance Uzbekistan from Western democracies that could reinforce secular values among the Uzbek population. And that means that Uzbeks will continue to turn to Muslim countries for economic engagement, thus reinforcing those same traditional values that are strengthening the role of religious leaders in local communities in rural and urban areas.

That said, Islam is a dynamic religion, and the demands that Islamic believers put on the state will change as the nature of Islam itself evolves. This dynamism has not been significantly affected by Uzbek policies toward religion. Nor has it been stifled by Abdurashid Bahromov's leadership of the Spiritual Administration of the Muslims of Uzbekistan, and he has lacked the learning or the talent to dominate or shape the debate.

At minimum, Mufti Bahromov has been overshadowed by Muhammad Sodiq Muhammad Yusuf. The self-styled sheikh continues to serve as a source for exposing an Uzbek audience to the religious debates going on in the Arab world in particular, through his preaching and his publications in print and in electronic form. The latter are particularly focused on the younger generation of Uzbeks.

The next *mufti* might enjoy more authority, especially if he is regarded as a theologically interesting and charismatic figure. But almost by definition if he has those qualities, he is likely to find theological justifications for pushing the government to grant a greater role for Islam in setting the moral values for the country—values that should be protected by law.

It will also be harder and harder over time for Uzbekistan's Spiritual Administration to serve as a moral guidepost. Twenty-first-century Uzbekistan has ties with a broader Islamic world. People travel to and from other Muslim countries and have access to ideas from all over the world, even in a place like Uzbekistan, where the relatively low standard of living limits the mobility of much of the population.

A younger generation of clerics has also emerged, many of whom have had some training outside of Uzbekistan, and an even larger number of whom have been able to travel in the Middle East. They bring their own views of developments to their work with their congregations, even if guidelines for sermons are still issued by the Spiritual Administration. Similarly, clerics who are teaching courses on the history of religion are able to inject their own views, despite the existence of a standardized curriculum. Teachers in the madrasas and Tashkent Islamic Institute have even more opportunities for shaping discussions on Islam, in the classroom and in informal contacts around their schools. There is a wealth of resources available on the web: the Uzbek sources referred to above and materials in Turkish, Russian, English, Arabic, and in other languages for those with the necessary linguistic skills.

Clerics whose views are shaped by the main body of Hanafi legal interpretation tend to be most accommodating toward the regime. But even Hanafi clerics (such as Muhammad Sodiq and those shaped by his teachings) seek ways to reinterpret the dominant Hanafi literature (sometimes through the use of less conformist Hanafi authors) so that it increases their ability to engage in independent political action. This often makes their attitude toward the relationship of the state to religion far closer to Salafi thinkers than to that of their own Hanafi brothers.

The question of the relationship between Islamic believers and the state is both critical and enduring. The resolutions that are offered to it will alternatively encourage, permit, or discourage the use of violence in the name of Islam. To a large degree, state authorities will inevitably remain bound to Islam, and Islamic clerics will continue to need to find ways to work with state authorities.

Without some participation by prominent clerics in state-sponsored activities, the Uzbek government would lose all credibility as a potential definer of acceptable religious space in society. Similarly, the clerics put their credibility at stake if they totally divorce themselves from the state. For whatever the unpopularity of President Islam Karimov and his entourage, Uzbek citizens have a love-hate relationship with the state. They simultaneously distrust authority but accept that state support confers legitimacy.

Religious authorities need both state support and popular loyalty, especially if they hope to retain their financial position as well as moral authority, both of which have become more valuable as a result of the return of religion to public life.

But the challenge for secular governments seeking to shape religious practice is a more difficult one, in that their leaders must be viewed as credible defenders of the faith—a particular challenge if they are not devout Muslims themselves. For this reason, over time it seems very likely that state-sponsored efforts to define Islam will be overwhelmed by the efforts of the Islamic community to define Islam for themselves.

Devout Muslims inevitably aspire to live under the rule of Sharia, even if they accept that it is unlikely in the country in which they are living. This aspiration is implicit in their faith and becomes a clearer goal for believers if the majority of citizens are of Muslim ancestry, but it often leads devout Muslims to be viewed as radical or even extremist by secular Muslims and non-Muslims in their midst. Similarly, most devout Muslims, like devout practitioners of many other faiths, believe that lapsed co-religionists can be brought back to the fold through exposure to their faith in schools and in public life.

Hanafi theology, which has dominated in the region, is quite tolerant and accepts the idea of subordination to the state, even an unjust one, if that serves to preserve the faith. But Hanafi Islam in Central Asia is no longer trapped in a colonial structure, and Islam is no longer the religion of the minority. Those conditions create new responsibilities for rulers and new vulnerabilities for those who do not meet them. The Hanafi clerics now loyally serving their governments are aware of their higher responsibility to spread the faith. This in turn requires new relationships with the government, which they recognize is not likely to be dominated by believers for one or two generations, if not more.

Barring cataclysmic changes in the relationship between religion and state in the larger Muslim world, and particularly the Muslim majority countries of the Middle East, it seems likely that sometime during the next quarter century, the current relationship between Islam and the Uzbek government will change.

Uzbekistan has always been at the outer edge of the Islamic world. Eighty years of religious near-isolation in the history of a faith that is nearly fifteen hundred years old does not make a region peripheral. In an era of global communication, this time gap will be rapidly erased. As contacts with global Islamic communities grow, tensions are likely to increase between the secular and religious elements in these societies, and divisions are likely to increase within the community of believers themselves. Through this process, a new role for Islam in society will eventually emerge and continue to evolve.

This book has described the changing relations between Islam and society in Uzbekistan. If the trends described in this book continue, those seeking to advance pro-Western, secular values in Uzbekistan will face a task that is ever more difficult, especially because the governing class will likely seek to reflect the values of the populations they rule.

As I have argued here, this scenario seems more likely than some form of revolutionary change analogous to Iran, in which religious elites take direct control of the government. But the middle of gradual movement toward the reassertion of religion and religious traditionalism is not one in which outside actors are likely to be able to assert much influence.

Over the past twenty years the government of Uzbekistan has pursued policies that have maximized the insular nature of Uzbek political development. They have not isolated the country from outside influences, just sought to mediate them wherever possible. This gives the United States and other international actors relatively limited leverage to use in Uzbekistan, particularly while President Karimov is still in charge. This is likely to still be the case when the regime changes, since there is little reason to expect a new elite with new political values to contest for power. In fact, one of the things that I have tried to demonstrate is how difficult it would be to undo the social changes that this book describes.

While the United States and other advanced democracies can continue to try to expose Central Asian youths to Western technologies and sociopolitical values, the number of those who are being trained is likely to continue to be relatively small—too small to tip the balance in favor of Western notions of secularism in the parts of Central Asia where society appears to be moving to reject them. Whatever positive reputation American values may enjoy in Uzbekistan, there is no "forward" position from which Washington can advance its cause to affect political outcomes in Central Asia.

The path of a "whirlwind of jihad" in Uzbekistan is not predictable, but developments over the past twenty years suggest that the greater jihad,

jihad al-nafs, the struggle for spiritual purification within each individual believer, is likely to continue to dominate over *jihad bil saif*, armed struggle in defense of Islam. Uzbekistan will continue to produce its share of armed jihadists, bent on overthrowing what they see as a godless and corrupt regime. But to the degree to which Uzbeks are focused on religion at all, the overwhelming majority seems concerned with their own personal religious struggles.

The way Uzbeks define their personal struggles is mostly shaped by events within their own country. But it is also influenced by developments in other Muslim countries, largely through the mediation of their clerics as well as through those who have made *hajj*. For the younger generation in particular, the internet is another connection to the global community.

The outside world has played a more limited role with regard to drawing Uzbeks into armed jihad. While the wars in Tajikistan and in Afghanistan have served as a training ground for young jihadists from Uzbekistan, their numbers have remained small, and Uzbek authorities have proved able to contain the security threat that they have created.

The Uzbek authorities remain far more concerned about risks of interethnic conflict spilling over from Kyrgyzstan or Tajikistan. But whatever might be the level of popular dissatisfaction with the political and economic choices made by President Karimov's regime, there is little evidence to suggest that people will turn to jihadist movements to express their dissatisfaction.

NOTES

PREFACE

1 Uzbekistan has been a labeled as a "Country of Particular Concern" by the U.S. Commission on International Religious Freedom. Starting in 2004, Uzbekistan failed to comply with its obligations under the bilateral 2002 Strategic Framework Agreement. As a result of both the government actions against U.S. implementing partners and U.S. government restrictions on aid, U.S. assistance to Uzbekistan in humanitarian aid, technical assistance, military-to-military funding, and microcredit support has decreased markedly from $101.8 million in 2004 to $20 million in 2006. See U.S. Department of State, "Uzbekistan: Background Notes," www.state.gov/outofdate/bgn/uzbekistan/index.htm.

2 The European Union imposed an arms embargo on Uzbekistan and decided to deny visas to top Uzbek officials, in response to the state's brutal suppression of the protest in Andijan and the Uzbek government's refusal to allow an international investigation into the events. The Andijan massacre occurred on May 13, 2005, when National Security Service troops fired into a crowd of protesters, killing and wounding hundreds of Uzbek civilians. "EU Imposes Sanctions on Uzbekistan Over Massacre," Human Rights Watch, October 2, 2005, www.hrw.org/en/news/2005/10/02/eu-imposes-sanctions-uzbekistan-over-massacre.

CHAPTER 1

1 The four schools of jurisprudence (*mazhabs*) within Sunni Islam are the 1) *Hanafi*, the oldest school of law, founded by Imam Abu Hanifa (d. 767); 2) *Maliki*, named for Malik ibn Anas (d. 795); 3) *Shafi*, founded by Muhammad ibn Idris al-Shafi (d. 820); and 4) *Hanbali*, named for its founder, Ahmad ibn Hanbal (d. 855). These schools differ in their observance of rituals and in the extent to which they rely on the four sources of Islamic law: the Quran, the *Sunna* (the actions and sayings of the Prophet that establish a model for Muslim conduct), reasoning by analogy, and the consensus of religious scholars.

2   Abu Bakr al-Kaffal ash-Shashi (d. 976) established the Shafi school in Shash (Tashkent); his burial site remains an important place of pilgrimage.

3   Mawarannahr, also known as the lands of Transoxiana, refers to the area between the Syr Darya and Amu Darya (rivers). The overwhelming majority of this territory is found in modern-day Uzbekistan (see map). Charles Warren Hostler, *Turkism and the Soviets* (London: George Allen & Unwin Ltd. and New York: Frederick A. Praeger, 1957), 10.

4   *Hadiths* are stories about the words and deeds of Prophet Muhammad that relate the different religious-legal sides of Muslim life. The *hadiths* are considered the second source of the Islamic law after the Quran.

5   It is challenging to find an appropriate term to use with reference to groups of Sufis, such as Kubrawiya or Yasawiya. It is common in English to refer to the followers of a particular noted teacher as constituting a brotherhood or a movement, given the shared religious philosophy of all the followers. Scholars of Sufism usually simply refer to Sufi teachings, while Sufis themselves often prefer to refer their adherents as following "the Sufi way."

6   The Kubrawiya was founded in the thirteenth century by Najm ad-Din al-Kubra (1145–1221); the Yasawiya was founded by Khoja Ahmed Yasawi (1103–1166); the Naqshabandiya originated near Bukhara and was founded by Abd al-Khaliq Ghijduvani (d. 1220). For more on Sufi history, see Martha Brill Olcott, "Sufism in Central Asia: A Force for Moderation or a Cause of Politicization?" Carnegie Paper 84 (Washington, D.C.: Carnegie Endowment for International Peace, 2007), www.carnegieendowment.org/files/cp84_olcott_final2.pdf.

7   In the second half of the nineteenth century, the Russian empire embarked on a sweeping campaign of occupation and annexation of Central Asian khanates, conquering Tashkent in 1865, Kokand in 1866, Bukhara in 1868, and Khiva in 1873. Seymour Becker, *Russia's Protectorates in Central Asia: Bukhara and Khiva, 1865–1924* (London: RoutledgeCurzon, 2004).

8   The Islamic Movement of Uzbekistan is a loosely consolidated jihadist movement that was formed in the 1990s in the Ferghana Valley; it has concentrated its activities in Central Asia and Afghanistan. For more information on the organization, see chapter 10.

9   The Muslim Spiritual Administration is an administrative body established by the Soviet authorities to supervise and regulate the religious life in the Soviet republics and territories with Muslim inhabitants. Spiritual Administrations were divided into four separate entities, each responsible for a different territorial unit. The four main Administrations were: Muslim Spiritual Administration for Central Asia and Kazakhstan, Spiritual Administration for Transcaucasia, Spiritual Administration for the European Soviet Union and Siberia, and Spiritual Administration for the North Caucasus and Dagestan.

10 The aforementioned Ferghana riots refer to the period of interethnic clashes between the Uzbek population and the Meskhetian Turks in Uzbekistan in May 1989. Kathleen Collins, *Clan Politics and Regime Transition in Central Asia* (New York: Cambridge University Press, 2006), 118–25.

11 Karimov was elected for a five-year presidential term after receiving 86 percent of the vote in what was widely seen as a rigged election. The only other candidate, the chairman of the party *Erk* (Freedom) Muhammad Solih, reportedly received 14 percent of the vote. Another major opposition party, *Birlik* (Unity), had been refused registration as an official party in time for the election. Glenn E. Curtis, ed. "Uzbekistan: A Country Study" (Washington, D.C.: Government Printing Office for the Library of Congress, 1996), http://countrystudies.us/uzbekistan/44.htm.

12 For instance, Absamat Masaliev, the leader of the Kyrgyz Soviet Socialist Republic, appointed for his party credentials, was ousted in 1990 after launching a highly unpopular campaign by promoting Kyrgyz clans from Osh at the expense of other ethnic clans and groups. Disillusioned by Masaliev's failures, the nation and the political elites chose to sack the Moscow-backed leader in favor of a more neutral candidate, Askar Akaev. In August 1990, with strong support from the newly elected reformist deputies and the majority of clan elites, Akaev was elected the first president of the Kyrgyz Republic with over 50 percent of the vote. Kathleen Collins, *Clan Politics*, 123–30.

13 After earning public disapproval following the bloodshed in Dushanbe and making powerful enemies among the political elites, Kakhar Mahkamov, Tajikistan's first president, lost his place under the sun to Rahmon Nabiev, Mahkamov's predecessor as first secretary (1982–1985). Deterioration of the economic situation in the country, coupled with Nabiev's reluctance to enter a power-sharing arrangement with the opposition, led to the eruption of riots and demonstrations in Dushanbe in April–May 1992, which grew into a bloody civil war in summer and fall 1992. The civil war rallied supporters along regional, clan, and ethnic lines in an attempt to resolve the ideological conflict between Islam and secularism and choose Tajikistan's future political leader. After failing to stop the war that claimed up to 100,000 dead and a million refugees, Nabiev resigned in September 1992. Minority Rights Group International, "World Directory of Minorities and Indigenous Peoples—Tajikistan: Overview," January 2008, available at www.unhcr.org/refworld/docid/4954ce14c.html.

14 Wahhabism is a more conservative form of Islam practiced in Saudi Arabia. *Wahhabi* was the popular term used for Islamists and extremists in much of the press of this time. For more about Wahhabis, see Ziauddin and Davies, *The No-Nonsense Guide to Islam*, 109, 110.

15 The following link "Musiqa zaralari—Shaykh Abduvali qori, Uzbek," (Translated as "Music is harmful—sermon of Abduvali qori in Uzbek") posted on YouTube by user IslomDini, www.youtube.com/watch?v=kwGV-mnVstI, is an example of one of Abduvali's many sermons that has been viewed thousands of times. As of March 2011, this particular link had over 12,000 hits since its original posting two years ago.

16 Salafi (derived from its Arabic root *salaf*, "to precede") is the term that denotes a follower of the Salafi movement of Islam. This movement calls for the return to the use of the Quran and the *Sunna* as the only sources for religious rulings. The modern form of Salafiya was established by Jamal ud-Din al-Afghani (1839–1897) and Muhammad Abduh (1849–1905) at the dawn of the twentieth century. Its core objectives were to restore Islam to its pristine form by condemning the mentalities of *taqlid* (blind imitation of legal precedence) and *jimud* (stagnation) among the Muslim

traditionalist clergy. See "Salafiyah," *Oxford Encyclopedia of the Modern Islamic World*, vol. III (New York: Oxford University Press, 1995), 463–68.

17 According to the UN World Population Prospects database, more than 51 percent of the population in Uzbekistan in 2010 is under the age of 24. See the demographic profile for Uzbekistan in the World Population Prospects: the 2008 Revision Population database, which can be found at United Nations, Population Division, http://esa.un.org/UNPP.

18 A *murid* is a Sufi disciple or student.

19 *Pir*, derived from Persian, is used by Sufis to describe a spiritual master (of Sufi adepts, craft apprentices, etc.).

20 A residential teaching center for Sufis that likely originated in Iran in the late tenth or eleventh century, AD. Although the etymological origin has been widely disputed, many believe that the term is of Persian origin, probably derived from *khana-gah* (the place of residence). Today *kanaqa* no longer includes residential quarters, although it still serves as a center for devotions, poetry, and the performance of the *zikr* and *sama* rituals. See "Khanaqah," *Oxford Encyclopedia of the Modern Islamic World*, vol. II (New York: Oxford University Press, 1995), 415–17.

21 Such as Uzbakayna and Bukharan, which according to Bakhtiyar Babadjanov, are still reportedly in existence.

22 In Muslim law, a *waqf* is a permanent nonperishable endowment (usually referring to land or buildings); its proceeds are spent for purposes designated by the benefactor. There are three main categories of *waqf*: religious, philanthropic, and family. Religious *waqf* refers to the house of worship (such as the mosque) and the real estate that provides revenue for its maintenance and expenses. Philanthropic *waqf* provides support to the struggling segments of the population by funding initiatives devoted to education, health services, and other charitable purposes. The third kind of *waqf* is a form of a real estate whose revenue is first given to one's descendants, and only the surplus is given to the poor. See "Waqf," *Oxford Encyclopedia of the Modern Islamic World*, vol. IV (New York: Oxford University Press, 1995), 312–16.

23 "Doklad o palomnichestve v svyashchennie goroda" (Report on the Pilgrimage to the Holy Cities), The Central State Archive of the Republic of Uzbekistan; Fund I-19; Case 16; Folders 127 and 3, as quoted by Bakhtiyar Babadjanov in unpublished materials shared with the author.

24 Jadidism is the Muslim reformist movement that emerged toward the end of the nineteenth century in response to the growing threat from the colonization of the region and the rapid industrialization and modernization of the West. Jadidists and their followers called for incorporation of various aspects of modernity to the base of Muslim identity to prevent spiritual and economic decay of the Islamic civilization. Staunch proponents of reforms in religious education system, empowerment of women, and greater economic productivity, Jadidists called for spiritual and intellectual reawakening and reassessment of the old way of life, while preserving inherently Islamic values and traditions to raise the quality of life for Muslims in Central Asia and to restore the power,

grandeur, and dignity of Islam in the world. The absence of a unified structure and centralized authority, as well as divergence of opinions among Jadid followers resulted in the weakening of the movement in the early twentieth century. See "Jadidism," *Oxford Encyclopedia of the Modern Islamic World*, vol. II (New York: Oxford University Press, 1995), 349–52. For an excellent account of their activities in Uzbekistan, see Adeeb Khalid, *The Politics of Muslim Cultural Reform: Jadidism in Central Asia* (Berkeley: University of California Press, 1998), www.netlibrary.com/urlapi.asp?action=summary&v=1&bookid=10042.

25 Sayyid Muhammad ibn Safdar Husayni, better known as Sayyid Jamal ud-Din al-Afghani (b. 1838–d. March 9, 1897), was an Islamic ideologist, philosopher, and political figure who lived and taught in India, Turkey, Afghanistan, Iran, Russia, and Europe. Al-Afghani's belief in Islam's compatibility with rationality, science, and nationalism of a linguistic and/or territorial variety, as well as his aversion to Western imperialistic ambitions, earned him the reputation of one of the "fathers of Islamic modernism." A staunch supporter of the fusion of Islam with Western sciences and institutions for self-strengthening purposes, al-Afghani penned numerous articles, a book on Afghan history, *Tatimmat al-bayan fi tarikh al-Afghan*, and a collection of polemics, "Al-Radd 'ala al-Dah riyyi" and "Refutation of the Materialists," where he advocated the instrumental use of Islamic identification and pan-Islamic unity to fend off the encroachments of Western imperialists. His innovative method of combining philosophical discourse with rigorous religious study to address contemporary social and political problems won him a group of devoted followers, including Muhammad Abduh, Adib Ishaq, Salim al-Anhuri, and Yaqub Sanu. Al-Afghani appreciated the central role newspapers play in helping to form public opinion and used this medium extensively to arouse nationalistic sentiments in the Middle East. Al-Afghani's power as a public orator, his strong connections with the leading intellectuals and political elites of the Muslim world, and his unconventional ideas often made him a subject of persecution, expulsion, and venomous verbal attacks from his critics. For additional information on al-Afghani, see Nikki R. Keddie, *Sayyid Jamal Ad-Din: A Political Biography* (Berkeley: University of California Press, 1972).

26 The Kokand Autonomy government (also known as the Muslim Provisional Government of Autonomous Turkestan) was a short-lived provisional government whose creation was declared at the Conference in Kokand in November 1917. The Kokand Autonomy government was dominated by local intellectuals and business interests; it created a small army and even issued money. The Kokand government's attitude toward Soviet authority in Moscow and its official representative, the Tashkent government, could best be described as the policy of ambivalent neutrality and compliance—recognizing Moscow as an almost legal government and even entering negotiations with the Tashkent government, while refusing to comply with orders issued from Tashkent on the basis of the nationalities' right to self-determination. After failing to gain popularity in the wider region outside of the Ferghana Province, the Kokand Autonomy ceased its independent existence in February 1918 after being defeated by the Red Army. See Serge A. Zenkovsky, *Pan-Turkism and Islam in Russia* (Cambridge, Mass.: Harvard University Press, 1967), 230–36.

27 The Khanates of Bukhara and Khiva, long-established religious centers in Central Asia, were occupied and annexed by the Russian empire in the end of the nineteenth century. Soviet forces

established control over Khiva in February 1920 after the military takeover of the khanate by the Red Army. Soviet authorities succeeded in consolidating their power in Bukhara (after several unsuccessful attempts in 1920) when the Red Army troops, politically supported by the local political groups—the Communist Party of Bukhara and the Young Bukharans—laid a two-day siege around the city and forced the Emir of Bukhara to escape. See Zenkovsky, *Pan-Turkism and Islam in Russia*, 238–49. For more information, see Becker, *Russia's Protectorates in Central Asia*.

28 Turkestan became an Autonomous Soviet Socialist Republic within the RSFSR with the promulgation of a new constitution on April 11, 1921. The Khanates of Khiva and Bukhara existed as independent entities, outside of Turkestan's supervision until 1924. In 1924 the borders between Turkestan and the two khanates were removed, resulting in a formation of four separate republics—Uzbekistan, Kyrgyzstan, Turkmenistan, and Tajikistan—built on strictly national principle. While Turkmenistan and Uzbekistan immediately became full-fledged members of the Soviet Union by receiving the status of Union Republic, Tajikistan did not acquire that privilege until 1929, and Kyrgyzstan in 1936. Zenkovsky, *Pan-Turkism and Islam in Russia*, 238–49; 252–53.

29 Khalid, *The Politics of Muslim Cultural Reform*.

30 For more information on Bobokhon, see Martha Brill Olcott and Diora Ziyaeva, "Islam in Uzbekistan: Religious Education and State Ideology," Carnegie Paper 91 (Washington, D.C.: Carnegie Endowment for International Peace, 2008), http://carnegieendowment.org/files/cp91_islam_uzbek_final.pdf and Martha Brill Olcott, "Roots of Radical Islam in Central Asia," Carnegie Paper 77 (Washington, D.C.: Carnegie Endowment for International Peace, 2007), http://carnegieendowment.org/files/cp_77_olcott_roots_final.pdf.

31 *Tafsir* (literally translated as "elucidation," "explanation," "interpretation") is an exegesis of the Quran. Most common topics of discussion in *tafsir* can be categorized as linguistic, juristic, or theological. The authority of the *tafsir* is determined based on its origin, the *tafsir* provided by the Prophet Muhammad being regarded as the most authoritative, while *tafsir bil-ray*, interpretation that is the outcome of personal reflection and logical deduction, is viewed as the least authoritative. Today, however, despite the initial opposition by Islamic jurists and theologians to one's heavy reliance on *tafsir bil-ray* for fear of interpretation being provided by unqualified people, *tafsir bil-ray* occupies a respectable niche in the greater literature of Islamic exegesis. See "Tafsir," *Oxford Encyclopedia of the Modern Islamic World*, vol. IV (New York: Oxford University Press, 1995), 169–75. *Qiyas* (translated as comparison or analogy) is one of the four "roots of jurisprudence" (*usul al-fiqh*). *Qiyas* is concerned with the comparison of the *hadiths* to the Quran and *Sunna*. Cyril Glasse, *Concise Encyclopedia of Islam* (San Francisco: Harper & Row, Publishers, Inc., 1989), 325, 361–62.

32 Unpublished material provided by Bakhtiyar Babadjanov.

33 Nikita Sergeyevich Khrushchev served as the first secretary of the Communist Party of the Soviet Union from 1953 until 1964. Leonid Ilyich Brezhnev served as the general secretary of the Communist Party of the Soviet Union from 1964 until 1982. See "Nikita Khrushchev," *Encyclopedia Britannica*,

www.britannica.com/EBchecked/topic/316972/Nikita-Sergeyevich-Khrushchev; "Leonid Brezhnev," *Encyclopedia Britannica*, www.britannica.com/EBchecked/topic/79098/Leonid-Ilich-Brezhnev.

34 Salafist intellectual writers who were highly influential among the Salafist circles in the 1950s and 1960s. Sayyid Abul Ala Maududi was the famed translator of the Quran into Urdu (*Tafhim al Quran*) and a founding father of the political Islamist movement *Jamaat e-Islami*, which strove to promulgate Islamic values and traditions in the region. Sayyid Qutb was an Egyptian scholar, author of 24 books (including the 30-volume masterpiece of commentary on the Quran), and theologian of the Egyptian Muslim Brotherhood. For more information, see Olivier Roy, *The Failure of Political Islam* (Cambridge, Mass.: Harvard University Press, 1994); Gilles Kepel, *Jihad: The Trail of Political Islam* (Cambridge, Mass.: Harvard University Press, 2002). To read the works by Maududi and Qutb, see http://islaam.com/Scholars.aspx.

35 For more information on the book, see Martha Brill Olcott, "A Face of Islam: Muhammad Sodiq Muhammad Yusuf," Carnegie Paper 82 (Washington, D.C.: Carnegie Endowment for International Peace, 2007).

36 Personal interviews conducted by the author in Tehran, February 1992.

37 Juma Namangani, a former Soviet paratrooper, jointly headed the IMU with Tohir Yuldoshev. He was killed in Afghanistan in late 2001. For more information, see Martha Brill Olcott, "Roots of Radical Islam in Central Asia," Carnegie Paper 77 (Washington, D.C.: Carnegie Endowment for International Peace, 2007), and Ariel Cohen, "Central Asia Beyond Namangani," *Central Asia-Caucasus Institute Analyst*, November 21, 2001, www.cacianalyst.org/?q=node/164.

38 In *Everyday Islam*, Poliakov describes Central Asian traditionalism as the hazardous ideology that "retards ... economic and social development" by "preserv[ing] the "outmoded" features of oriental society" (p. 142). In particular, Poliakov charges Islamic traditionalism with opposition to the modernization of the "old ways" and the advocacy of the ultimately unstable and inefficient economic base—"petit bourgeois mode." Sergei Petrovich Poliakov and Martha Brill Olcott, *Everyday Islam: Religion and Tradition in Rural Central Asia* (Armonk, N.Y.: M. E. Sharpe, 1992).

39 Sayid Abdulloh Nuri (1947–2006) was a Tajik politician and religious leader of the Opposition Islamic Renaissance Party in Tajikistan during the Tajik Civil War (1992–1997). After launching his career as the leader of the illegal Islamic educational organization Nahzat-i Islomi in the 1970s, Nuri became involved with the Islamic Renaissance Party, a political Islamic organization that sought to establish an Islamic state on the territory of Tajikistan. Following the 1997 peace agreement that put an end to the civil war, he formed a coalition with his former political archenemy, President Emomali Rakhmon(ov), and chaired the Commission on National Reconciliation. Conciliation Resources, "Said Abdullo Nuri," www.c-r.org/our-work/accord/tajikistan/profiles.php. Muhammad Sharif Khimmat-zoda (1951–2010) was an opposition leader and a member of the United Tajik Opposition (UTO) in exile during the Tajik Civil War, and the deputy chairman of the Islamic Renaissance Movement in Tajikistan. Saodat Olimova, "Political Islam and Conflict in Tajikistan," CA&CC Press, AB, www.ca-c.org/dataeng/11.olimova.shtml. Stephane A. Dudoignon,

"From Ambivalence to Ambiguity? Some Paradigms of Policy Making in Tajikistan," in *Tajikistan at a Crossroad: The Politics of Decentralization*, edited by Luigi De Martino (Geneva: Cimera Publications, 2004). Sodikjon qori Kamalludin (Kamalov) (1950–present) is a prominent religious leader and a former *mufti* of Osh, Kyrgyzstan. He was a deputy of the Kyrgyz parliament from 1990 to 1995 and currently serves as the head of the International Center for Islamic Cooperation. Mahamadzhan Urumbaev, "Intervyu na temu" (Interview with Sodikjon qori Kamalov), *Tazar*, June 20, 2007, www.tazar.kg/news.php?i=4893.

40 The Congress of People's Deputies was a political institution established in 1988 as part of Gorbachev's glasnost and perestroika campaign. Each republic had its own Congress, whose candidates were chosen on a democratic basis, regardless of their party affiliation—although the Communist Party candidates still constituted a majority of the Congress. Vladimir N. Brovkin, "The Making of Elections to the Congress of People's Deputies (CPD) in March 1989," *Russian Review*, vol. 49, no. 4 (October 1990): 417–42. Available at www.jstor.org/stable/130524.

41 *Iftar* is an evening festive meal to break the daytime fast during the Islamic month of Ramadan. See "Ramadan," *The Oxford Encyclopedia of the Modern Islamic World*, vol. III (New York: Oxford University Press, 1995), 408–10.

42 As quoted by Bakhtiyar Babadjanov in his unpublished manuscripts prepared for the Carnegie Endowment for International Peace.

43 Obidkhon qori (Nazarov) (1958–present) is one of the most famous Uzbek theologians and preachers. His sermons at the Tashkent mosque Tukhtaboy in the 1990s earned him hundreds of followers. Following his public criticism of the Uzbek authorities' ban on beards and the *hijab* (traditional head covering worn by Muslim women), Nazarov fled Uzbekistan to avoid detention and was later granted refugee status through the United Nations High Commissioner for Refugees. Audiocassettes and videotapes of his sermons are still widely circulated in Uzbekistan. Igor Rotar, "V Uzbekistane idut novie aresti musul'man" (New arrests of Muslims in Uzbekistan), Interfax, April 13, 2006, www.interfax-religion.ru/yz/?act=print&div=3360.

44 According to Bakhtiyar Babadjanov, in the unpublished work that he prepared for the Carnegie Endowment for International Peace, Mavlavi Abdulkhai Iskandarov, a former student of Hindustani, was the "minister of education" in the "government-in-exile" that the IRP organized. By this account, he used to regularly travel to Pakistan to try to ensure that children were getting an acceptable Islamic education according to traditional Hanafi teachings rather than the more radical neo-Deobandi teachings that were becoming popular there.

45 "Special Section: Terrorist Attacks on America—Islamic Movement of Uzbekistan (IMU)," James Martin Center for Nonproliferation Studies, http://cns.miis.edu/archive/wtc01/imu.htm; U.S. Department of State, "Country Reports on Terrorism," 2004–2009, www.state.gov/s/ct/rls/crt/index.htm; Jane's Information Group, "Islamic Movement of Uzbekistan (IMU) (Uzbekistan)," www.janes.com/articles/Janes-World-Insurgency-and-Terrorism/Islamic-Movement-of-Uzbekistan-IMU-Uzbekistan.html; Jim Nichol, "Central Asia: Regional Development and Implications for

U.S. Interests," Congressional Research Service, November 20, 2009, http://books.google.com/books?id=wyV6fZJSrRMC&dq=IMU+1999+incursion&source=gbs_navlinks_s, 10–12; Australasian Legal Information Institute, Criminal Code Amendment Regulations 2007 (no. 4) (Select Legislative Instrument 2007 no. 48, 2007), www.austlii.edu.au/au/legis/cth/num_reg_es/ccar20074n48o2007414.html.

46 Hanafi, the oldest school of law dominant in most countries, was founded by Imam Abu Hanifa (d. 767). Out of four schools of law, Hanafi philosophy is known to be the least averse to modern ideas while adhering to the strictest interpretation of Islamic law.

47 These slogans were provided by Bakhtiyar Babadjanov and Diora Ziyaeva, who encountered them in Tashkent.

CHAPTER 2

1 See Jurgen Paul, "The Histories of Samarqand," *Studia Iranica* 22, 1993, 69–92.

2 The clerics of the Seljuk dynasty introduced Shafiya law in the region, which continued to be practiced in Turkmenistan even after their decline. In Tashkent, many Shafi customs continued through the end of Russian colonial rule. However, Shafi interpretation on questions of rule by *ghayr-i din* and *kafir* were not dissimilar from those of the Hanafi rulers.

3 I wish to acknowledge assistance from Bakhtiyar Babadjanov, who helped with this analysis by preparing unpublished material on the role of Sufism in Uzbekistan since the twelfth century.

4 The shrine was a site of strong spiritual and historic importance during the period of the Kazakh Khanate, especially for the khans of the Middle Horde, as burial there was viewed as interment on sacred ground.

5 Turkish Yasawiya groups have been funding projects in southern Kazakhstan near Yasawi's mausoleum since the early 1990s. There is now a Yasawi International Kazakh-Turkish University in the Kazakh city of Turkestan.

6 Gijduvani (d. 1220) of Gijduvan in Bukhara Province was the fourth *khalifa*, successor to Khoja Yusuf Hamadani (a Sufi from Merv), and the absent master of the Uwaysi (Sufi who can be guided by a master who is absent in space or time). See Svat Soucek, *A History of Inner Asia* (New York: Cambridge University Press, 2000), 137–38.

7 I wish to thank Elyor Karimov for helping me understand the origins of the Naqshabandiya.

8 For an introduction to the life and works of Khoja Ahror, see Jo-Ann Gross and Asom Urunbaev, eds., *The Letters of Khwaja Ubaydallah Ahrar and his Associates* (Leiden: E. J. Brill, 2002).

9 Bakhtiyar Babadjanov reports that one of the files at the Committee for Religious Affairs, the Cabinet of Ministers of Uzbek Soviet Socialist Republic, contains many years of correspondence in which

local authorities warn Tashkent and Moscow that Khoja Ahror's mosque should not be closed down, as it might "lead to disturbances" because of its exceptional popularity (Central State Archive of Uzbekistan, Fund R-5427, file 17).

10 From Bakhtiyar Babadjanov's unpublished manuscript prepared for the Carnegie Endowment Islam project.

11 Gross bases her information on an article from *Turkestanskie Vedomosti*. See Jo-ann Gross, "The *Waqf* of Khoja 'Ubayd Allah Ahrar in Nineteenth Century Central Asia: A Preliminary Study of the Tsarist Period," in *Naqshabandis in Western and Central Asia: Change and Continuity: Papers Read at a Conference Held at the Swedish Research Institute in Istanbul, June 9–11, 1997*, edited by Elisabeth Ozdalga, vol. 9 (Istanbul: Swedish Research Institute in Istanbul, 1999), 48–49.

12 Bakhtiyar Babadjanov, unpublished materials prepared for Carnegie Endowment study on Sufism.

13 Annemarie Schimmel, *Mystical Dimensions of Islam* (Chapel Hill, NC: University of North Carolina Press, 1975), 366.

14 Adeeb Khalid, *Islam After Communism: Religion and Politics in Central Asia* (Berkeley, CA: University of California Press, 2007), 29.

15 Travel guide to Turkestan and Middle-Asian and Tashkent railroads, Saint Petersburg, 1912, 274, as quoted in Bakhtiyar Babadjanov, "The Old City," unpublished manuscript. The population of the Tashkent region in this period was some hundred thousand people.

16 Abror M. Khudaikulov, "Prosvetitel'skaya deyatel'nost' djadaistov Turkestana (konets XIX-nachalo XX v)" Educational Activities by Turkestan's djadaists (late XIX–early XX century), doctoral dissertation synopsis, Tashkent, 1995, 3.

17 Bakhtiyar Babadjanov argues that Yasawiya, Ishquiya, and Qalandariya Sufi leaders strongly opposed the efforts of Bukhara's Hazrat Shah Murad (ruled 1785–1800) and Emir Haydar (ruled 1800–1825) to codify Sharia principles. See Bakhtiyar Babadjanov, "From Colonization to Bolshevization: Some Political and Legislative Aspects of Molding a 'Soviet Islam' in Central Asia," in *Central Asian Law: An Historical Overview*, edited by Wallace Johnson and Irina F. Popova (Lawrence, KS: Society for Asian Legal History, 2004), 154–55.

18 Babadjanov, "From Colonization to Bolshevization," 155–56.

19 Adeeb Khalid, *The Politics of Muslim Cultural Reform: Jadidism in Central Asia* (Berkeley, CA: University of California Press, 1998), 46.

20 This is the view of Adeeb Khalid, who has done extensive research into this period. See his "Society and Politics in Bukhara 1868–1920," *Central Asian Survey* 19, no. 3/4 (2000), 367–96, and especially 370.

21 "Russian Tartary: Troubles in Bokhara—A Revolution Against the Ameer Imminent," *New York Times*,

July 3, 1871, http://query.nytimes.com/mem/archive-free/pdf?_r=1&res=9D0CEED9103EEE34BC4B53DFB166838A669FDE. The article is report of a letter from Tashkent, dated April 26, 1871, which appeared in the *Russian Exchange Gazette*.

22 Khalid, "Society and Politics," 372.

23 The administrative structure of the "Steppe Region" (Turgai, Akmolinsk, Uralsk, and Sempialitansk Oblasts) was set forth in the "Steppe Statute" of 1868. See Martha Brill Olcott, *The Kazakhs* (Stanford, CA: Hoover Institution Press, Stanford University, 1987), 58.

24 The administrative structure of Turkestan (Semireche and Syr Darya Oblasts) was set forth in the "Statute on the Administration of Turkestan" of 1867, Olcott, *The Kazakhs*, 77.

25 See Robert D. Crew, *For Prophet and Tsar: Islam and Empire in Russia and Central Asia* (Cambridge, MA: Harvard University Press, 2006) for a discussion on Russia's policy toward Islam during the colonial period—especially the chapter "Civilizing Turkestan."

26 Crew, 274–75.

27 "Provision on administrating the Turkestan region," Tashkent, 1903, *Svod Zakonov Rossijskoj Imperii* (Code of Laws of the Russian Empire) vol. 2, 1892 edition. This provision was written and entered into force as early as 1886 and was sanctioned by the Emperor. The full text of the provision can be accessed at www.hrono.ru/dokum/turkestan1892.html.

28 As quoted by Hisao Komatsu, "Dar al-Islam under Russian Rule as Understood by Turkestani Muslim Intellectuals," in *Empire, Islam and Politics in Central Eurasia*, edited by Tomohiko Yuama (Sapporo, Japan: Slavic Research Center, 2007), 7. Available at: http://src-h.slav.hokudai.ac.jp/coe21/publish/no14_ses/01_komatsu.pdf.

29 *Fiqh* is Islamic law.

30 See Robert D. McChesney, *Central Asia: Foundations of Change* (Princeton, NJ: Darwin Press, 1996). See especially chapter 3.

31 This was part of the Stolypin reforms, introduced by Pyotr Stolypin, prime minister of Russia from 1906 to 1911, and designed to offer "unused" lands to those willing to settle in "Siberia," which for purposes of the reforms included all of present-day Kazakhstan and parts of present-day Kyrgyzstan and Uzbekistan.

32 The following sketch on Dukchi Ishan was adapted from the account written by Bakhtiyar Babadjanov that appeared in *Islam na territorii byvshei Rossiskoi imperii: Entsiklopeicheskii slovar* (Islam in the territory of the Previous Russian Empire: Encyclopedic Dictionary) (Moscow: Russia, Vostochnaya Literatura 1999), 35.

33 Komatsu, "Dar al-Islam," 11.

34 Bakhtiyar Babadjanov's unpublished manuscript prepared for a Carnegie Endowment study on Sufism in Uzbekistan.

35 A *fatwa* is a legal opinion based on Sharia law, offered by an Islamic religious leader.

36 Ibid.

37 *Sayyids*—purported descendants of the Prophet Muhammad.

38 According to Bakhtiyar Babadjanov in unpublished materials prepared for a Carnegie Endowment study on religious education in Uzbekistan.

39 See Hisao Komatsu, "Bukhara and Istanbul," in *Islam in Politics in Russia and Central Asia: Early Eighteenth to Late Twentieth Centuries*, edited by Stéphane A. Dudoignon and Hisao Komatsu (London, New York, Bahrain: Kegan Paul, 2001), 168. Muhammed Abduh (1849–1905) was an Islamic reformer who began a revival movement within Islam known as Salafism in the mid-nineteenth century with the intellectuals Jamal al-Din Afghani (1839–1897) and Rashid Rida (1865–1935). He became known as the father of Islamic modernism. See Shireen Hunter, ed., *Reformist Voices of Islam* (New York: Armonk, 2004), 14. See Zianddin Zardar and Merryl Wyn Davies, *No Nonsense Guide to Islam* (Oxford: New Internationalist Press, 2007) for more about reformers in Islam.

40 The new method referred to how the Arabic alphabet was taught. Khalid, *Islam After Communism*, 41.

41 During his studies in Moscow, Gasprinski boarded with the family of M. Katkov, an owner and editor of the Russian newspapers *Moskovskie Vedomosti* and *Russki Vestnik*. Katkov's house often served as a gathering place for many Russian writers and intellectuals, including Tolstoy, Ostrovski, and Turgenev.

42 *Tercuman* (*Perevodchik*) was published from 1883 to 1918, in both Tatar and Russian. For more information about Gasprinsky and *Tercuman*, see Edward Lazzerini, "Ismail Bey Gasprinskii's Perevodchik/Tercuman: A Clarion of Modernism," in *Central Asian Monuments*, edited by H. B. Paksoy (Istanbul: Isis Press, 1992), 143–56. For more about Jadids and Tatar reformers, see Azade-Ayse Rorlich, *The Volga Tatars: A Profile in National Resilience* (Stanford, Calif.: Hoover Institution Press, Stanford University, 1986), chapters 6–9.

43 During the first month of its existence, *Tercuman* had only nine subscribers.

44 Shoshanna Keller, *To Moscow, Not Mecca: Soviet Campaign against Islam in Central Asia, 1917–1941* (Westport, Conn.: Praeger, 2001), 23.

45 Edward Allworth, *The Uzbeks* (Stanford, Calif.: Hoover Institution Press, 1990), 131.

46 Sayid Mir Alim Khan replaced his father, Sayid Abdul Ahad, in January 1910. Abdul Ahad had done the same upon the death of his own father, Muaazfar ad-Din, in 1885.

47 Khalid, "Society and Politics," 379.

48 Keller, *To Moscow, Not Mecca*, 25.

49 Numandjon Gafarov, "Istoriia kul'turno-prosvetitel'skoi deyatel'nosti dzhadidov v Bukharskom emirate (nachalo XX veka) (History of the Cultural Contributions of the Jadids in the Bukharan Emirate) (Khujand: Tadzhiksii Gosudarstvennyi universistet prava, biznesa i politiki, 2000), 58.

50 Khalid, *The Politics of Muslim Cultural Reform*, 81.

51 Komatsu, "Dar al-Islam," 19.

52 For a detailed portrait, see Khalid, *The Politics of Muslim Cultural Reform*.

CHAPTER 3

1 For a discussion of the *basmachi* resistance, see Glenda Fraser, "Basmachi-I," *Central Asian Survey*, vol. 6, no. 1, 1987, 1–73, and Glenda Fraser, "Basmachi-II," *Central Asian Survey*, vol. 6, no. 2, 1987, 7–42.

2 Madamin Bek was a member of a tariqa led by Mavlana Makhdum, a descendant of Makhdum Azam and of Khoja Ahror.

3 Shoshana Keller, *To Moscow, Not Mecca: The Soviet Campaign Against Islam in Central Asia, 1917–1941* (Westport, Conn. and London: Praeger Books, 2001).

4 Ibid., 41.

5 Ibid., 46.

6 After the Russian Revolution formally transferred power to the Tashkent Executive Committee, whose policies and appointments were criticized by local Mensheviks. They, in turn, seized power in the name of the Tashkent Soviet of Workers' Deputies which in turn handed civil authority to the Turkestanian Committee, and the Regional Congress of Soviets elected the SOVNARKOM (Soviet of People's Commissars) as the governing body of the region. See Dov B. Yaroshevski, "Russian Regionalism in Turkestan," *Slavonic and East European Review*, vol. 65, no. 1 (January 1987), 77–100, available at www.jstor.org/stable/4209432.

7 Paolo Sartori, "What Went Wrong? The Failure of Soviet Policy on Sharia Courts in Turkestan, 1917–1923," *Die Welt des Islams* 50 (2010), 397–434.

8 Keller, 44.

9 Ibid., 70–72.

10 It is interesting that one of the issues that the *qurultoy* took up was the high cost of traditional

ceremonies such as burials and weddings, as well as the high costs of continuing the payment of *qalins* (dowries), which were seen as further damaging the already stressed economy of the region. Their presentation of the problem mirrors current debates, as well as those of the late Soviet period.

11 Keller, 75, offers a lengthy discussion of the *qurultoy*.

12 Keller, 80.

13 This campaign targeted the Uzbek and Tajik population; Kyrgyz and Kazakh women generally wore open-faced but modest garb.

14 There are two excellent books on the Stalin-era policies toward women: Marianne Kamp, *The New Woman in Uzbekistan: Islam, Modernity and Unveiling under Communism* (Seattle and London: University of Washington Press, 2006), and Douglas Northrop, *Veiled Empire: Gender and Power in Stalinist Central Asia* (Ithaca, N.Y. and London: Cornell University Press, 2004).

15 Keller, 54.

16 Ibid., 97.

17 Ibid., 135.

18 Her conclusion is based on materials from Uzbek Communist Party and Uzbek state archives. See Keller, 139.

19 "Postanovlenie VTsIK i SNK RSFSR o religioznykh ob'edineniiakh," Sobranie uzakonenii i rasporiazhenii raboche-krest'ianskogo pravitel'stva RSFSR ("Resolution of the Central Executive Committee and the CPC of the RSFSR on the Religious Unification," Collection of Laws and the disposal of the Worker-Peasant Government of the RSFSR (1929), no. 35, http://onlinehistories.ssrc.org/centralasia/cultural/default.aspx?id=602.

20 "1936 Constitution of the USSR," available at www.departments.bucknell.edu/russian/const/1936toc.html.

21 Keller, 188.

22 Ibid., 218.

23 Keller reproduces archival materials that showed that some 686 legally registered mosques and 2,588 unregistered mosques were noted by Uzbek authorities as functioning on January 1, 1936. These data include 100 mosques in the Kyrgyz ASSR. Keller, *To Moscow, Not Mecca*, 223.

24 Ibid., 225.

25 Document from November 15, 1944, quoted in Yaacov Roi, *Islam and the Soviet Union* (New York:

Columbia University Press, 2000), 93.

26 *Muezzin*—the crier of a mosque who summons Muslims to prayer five times daily; he is not considered a cleric.

27 Roi, 62 and 66.

28 Report of the Central Committee of the CPSU to the 22nd Congress of the Communist Party of the Soviet Union, delivered by Nikita S. Khrushchev, October 17, 1961. Khrushchev served as general secretary of the Communist Party of the Soviet Union from September 7, 1953, to October 14, 1964. See Martin McCauley, *The Soviet Union 1917–1991*, second edition (New York: Longman, 1993). See chapters 6, 7, and 8 for more about Khrushchev and his successors.

29 Anisa Abdullaeva, "Youth, tolerance and national values," Uzbekistan Today Information Agency, www.ut.uz/eng/opinion/youth_tolerance_and_national_values.mgr.

30 United Nations, "Population by sex, residence, and intercensal rates of increase for total population, each census: 1948–1997," UN Statistics Division, http://unstats.un.org/unsd/demographic/products/dyb/DYBHist/HistTab03.pdf.

31 Roi, 106.

32 *Eid ul-Fitr/Ramazan hayit*, a three-day celebration/feast marking the end of the 30-day fast of Ramadan, or *Ruza hayit*.

33 *Eid ul-Adha/Qurbon hayit*, marks the end of the *hajj* and is celebrated approximately 70 days after end of the month of Ramadan. It commemorates Abraham's willingness to sacrifice his son as an act of obedience to God.

34 Roi, 71.

35 Ibid., 85.

36 Ibid., 91.

37 Ibid., 89–91.

38 Ibid., 67.

39 Ibid., 68.

40 Ibid., 162.

41 Al-Azhar University dates back to the middle of the tenth century, www.islamfortoday.com/alazhar.htm.

42 Ibid., 174.

43 For example, SADUM was not able to print an edition of the Quran until 1956, when 2,000 copies were printed, and it was reprinted again with 2,250 copies in 1961, with further editions in 1969, 1976, 1977, and 1979, but Roi provides no numbers for how many of each of these later editions were printed. See Roi, 170–71.

44 Leonid Brezhnev served as general secretary of the Communist Party from October 14, 1964, to November 10, 1982. See McCauley, *The Soviet Union 1917–1991*, ch. 7.

45 For details, see Martha Brill Olcott and William Fierman, "The Challenge of Integration: The Political Socialization of the Muslim Conscript," in *Soviet Union*, vol. 14, no. 1 (1987): 65–102.

46 See the address by Yegor Ligachev, second secretary (1985–1990) of the Central Committee of the Communist Party of the Soviet Union, *Bakinsky rabochii*, December 22, 1985. Ligachev had much of the primary responsibility for supervising the seemingly recalcitrant republic communist parties and was able to put some of his own people into the post of first secretary. Saparmurat Niyazov, initially first secretary and then president of Turkmenistan, was a protégé of Ligachev's.

47 Sharaf Rashidov served as the first secretary of the Central Committee of the Communist Party of Uzbekistan from March 14, 1959, to October 30, 1983. He was succeeded by Imanjon Usmankhojaev (November 3, 1983–January 12, 1988), Rafik Nishanov (January 12, 1988–June 23, 1989), and Islam Karimov (June 23, 1989–November 3, 1991). For more about them, see Neil Melvin, *Uzbekistan: Transition to Authoritarianism on the Silk Road* (Amsterdam: Overseas Publishers Association, 2000).

48 For details, see Martha Brill Olcott, "Perestroika in Kazakhstan," *Problems of Communism*, vol. 39, no. 4 (July–August 1990).

49 During Gorbachev's tenure, troops were dispatched to Central Asia to quell riots in Kazakhstan after the placement of Gennady Kolbin, a Russian, as president in 1986, to subdue protests near Ferghana in 1989, and to stop ethnic violence in Osh and Uzgen in Kyrgyzstan in 1990. For more on these and later conflicts, see Valery Tishkov, *Ethnicity, Nationalism, and Conflict in and After the Soviet Union* (London: Sage Publications, 1997).

50 See pages 186–87 of Mehrdad Haghayeghi, "Islam and Democratic Politics in Central Asia," *World Affairs*, vol. 156, no. 4 (Spring 1994): 186–98.

51 For more about Islam in this transitional period in Uzbekistan and the rise and fall of the IMU, see Vitaly Naumkin, *Radical Islam in Central Asia: Between Pen and Rifle* (Lanham, Md.: Rowman & Littlefield, 2005).

CHAPTER 4

1 A *sura* is a Quranic chapter.

2 See Alexandre Bennigsen and Chantal Lemercier-Quelquejay, *Islam in the Soviet Union* (London:

published in association with the Central Asian Research Centre by Pall Mall Press, 1967), and Alexandre Bennigsen and S. Enders Wimbush, *Mystics and Commissars: Sufism in the Soviet Union* (Berkeley: University of California Press, 1985).

3   Unpublished work by Bakhtiyar Babadjanov.

4   *An Islamic Biographical Dictionary of the Eastern Kazakh Steppe, 1770–1912*, edited by Qurban-Ali Khalidi, Allen J. Frank, and Mirkasyim A. Usmanov (Leiden: Brill, 2005).

5   Dru C. Gladne, "The Salafiya Movement in Northwest China: Islamic Fundamentalism among the Muslim Chinese," in *Muslim Diversity: Local Islam in Global Context*, edited by Leif Manger (Surrey, UK: Curzon Press, *Nordic Institute of Asian Studies*, no. 26, 1999), 102–49.

6   Ashirbek Muminov, "Fundamentalist Challenges to Local Islamic Traditions in Soviet and Post-Soviet Central Asia," in *Empire, Islam, and Politics in Central Eurasia*, edited by Tomohiko Uyama (Sapporo, Japan: Slavic Research Center, Hokkaido University, 2007), 254–55.

7   As quoted in Muminov, "Fundamentalist Challenges to Local Islamic Traditions in Soviet and Post-Soviet Central Asia," in Uyama, ed., *Empire, Islam, and Politics in Central Eurasia*, 255.

8   Bakhtiyar Babadjanov, Ashirbek Muminov, and Martha Brill Olcott, "Muhammadjon Hindustani i religioznaya sreda yego epokhi" (Muhammadjon Hindustani and the Religious Atmosphere of his Epoch), *Vostok (Orient)*, no. 5, 2004, 28.

9   *Namaz* (or *salah* in Arabic), the ritual prayer offered 5 times daily, is one of the five pillars of the faith.

10 Akramiya was a group formed by Akrom Yuldoshev, who wrote the 1992 brochure "The Path to Belief" after he left the group Hizb ut-Tahrir. One source indicates that Yuldoshev was inspiring to business people, others that he wanted to begin an Islamic state, and others that he was a reformer. Yuldoshev has been imprisoned since 1999 following his conviction for responsibility for the bombings in Tashkent. For more about Yuldoshev and the controversy that surrounds him, see Bakhtiyar Babadjanov, "Akramia: A Brief Summary"; Alisher Ilkhamov, "'Akromiya': Islamic Extremism or the Islamic Brand of Social Democracy?"; Zuhriddin Husniddinov, *Islam: Directions, Factions, and Movements*; or Sarah Kendzior, "Inventing Akromiya: The Role of Uzbek Propagandists in the Andijon Massacre."

11 In addition to the *Mariftachilar* or Akramiya movement, which began its activity in the 1990s, these groups include the more recent *Shokhidiylar*, whose members were sentenced to prison in December 2010. See Catherine A. Fitzpatrick, "25 Muslims Sentenced in Andijan," Eurasianet.org, December 17, 2010, www.eurasianet.org/node/62587. In neither case is it clear that these schismatic movements saw themselves as taking their inspiration from the *Ahl-i Quran* movement.

12 See Martha Brill Olcott, "Roots of Radical Islam in Central Asia," Carnegie Paper 77, July 2007 (Washington: Carnegie Endowment for International Peace, 2007), 15.

13 Unpublished material provided by Bakhtiyar Babadjanov.

14 Shihab al-Din Marjani was an *alim* (scholar of Islamic law) from Kazan. Having studied in both Bukhara and Samarkand, Marjani brought reformist thought with him back to Russia. For more information, see Stéphane A. Dudoignon, "Echoes to al-Manar among the Muslims of the Russian Empire: A Preliminary Research Note on Riza al-Din b. Fakhr al-Din and the Sura (1908–1918)," in *Intellectuals in the Modern Islamic World: Transmission, Transformation, Communication*, edited by Stéphane A. Dudoignon, Komatsu Hisao, and Kosugi Yasushi (Abingdon, Oxon, and New York: Routledge, 2006), 85–116; and Ahmet Kanlidere, *Reform Within Islam: The Tajdid and Jadid Movement Among the Kazan Tatars (1809–1917): Conciliation or Conflict?* (Istanbul: Eren, 1997).

15 Muminov, "Fundamentalist Challenges to Local Islamic Traditions in Soviet and Post-Soviet Central Asia," in Uyama, ed., *Empire, Islam, and Politics in Central Eurasia*, 257.

16 These include Tajibay domla, Turdibay domla, and Abu Turab Yunusov (all died at the beginning of the 1980s), according to Bakhtiyar Babadjanov's unpublished materials prepared for the Carnegie Endowment.

17 Muminov writes, for example, that after the arrest of Jamal Khoja Ishan, the leadership of the group passed to Mullah Nafiq, Mullah Ghaybullah, and Muhammad Amin Domulla. At the time of Muminov's writing he identifies the group's leader as Mash-Tabib (Abd al-Jabbar Azimov). See Muminov's citation on page 257 in Muminov, "Fundamentalist Challenges to Local Islamic Traditions in Soviet and Post-Soviet Central Asia," in Uyama, ed., *Empire, Islam, and Politics in Central Eurasia*, 249–62.

18 Included in their number were Jamal Khoja Ishan (killed 1937), Said Abu Nasr Mubashshir al-Tarazi (1896–1977), Mullah Yunus Khakimdjanov (1893–1974), Abd al-Qadir Muradov (1893–1976), Ibrahim qori Ishakov, Shaykh-Ikram Shaykh-Islamov, Mullah Abd as-Samad (killed in 1937, at age 26), Zain ud-Din qori (d. 1983). See Muminov, "Fundamentalist Challenges to Local Islamic Traditions in Soviet and Post-Soviet Central Asia," in Uyama, ed., *Empire, Islam, and Politics in Central Eurasia*, 256.

19 Eshon Bobokhon (1861–1957). For more about the Bobokhon family, see Sebastien Peyrouse, "The Rise of Political Islam in Soviet Central Asia," in *Current Trends in Islamist Ideology*, vol. 5 (Washington, D.C.: Hudson Institute, 2007), or Amirsaidkhan Usmankhodzhaev, *Zhizn muftiev Babakhanovykh: sluzhenie vozrozhdenii u Islama v Sovetskom Soiuze* (Life of the Muftis of the Bobokhonov Family: Service of the Revival of Islam in the Soviet Union) (Moscow: Medina Publishing, 2008).

20 Vitaly Naumkin. *Radical Islam in Central Asia: Between Pen and Rifle* (Lanham, Md.: Rowman & Littlefield, 2005), 39.

21 Bakhtiyar Babadjanov says this was in fact the term that Salim Hajji himself used, at least as reported to Babadjanov by one of Salim Hajji's must trusted students.

22 Bakhtiyar Babadjanov was able to interview several students of Salim Hajji, most notably Abdulloh mahsum (aged 76), Gaffor mahsum (aged 83), and the latter's son, Sallohiddin Mahsum-domla (aged 49). The latter is the imam of the Katartal Mosque in Tashkent, while the former two live in the Buke region in Tashkent Oblast. Abdulloh mahsum and Gaffor mahsum remain strong defenders of their late teacher.

23 Naumkin, *Radical Islam in Central Asia*, 43.

24 Bakhtiyar Babadjanov, unpublished manuscript on *fatwas*, 2.

25 "Bu qogoz vijdonimizga putur etkazdi, ammo islom va musulmonlarning manfaatini himoya qildi."

26 N. K. Mirmahmudov, *Islam na territorii byvshey Rossiyskoy imperii—Enciklopedicheskiy slovar* (Islam on the Territory of the Former Russian Empire—Encyclopedic Dictionary), vol. 3 (Moscow: Vostochnaya Literatura, 2001), 75.

27 Bakhtiyar Babadjanov's unpublished materials prepared for the Carnegie Endowment for International Peace.

28 They included most prominently Alikhon tura Saguni (d. 1976).

29 The Russian word/slang expression *krysha* means "roof," that is, a place, an organization, or a person or group of persons that offer protection.

30 *Hatib*—Islamic preacher. He delivers the sermon at Friday prayer. A *hatib* is usually, but not always, the imam. As the prayer leader, he must be a male who has reached puberty. Ziauddin Sardar and Merryl Wyn Davies, *The No-Nonsense Guide to Islam* (Oxford: New Internationalist Press, 2007).

31 Abdulkhay domla, of the Gumbaz Madrasa in Namangan, the former center of the "Wahhabi" movement in Namangan (during the early 1990s), which was then restored to the Hanafi tradition, is also a former student of Hindustani's, although Abdulkhay domla studied with Hindustani for only six months.

32 Gafurov was born near Khujand in 1908, studied journalism in Moscow, served as first secretary of the Tajik Communist Party from 1946 to 1956, and as director of the Institute of Oriental Studies of the Tajik Academy of Sciences from 1956 to 1977, when he died. See www.iranica.com/articles/gafurov- or Iraj Bashiri, "Prominent Tajik Figures of the Twentieth Century," www.angelfire.com/rnb/bashiri/TajikFigures/TajikFigures.pdf.

33 See page 7 of Martha Brill Olcott and Diora Ziyaeva, "Islam in Uzbekistan: Religious Education and State Ideology," Carnegie Paper no. 91 (Washington D.C.: Carnegie Endowment for International Peace, 2008), http://carnegieendowment.org/2008/09/10/islam-in-uzbekistan-religious-education-and-state-ideology/4u3.

34 Informal communications with the author.

35 Hojji Ahmadjon Makhdum was born in 1939 in the village of Zar-i Kon in the Sarasiya district of Surkhandarya Oblast, where he died in 2002.

36 Bobo Muhammad served six months in jail for his criticism of Ayni; Ayni successfully pressed for Bobo Muhammad's release, according to the unpublished writings of Bakhtiyar Babadjanov.

37 Mahdum Bobo-vi Andaqi, d. 1971, was from a *sayyid* family and studied first in Samarkand and then in Bukhara. He fled in the late 1920s and early 1930s to Hisar, then returned to his native village during World War II.

38 For an in-depth account of Muhammad Hindustani's life and works, see Bakhtiyar Babadjanov and Muzaffar Kamilov, "Muhammadjon Hindustani and the Beginning of the 'Great Schism' Among Muslims of Uzbekistan," in *Islam in Politics in Russia and Central Asia: Early Eighteenth to Late Twentieth Centuries*, edited by Stéphane A. Dudoignon and Hisao Komatsu (New York: Kegan Paul, 2001), 195–220.

39 Jalal ad-Din Muhammad Balkhi (1207–1273) was born in Balkh and went on to become the most famous poet in Persia, if not the world. He is known in the West as Rumi for the name of his dwelling place, Anatolian Rome, and in the East as Mawlavi for the name of his Sufi Brotherhood. For more on him and Sufi poetry, see Franklin D. Lewis, *Rumi Past and Present, East and West: The Life, Teaching and Poetry of Jalal al-Din Rumi* (Oxford: Oneworld, 2000). Or see John A. Moyne, *Rumi and the Sufi Tradition* (Costa Mesa, Calif.: Mazda, 2009).

40 Abdul-Qader Bidel (1665–1722) was an Afghan poet who was influenced by Rumi but adopted his own style. See Lewis, *Rumi Past and Present*, 488.

41 Abdurahmonjon's students included Khofizkhon Eshon of Kokand, who died in 1982, and was a teacher of Ibrahim Hazrat, the aforementioned well-known Sufi in the Ferghana Valley.

42 Bakhtiyar Babadjanov and Sh. Vahidov, "Faqiri," in *Islam na territorii byvshey Rossiiskoy imperii. Enciklopedicheskiy slovar*, vol. 3 (Islam on the Territory of the Former Russian Empire—Encyclopedic Dictionary, vol. 3) (Moscow: Vostochnaya literatura, 2001), 107–108, and Bakhtiyar Babadjanov and Sh. Vahidov, "Ravnaqi," in *Islam na territorii byvshey Rossiiskoy imperii*, 81–82.

43 This account is based on an account by Bakhtiyar Babadjanov prepared for the Carnegie Endowment for International Peace. See Hoji Ahmadjon Makhdum Xanafiy Naqshabandiy-Muhaddidiy, *Risalat ul-komila fi Qada il-fatiya* (Tashkent: Mouwarannahr, 2005).

44 Bakhtiyar Babadjanov and Sh. Vahidov, "Ravnaqi," 81–82.

45 Faqiri was born in Sarasia village of the Kitab district of Kashkadarya (Qashqadaryo) Oblast. Mirak Shah khoja, who served as a judge for Abd al-Aziz Khan II (1645–1681) in Balkh, was the founder of his distinguished family, which included *otin oyis* (women with theological education; literally translated an *otin* is a female religious teacher, and *oyi* is an term of endearment for one's mother.)

46 Bakhtiyar Babadjanov and Sh. Vahidov, "Faqiri," 107–108.

47 He was from Dahbid in Kashkadarya Oblast.

48 This means that there was a direct connection between Faqiri and Makhdum Azam, through a continuous line of teachers.

49 Quiet *zikr* is based on alternating concentration (*tavdjjuh*) on specific "points" (*nuqtas*) or "bodies" (*lataif*) located in different parts of the thorax. Each one of them (or their combination) had a specific name, which corresponded to one of the phases of *zikr* (*qalb, rukh, sirr, hafi, akhfa, sultan*) and methods of spiritual concentration (*rabita, tawajjuh, nafi-yi isbat, muraqaba-yi khafi*). Concentration on each one of these points (or a group of points) was accompanied by a mental iteration of Allah's words or a formula of the belief's symbols (*Laillaha illa-Llahu*) for a number of times.

50 These include *Risala-yi tariq-i zikr*, *Risala-yi tariqat-i suluk*, and *Risala-yi tariqat-i Kubraviya*.

51 These include thirty volumes of manuscripts (mainly, Sufi essays, incomplete collection of letters) and essays on *fiqh* and *kalam*.

52 Hojji Ahmadjon Makhdum was the great grandson of Ashur Hisari (who died in the middle of the nineteenth century), who was a very well-known Mujaddidiya sheikh in Eastern Bukhara. Ahmadjon Makhdum's father, Makhdum qori, studied in Bukhara with several Mujaddidiya sheikhs, but he never had any formal students.

53 Eshon Abdurahmanjon died in 1971 at the age of 89.

54 Eshon Shaykh Asadulloh died in 1980.

55 Bakhtiyar Babadjanov, unpublished materials prepared for the Carnegie Endowment for International Peace.

56 The succession line of Abd al-Wahid Turkestani consists of following persons: Ahmad Sirhindi (d. 1624), also known as "Mujaddad alf as-sani" or "the Reformer of the Second Millennium," as he lived at the beginning of the second millennium of the Muslim chronology → Sayyid Muhammad → Sheikh Abdallah → Mawlana Miyan Abid Sheikh → Muhammad Musa Khan Dahbidi (d. 1789) → Khalifa Siddiq (d. 1795) → Khalifa Husayn (d. 1833 or 1834) → Khalifa Abd al-Sattar ibn Khalifa Husayn → Khalifa Salih Muhammad → Khalifa Muhammad Amin → Khalifa Abd al-Wahid Turkestani (d. 1940 or 1941). This is according to Bakhtiyar Babadjanov.

57 Kushata, also known as Kushchi-ata, is located 15–17 kilometers northeast of Turkestan, which is part of today's Kazakhstan.

58 Referring to the ritual of *zikr*.

59 There are also references to his having died in 1978.

60 Gulom ota was still alive in 2005.

61 Bakhtiyar Babadjanov says that the village of Tuda near Chustom in Namangan was one favored site of such meetings.

62 Bakhtiyar Babadjanov reports that Gulom ota's knowledge of Arabic was limited.

63 Several years ago, Dovudkhon was caught allegedly engaging in intimate intercourse with his young students, boys ages 12–15. However, the boys' parents did not press charges, and Dovudkhon continues to accept students and serves as the imam of his mosque in Namangan. If these accusations are in fact true, they would be in keeping with what some maintain was common practice among sheikhs of Sufi brotherhoods.

64 Hakimjon qori was viewed as wealthy by local standards, and his sons owned some local stores. One of them chaired a silk processing guild, while another—Abdulbosit Vosiev, the youngest son—followed in his father's footsteps. He teaches at the Kukaldosh Madrasa in Tashkent.

65 For a discussion of Rahmatulla-alloma, see Abdujabar Abduvakhitov, "Islamic Revivalism in Uzbekistan," in *Russia's Muslim Frontiers: New Directions in Cross-Cultural Analysis*, edited by Dale F. Eickelman (Bloomington: Indiana University Press, 1993), 79–97; and Abdujabar Abduvakhitov, "The Jadid Movement and Its Impact on Contemporary Central Asia," in *Central Asia: Its Strategic Importance and Future Prospects*, edited by Hafeez Malik (New York: St. Martin's Press, 1994).

66 The essay was written in approximately 1977–1978. We only have a detailed narration of the essay's content, dictated by one of the author's students. The author described an ideal country "Musulmon-obod," where Islam prospers, people are equal and "worship only to God, but not to any of parties, living or dead leaders." Generally, the essay (this is a conditional name) reminds us of a famous essay by Tomazzo Campanella, "The City of Sun."

67 *Ijtihad*—In Islamic law, the independent or original interpretation of issues not precisely covered by the Quran, *hadith*, and *ijma*.

68 This was all reported by Bakhtiyar Babadjanov, who interviewed Ayubkhon Homidov. At the time of the interview, Ayubkhon Homidov was a teacher of *fiqh* and *tafsir* at the Higher Islamic Institute under the Spiritual Governance of the Republic of Uzbekistan. In 1988 he studied with Abduvali qori. After Muhammad Sodiq Muhammad Yusuf became the *mufti*, Ayubkhon was accepted at the Supreme Islamic Institute and became his student. Muhammad Sodiq Muhammad Yusuf advised Ayubkhon to start by strengthening his religious knowledge and then move to policy issues. Ayubkhon, together with Azamkhon, an instructor at the Department of Islamic Science at the State Institute of Oriental Studies, quite often debated Muhammad Sodiq Muhammad Yusuf on his "lesson on *hadiths*."

69 His work *Tafsir al-furqan* was written at that time.

70 *Tahajjud* (in Arabic, ritual)—the night prayer, which is generally not considered obligatory and not counted among the five daily prayers.

CHAPTER 5

1. He maintains a Russian language site, islam.uz, and three principal Uzbek language sites, islom.uz, quran.uz, and muslimaat.uz, which also have additional Uzbek sites that are linked to them.

2. The only real competition might come from Tajikistan, but Khoji Akbar (Qaharov) Turojonzod divides his time between his economic activities and religious affairs, while Sayid Abdulloh Nuri died in 2006. See "Tajikistan: Influential Islamic Politician Remembered," Radio Free Europe/ Radio Liberty, August 10, 2006, www.rferl.org/content/article/1070492.html. For more background, see Martha Brill Olcott, "Islam and Fundamentalism in Independent Central Asia," in *Muslim Eurasia: Conflicting Legacies*, edited by Yaacov Roi (Portland, OR: Frank Cass Publishing, 1995), and Vitaly Naumkin, *Radical Islam in Central Asia: Between Pen and Rifle* (Lanham, Md.: Rowman & Littlefield, 2005), ch. 4.

3. I have met Muhammad Sodiq Muhammad Yusuf on four occasions, twice while he was *mufti*, and twice since his return from exile.

4. Mansur Hajji's educational activities led to his arrest in 1936. After nearly six years in prison, he was released to serve in the penal battalions, returning to Uzbekistan in 1946. Mansur Hajji returned to teaching after Stalin's death and continued to work until his own death in 1971.

5. For more about Muslims of the Soviet East and the relation of religion and the state in Uzbekistan, see Christian Larson. *Official Islam in Central Asia: Continuity and Oscillation in the Religio-Political Relationship, 1867–2003*, Thesis (M.A.). Bloomington: Indiana University, Department of Central Eurasian Studies, 2008.

6. Gulbuddin Hekmatyar, head of Afghanistan's Islamic Party, led in the *mujahideen* resistance against the Soviets and was Afghan prime minister from 1993 to 1994. In a 2001 interview with *Jane's Defense Weekly*, he said, "I defeated the Soviet Union; I will defeat the USA, in the same way. Americans are repeating the same mistakes." In recent years, he has been near Peshawar, Pakistan, and met with Afghan President Karzai's government in 2010. James Lamont and Farhan Bokhari, "Kabul in Talks with Leading Militants," *Financial Times*, March 23, 2010. For more on his relation to Pakistan, see C. Christine Fair, "The Militant Challenge in Pakistan," *Asia Policy*, no. 11, January 2011, 105–137.

7. See Muhammad Sodiq Muhammad Yusuf, *Esli by my vse byli nabozhnymi* (If We Were All Devout) (Tashkent: Chulpan, 1992).

8. TASS March 14, 1989, as quoted by *FBIS Daily Report: Soviet Union*, FBIS-SOV-89,049, March 15, 1989.

9. Kuwaiti al-Anbaa Newspaper, May 11, 1989, as translated in *FBIS Daily Report: Soviet Union*, FBIS-SOV-89-096, May 19, 1989, 85.

10. Muhammad Sodiq Muhammad Yusuf, *Esli by my vse byli nabozhnymi*, 40, as quoted in a May 12, 1989, article in *Literatura i iskusstvo Uzbekistana* (Literature and Art of Uzbekistan).

11 Muhammad Sodiq Muhammad Yusuf, *Esli by my vse byli nabozhnymi*, 10.

12 M. Alimov and A. Mursaliev, "My-Partiya Allakha" (We are the Party of Allah), *Komsomolskaia Pravda*, December 8, 1990, 1, and M. Alimov, "Muftiy znait chto govorit" (The Mufti Knows What He is Saying), *Komsomolskaia Pravda*, April 3, 1991, 1.

13 Mehrdad Haghayeghi, "Islam and Democratic Politics in Central Asia," *World Affairs*, Farmington Hills, Mich., March 22, 1994. Available at www.highbeam.com/doc/1G1-15232351.html.

14 In 1995, Muhammad Sodiq published a book titled *The Essence of Contradictions* (Ixtiloflar haqida), dedicated to the theological analysis of the disagreements that separated the two groups.

15 All arrangements with the "Arabs" were being done by A. Gafurov, Muhammad Sodiq Muhammad Yusuf's personal representative to the Ferghana Valley.

16 Bakhtiyar Babadjanov reports that some Saudi Arabian millionaires who were ethnic Uzbeks from Tashkent financed the construction of some of the largest mosques in Tashkent directly, without any involvement from the *mufti*'s office. (For example, Kukcha Mosque, Kukeltash Madrasa, and others.)

17 Other members of the opposition to Muhammad Sodiq included Fozil qori, the imam of Khoji Alambardor Mosque; Abdulaziz Mansurov, the former head of the *fatwa* department of the *mufti*'s office; Faizur Rahmon, the imam of Said Waqqa's mosque; Ghulam-qadir, the imam of Allon Mosque, and Obidkhon qori Nazarov.

18 There was no unity among Muhammad Sodiq Muhammad Yusuf's supporters either. One of these groups was led by Namangan leaders of religious organizations of the youth, similar to *Islom lashkarlari* (Fighters of Islam), and another by Muhammad Sodiq Kosimov (born in 1960), a former disciple of Hindustani, who was not so well known then and is currently the imam of the main mosque in Andijan.

19 *Fitnalarni toxtataylik* (Let's Stop the Conspiracies), *Toshkent haqiqati* (Tashkent's Truth), July 10, 1991. Publications like that once again prove that state agencies were backing Muhammad Sodiq Muhammad Yusuf's opponents.

20 "*Islom nuri*" (The Light of Islam), July 1–15, 1991, 2–3.

21 This is based on my interviews in the Ferghana Valley in 1992 and 1993.

22 Bakhtiyar Babadjanov reports that Abduvali qori's political goals during this period were to see the integration of the Islamic state of Turkestan that would unify the territory of the whole Central Asia.

23 Tashkent Radio, February 26, 1992, *FBIS Daily Report: Central Eurasia*, FBIS-SOV-92-045, March 6, 1992, 59.

24 Aleksei Volosevich, "Neutralization of Student Disturbances in Tashkent in 1992: What It Was Like," Fergana News Agency, January 24, 2006, http://enews.fergananews.com/article.php?id=1248.

25 For a more detailed analysis, see Martha Brill Olcott, "Roots of Radical Islam in Central Asia," Carnegie Paper 77 (Washington, D.C.: Carnegie Endowment for International Peace, 2007).

26 Uzbeks continue to use the Soviet-era term "Oriental" (*sharqiy*) studies, for research on Islam, and for studies on Asian societies.

27 Bakhtiyar Babadjanov, unpublished materials; dates of the videotape and conference are not provided.

28 "Uzbek Sports Journalist Accused of Islamist Leanings," Institute for War & Peace Reporting, January 26, 2010, http://iwpr.net/report-news/uzbek-sports-journalist-accused-islamist-leanings.

29 This is a point that he raised in meetings with Alexei Malashenko and the author.

30 These include Ayubkhon Homidov, a lecturer at the Highest Islamic Institute; Muzaffar Kamilov, the deputy rector in the State Institute of Oriental Studies; Azamkhon Kayumov, a lecturer at the Tashkent State Institute of Oriental Studies; and Rahmatulla qori, imam of a mosque in Tashkent and at the same time lecturer at the State Islam University in Tashkent.

31 This section is based wholly upon materials provided by Bakhtiyar Babadjanov.

32 His main works include: *Commentary on the Quran* (Tafsir-i Hilal), 2003; *Hadiths and Life* (Hadis va hayot), completed in 2000 (Tashkent); *Islam and Democracy* (Islom va demokratiya), Osh 1995; *The Sunni Credo of Faith* (Sunniy aqidalar), Tashkent 2004; *The Essence of Contradictions* (Ixtiloflar haqida), Osh 1995, reissued in expanded form, Tashkent 2000; and *Religion Is Edification* (Din nasihatdir), Tashkent 2005.

33 *Mujahid*—a Muslim engaged in jihad; the proper Arabic plural is *mujahideen*.

34 Dawud: Book 14: *Hadith* 2639, "Narrated Jarir ibn Abdullah: The Apostle of Allah (peace be upon him) sent an expedition to Khatham. Some people sought protection by having recourse to prostration, and were hastily killed. When the Prophet (peace be upon him) heard that, he ordered half the blood-wit to be paid for them, saying: I am not responsible for any Muslim who stays among polytheists. They asked: Why, Apostle of Allah? He said: Their fires should not be visible to one another." See www.quranexplorer.com/Hadith/English/Index.html [search terms *hadith* 2639].

35 "Verily, this [religion] is an admonition: therefore whosoever will, let him take a Path to His Lord!" (*al-Muzzammil*, chapter 73, verse 19), www.searchtruth.com.

36 Muhammad ibn Ismail al-Bukhari (810–870 AD) was a religious scholar best known for authoring the *hadith* collection named *Sahih Bukhari*. He was born in Bukhara and is buried near Samarkand. For more about the life of imam al-Bukhari, see Ghassan Abdul-Jabbar, *Bukhari* (New York: Oxford University Press, 2007).

37 Abu Isa Muhammad al-Termizi (also spelled Tirmizi) wrote one of the six canonical *hadith* compilations used in Sunni Islam. He was born and died in Bagh, near what is now Termez, Uzbekistan. For more about him, including the annotated translations of two of his writings, see Bernd Radtke and John O'Kane, *The Concept of Sainthood in Early Islamic Mysticism* (Surrey, UK: Curzon Press, 1996).

38 He says that Hizb ut-Tahrir wrongly denies that there will be suffering on Judgment Day and second, that on Judgment Day, the Messiah will appear in the forms of Jesus Christ and the False Messiah. Muhammad Sodiq cites the Quran and *Sunna* to prove that these beliefs are in fact firmly rooted in Islamic dogma.

39 Literally Arabic for "witness," a *shahid* is a martyr who sacrifices his life to fulfill a religious commandment or defend his country or family.

40 The author of *Who Is to Blame?* (1847), Alexander Herzen (1812–1870), was a Russian writer and thinker who assisted in creating a political climate that led to the emancipation of the serfs in 1861. The author of *What is to Be Done?* (1863), Nikolay Chernyshevsky (1828–1889), was a radical journalist and politician who influenced the young Russian intelligentsia and was considered to be a forerunner of Vladimir Lenin. For more on these men and their connection to early Russian populism, see Franco Venturi, *Roots of Revolution: A History of the Populist and Socialist Movements in Nineteenth Century Russia* (New York: Grosset & Dunlap, 1966), chapters 1, 5.

41 Dr. Muhammad Said Ramadan al-Buti is a prominent Islamic scholar and religious leader who is the head of the Beliefs and Religions Department in the faculty of the Islamic Law, Damascus University. He has a Facebook page, www.facebook.com/group.php?gid=9842892919, and a website, www.bouti.com. For more information, see Andreas Christmann, "Islamic Scholar and Religious Leader: A portrait of Sheikh Muhammad Said Ramadan al-Buti," *Islam and Christian-Muslim Relations*, volume 9, issue 2, 1998, 149–69. For an example of his sermons, see www.youtube.com/watch?v=Fcgfj-iCLZI.

42 For more about al-Afghani, see Nikki R. Keddie, *An Islamic Response to Imperialism: Political and Religious Writings of Sayyid Jamal ad-Din "al-Afghani"* (Berkeley: University of California Press, 1983). In his book, Afghani emphasizes that there is a strong intellectual tradition in Islam, "Regarding the religions that we have before us, we remark that the religion of Islam was established on a strong base of wisdom." Jamal ud-Din al-Afghani, *Refutation des materialistes: 3e edition Arabe avec introduction et notes* (translated into French by A. M. Goichon) (Paris: P. Geuthner, 1942), 158.

43 "Orientalism was ultimately a political vision of reality whose structure promoted the difference between the familiar (Europe, West, 'us') and the strange (the Orient, the East, 'them')." Edward W. Said, *Orientalism* (New York: Vintage Books, 1979), 45. For an introduction to Edward Said, see www.lehigh.edu/~amsp/2004/09/introduction-to-edward-said.html.

44 "With Reference to (especially Central) European Universities: The Action or Process of Recognizing Foreign Degrees." See Oxford English dictionary, www.oed.com/view/Entry/234102?redirectedFrom=nostrification#. In this case, the degrees would be conferred by unsanctioned institutions.

CHAPTER 6

1. Bakhtiyar Umarov, a government sociologist, headed the research team and was responsible for choosing the survey researchers who conducted the interviews. He undertook the study in a private capacity, running the project from a private research organization that he had organized. This study was initially intended to cover three countries—Uzbekistan, Tajikistan, and Kazakhstan—but the civil war in Tajikistan made data collection there impossible. The Kazakh data were collected, but the data collection process was subject to a tightly structured interview protocol, making it non-comparable to the research materials collected in Uzbekistan. The funding for this study was received by Colgate University from the National Council for Soviet and East European Research, now known as the National Council for Eurasian and East European Research. Some of the materials in the study appeared in an article, Martha Brill Olcott, "New States and New Identities: Religion and State Building in Central Asia," in *Ethnic Conflict and International Politics in the Middle East*, edited by Leonard Binder (Gainesville, Fla.: University Press of Florida, 1999).

2. A fifth community was selected, in Khiva Oblast, and the interviews were supposedly conducted. But I never received them and never got a fully clear explanation of whether they were seized by the government, or whether Umarov had been told not to give them to me, or whether his local scholar had simply absconded with the money and never did the interviews. The survey was conducted at a time of fairly strong secessionist views in Khiva.

3. I did not visit the community chosen in Samarkand but met with the researcher who did the interviews. In all other cases, I met with the researchers and spent a few days in the villages or communities that we chose, but I was deliberately not present during the interviews. I did work directly with the research team in Tashkent Oblast when we did a series of pilot interviews, to make sure that the team members understood the "conversational" format that we chose for the interviews—just a few informational questions to break the ice, and then a minimally directed free-flowing conversation on the role of religion in the community and in their own lives.

4. Unfortunately, about ten years ago, my copies of the original interviews, transcribed and translated from Uzbek to English in the United States by another Uzbek-trained social scientist, were accidentally discarded in the breaking up of my household effects in a move from Hamilton, New York, to Washington, D.C. I have never at any time questioned the authenticity of the interviews.

5. Baisun was the only community in the study that was not subject to Russian colonial rule, and thus did not experience governance by Russians until after the Russian Revolution.

6. There is a visa regime in place between the two countries, and someone going from Baisun to Dushanbe would first have to travel to Tashkent to get a visa, and then could travel to Dushanbe. There is currently no commercial air or bus service between Uzbekistan and Tajikistan.

7. Thirty interviews were done in Baisun, both in the district center and in the surrounding regions of the district in October 1992. The tapes of two interviews proved to be defective, so that a total of twenty-eight interviews (twenty-four with men and four with women) survive; seventeen families

are represented in the sample. A few of the interviews were done with family members from the city of Baisun, and the rest took place on the farm itself. The interviews were conducted by someone originally from the town of Baisun, aided by an assistant from Tashkent.

8   In the Turkipoen sample, two of the thirty people interviewed came from the neighboring village of Turki Bola. Fifteen families were interviewed; thirteen pairs of fathers and sons, one mother and daughter, and one father and daughter. The oldest resident interviewed was born in 1915, the youngest in 1960. One respondent was half Tajik; all the rest were Uzbeks. The interviewer in this case was a woman, born in the village. The interviews were conducted just after the conclusion of Ramadan in 1992, when she had come back to the village to celebrate *Ramazan hayit* with her relatives. There is no evidence to suggest that the use of a female interviewer had any impact on the answers.

9   For example, one of the interviewees, born in 1927, recalled with pride a trip to Mecca by his own ancestor, whose *hajj* was more of an exception than the rule. "The mother of my mother, Asalmomo, died when she was 97. Her husband went on *hajj* and was taken as a *hajj* there, where he died. His friend, who had traveled with him, returned and gave Asalmomo his *chalma* (turban) and his clothes.... They traveled there for several years. They even had to beg for bread. They had no place to stay and had to ask for shelter. They were holy people. We are the children of great people. Our ancestors were great people."

10 Only eight of the thirty people interviewed in Turkipoen had received some form of religious instruction prior to 1989; for six of these eight, their knowledge of Islamic teachings and practice still seemed limited. The exceptions were two respondents who had "returned" to Islam in the 1970s. Six of the eight were fathers and sons, the sons having been taught by the fathers. Two of the three fathers (born in 1919 and 1915, respectively) had received several years of formal religious instruction in local schools, prior to the collectivization drive of 1929–1934. The former is the last in a long line of ritual butchers.

11 The shrine is 7.5 miles north of Samarkand, and the Chelak region center is about 10 miles north of that.

12 For more about the tradition of "Seven Fathers," see Saulesh Yessenova, "'Routes and Roots' of Kazakh Identity: Urban Migration in Postsocialist Kazakhstan," *Russian Review*, vol. 64, no. 4, October 2005.

13 The Kuva sample consists of eighteen families and a total of 28 interviews, of which 23 are with men. The oldest person interviewed was born in 1911; the youngest person interviewed was born in 1972. All but three of those interviewed were born in the three villages that made up the Kuva sample. It includes several village notables and many people with advanced secondary or higher education, among them eight teachers and a doctor.

14 Only seventeen people were interviewed in Tova, because the local interviewer reported that he was unable to do the second round of studies as the political situation in the Namangan region

had grown more tense since the first round. Our contact in the village was an instructor in the philosophy department at Namangan Pedagogical Institute, Namangan's sole university. The professor, a specialist in "scientific atheism," was very critical of the growing political strength of Islamic revivalists in the city of Namangan and complained of their growing influence within his *kishlak* as well. Perhaps that is why none of the respondents seem to have been members of revivalist Islamic groups, although the activities of such groups are certainly described in the interviews, sometimes at considerable length. The two oldest in the group were born in 1925; the youngest, a student at the Namangan Pedagogical Institute, was born in 1972. The sample included four teachers, three engineers or technicians, and four collective farmers; about half the sample had attained higher education. Unfortunately, the sample included only three women—the mother and wife of a respondent, and another female respondent.

15 Given the biases of our contact in the community, it is unlikely that the study was deliberately steered toward people with roots in Namangan's religious community.

16 Although his house was set up in traditional Uzbek style, with a few family rooms and a separate guest house in which we spent the night, the *sayyid* professor of atheism kept a secular home. His wife and grown daughter dressed modestly but were welcome both to eat and to drink spirits with us. Not even the most symbolic of prayers were offered during our visit, which is quite unusual in rural Uzbekistan. He, like his colleague in Kuva, included himself in the survey, and the comments about his not having had religious education come from his interview.

17 *Hayit nomoz*—prayers for *Eid al-Adha* (*Qurbon hayit*), the feast of the Sacrifice (of Isaac by Abraham). Roi, 70.

18 This would have been a journey of several days.

19 Faizulla Khodjaev was a Bukharan Jadid who fought along with the communists to overthrow the Emir of Bukhara in 1920. He was appointed the first president of the Bukhara SSR in 1922 and was a victim of the purges.

20 Akmal Ikramov was the first secretary of the Uzbek Communist Party alongside Chairman of the Council of People's Commissars of the Uzbek SSR Faizulla Khodjaev. Both were executed on March 13, 1938. See Donald Carlisle, "Geopolitics and Ethnic Problems of Uzbekistan and Its Neighbours," in *Muslim Eurasia: Conflicting Legacies*, edited by Yaacov Roi (Portland, Ore.: Routledge, 1995), 74–78.

21 Translated from Uzbek, *buvi* means grandmother. Hence, an *otin buvi* is an older female religious teacher.

22 *Aka* means "older brother" and is used as a term of respect after a man's name.

23 Sharaf Rashidov was first secretary of the Uzbek Communist Party from 1959 to 1983. He was born in Jizzakh, 65 miles from Samarkand. Though many ordinary Uzbeks identified with him as an advocate of the republic's needs, his critics maintain that corruption and clan politics were prevalent during his rule. For more about him and the reaction to his policies, see Nancy Lubin,

"Uzbekistan," in *Kazakstan, Kyrgyzstan, Tajikistan, Turkmenistan, and Uzbekistan: Country Studies*, edited by Glenn E. Curtis (Washington: Federal Research Division, Library of Congress, 1996).

24 She was not interviewed, so there are no personal data on her.

25 In the Soviet Union, most of the so-called sanitoria were really more like health spas, places where people could combine vacation and "healing," using sick days rather than vacation days to "pay" for their visits.

26 *Kalima* (Arabic)—"a saying." In this context, it could be a profession of faith.

27 From "Muhammad's Birth and Forty Years Prior to Prophethood," www.alsiraj.net/English/sira/html/page00.html (a Sufi legend from an unidentified source about the dervish Adham and Princess Malika). It is possible that the *otin* was alluding to the compilation of legends about the great Sufi dervish, Sheikh Ibrahim ibn Adham, whose righteous father, Adham, married a princess.

28 Imonjon Usmankhojaev was the first party secretary after Rashidov (1983–1988), whom the Soviets installed in an unsuccessful effort to end corruption in the local Communist Party. He was quickly replaced by Rafiq Nishonov, who was seen as leaning more toward Moscow. See Nancy Lubin, "Uzbekistan," for an overview and Kathleen Collins, "The Logic of Clan Politics: Evidence from the Central Asian Trajectories," *World Politics*, vol. 56, no. 2 (January 2004): 224–61, for more about clan politics.

29 *Khudoya* (Persian), literally, "Oh, God."

30 *Fatiha* is the first *sura* of the Quran and is said to contain its essence of monotheism, piety, the straight path, and the afterlife:

In the name of Allah, the most gracious, the dispenser of grace: All praise is due to Allah alone, the sustainer of all the worlds, the most gracious, the dispenser of grace, lord of the day of judgment, thee alone do we worship, and unto you do we turn for aid. Guide us on the straight path, the way of those upon whom you have bestowed the blessings, not of those who have been condemned by you, not of those who go astray (1:1–7), as translated in Diane Morgan, *Essential Islam: A Comprehensive Guide to Belief and Practice* (Westport, Conn.: Praeger, 2010), 24.

These words are incorporated into all daily prayers and are traditionally read into the ears of the dying.

31 We asked, "Please tell me, how do you explain for yourself the sense and content of the understanding 'Muslimness'?" And, "What does it mean to fulfill the demand *musulmonchilik qilish kerak*" (one must act like a Muslim)? These questions were in response to the common statement, "*Bu musulmonchilik emas*" (This is not Muslimness).

32 This respondent was responsible for the survey in Kuva and had his assistant in the project conduct this interview as well as one with his father.

CHAPTER 7

1. Alisher Navoi—an Uzbek poet (1441–1501), who lived during the reign of the Timurid dynasty. Navoi is the author of the lyrical work "Treasure of the Thought," as well as a number of other literary and scientific works in philosophy, linguistics, and history. Navoi's most famous poems are: "Wonders of Good People," "Leili and Medjnun," "Farkhad and Shirin," "Seven Travellers," and "Dam of Iskander." For more information on Alisher Navoi and the early poetry in Central Asia, see Aftandil Erkinov, "The Poetry of Nomads and Shaybani Rulers in the Process of Transition to a Settled Society," in *Central Asia on Display: Proceedings of the VII. Conference of the European Society for Central Asian Studies*, edited by Gabriele Rasuly-Paleczek and Julia Katschnig (Vienna: Central Asian Studies, 2005).

2. Moulana Mahammad Suleyman oglu Fizuli Baghdadi (1494–1556) was an Azerbaijani poet, thinker, and writer in Turkish, Arabic, and Persian languages. Fizuli is especially famous for his lyrical poetry in Turkish. His most known masterpiece is "Leyli and the Madman"—the Romeo and Juliet of the East. For more information on Fizuli and the poetry of Azerbaijan, see Inna Naroditskaya, "Dervishes in Modern Azerbaijan: Absence and Presence," in *Manifold Identities: Studies on Music and Minorities*, edited by Ursula Hemetek et al. (Cambridge: Scholars Press, 2004); and Mirza Ibrahimov, ed., *Azerbaijanian Poetry: Classic, Modern, Traditional* (Moscow: Progress, 1969).

3. *Hashar*—voluntary contributions, often in the form of work such as construction or cleaning, from all the members of a *mahalla*. During Soviet times, this was known as *subotnik* (Saturday work).

4. Veiled cloak worn by devout Muslim women.

5. *Ruza hayit*—the Uzbek term for the 30 days of fasting during Ramadan.

6. *Kadisoia* is likely a dialect version of the *hadiths*.

7. *Mutaval*—proprietor of a religious foundation.

8. *Karnay*—Uzbek trumpet used for ceremonial announcements.

9. There was a virtually identical statement made by another teacher in Kuva, born in 1965.

10. During the Soviet era the *mahalla* had become a partially Soviet institution, making sure that state holidays were observed and that any state funds that may have been allotted were properly used. Even during the years of religious repression, though, when no mosques were in evidence, the *mahalla* committee continued trying to ensure that some of the traditional practices were preserved. Once Soviet power evaporated, however, the institution of the *mahalla* committee was wholly restored to its former function.

11. This quote, and complaint, comes from a couple born in the 1950s, both of whose ancestors were religious figures.

12 He was interviewed in Turkipoen, but was a visitor to the region from another unspecified part of Uzbekistan.

13 In Uzbek folklore, a *palvan* is a defender of truth and justice, a protector of the oppressed ones. Today this term is applied more broadly, usually connoting such traits as bravery, courage, might, and valor.

14 Sangak Safarov was a Tajik barman who spent twenty-three years of his life in prison for committing offenses of varying degrees of gravity, including a murder and an organized prison revolt. By mid-1992, when the region of Kulyab seceded from the central government, Safarov established a military organization, which was described in media reports as "the Popular Front," "the Kulyab brigade," or "the Safarov gang." This heavily armed but poorly run militia received backing from Russia and Uzbekistan and was notorious for looting and atrocities. Later in 1992, Safarov handpicked Emomali Rahmon as his protégé, who was then selected as the chairman of the Supreme Court in November 1992. Safarov was shot in a brawl with another Popular Front official. See International Crisis Group, *Tajikistan: On the Road to Failure*, Asia Report 162, February 12, 2009.

CHAPTER 8

1 Laura Adams has written extensively on the state-building policy of Islam Karimov's government. In *The Spectacular State*, she makes a very convincing argument that the efforts at ideology building on the part of the Uzbek government have been better thought out and more sophisticated than often credited by outside observers, noting that the depiction of national history is but one part of a three-part strategy that includes ethnic and international components and seeks to depict Uzbek national culture as a "normal" national culture. See Laura Adams, *The Spectacular State: Culture and National Identity in Uzbekistan* (Durham, N.C.: Duke University Press, 2010), 38–43.

2 While Western scholars, such as Edward Allworth, *The Modern Uzbeks: From the 14th Century to the Present* (Stanford, Calif.: Hoover Institution Press, 1990), would take issue with this, the Uzbek government's history books—A. Askarov, *Uzbekiston xalqlari tarixi* (The History of the Peoples of Uzbekistan) Tashkent: Fan, 1993—assert the "truth" of this in no uncertain terms.

3 This group is also known as the Islamic Jihad Group (IJG), *al-Jihad al-Islami*, and *Jamaat Mujahidov*.

4 Islam Karimov, the president of Uzbekistan, in a speech to the special meeting of the Oliy Majlis (national parliament), August 1991. As cited in Martha Brill Olcott, "Islam in Uzbekistan: Religious Education and State Ideology," Carnegie Paper 91 (Washington: Carnegie Endowment for International Peace, 2008), 30.

5 According to Babadjanov, literary works of late nineteenth- and early twentieth-century writers, such as Abdulla Qahhar, Avloni, Saloh ad-Din, and Ghofur Ghulom, were written primarily in Chagatai (the precursor to modern Uzbek) and some in Farsi as well.

6   Bakhtiyar Babadjanov's unpublished materials prepared for the Carnegie Endowment for International Peace.

7   Muhammad Abu Mansur al-Maturidi (d. 944) of Maturid in Samarkand province wrote many tracts about Hanafi doctrine, including the *Book of Monotheism and the Book of Interpretations of the Quran*, as well as three refutations of an opposing doctrine to Hanafi, that of Mutazila. See www.sunnah.org/history/Scholars/al_maturidi.htm.

8   Bakhtiyar Babadjanov, unpublished materials prepared for the Carnegie Endowment for International Peace.

9   The monitoring of these Uzbek language radio stations was done by Bakhtiyar Babadjanov and Diora Ziyaeva.

10 The program was hosted by Sanjar Sadullaev and Muhammadali Abduqunduzov, a former deputy minister of culture of Uzbekistan.

11 Much of this programming features Anvar qori, *imam-hatib* of Tashkent.

12 As already mentioned in earlier sections of the book, this is a point of contention between traditionally-oriented Hanafi clerics and their more doctrinal-oriented Hanafi colleagues. Salafist clerics reject these garish ritual celebrations.

13 While Uzbeks and other Central Asians complain about the biases of Russian language broadcasting produced in Russia, those with cable have access to independent Russian language broadcasting such as CNN, BBC, and Euronews in Russian. Similarly, they have access to a wide range of independent Turkish language broadcasting.

14 The comments about physical access to the Internet reflect the author's own experiences and those of ordinary Uzbeks with whom she has conversed during trips to Uzbekistan which focused on questions relating to information technology. Physical access to the Internet refers to the ability to connect to the internet, and does not imply free access to all information found on the Internet.

15 One of the things that Uzbek authorities have done to try to counter this is to ask Internet café owners to record passport numbers of users, although there is no information on whether this is being enforced. Furthermore, there has been no mention of people being arrested for downloading seditious material on the Internet either in cafés or in their homes.

16 See the Uzbek constitution, available at www.gov.uz./en/constitution. December 8 was "Constitution Day" in the USSR, something that was obviously considered by the Uzbek government in its choice of date.

17 According to the criteria employed by Human Rights Watch, freedom of religion has been repressed (after a brief thaw) since 1994. The group notes in its 2011 report on Uzbekistan that religious practitioners—whether Muslim, Baptist, or Hare Krishna—are often imprisoned. Many scholars

argue that by labeling conservative Islam "Wahhabism," Uzbek authorities have demonized it. However, Zeyno Baran, Fred Starr, and Svante Cornell argue that in the early 1990s, Islamic radicalism caused repression of Islamic groups and that there is no correlation between radicalism and levels of repression. See Human Rights Watch, "January 2011 Country Summary: Uzbekistan," 3–4; Baran, Starr, Cornell, "Islamic Radicalism in Central Asia and the Caucasus: Implications for the EU"; and Alexander Knysh, "A Clear and Present Danger: 'Wahhabism' as a Rhetorical Foil."

18 Radio Free Europe/Radio Liberty indicates that 400 people have been killed by land mines on the Uzbek-Tajik border, where mines have been since the Tajik Civil War of 1992–1997. The Landmine and Cluster Monitor indicates that Uzbekistan has mined its borders with Kyrgyzstan, Tajikistan, and Afghanistan. The Afghan border has been mined since the Soviet era. See "Landmine and Cluster Munition Monitor: Uzbekistan Country Report," June 18, 2010.

19 Igor Rotar, "'Nash dolg priobshchit' kommunistov k isalmu'" (It is our Duty to Involve the Communists in Islam), *Nezavisimaya gazeta*, January 7, 1992, 3.

20 Mukhtarkhon Abdullaev (1993–1996, died in 2003) headed Mir-i Arab Madrasa in Bukhara. During the first presidential election in Uzbekistan in 1991, Abdullaev had campaigned for Karimov.

21 Bakhtiyar Babadjanov says that a number of imams from Tashkent's "Old City," including Obidkhon qori Nazarov, Rukhitdin Pahritdinov, and Rahmatulla Obidov, actually formally boycotted Abdullaev as *mufti*.

22 Tohir Yuldoshev was a founder and leader of the Islamic Movement of Uzbekistan. Born in 1967, he acted as an underground imam in the 1990s. His location is currently unknown, but there are rumors that he is in Pakistan. See Martha Brill Olcott, "Roots of Radical Islam in Central Asia." Also see "Representatives of the Islamic Movement of Uzbekistan Claim That Tohir Yuldoshev Is Alive," Ferghana.ru, April 9, 2007, http://enews.ferghana.ru/article.php?id=1917.

23 The camps in Tajikistan were liquidated only after substantial pressure was exerted by Karimov on Tajikistan's president, Emomali Rahmon, to drive these irregulars across the border into Afghanistan. The IMU went from Tajikistan to Batken in August 1999. See Rashid, *Jihad*.

24 See U.S. Department of State, "Uzbekistan: Country Reports on Human Rights Practices, Bureau of Democracy, Human Rights, and Labor, 1999," February 23, 2000, www.state.gov/g/drl/rls/hrrpt/1999/369.htm.

25 The Russian human rights group Memorial estimates that more than 83 percent of the approximately 10,000 independent Muslim worshippers who were prosecuted in 1998–2003 were charged with violation of Article 159 of the Criminal Code. In the majority of these cases, charges under other articles of the Criminal Code were added to the "attempt to overthrow the constitutional order." Memorial has gathered and made public the names of 4,304 of those charged under Article 159. Most of them continue to languish in prison. In 2004, several hundred more people were added to this number.

26 People charged with violations of administrative codes are fined, whereas those found guilty of violations of the criminal code are sent to prison. Uzbek authorities have a great deal of leeway in deciding whether to charge people according to criminal or administrative codes.

27 Hizb ut-Tahrir is an Islamist political party whose goal is to re-establish the caliphate within the Muslim world. The organization was founded by Sheikh Taqiuddin al-Nabhani, a judge from Jerusalem in 1953.

28 The idea that members of Hizb ut-Tahrir would be responsible for such violent acts struck most outside observers as unlikely, given that the group is committed to nonviolent struggle during the current phase of its efforts to create an Islamic caliphate.

29 U.S. Department of State, "Uzbekistan: Country Report on Human Rights Practices–2000," February 23, 2001, www.state.gov/g/drl/rls/hrrpt/2000/eur/858.htm.

30 Mansurov was Karimov's adviser on religion from 1998 to 1999. According to Babadjanov, Mansurov is a "fairly erudite Hanafi cleric." He was born in Andijan and received his religious education at a madrasa in Bukhara. He wrote the first official Uzbek translation of the Quran (in 2001, second edition in 2003).

31 I got to interview a half-dozen people who returned to Uzbekistan under this amnesty program, one of whom was subsequently rearrested after the violence in Andijan in May 2005. It should not be presumed that all who returned to their communities live "normal" lives. The authorities certainly know where they live, but it is impossible for me to know whether or not they were stigmatized by neighbors or employers.

32 In late March, bombs exploded in Bukhara followed by more explosions a day later in Tashkent. The incidents killed 47 people and were the first suicide bombing attacks in Central Asia. The government accused the IMU and Hizb ut-Tahrir of conducting the attacks. For more information, see Gulnoza Saidazimova, "Uzbekistan: Effect of Tashkent Explosions Still Felt Two Years Later," Radio Free Europe/Radio Liberty, March 27, 2006, www.rferl.org/content/article/1067140.html.

33 On July 30, 2004, simultaneous explosions occurred in Tashkent outside of the U.S. and Israeli embassies and the headquarters of the Uzbek chief prosecutor. The attacks killed four Uzbek law enforcement personnel and the three suicide bombers. Evidence from Kazakhstan's National Security Committee suggested that the IMU was involved in carrying out the attacks. See Susan B. Glasser, "U.S., Israeli Embassies Hit in Uzbek Bomb Attacks," *Washington Post*, July 31, 2004, www.washingtonpost.com/wp-dyn/articles/A26869-2004Jul30.html, and Daniel Kimmage, "Analysis: Kazakh Breakthrough on Uzbek Terror Case," Radio Free Europe/Radio Liberty, November 15, 2004, www.rferl.org/content/article/1055882.html.

34 Said Nursi (1878–1960) was a Turkish Kurd who promoted the adoption of Sharia, encouraged the acceptance of Christians in the Ottoman Empire, and wrote a book of commentary on the Quran. One of his contemporary followers, Fethullah Gulen, a charismatic leader who broke with the mainstream movement founded by Nursi, organized a network of more than 1,000 schools in Turkey

and 100 countries worldwide. These schools were introduced into Central Asia in the early 1990s. For more, see Ian Markham and Suendam Birinci Pirim, *An Introduction to Said Nursi: Life, Thought, and Writings* (Surrey, UK: Ashgate Publishing, 2011), and Helen Rose Ebaugh, *The Gulen Movement: A Sociological Analysis of a Civic Movement Rooted in Moderate Islam* (New York: Springer, 2010).

35 "Uzbekistan," *International Religious Freedom Report 2010*, U.S. Bureau of Democracy, Human Rights, and Labor, November 17, 2010, www.state.gov/g/drl/rls/irf/2010/index.htm.

36 Johan Rasanayagam, *Islam in Post-Soviet Uzbekistan: The Morality of Experience* (New York: Cambridge University Press, 2011), 40–85.

37 Ibid., 47.

38 Ibid., 67.

39 For a more detailed description of a *mahalla*'s function, as well as a comprehensive account of different kinds of *mahallas* and their relationship with the government, see Rasanayagam, *Islam in Post-Soviet Uzbekistan*, 49–64, 110–120.

40 Ibid., 119.

41 While the relegation of the distribution of services from the state-level apparatus to *mahalla* committees seemed to be a positive democratic development that strengthened the power wielded by regional institutions, it has also inflicted much harm on certain social groups. In her article "Between Women and the State: Mahalla Committees and Social Welfare in Uzbekistan," Marianne Kamp discusses how the government's choice to vest welfare decision-making power in the hands of *mahalla* committees resulted in increased discrimination and marginalization of those groups, which already lacked social capital and had no recourse to justice. Uzbekistan's welfare system encourages generous provision of subsidies to mothers who do not have adequate financial means to raise their children. In 1994 *mahalla* committees were entrusted with the distribution of such maternal entitlements. Women do not have much influence in the *mahalla* committee—in fact, the government requires that only one vice chair be a woman; for the most part, however, the *mahalla* committee is dominated by elderly men, who often choose to slight single mothers, who are seen by the committee as dissenters from the *mahalla*-approved conservative moral values. As such, *mahalla* committees often prefer to please the central government by pointing at the reduction in poverty and local welfare assistance, which comes at the expense of single mothers, deprived of their entitlements. For more information, see Kamp's chapter in *The Transformation of Central Asia: States and Societies from Soviet Rule to Independence*, edited by Pauline Jones Luong (Ithaca, N.Y.: Cornell University Press, 2004), 29–58.

42 Rasanayagam, *Islam in Post-Soviet Uzbekistan*, 112.

43 Royiq Bahadirov was born in Tashkent in 1953. He comes from a secular Uzbek family. Bahadirov graduated from Tashkent State Institute of Oriental Studies, is fluent in Arabic, and worked in Syria and Egypt. Both of his postgraduate dissertations were on the history of Muslim science. Since

1990, he has worked in the presidential administration. From 1996 to 1999, he was the president's adviser on religious affairs. He joined the Ministry of Foreign Affairs in 1999.

44 Materials prepared for Bakhtiyar Babadjanov for the Carnegie Endowment study on Islam.

45 This is in clear violation of Article 15 of the 1998 "Family Code" of Uzbekistan, which sets the minimum age for marriage at seventeen—sixteen with extenuating circumstances.

46 Materials prepared for Bakhtiyar Babadjanov for the Carnegie study on Islam.

47 Bakhtiyar Babadjanov argues that most of the security services' paid informers also seem to have suffered from a selection bias. More devout students seem to have been less willing to serve as informers, while those who opt to serve this role frequently have generally poorer foreign language skills or seem uninterested in paying close attention to the content of textbooks.

48 Research done by Bakhtiyar Babadjanov for the Carnegie Endowment project on Islam.

49 While all of the analysis in this section is mine, the materials on Tashkent Islamic University were collected by Bakhtiyar Babadjanov.

50 Karomatov, appointed ambassador to Japan in 2009, was deputy foreign minister in 2008. He is also the head of the University of World Economy and Diplomacy in Tashkent. He served as the first deputy prime minister from 1999 until 2003, and during part of that time he concurrently occupied various posts within the government, and served as ambassador to France from 2003 to 2005. He has published a number of books through the Tashkent Islamic University. See Olcott, "Islam in Uzbekistan: Religious Education and State Ideology," 30.

51 Zuhriddin Husniddinov was the rector at Tashkent Islamic University in 2004 and was an adviser to President Karimov from 1999 to 2005. He has held various government positions, including assistant chief of the Main Department of Detention Centers, and has written several books, including *Educational-Methodological Manual on "The Directions in Islam: Khorijiys and Shias," The Light of Islam Over the Uzbek Nation, Our Great Ancestors*, and *Islam and Directions*. See www.tiu.uz/index.php/uz/kafedralar/--/index.php?option=com_content&view=article&id=34&Itemid=34&lang=en, or "Central Asia: Islam and the State," ICG Asia Report 59, July 10, 2003, www.crisisgroup.org/~/media/files/asia/central-asia/059%20central%20asia%20islam%20and%20the%20state.pdf.

52 There are unconfirmed rumors of the corruption of both men, who were said to have profited from the travel to Saudi Arabia and other Arab countries by pilgrims, students, and others with trading interests in the region. Personal communication with the author.

53 Yovkochev was born in Tashkent in 1964. He graduated from the Oriental Studies Department of Tashkent State University and worked for several years as an interpreter in Egypt. From 1991 to 1996, he worked in the Ministry of Foreign Affairs and was subsequently appointed as first secretary of the Embassy of Uzbekistan in Egypt. Since 2000, he has worked in the Department of

International Relations at Tashkent State Institute of Oriental Studies, while defending his Ph.D. dissertation on the topic of radical Islamic organizations in Egypt. From 2004 to 2005, he worked as the director of the Institute for Strategic and Regional Studies, under the auspices of the Presidential Office.

54 Shukhrat Yovkochev, "O vliyanii radikal'nykh islamistskikh organizatsiy i dvezheniy egipta na sozial'no-politechskuiu situatsiiu v strane" ("On the Influence of Radical Islamic Egyptian Organizations and Movements on the Social-Political Situation in the Country"), *Vostok. Afro-Aziatskie Obshestva: istoria I sovremennost* (East, Afro-Asian Society: Past and Present), no. 6, 2007, 116–24.

55 Babadjanov attributes much of the success that TIU has had with this strategy to Abdulaziz Mansurov, the vice principal of TIU, who was charged with its implementation. Abdulaziz Mansurov previously worked in the Spiritual Administration (with Soviet-era *mufti* Ziyauddin Bobokhon [1982–1989]), later worked at the Oriental Institute of the Academy of Science of the Republic of Uzbekistan, in the State Committee on Religious Affairs, and then spent six months in 1999 as President Karimov's adviser on religious issues.

56 Based on information from Jaloliddin Nuriddinov, *The Educational System of Muslim Board of Uzbekistan* ("Uzbekiston musulmonlari idorasi talim tizimi") Tashkent: 2003.

57 During 2002 and 2003, these materials included *Mukhtasar Ul-Vikoya, Shifohiya, Durusun nahviya, Nurul Yakin, Sharhu Aqaidut-Tahoviya, Tajvid*, and *Balagat*.

58 The Juybori Kalon School is located in a seventeenth-century building and has a relatively extensive library with more than 1,500 books.

59 It was initially suggested that the Kadichai Kubro School be named for Eshon Bobokhon.

60 Abu Rayhan Muhammad ibn Ahmad al-Biruni (973–1048) was an astronomer, mathematician, ethnographer, anthropologist, historian, and geographer, and wrote more than 60 volumes on those subjects. He was born in Khiva, which is now in Uzbekistan, during a time of political upheaval and Islamic renaissance and was a contemporary of Ibn Sino.

61 B. Qodirov is the chair of the Committee on Religious Affairs. For more about the committee in Uzbek and Russian, see www.religions.uz/uzb/index.html.

62 Those who went in the first groups were able to serve as guides on pilgrimages in subsequent years, so for some going was not only status, but also a guarantee of further livelihood. Even today, when pilgrims pay their own way, those seeking a place from Uzbekistan's quota are forced to pay bribes of $250–$350.

63 The Uzbek government has always maintained diplomatic relations with Iran. Trade relations between the two countries have steadily improved, especially when Iran was willing to purchase Uzbek cotton after the sale of this important Uzbek government trade monopoly was restricted in the European Union following the Andijan events in 2005.

64 In his unpublished writings on Islam, he detailed accounts of such sums being directly transferred by the Saudis and by the Malaysian embassies.

65 Ozal was prime minister of Turkey from 1983 to 1989, and president from 1989 to 1993. See Feride Acar, "Turgut Ozal: Pious Agent of Liberal Transformation," in *Analyzing National and International Policy: Theory, Method, and Case Studies*, edited by Laure Paquette (Oxford: Lexington Books, 2003).

66 He is said to have brought back gifts of valuable rugs (rumored to be worth about $50,000 each) as donations from prominent Turkish religious leaders, some of which were rumored to have found their way into Abdullaev's personal possession.

67 Abramson says that 43 Uzbek students were studying at Al-Azhar University in 2008 and 2009, and he estimates that 100 to 600 Uzbek students total may have been studying in Egypt in 2009. He offers no estimates on the number of Uzbek students studying in Saudi Arabia, Turkey, Iran, or Pakistan during that same year, although he offers statistics for Kyrgyz and Tajiks studying in these countries. David M. Abramson, "Foreign Religious Education and the Central Asian Islamic Revival: Impact and Prospects for Stability," Central Asia-Caucasus Institute Silk Road Studies Program, 2010, www.silkroadstudies.org/new/docs/silkroadpapers/1003Abramson.pdf. See especially the appendices.

68 The pro-Islamic party now known as the Justice and Development Party has been involved in Turkish politics since 1970. It began as the National Order Party (1970–1971), then the National Salvation Party (1972–1980), the Welfare Party (1983–1998), the Virtue Party (1998–2001), and the Justice and Development Party (2002–). These parties are connected through an ideology known as "Milli Gorus," National View, that is conservative, pro-Islam with an eye on Ottoman heritage. The Justice and Development Party won 34 percent of the votes of the Turkish General Election of 2002, and its grandfather party, the Welfare Party, won 21 percent in 1995, enough for its pro-Islamic leader, Necmettin Erbakan, to become prime minister. See Fulya Atacan, "Explaining Religious Politics at the Crossroad: AKP-SP," in *Religion and Politics in Turkey*, edited by Ali Carkoglu and Barry M. Rubin (New York: Routledge, 2006).

69 Abramson notes that the closure of the Gulen schools served as a great disappointment to many non-religious Uzbeks as well, because secular Uzbeks were also attending these schools to become fully bilingual in Turkish in order to gain admission to Turkish universities. Travel and study in Turkey is easier for Uzbeks than in many other foreign countries because Turkey does not require visas from any citizens of the Soviet successor states.

70 Igor Rotar of Forum 18 reports that effectively *Tablighi* was banned under the 1998 law that prohibits mission work and private religious teaching, because *Tablighi* is by its nature a missionary and educational organization. See Igor Rotar, "Uzbekistan: Why Were Some Tabligh Members Given Lesser Jail Terms Than Others?" Forum 18 News Service, December 3, 2004.

CHAPTER 9

1. Alexandre A. Bennigsen and S. Enders Wimbush, *Muslim National Communism in the Soviet Union: A Revolutionary Strategy for the Colonial World* (Chicago: University of Chicago Press, 1979), and Hélène Carrère d'Encausse, *Decline of an Empire: The Soviet Socialist Republics in Revolt* (New York: Harper & Row, 1981).

2. This is based on *taqiyya*, a practice that comes from Sharia that allows Muslims to feign apostasy rather than be killed. It is based on a verse in the Quran that forbids a Muslim to be instrumental in his own death. See Raymond Ibrahim, "How Taqiyya Alters Islam's Rules of War: Defeating Jihadist Terrorism," *Middle East Quarterly*, Winter 2010, available at www.raymondibrahim.com/7377/taqiyya-islam-rules-of-war.

3. Hakimjon qori's students in this period also Rajab Ali Quqoniy, who sparred with Ismoil qori Quqoniy, the imam of a major mosque in Kokand, for influence in Kokand (taking the latter captive in 1992), and who subsequently received a lengthy prison sentence.

4. Bakhtiyar Babadjanov and Muzaffar Kamilov, "Muhammadjan Hindustani and the Beginning of the 'Great Schism' among Muslims of Uzbekistan," in *Politics in Islam in Russia and Central Asia*, edited by Stéphane Dudoignon and Hisao Komatsu (New York: Routledge, 2001), 200.

5. The specific objections were to the placement of the hands during the *takbir* (*rafi al-yadayn*) and *qiyam*, and to the recitation of *amin* to oneself (*mahfi*), rather than aloud, as the young radicals desired. (*Takbir* is the Arabic word for announcing the greatness of God.)

6. Babadjanov and Kamilov, "Muhammadjan Hindustani and the Beginning of the 'Great Schism' Among Muslims of Uzbekistan," appendix, 216-17.

7. As quoted in the translation of this text, which appears in an appendix in Babadjanov and Kamilov, "Muhammadjan Hindustani and the Beginning of the 'Great Schism'," 205.

8. Babadjanov and Kamilov (appendix).

9. Abdujabar Abduvahitov writes of seeing a copy of Maududi's books bound in the cover of "Materials of the XXVth Conference of the CPSU." See Abdujabar Abduvahitov, "Islamic Revivalism in Uzbekistan," in *Russia's Muslim Frontier*, edited by D. F. Eickelman (Bloomington: Indiana University Press, 1993), 83.

10. My visits to the Ferghana Valley in 1992 and 1993 were made with Dr. Abdujabar Abduvahitov, whom I had met in the late 1980s when he worked in the Institute of Oriental Studies of the Academy of Sciences of the USSR and I was a visiting scholar there.

11. This analysis relies heavily on Bakhtiyar Babadjanov's interpretation of Abduvali's lectures and *tafsir*. There is also an edition of Abduvali and Obidkhon qori's writings, containing both Uzbek language originals and their translations by Allen Frank and Jahangir Mamatov. I have not made direct use of that edition due to Babadjanov's claim that the Frank texts are less complete than the

audiocassettes Babadjanov has in his possession (obtained directly from contacts in the Ferghana Valley) and because Babadjanov finds some flaws in Frank's translation. For more information, see Allen J. Frank, *Uzbek Islamic Debates: Texts, Translations and Commentary* (Hyattsville, Md.: Dunwoody Press, 2006).

12 Bakhtiyar Babadjanov, who is the source of our information about this book, says that in the version of the *tafsir* that he saw, Abduvali qori was listed as author in the Arabic style, Skaykh Abduvali qori, son of Ashurali Andijani, and although the publishing house was listed as the printing house of King Fahd, Medina, 1425/2005, in reality Babadjanov believes that its publication was arranged by Abduvali qori's eldest son, and that it was printed in underground shops.

13 Ibid.

14 "And when ye said: O Moses! We are weary of one kind of food; so call upon thy Lord for us that He bring forth for us of that which the earth groweth of its herbs and its cucumbers and its corn and its lentils and its onions. He said: Would ye exchange that which is higher for that which is lower? Go down to settled country, thus ye shall get that which ye demand. And humiliation and wretchedness were stamped upon them and they were visited with wrath from Allah. That was because they disbelieved in Allah's revelations and slew the prophets wrongfully. That was for their disobedience and transgression."

15 This is a hint to the slogan chosen by Uzbekistan in its first years of independence—"Uzbekistan is a country of great future."

16 "Let not their wealth nor their children please thee! Allah purposeth only to punish them thereby in the world, and that their souls shall pass away while they are disbelievers."

17 "Allah hath made ready for them Gardens underneath which rivers flow, wherein they will abide. That is the supreme triumph."

18 "Not unto the weak nor unto the sick nor unto those who can find naught to spend is any fault (to be imputed though they stay at home) if they are true to Allah and His messenger. Not unto the good is there any road (of blame). Allah is Forgiving, Merciful."

19 "And as for those who chose a place of worship out of opposition and disbelief, and in order to cause dissent among the believers, and as an outpost for those who warred against Allah and His messenger aforetime, they will surely swear: We purposed naught save good. Allah beareth witness that they verily are liars."

20 This is a quote from one of Islam Karimov's early speeches.

21 Babadjanov bases this notion of religious authority on P. Crone and M. Hinds, *God's Caliph: Religious Authorities in the First Centuries of Islam* (Cambridge, U.K.: Cambridge University Press, 1968), 7–12, 14–16.

22. Abduvali qori could be found on 552 videos from a Google video search as of June 2, 2011. His videos are available on the "normal" sources: YouTube, Dailymotion, Vimeo, and Metacafe, as well as rutube.ru, and a website called carcarecompany.com. Also these videos are available on the IMU website and others mentioned in chapter 11.

23. Two of these interviews were conducted in the presence of Abdujabar Abduvahitov, but I met with Obidkhon qori a third time in the presence of Bahodir Umarov, a sociologist from Tashkent.

24. Though born in Namangan, Obidkhon qori is included with the Andijan clerics because he was a disciple of Abduvali's.

25. The information on O. Nazarov's biography and activities was gathered by Bakhtiyar Babadjanov during an interview with religious figures and common residents of Namangan, Tashkent, and South Kazakhstan.

26. The Tukhtaboy Vacha Mosque was built at the end of the nineteenth century by a Tashkent merchant, Tukhtaboy. In 1933 it was closed down, and in 1936 a medical office was set up in the building. It was not until 1988 that the believers from nearby *mahallas* insisted on the mosque's being returned to them.

27. Bakhtiyar Babadjanov reports that Obidkhon qori originally sought the post of *imam-hatib* of the more prestigious Tilla Sheikh Mosque in which he was serving as assistant. However, the mosque community (*qawm*), which consisted of residents of the old city, did not want to see him as their *imam* and held a prayer sit-in to get their way.

28. For a discussion of Islamic clerical attire in Uzbekistan, see Olga Sukhareva. "Chalma Voobshe I Chalma Po-Sredneaziatski" (The Turban in General, The Turban in Central Asia), *Tatarski Mir*, issue 5, 2005, www.sanat.orexca.com/rus/archive/1-08/semcha.shtml.

29. Babadjanov was able to interview a former member of a *jamoa* and reports that the course of study included Arabic language instruction through textbooks used in medieval madrasas (*Muallim al-avval, Muallim as-sani*, and others). Other subjects included reading of the Quran, listening to and commenting on video and audio recordings of Abduvali qori (especially his commentary on the Quran, "Tafsir ul-furqan"), "Conversation on free issues" (*Erkin mavzudagi suhbat*), discussions on political problems in Uzbekistan and neighboring countries, and issues of international politics, especially in the Islamic world, in which publications of Arab Islamists were used.

30. Babadjanov notes that the seventeen-page pamphlet does not list the author's name or publication date, although Obidkhon qori has never denied authorship.

31. Babadjanov reports that by 1993 there was at least one *jamoa* in the Piskent, Toytepa, and Buka regions of Tashkent Oblast.

32. Babadjanov had the opportunity to examine one of these contracts in the Eski Juva Bazaar, noting

that virtually the only difference with traditional contracts was the addition of the oaths "I call Allah as my witness" and "Let Allah punish me if I renege on this obligation."

33 Babadjanov notes that he heard reports that Obidkhon qori even took money from those selling spirits, knowing that Uzbeks were buying vodka and other alcoholic products from these people.

34 Babadjanov believes that not all the arrests were for narcotics planted on people, or so he claims in his published writing, stating that in Andijan on May 2, 1990, there were drunks and people smoking drugs among the crowd of Islamists. (For more on that, see Bakhtiyar Babadjanov, "Debates Over Islam in Contemporary Uzbekistan: A View from Within," in *Devout Societies vs. Impious States? Transmission of Islamic Learning in Russia, Central Asia and China, through the Twentieth Century*, edited by Stéphane A. Dudoignon (Berlin: Klaus-Schwarz-Verlag, 2004), 51.

35 The date is inferred, because of the date of the trial, and the fact that foreign journalists were in attendance.

36 This is a clip from a video film "*Ular*," shot by Jundulla Film Studio of the Islamic Movement of Uzbekistan.

37 Meaning the trial and the false accusations.

38 The interview was conducted by Bakhtiyar Babadjanov.

39 Babadjanov reports that the level of Obidkhon qori's religious knowledge is estimated as mediocre by education.

40 Abduhvahitov, "Islamic Revivalism in Uzbekistan."

41 Vitaly Naumkin's interpretation of the emergence of *Adolat* is somewhat different from the information presented here. He writes that *Islom lashkarlari* was established before *Adolat* in the early 1990s. Shortly afterwards, however, "Islom lashkarlari" split into two separate entities, with one of the wings being *Adolat*. See Vitaly Naumkin, *Radical Islam in Central Asia: Between Pen and Rifle* (Lanham, Md.: Rowman and Littlefield, 2005), 58.

42 Hakimjon Sattimov seems to have been the initial organizer of the group. He was a student of Hindustani's and was considered to be the "father" of the Wahhabi groups in Ferghana. *Adolat* emerged in 1988 under his leadership. Muminov indicated that *Adolat* was made up of groups of young men who patrolled the street as a neighborhood watch-type group, unlike the militant group that was based in the same mosque. See Vitaly Naumkin, *Radical Islam in Central Asia*, 58.

43 For more information on Yuldoshev and his leadership, see Vitaly Naumkin, *Radical Islam in Central Asia*, 72–95.

44 According to Naumkin, *Adolat* did not embrace immediately the tenets of radical Islam. In fact, Naumkin states that initially *Adolat* was nothing more than a militarized structure without any ideological affiliation. In his *Radical Islam in Central Asia*, Naumkin cites an episode, related to him

by the Tashkent scholar A., in which a meeting took place between a group of religious activists, the *imam* of the Gumbaz Mosque, Abdul Ahad, and Abdirahim Pulat(ov), the leader of the secular opposition *Birlik partiyasi*. In the course of the meeting, Pulat urged the militants to work more actively with the army. After the militants objected, citing as an argument their unwillingness to work with army personnel that were mostly ethnically Russian, Pulat retorted that the problem could be resolved by "convert[ing] Russians to Islam." This insensitive blunder later cost him the positions the *Birlik partiyasi* could gain by aligning themselves with an increasingly militarized structure. Shortly thereafter, *Adolat* fully embraced the radical Islamic ideology.

45 This section is based on materials collected by Bakhtiyar Babadjanov, mainly interviews, done in 2003–2004.

46 Bakhtiyar Babadjanov reports that by R. Akramov's estimates, Tohir Yuldoshev had a maximum of 2,000 fighters. Namangan's population was about half a million people, as of the 1989 Census. Rahimjon Akramov was born in 1942 in Namangan and graduated from the Pedagogical Institute in Tashkent. He worked as a history teacher, and then served as deputy and finally as director of a local school. In 1989 he was appointed to the Namangan Oblast department on religious cults attached to the Oblast Executive Committee, and then moved to the Namangan *hokimiyat* in 1991. He shared his recollections of this period with Babadjanov in a number of meetings held in 2002 through 2004.

47 This is based on information gathered by Bakhtiyar Babadjanov in Namangan, but the exact date was not provided. Also see Bakhtiyar Babadjanov, *Jihad kak Ideologia Izgoev* (Jihad: The Ideology of Pariah Groups), www.knyazev.org/biblio/Jihad_ifeac.pdf.

48 In common usage, this verb (*yurishmoq*) signifies that a group of people walked together.

49 Umarkhon domla was born in Namangan in 1950, and finished eight grades of education (middle school), claiming that he was always more interested in religious education than receiving secular training.

50 Zokirjon domla served for a while as imam of the mosque in his native northeastern district of Tashkent (Chuqursay) but left the post after a fight with Shamsuddin Bobokhonov. His theological position had always been critical of both the SADUM clerics and their opponents. He maintained his religious school, which generally had about ten students, in a workshop that made traditional caps (*duppis*). He appears to have been questioned regularly by Uzbek state security in 1994, but then suffered a stroke that year and died at age 53 or 54. Those who attended his funeral maintained that his death was brought on by an interrogation by the authorities.

51 It was one of the marvels of Soviet-era Uzbekistan that even when private property was technically banned, people could find ways to own and operate small enterprises in the service sector, such as bakeries making *non* or *lepyoshkas*, home-style baked breads.

52 Bakhtiyar Babadjanov met with Umarkhon domla both together and individually, as I met with him with Abdujabar Abduvahitov in 1992 and 1993.

53 My Uzbek interlocutor met with him at his home two days after his release from prison, and noted that Umarkhon domla was quite fat, and his hands were soft, showing no signs of physical labor, giving some substance to the charges that he expropriated large amounts of money in his official position, because obtaining a soft perch in jail is very costly.

54 Mirsaidov served as prime minister of Uzbekistan in the early 1990s, and Gafurov was one of the intermediaries between Mirsaidov and the group around Muhammad Sodiq. While this would have been a source of influence for Gafurov initially, once Mirsaidov's office (the vice presidency) was abolished by Karimov in 1992, the association became an additional liability for Gafurov.

55 Babadjanov says that Gafurov had enough money to rent a Tu-154 to fly his family to Saudi Arabia to make *hajj* in the early 1990s.

56 Based on information obtained by Bakhtiyar Babadjanov.

57 Olcott, "Roots of Radical Islam in Central Asia," 23. Gafurov's financial dealings also provided the Karimov government with a handle to use in removing him from the scene in the mid-1990s, sentencing him to six years in prison for fraudulent financial dealings and the loss of property, but releasing him after three years.

58 Much of the discussion on Barnaev comes from materials provided by his sister in interviews with Bakhtiyar Babadjanov conducted as part of the Carnegie Endowment for International Peace project on Islam.

59 See Olcott, "Roots of Radical Islam in Central Asia," 24–25; Naumkin, "Radical Islam in Central Asia," 59, 67.

60 See Olcott, "Roots of Radical Islam in Central Asia," 24–25.

61 Ishan Khan-tura was exiled in the 1930s to Omsk, then transferred to Orenburg, and then sent to Kokand prison, where he was released in 1933, only to be rearrested in 1937 and executed.

62 Throughout the period of the early 1990s, he was arrested and released numerous times, and in 1994 he was held in jail for three months, but has not been jailed since. Some claim this is because he was willing to provide evidence in cases against other clerics from Namangan. He claims that shortly before this last arrest the authorities came to him and tried to get him to immigrate to Turkey, but he refused, because, as he said, all of his ancestors are buried in Central Asia.

63 This quote comes from an interview with Umarkhon domla that was commissioned by Bakhtiyar Babadjanov, which he substantiated as basically accurate in a later interview with Muhammad Sodiq. These interviews were held in 2004 in Tashkent and Namangan.

64 Rahimjon Akramov was born in 1942 in Namangan and graduated from the Pedagogical Institute in Tashkent. He worked as a history teacher, and then served as deputy and finally as director of a local school. In 1989 he was appointed to the Namangan Oblast department on religious cults

attached to the Oblast Executive Committee, and then moved to the Namangan *hokimiyat* in 1991. He shared his recollections of this period with Babadjanov in a number of meetings held in 2002 through 2004.

65 I have a copy of this rally on videotape.

66 According to R. Akramov, this demand was included by unofficial order of Muhammad Sodiq Muhammad Yusuf, who was also in Namangan at that time, but as a precautionary measure did not participate in the rally. Muhammad Sodiq Muhammad Yusuf claims that this information is wrong.

67 Babadjanov says that Yuldoshev made mistakes in reading them and he believes that Yuldoshev was seeing the list for the first time.

68 From interviews done by Bakhtiyar Babadjanov with participants at the meeting.

69 Golos Ukrainy, July 3, 1992, as quoted by FBIS Daily Report Central Eurasia, FBIS-USR-92-077, June 24, 1992, 112. This attempted Congress had been put together largely through the combined efforts of *Birlik* and *Erk*, both organizations that are dominated by secularized intellectuals.

70 *Birlik* started as an "informal political group" but was registered as a political organization in Uzbekistan in 1991, although its presidential candidate was not registered in the election. In 1992 its members began to be targeted by Uzbek authorities, and its head, Abdurahim Pulat, was nearly beaten to death by a group of unidentified assailants. He then fled the country, initially living in Turkey, and then went to the United States as a political refugee.

CHAPTER 10

1 For example, the Taliban, Tehrik-e Taliban Pakistan.

2 From the start, the IMU leadership and its followers were disillusioned with the IRP's mission and its reluctance to undertake brash actions in the political arena. As one of the young men, a follower of the *Adolat*, stated, "The IRP is in the pay of the government; they want to be in parliament. We have no desire to be in parliament. We want an Islamic revolution here and now—we have no time for constitutional games." Both Yuldoshev and Namangani fled to Tajikistan and enlisted with the Tajikistan IRP once the Uzbek government launched a decisive crackdown on IMU followers in the Ferghana Valley region. When war broke out in Tajikistan, Yuldoshev left for Afghanistan, where he continued to spread IRP propaganda from Taloqan. That is when Yuldoshev began to travel to other Islamic countries around the world to learn about their movements and build new contacts with religious communities and intelligence agencies, from which he had sought financial support for the IMU activities. For more information on the history of this period in Tajikistan and in Afghanistan, as well as the IMU's relationship to it, see Ahmad Rashid, *Jihad: The Rise of Militant Islam in Central Asia* (New York: Penguin Books, 2002), 137–55.

3   Most of the Afghan materials came from information collected by C. J. Chivers in Afghanistan, which he allowed local translators to copy. Chivers is aware that I have copies of some of this material, but all responsibility for the translation of it, or its analysis, rests with me. He and I have chatted a few times but have never compared analyses of this material.

4   Saifullo Dalilov, a prosecutor in the Siab region of Dushanbe between 1981 and 1992, claims to have been taken hostage by Turajonzoda in 1992 as punishment for having ordered the arrest and beating of pro-Islam demonstrators.

5   From author's interviews with Muhammad Sodiq Muhammad Yusuf.

6   Samir Saleh Abdullah al-Suwailem (1969–2002), known as Khattab, is said by some to be half Circassian. He first came to Afghanistan to fight the Soviets and then remained there, and sought to gather fighters to join in the Chechen cause (and IMU members were enlisted in this). He returned to Afghanistan, and then to Tajikistan, during the lulls in fighting in Chechnya, and he apparently sought to wrest leadership of the IMU from Tohir Yuldoshev and Juma Namangani.

7   For an extensive discussion of the connections between the IMU, the United Tajik opposition, and the Afghan situation, see Mariam Abou Zahab and Olivier Roy, *Islamist Networks: The Afghan-Pakistan Connection*, trans. John King (New York: Columbia University Press, 2004).

8   It is hard to get much information about this community—which was made up of those who were living in and around the holy sites maintaining Turkestani *waqfs* when the Soviets took power, and Uzbeks who came to the holy cities when fleeing Soviet rule.

9   This was in a box of documents collected by C. J. Chivers and given to an Uzbek colleague for translation.

10 He sought to study at a madrasa in Hayatabad, a suburb of Peshawar near the Khyber Pass.

11 Pulat maintains that Solih agreed to take a post from Tohir Yuldoshev and shared information with him. There is no formal proof of this.

12 Some of this material appears in my article, "The Failure of Jihad in Uzbekistan," in a forthcoming book edited by David Cook.

13 Bakhtiyar Babadjanov bought some of the cassettes himself and seems to have gotten some of the materials from people who served on expert commissions for the Uzbek government to examine "extremist literature." Vitaly Naumkin, who seems to have had access to some of the same information, noted that the use of illicit materials contains some risk, including the possibility that this material may have been forged by the Uzbek authorities. See Vitaly Naumkin, *Radical Islam in Central Asia: Between Pen and Rifle* (Lanham, Md.: Rowman and Littlefield, 2005), 98. While it is possible that this is the case, I feel that is unlikely.

14 Babadjanov believes that the tapes had to have been recorded before 1999, given the diacritical marks in the printed Uzbek version that he received, which were no longer in use after that date.

15 Babadjanov further argues that in the text in particular, a lot of local (Ferghana Valley-specific) slang is used, and that the spoken language on the tapes is of an Uzbek who grew up in the Ferghana Valley.

16 These interviews were done between 2001 and 2005.

17 "There is no god but God (Allah) and Muhammad is his prophet/messenger."

18 Most of these came to me through Babadjanov, who was assured that they came from concerned Uzbek citizens sharing materials with authorities that they thought were seditious.

19 Martha Brill Olcott and Bakhtiyar Babadjanov, "The Terrorist Notebooks," *Foreign Policy*, March/April 2003, 30–40.

20 These study circles were often termed "Wahhabist" by Uzbek authorities; many were Salafist or quasi-Salafist in content, and the content of their teachings was generally distinct from those of the Hanafi madrasas run by SADUM or its successor, the UMU.

21 I have used none of the last names of the former members of the IMU in respect for their privacy.

22 He maintained that he went to Tajikistan for religious reasons, while others from his town say he was fleeing the authorities after having accidentally killed another youth.

23 Notebook four is by a writer from Andijan and is dated January 1995. It includes a block on "The Theology of Jihad." The section starts by stating that the call for *jihad* (*farz-i ayn*) is based on *sura al-anfal* (*sura* 8), *ayats* 15 and 45, which are referred to in the text, but are not reproduced, as well as *al-tawba sura* 9), *ayat* 38. The text then goes on to name four forms of jihad—*nafs, shaitan, munafik, kafir*—referring again to *sura* 8, *ayats* 15, 45, and now 60 as well, and then some citations to *hadiths* as to who is obliged to make jihad (when it is *farz-i ayn*). Bakhtiyar Babadjanov notes that this presentation ("let him be Muslim, in full command of his faculties, 15 or older, free and not a slave and have means of subsistence") follows the presentations of medieval books of commentary such as Bukhan ad-Din Margilani's *al-Khidaia al-Furu*. This is followed by a discussion of who is not permitted to participate in jihad (from *an-nisa, sura* 4, *ayat* 98), and those not able to (*at-Tawba, sura* 9, *ayats* 91 and 92, *an-nisa, sura* 4, *ayat* 95) and those exempt from fighting (*at-Tawba, sura* 9, *ayat* 8). Babadjanov translated the materials in the notebooks into Russian and analyzed them with me.

24 This was from the notebook labeled number seven, 50a–59b.

25 When this trade was restricted—to benefit Russian wholesalers, not because of any terrorist threat from Uzbekistan—it had a negative impact on the Uzbek economy and on Russian-Uzbek bilateral relations. Russia briefly banned Uzbek exports of fruits and vegetables after a dangerous pest was discovered in them in May 2008. The Russian ban was preceded by a ban imposed by the Uzbek authorities in summer 2007 that forbade the export of fruits and vegetables to Russia under the pretext of ensuring an adequate supply of fresh produce to the local market and stabilization of

food prices. A similar ban was imposed by the Uzbek government in 2008 and 2009. "Uzbekistan ne vipuskaet frukti i ovoshi, kuplennie rossijskimi predprinimateliami" (Uzbekistan prohibits exports of fruits and vegetables purchased by Russian entrepreneurs), Fergana News, August 25, 2009, www.fergananews.com/news.php?id=12794.

26 "They will not fight you all except within fortified cities or from behind walls. Their violence among themselves is severe. You think they are together, but their hearts are diverse. That is because they are a people who do not reason." See http://quran.com/59.

27 In a former Tajik film studio sanitorium in the mountains between Dushanbe and Nurek, as reported by former members of the IMU.

28 See Rashid, *Jihad*, 165–67.

29 This information comes from former IMU members, and they may have been simply referring to audiotapes, but it is possible that IMU material was broadcast by their Arab sponsors.

30 This comes from a box of materials collected by C. J. Chivers in Afghanistan and shared with an Uzbek colleague.

31 "Karimop" is as said in the film.

32 In the Namangan region, a local journalist sat in on the interviews, and in Kokand, someone from the *hokimiyat* showed us the houses, but remained in his car throughout the interviews.

33 Alauddin Mansur lived on the Kyrgyz side of Kara Suu and had his own Quran study center, which I was able to visit in 2005.

34 *Farz* (or *fard* in Arabic) means "mandatory" and is used to describe a religious duty.

35 Mirzo Ziyoev was a leader in the Tajik civil war, then minister of Emergency Services. He was allegedly involved with a drug gang, which engaged in a firefight with Tajik Security Forces in July 2009. See "Tajik Ex-Minister Dies in Ambush," BBC News, July 12, 2009, http://news.bbc.co.uk/2/hi/asia-pacific/8146989.stm.

36 There is an irony in the title, because Uzbek authorities always referred to Islamic extremists including the IMU as "them," creating a mirror image sense of alienation.

37 "Wahhabites" referred to all people who followed a local way of living, *khanafism*, as *mushrikams*. In *khanafism*, there is a special status for saints and people visit their graves. The spirit of saints can be a mediator between God and people even after death.

38 Here this is probably a government official.

39 My Allah! Is there another way to "find paradise"?

40 This is a reference to Karimov, who mentioned in one of his interviews that members of the military opposition fight not on religious grounds but because they get paid $700 a month.

41 In general, Yuldoshev seems to recognize that *mujahideen* earn their salaries in dollars. Perhaps $700 is an accurate amount.

42 Yuldoshev is confusing the two battles. The Budre battle was in 624. The Uhud battle, when Musab ibn Umar was killed, was in 625.

43 *Kafan* is a white cloth in which the deceased are wrapped.

44 This is a famous story from the early Muslim "agiographia." "On his way to Allah," Musab ibn Umar gave his treasures to Muslims and became a martyr, finding the treasures of a different world.

45 This film is in the personal archives of the author.

46 These come from the same box of materials picked up in the camps in Afghanistan by C. J. Chivers and passed to me through an Uzbek colleague. The authenticity of the materials was verified by Chivers.

47 "In the name of Allah, the Entirely Merciful, the Especially Merciful. [All] praise is [due] to Allah, Lord of the World—The Entirely Merciful, the Especially Merciful, Sovereign of the Day of Recompense. It is You we worship and You we ask for help. Guide us to the straight path—The path of those upon whom You have bestowed favor, not of those who have evoked [Your] anger or of those who are astray." See http://quran.com/1.

48 It is possible that the Uzbek authorities gave the returning IMU members certain "set pieces" that they had to repeat in interviews to discredit the movement, and this may have been one of them. But the interviews left me in no doubt of the brutality of the IMU, and the former sentry, who unsuccessfully sought to escape, was obviously physically damaged. If this had been done at the hands of Uzbek authorities, they would never have provided me with his name and address.

49 In *sura al-Baqara*, Muslims are given permission to fight for the purposes of self-defense. It is important to mention that the Quran does not prescribe the initiation of warfare; on the contrary, *ayats* 190–193 forbid Muslims to initiate hostilities unless experiencing persecution or a military attack. "Fight in the way of Allah against those who fight against you, but begin not hostilities.... And fight them until persecution is no more, and religion is for Allah."

50 Sura al-Anfal contains the discussion of the laws of warfare, introducing the injunction to wage war against the enemies of Islam. Unlike the *sura al-Baqara*, *al-Anfal* reveals a new dimension of the warfare, allowing Muslims to initiate the fighting in order to facilitate the spread of Islam. As the *ayats* 36–39 state: "those who disbelieve spend their wealth in order that they may debar men from the way of Allah … then they will be conquered.… And fight them until there is no more tumult or oppression, and there prevail justice and faith in God altogether and everywhere." It is important to mention that the very same *sura* also impels Muslims to embrace peace, if their

enemies have an inclination to it; 8:61: "And if they incline to peace, incline thou also to it, and trust in Allah."

51 While suicide is strictly proscribed in Islam, martyrdom for the purpose of spreading Islam is viewed as the incumbent religious duty. Rewards for martyrdom in the afterlife are so great that "Nobody who enters Paradise will ever like to return to this world even if he were offered everything, except the martyr who will desire to return to this world and be killed 10 times for the sake of the great honor that has been bestowed upon him" [*Sahih Muslim*, chapters 781, 782, *The Merit of Jihad*, and *The Merit of Martyrdom*]. The martyr's/righteous person's experience in paradise is rendered in lush and rich sensual details in *suras* 55, 56, and 76. "And theirs shall be the dark-eyed *houris*, chaste as hidden pearls: a guerdon for their deeds.... We created the *houris* and made them virgins, loving companions for those on the right hand...." The Quran itself, however, does not specify the exact number of virgins in paradise.

52 Again, this is also from the material brought out of Afghanistan by C. J. Chivers.

53 The Japanese government wound up paying approximately $3 million for the release of the group of Japanese geologists taken hostage by IMU supporters.

54 Namangani died in November 2001, and Yuldoshev died in August 2009. See Vitaly Naumkin, *Radical Islam in Central Asia*, and David Witter, "Uzbek Militancy in Pakistan's Tribal Region," 1, 2, 13. For the statement about Yuldoshev's death (in Uzbek), see http://furqon.com/shahidforuq/Usmonodil-08.2010.html.

CHAPTER 11

1 Many religious groups, including Jehovah's Witnesses, Baptists, and Muslims, have not been allowed to register with the state, and activity by unregistered groups is a criminal offense, as are proselytizing (something that could be as simple as sharing beliefs) and meetings for religious purposes in private homes. Religious communities are often raided, and their members threatened, assaulted, and even tortured. Prisoner of conscience numbers are increasing. See Mushfig Bayram and John Kinahan, "Uzbekistan: Religious Freedom Survey, August 2008," Forum 18 News Service, August 14, 2008.

2 The IJU is thought to have conducted several attacks in Kyrgyzstan in 2002 and 2003, including alleged attempts to kill Kyrgyz National Security Council Secretary Misir Ashirkulov in September 2002, a bombing in the Oberon Bazaar in Bishkek, and two explosions in Osh in May 2003. Chaudet indicates that the perpetrators were local cell members set up by Namangani. Kyrgyz sources cited by Weitz allege that they worked with members of the Eastern Turkestan Islamic Movement on the attacks and planned the murder of nineteen Chinese citizens in March 2003. See Didier Chaudet, "Islamist Terrorism in Greater Central Asia: The 'Al-Qaedaization' of Uzbek Jihadism," *Russie.Nei. Visions* 35 (December 2008), 22–23, and Richard Weitz, "Storm Clouds over Central Asia: Revival of the Islamic Movement of Uzbekistan?" *Studies in Conflict & Terrorism* (August 2004), 512–13.

3   According to Vitaly Naumkin, conflicting accounts of Namangani's death were made by General Abdul Rashid Dostum, the Taliban, and the son of an Uzbek militant who said he attended the funeral in November. Witter puts his death in November 2001 in northern Afghanistan, stating that although there were conflicting opinions, he likely died fighting near Kunduz. See Vitaly Naumkin, *Radical Islam in Central Asia: Between Pen and Rifle* (Lanham, Md.: Rowman & Littlefield, 2005), and David Witter, "Uzbek Militancy in Pakistan's Tribal Region," Institute for the Study of War, January 27, 2011, 1, 2, 13. I was told a different version by one of Namangani's relatives—that Namangani was shot in the back by his own men.

4   Witter, "Uzbek Militancy in Pakistan's Tribal Region."

5   On May 12, 2003, Kyrgyz authorities announced that they had apprehended suspected IMU members in connection with the May 2003 Osh bombings. These same suspects were accused of the December 2002 bombings in Bishkek, and the announcement also mentioned the apprehension of twelve accused members of Hizb ut-Tahrir. See Alisher Khamidov, "Officials in Kyrgyzstan Suggest Islamic Militant Group Is Active Again," Eurasianet, May 14, 2003, available at www.unhcr.org/refworld/docid/46cc320d23.html.

6   Witter names two key IJU players: Najmiddin Jalolov, or Abu Yahya Muhammad Fatih, the co-founder and overall commander of the IJU until his death in September 2009, and Suhayl Fatilloevich Buranov, co-founder and deputy chief of the IJU. Buranov is an explosives expert and likely assumed command of the IJU after Jalolov's death. David Witter, "Uzbek Militancy in Pakistan's Tribal Region."

7   Interviews in Uzbekistan, 2002–2005.

8   Both Sandee and Kimmage estimated that 50 people died overall in the 2004 attacks. Sandee notes that 47 people were killed in the attacks from March 28 to March 31, 2004, among them ten policemen, three civilians, and 33 IJG fighters, including their leader, Ahmad Bekmirzaev. Sanderson estimates a total of 19 dead and 63 wounded in Uzbek attacks in 2004. See Ronald Sandee, "The Islamic Jihad Union (IJU)," NEFA Foundation Special Report, 14 October, 2008, www.nefafoundation.org/miscellaneous/FeaturedDocs/nefaijuoct08.pdf; Daniel Kimmage, "Kazakh Breakthrough on Uzbek Terror Case"; or Thomas M. Sanderson et al., "From the Ferghana Valley to South Waziristan."

9   Kimmage reported that three Kazakh citizens—Avaz Shoyusupov, Isa Eruov, and Mokhira Ibragimova—were the suicide bombers in Tashkent. Sandee reports that two female suicide bombers, identified as Dilnoza Kholmanadova and Shahnoza Inoyatova, blew themselves up in the Chorsu Bazaar on March 29, 2004. They were identified as studying Arabic in the Egyptian Embassy's Cultural Center in Tashkent, and it was reported on March 31 that Qilichbek Azimbekov blew himself up in Tashkent.

10   For more information, see Gulnoza Saidazimova, "Uzbekistan: Effect of Tashkent Explosions Still Felt Two Years Later," Radio Free Europe/Radio Liberty, March 27, 2006, www.rferl.org/content/article/1067140.html.

11 I was later shown some of these letters, and they were also used at the trials that followed. Some were shown on Uzbek television.

12 Al-Qaeda in Europe made unsubstantiated claims of responsibility for terrorist attacks on Madrid commuter trains in March 2004, where 191 were killed and 1,800 injured. The Moscow bombings occurred in February 2004, and ten were killed, 50 injured. For more about those and other transportation bombings, see "Background Report: On the Fifth Anniversary of the 7/7 London Transit Attack," National Consortium for the Study of Terrorism and Responses to Terrorism, July 2010, www.start.umd.edu/start/announcements/July07_LondonMetroBombing_2010.pdf.

13 According to Sandee, they reported this information on April 3, 2004, by an e-mail to the website www.stopdictatorkarimov.com. Carnegie researchers were unable to verify this. However, the U.S. State Department named them as the attackers when it designated the IJU as a terrorist group in a May 2005 press release, http://2001-2009.state.gov/r/pa/prs/ps/2005/46838.htm. Another theory was that some bombings occurred because people were upset over police brutality. See "Uzbekistan: Effect of Tashkent Explosions Still Felt Two Years Later," Radio Free Europe/Radio Liberty, March 27, 2006, www.rferl.org/content/article/1067140.html.

14 NEFA cites Uzbek television Channel 2 in naming Mavlon Mirzaqulov and Qodirjon Toychiev as members of the IJU in Uzbekistan in a televised court appearance. In a lengthy quotation, the Uzbek state prosecutor named the suicide bombers and the IJU leadership, and talked of the IJU's weapons, literature, and jihad. See Ronald Sandee, "The Islamic Jihad Union (IJU)."

15 The Islamic Jihad Group claimed responsibility for the blasts, saying they were a protest against injustice and in support of Palestinian, Iraqi, and Afghan fighters. This is confirmed via a Russian news site, which indicated that a communiqué was posted on www.stopdictatorkarimov.com, and reposted that communiqué. See Oleg Shchedrov, "Uzbekistan Points to Islamists in Suicide Bombings," Reuters, July 31, 2004, and "*Uzbekistan: Srochnoye soobsheniye. Gruppa Islamskiy Dzhihad opiat' beret na sebia...*" (Uzbekistan: Urgent Message. Islamic Jihad Group Takes Responsibility Upon Itself...), CentrAsia News, July 31, 2004, www.centrasia.ru/newsA.php?st=1091217600.

16 See Susan B. Glasser, "U.S., Israeli Embassies Hit in Uzbek Bomb Attacks," *Washington Post*, July 31, 2004, www.washingtonpost.com/wp-dyn/articles/A26869-2004Jul30.html; Daniel Kimmage, "Analysis: Kazakh Breakthrough on Uzbek Terror Case," Radio Free Europe/Radio Liberty, November 15, 2004, www.rferl.org/content/article/1055882.html. On Kazakh ties, the government of Kazakhstan has recently detained individuals suspected of organizing these latest attacks. See "Country Reports on Terrorism," Office of the Coordinator for Counterterrorism, April 27, 2005, www.state.gov/s/ct/rls/crt/45388.htm.

17 See Gulnoza Saidazimova, "Uzbekistan: Dissident Imam Reaches Safety After Eight Years in Hiding," Radio Free Europe/Radio Liberty, March 16, 2006, www.rferl.org/content/article/1066744.html.

18 From Bakhtiyar Babadjanov's unpublished materials prepared for the Carnegie Endowment.

19 Ruhiddin Fahriddinov is a former imam at the Khoja Nasreddin Mosque in Tashkent. He and Tohir Abdusamatov were wanted by the Uzbek government for "attempting to overthrow the constitutional order." Kazakh authorities arrested them along with eight other followers of Obidkhon qori in late November 2005. In September 2006 Fahriddinov was sentenced to seventeen years in prison for extremist activities and involvement in the 1999 Tashkent car bombing. See *International Protection Considerations Regarding Asylum-Seekers and Refugees From the Republic of Uzbekistan*, "Uzbekistan: International Religious Freedom Report 2007," or "Kazakhstan: Further Information on Fear of Forcible Return/'Disappearance.'" Google searches for Fahriddinov brought up Human Rights Watch and Amnesty International reports on rights abuses in Uzbekistan. *Creating Enemies of the State: Religious Persecution in Uzbekistan* has a confession about acquiring non-state-sanctioned knowledge:

> We were secretly acquiring knowledge ... we later embarked on the Wahhabi path. I swear to Allah that I'm never going to return to that path and if I decide that I'm going to acquire knowledge, like the respected imam said, everyone should go to his local mosque and if this is asked of them the imams will help to the extent that they are able.

20 See Saidazimova, "Uzbekistan: Dissident Imam Reaches Safety After Eight Years in Hiding."

21 According to the Voice of America, his family members were in a deadly car accident in 2007. See Alisher Soipov, "*Shayx Abduvali qori Mirzayevning oila azolari avtohalokatga uchragan*" (The Family Members of Skaykh Abduvali qori Mirzaev Were Involved in a Motor Vehicle Accident), Voice of America, September 29, 2007.

22 See Alla Pyatibratova, "Kyrgyz Mufti Fends Off Extremism Charges: Muslim Leader Denies Claims That He's a Key Figure in the Hizb ut-Tahrir Movement," Institute for War and Peace Reporting, RCA issue 318, February 21, 2005, http://iwpr.net/report-news/kyrgyz-mufti-fends-extremism-charges.

23 Bakhtiyar Babadjanov and Zuhriddin Husniddinov have portrayed Yuldoshev as an extremist. Alisher Ilkhamov and Sarah Kendzior have depicted him in a less threatening light as a businessman and amateur scholar, as well as possibly a victim of overactive prosecutors. Sarah Kendzior, "Inventing Akromiya: The Role of Uzbek Propagandists in the Andijon Massacre," *Demokratizatsiya: The Journal of Post-Soviet Democratization*, vol. 14, no. 4, Fall 2006, 545–62.

24 See Kendzior, "Inventing Akromiya," 3.

25 According to the most recent U.S. State Department human rights report, police regularly detain citizens for lengthy periods of time to collect bribes or to intimidate their families and are rarely prosecuted for this. For more information and examples, see "2010 Human Rights Report: Uzbekistan."

26 This occurred in Osh in early 2006.

27 Sodikjon qori Kamaluddin was *qadi* of Kyrgyzstan from 1987 to 1990, a deputy of the Kyrgyzstan Congress from 1990 to 1994, and nominated Akaev president in 1990. He was also president of the Kyrgyzstan Islamic Center. See Leonid Levitin, "Liberalization in Kyrgyzstan," 190.

28 According to Igor Rotar of Forum 18, the details of his death were unclear, but the Uzbek National Security Service issued a statement that the terrorists had probably taken him hostage for a human shield, thinking that if he died, they could use his name to provoke conflict between Muslim believers and the authorities. Igor Rotar, "Kyrgyzstan: Imam's Killing Seen as Attack on Independent Islam," Forum 18, August 24, 2006, http://wwrn.org/articles/22526/?&place=central-asia&section=islam.

29 Unpublished materials prepared by Bakhtiyar Babadjanov for the Carnegie Endowment.

30 Witter indicates that the IMU had settled into farming roles in South Waziristan and that it was fighting with Waziri tribesmen and the Pakistani military that led to Yuldoshev's death.

31 Witter indicates that the IMU had a history with Bin Laden from the time they were his guests in Afghanistan, which is what led the United States to designate the IMU as a terrorist group. See David Witter, "Uzbek Militancy in Pakistan's Tribal Region," 1. Also see www.furqon.com for an idea of the importance of Bin Laden as a motivation for the IMU.

32 Witter names eleven key players in the history of the IMU: Juma Namangani (d. 2001); Tohir Yuldoshev (d. 2009); Nek Mohammad (d. 2004); Mullah Nazir (Maulvi Nazir); Saifullah Rahman Mansour; Baitullah Mehsud (d. 2009); Hakimullah Mehsud; Jalaluddin Haqqani; Sirajuddin Haqqani; Najmiddin Jalolov, also known as Abu Yahya Muhammad Fatih, co-founder and overall commander of the IJU (d. 2009); Suhayl Buranov, co-founder of IJU and likely assumed command after Jalolov's death. The IMU website lists four members by name: Abbos Mansur, army commander; Abdul Fattoh Ahmadiy, publisher; Yusuf Oshiy, poet; and Usman Odil, leader. See David Witter, "Uzbek Militancy in Pakistan's Tribal Region," 3, or www.furqon.com.

33 According to the Institute of War and Peace Reporting, he is married to Yuldoshev's eldest daughter. His posting on the IMU web site to announce Yuldoshev's death did not have any personal information. See http://furqon.com/shahidforuq/Usmonodil-08.2010.html or "Institute for War and Peace Reporting: Militant Islamic Force Signals Return to Central Asia," October 13, 2010, www.ecoi.net/local_link/147867/2490bbb15_en.html.

34 According to Andrew McGregor of the Jamestown Foundation, twelve people were arrested in Tajikistan in connection with the IMU during the summer of 2009. Charges included weapons possession, connection to the murder of police in 2005, and membership in the IMU. The Tajik government has blamed some of this trouble with militants in the IMU and has made that connection through Mirzo Ziyoev and Shaykh Nemat Azizov, who both led Islamic forces in the Tajik civil war and were killed in separate events in the area of Tavildara, a former IMU stronghold, in July 2009. See Andrew McGregor, "Counterterrorism Operations Continue in Tajikistan," *Terrorism Monitor*, vol. 7, no. 25, August 13, 2009.

35 This suicide bombing claimed four lives; in addition to the bomber, Akmal Karimov, three police officers were killed, and 28 were injured. Akmal Karimov and his brother Firdavs, who had connections to the IMU, were held responsible. Tajik prosecutors also blamed a new group, *Jamaat*

Ansarullah, for the action. See "Russia arrests 3 Tajiks for Khujand police bombing," Central Asia Security Newswire, December 7, 2010.

36 There were two attacks in May that killed one police officer. See "Uzbekistan: 2009 Country Reports on Terrorism," August 5, 2010.

37 Bruce Pannier, "Motives Behind Attack on Uzbek Imam Remain Unclear," Radio Free Europe/Radio Liberty, August 4, 2009, www.rferl.org/content/Motives_Behind_Attack_On_Uzbek_Imam_Remain_Unclear/1792475.html?utm_source=wordtwit&utm_medium=social&utm_campaign=wordtwit.

38 See "Islamic Jihad Union (IJU)," National Counterterrorism Center Calendar, www.nctc.gov/site/groups/iju.html.

39 A search conducted on YouTube in March 2011 for the term "Abduvali qori" led to 205 different results.

40 There was even footage of the riots put to the pop music of Yulduz Usmonova on YouTube.

41 For Uzbeks residing in southern Kyrgyzstan, the June 2010 ethnic riots were a wrenching experience. Many were left bereaved, losing both their homes and their loved ones. The Uzbek government, which had maintained tight controls on the border since 1999, agreed to accept some 100,000 refugees, the maximum number it felt able to safely provide for. Meanwhile, nearly three times that number remained on the Kyrgyz side of the border. See "Spillover Effects of Kyrgyzstan's Crisis: Uzbekistan Strives to Cope," http://kyrgyzstan.carnegieendowment.org/2010/06/spillover-effects-of-kyrgyzstan%e2%80%99s-crisis-uzbekistan-strives-to-cope.

42 Many of the websites associated with Muhammad Sodiq Muhammad Yusuf have information about the events in Kyrgyzstan, including updates about the situation. The sites mostly have re-postings of articles from RFE and Eurasianet and other news sources. See http://info.islom.uz/content/category/1/40/1027. Also, Imam Yusuf signed a document in 2007 promoting peace between Christians and Muslims, www.acommonword.com/index.php?lang=en&page=signatories.

43 Obidkhon qori's website has a page about the events in Kyrgyzstan, where it says that people should help each other. See www.islomovozi.com/?cat=32.

44 As I have argued earlier, I do not accept the notion that the civil war in Tajikistan was a form of jihad, and it is not conventionally considered to be a religious war, but a battle between competing political factions for power.

GLOSSARY

A

adat
custom [Arabic]

Akramiya
the group formed by Akrom Yuldoshev, who wrote the 1992 brochure "The Path to Belief" after leaving the group Hizb ut-Tahrir. Yuldoshev has been in prison since 1999, following his conviction for the bombings in Tashkent.

alem al-ulama
learned of the learned [Arabic]

aqiqa toy
celebration in honor of the birth of a child [Uzbek]

ashabs
companions of the Prophet Mohammad [Arabic]

avliyo
saint [Uzbek]

ayat
verse from the Quran [Arabic]

B

basmachi
(from the Russian word "baskinji" or *attacker*); name of the resistance movement that fought for the liberation of Central Asia from the Bolsheviks

bayonet
statement [Uzbek]

bidat
heresy [Uzbek]

bitim
accord, agreement [Uzbek]

bogatyr
soldier [Russian]

C

chaikana (choyxona)
teahouse [Uzbek]

chalma
turban [Uzbek]

Chingizids
descendants of Chingiz Khan's family

D

dar al-harb
(also known as *dar al-kufr*, meaning "territory of war"); refers to non-Muslim countries that are considered by Muslim scholars as potentially at war with Muslim countries [Arabic]

dar al-Islam
(literally "territory/world of Islam"); refers to the Muslim countries in which the life is completely regulated by Sharia [Arabic]

davat
a call/summons to the faith [Uzbek]

davatchi
one who summons others to the join the Islamic faith [Uzbek]

divon
a collection of decrees, works, or documents [Uzbek]

domla
(or domulla in Arabic)
religious teacher of Islam; expert of Muslim rituals, religious clerk, well-educated man and scholar [Uzbek]

druzhinniki
a nominally voluntary public group created by organizations, factories, and other enterprises to help prevent crime in public places [Russian]

dukchi
manufacturer of spindles [Uzbek]

dua
prayer [Arabic]

Duma
the Russian parliament

E

emir
title used for Muslim rulers [Arabic]

F

farz
(or fard in Arabic)
meaning "mandatory," the term describes religious duties within Islam [Uzbek]

fatwa
a legal opinion based on Sharia law, offered by an Islamic religious leader [Arabic]

fiqh
("deep knowledge and understanding"); Islamic law [Arabic]

fura al-fiqh
judgments [Arabic]

G

gaps
male social gatherings, in which 7–15 men gather at a home or a chaikana to dine together and discussing topics of mutual interest [Uzbek]

gariba
exile [Arabic]

ghayr-i din
non-believer [Arabic]

ghazavat
holy war [Arabic]

H

hadith(s)
(meaning "news" or "story"); stories about the words and deeds of Prophet Muhammad that relate the different religious-legal sides of Muslim life. The *hadiths* are considered the second source of the Islamic law after the Quran. [Arabic]

hajj
pilgrimage to Mecca [Arabic]

hajjis
pilgrims going on *hajj* [Arabic]

Hanafi
the oldest of the four *mazhabs*, the Hanafi school was founded by Imam Abu Hanifa (d. 767). Ninety percent of Uzbekistan's population is, at least nominally, of this school.

hashar
voluntary participation from the other members of one's *mahalla*, typically with chores such as the construction of mosques, homes of community members, community buildings, or canals. [Uzbek]

hatib
Islamic preacher who delivers the sermon at Friday prayer. A *hatib* is usually, but not always the imam. As the prayer leader, he must be a male who has reached puberty. [Turkish]

Hayit nomoz
a prayer said during *Ruza hayit* or *Qurbon hayit* [Uzbek]

hijab
a veil that Muslim woman wear outside of their homes [Arabic]

hijra
migration [Arabic]

Hizb ut-Tahrir
Islamist political party whose goal is to re-establish the caliphate within the Muslim world

hokim
the governor of a *viloyat* [Uzbek]

hokimiyat
government, may refer to that of a single region (*viloyat hokimiyati*) or of the Uzbek nation-state (*davlat hokimiyati*) [Uzbek]

houris
virgins, one of the rumored rewards of a *shadid* [Arabic]

hujra
a cell or classroom in a madrasa; an illegal religious school in the home of a sheikh, imam, or ishan [Arabic]

I

iftar
a festive evening meal to break the daytime fast during the month of Ramadan [Arabic]

ijma
("consensus"); the infallible agreement of the Islamic community on a religious principle [Arabic]

ijtihad
in Islamic law, the independent or original interpretation of issues not precisely covered by the Quran, *hadith*, and *ijma* [Arabic]

IJU
Islamic Jihad Union

ilm
knowledge, science [Uzbek]

imam
(derived from the word "amma," to stand ahead of or lead); the head of a Muslim community, leads prayers in a mosque [Arabic]

imam mecheti
the imam of a mosque [Russian]

IMU
Islamic Movement of Uzbekistan

irshad
guidance transmitted from a Sufi master to his students [Arabic]

ishan
(or eshon in Uzbek)
religious functionary in Islam, honorific title for sheikhs [Arabic]

Islomiy davlat
Islamic state [Uzbek]

isyonchi
insurgent [Uzbek]

J

Jadidism
(literally "renewal"); emerging at the end of the nineteenth century in Central Asia, this movement called for the addition of modern practices, such as educational reforms and the empowerment of women, into their Muslim identity in order to prevent spiritual or economic decay

jamoa
community [Uzbek]

jamoa Islomi
community of Islam [Uzbek]

janaza
a prayer read at funerals [Arabic]

jihad al-nafs
the "greater jihad," a struggle to rid evil from within oneself, in which all Muslim believers engage in [Arabic]

jihad bil saif
the "lesser jihad," where believers engage in an armed struggle in defense of Islam [Arabic]

jimud
stagnation [Arabic]

jinaz
religious burial [Arabic]

K

kafan
a white cloth in which the deceased are wrapped [Arabic]

kafir
infidel [Arabic]

kalima
("a saying"); a profession of faith [Arabic]

kanaqa
residential teaching center for Sufis that likely originated in Iran in the late tenth or eleventh century. Although the etymological origin has been widely disputed, many believe that the term is of Persian origin, probably derived from *khana-gah* (place of residence). Today *kanaqa* no longer includes residential quarters, although it still serves as a center for devotions, poetry, and the performance of the *zikr* and *sama* rituals.

karnay
Uzbek trumpet used for ceremonial announcements; wedding parties, celebrations [Uzbek]

khalifa
a Muslim who becomes the spiritual successor to his teacher [Arabic]

khalqa
literally a circle or chain, the term refers to a united group of believers [Uzbek]

khodoya
(meaning "Oh God"); celebration of the prayers on the third day after death [Persian]

kibla
direction to Mecca, toward which all Muslims should pray [Arabic]

kishlak (qishloq)
village [Uzbek]

kolkhoz
collective farm [Russian]

Komsomol
Young Communist League

krysha
(literally "roof"); slang terminology for a place or organization that provides protection [Russian]

kulak
affluent peasant [Russian]

kurort(s)
Soviet-style resorts [Russian]

M

madrasa
Muslim religious school [Arabic]

mahalla
a neighborhood community within a city [Uzbek]

majnun
madman [Arabic]

maktab
school [Arabic]

malun
apostates [Arabic]

manaviyat
ethics, spirituality [Uzbek]

marifat
enlightenment [Uzbek]

maruza
lecture [Uzbek]

mazar
Muslim cemetery [Persian]

mazhab(s)
a religious sect or school of jurisprudence [Arabic]

mudarris
head of a madrasa [Arabic]

muezzin
the crier of a mosque who summons Muslims to prayer five times daily [Arabic]

mufti
("a religious leader who issues *fatwas*"); expert on Sharia who provides detailed explanation of its basic provisions and resolves disputes on its principles and precedents [Arabic]

muftiyat
council of *muftis* [Arabic]

Mujaddidiys
those favoring renewal within the faith, also known as *Javononi islomi* (the Youth of Islam)

Mujahid
(plural: *mujahideen*)
Islamic cleric [Arabic]

mullah
Islamic cleric [Arabic]

murid
a Sufi disciple or student [Arabic]

musulmonchilik
Muslimness [Uzbek]

mutaval
proprietor of a religious foundation [Arabic]

N

namaz
Islamic ritual prayer practiced five times daily [Arabic]

nikoh toy
religious wedding ceremony [Uzbek]

nisbat
spiritual connections [Uzbek]

nutq
oratory, speech [Uzbek]

O

Oliy Majlis
the Uzbek parliament

oq soqoli
(literally "one possessing a white beard"); a learned and respected old man, the *mahalla* elder [Uzbek]

oq suyak
(meaning "white bone"); the term described the behavior of the descendants of Sufi clans in Central Asia. These clans were secluded, married only within similarly high-ranking families, and were considered blue-blooded. [Uzbek]

otin buvi
as *buvi* means grandmother, and an *otin* is a female religious teacher, an *otin buvi* is an older female religious teacher [Uzbek]

otin oyi
a woman with theological education; literally translated an *otin* is a female religious teacher, and *oyi* is an endearing term for one's mother [Uzbek]

P

paranja
a veiled cloak for devout Muslim women [Persian]

pir
a Sufi spiritual master (of Sufi adepts, craft apprentices etc.) [Persian]

podishoh
king [Uzbek]

pok
pure [Uzbek]

Q

qadi
(or qozi in Uzbek)
a judge of Sharia [Arabic]

qadi kalan
senior judge of Sharia [Arabic]

qasam
oath [Uzbek]

qawm
mosque community [Arabic]

qiraat
private lessons on reading the Quran [Arabic]

qiyas
(translated as "comparison" or "analogy"); concerned with the comparison of the *hadiths* to the Quran and *Sunna* [Arabic]

qori
one who has memorized the Quran [Arabic]

qori pochcha hujra
limited religious education continued within families by a relative able to read the Quran. This instruction was generally restricted to learning some basic prayers and some verses of the Quran, normally the first chapter, the last verses of the *Ayat ul-Kursi* (Quran, 2:251), and some prayers of personal supplication. [Uzbek]

Quran
Holy Book of Islam

Qurbon hayit
(or Eid ul-Adha in Arabic, "feast of the sacrifice") an Islamic holiday marking the end of the *hajj*, which is celebrated approximately seventy days after the month of Ramadan. It commemorates Abraham's willingness to sacrifice his son as an act of obedience to God. [Uzbek]

qurultoy
a congress [Uzbek]

R

Ramazan hayit
(or Eid al-Fitr in Arabic) a three-day celebration feast marking the end of the thirty-day fast of Ramadan [Uzbek]

raqs
dance [Uzbek]

raykom (rayon komitet)
a district committee of the Communist Party [Russian]

rayon
administrative unit, district, neighborhood [Russian]

risola
treatise [Uzbek]

Ruza hayit
the thirty days of fasting during Ramadan [Uzbek]

S

SADUM
The Spiritual Administration of the Muslims of Central Asia and Kazakhstan, or DMU (as it was later renamed), was the official body governing Islamic activities in the Central Asian republics of the Soviet Union. Founded in 1941, it was housed in Tashkent for fifty year before the dissolution of the Soviet Union.

sahih(s)
("reliable, correct"); recognized canon of *hadith* studies [Arabic]

Salafi(s)
(based on the Arabic word *salaf* for "ancestors"/"predecessors"); a follower of the Salafi movement of Islam. This movement calls for the return to the use of the Quran and the *Sunna* as the only sources for religious rulings. Its core objectives were to restore Islam to its pristine form by condemning the mentalities of *taqlid* and *jimud* among the Muslim traditionalist clergy.

sarts
urban dwellers [Uzbek]

sayyid(s)
purported descendants of the Prophet Muhammad [Arabic]

shahid
a Muslim who sacrificed his life for faith and who died as a martyr [Arabic]

sheikh ul-Islam
(the "elder of Islam"); the head cleric or leader of Islam [Arabic]

shuro
council [Uzbek]

silsila
spiritual succession [Arabic]

sovkhoz
state-owned farm [Russian]

sovremennyi chelovek
a modern person [Russian]

Sunna
("custom" or "example"); the use of the Prophet Muhammad's life as an example and guide for the Muslim community [Arabic]

sunnat
prayer read before the beginning of the formal prayer session [Arabic]

sunnat toy
circumcision ceremony [Uzbek]

sura
a chapter of the Holy Quran [Arabic]

T

tabib
a healer who uses traditional medicine [Uzbek]

tafsir
(translated as "elucidation," "explanation," or "interpretation"); an exegesis of the Quran. Most common topics of discussion in *tafsir* can be categorized as linguistic, juristic, or theological. The authority of the *tafsir* is determined based on its origin, with the *tafsir* provided by the Prophet Muhammad regarded as the most authoritative, while *tafsir bil-ray*, interpretation that is the outcome of personal reflection and logical deduction, is viewed as the least authoritative. [Arabic]

tahajjud
("ritual"); the night prayer, which is generally not considered obligatory and not counted among the daily prayers [Arabic]

takbir
announcing the greatness of God by saying "Allahu akbar" (God is Great) [Arabic]

taqlid
("copy or imitation"); the application of reason based on legal precedent [Arabic]

taqlidchi
a religious traditionalist, one who imitates religious precedents (as opposed to the *Mujaddidiys*) [Uzbek]

taqiyya
a practice that comes from Sharia that allows Muslims to feign apostasy rather than be killed. It is based on a verse in the Quran that forbids a Muslim to be instrumental in his own death. [Arabic]

tariqa
a Sufi brotherhood

technikum
technical-training college [Uzbek]

toy
ceremony, celebration [Uzbek]

U

ulama
(plural of "alim," meaning "scholar"); local class of clerics [Arabic]

umma
the Muslim community [Arabic]

UMU
the Spiritual Administration of the Muslims of Uzbekistan, the Uzbek successor to SADUM

upolnomochennye
authorized [Russian]

urf wa adat
customary practices [Arabic]

uzun soqolis
("those possessing long beards"); used to describe the Ahl-i Quran movement [Uzbek]

V

viloyat
region, oblast [Uzbek]

W

Wahhabism
a more conservative form of Islam practiced in Saudi Arabia, and a popular term used for Islamists and extremists in much of the press. In Uzbekistan, the term often refers to those who preached a politicized form of Islam, by re-emphasizing the uniqueness of "Uzbek" Islam. The movement derives its name from its founder Muhammad ibn Abd al-Wahhab Tamimi (1703–1792).

waqf
In Islamic law, a permanent nonperishable endowment, usually referring to land or buildings, the proceeds of which are used for the purposes designated by the benefactor. There are three main categories of *waqf*: religious, philanthropic, and family. Religious *waqf* refers to the house of worship (such as the mosque) and the real estate that provides revenue for its maintenance and expenses. Philanthropic *waqf* provides support to the struggling segments of the population by funding initiatives devoted to education, health services, and other charitable purposes. The

third kind of *waqf* is a form of real estate whose revenue is first given to one's descendants, and only the surplus is given to the poor. [Arabic]

Y

yot
alien [Uzbek]

yurish
medieval term for military expeditions [Uzbek]

Yurtbashi
father of the homeland [Uzbek]

Z

zakot
alms that Muslims were expected to offer to religious institutions [Arabic]

zastoy
("stagnation"); a period of economic stagnation in the 1970s–1980s under the rule of Soviet Communist Leader Leonid Brezhnev [Russian]

zikr
an Islamic devotional act with the intent of remembering God. *Zikr* is conducted out loud, or internally, and is considered to lead Sufi believers closer to God. [Arabic]

ziyorat
visit, pilgrimage [Uzbek]

BIBLIOGRAPHY

Abdul-Jabbar, Ghassan. *Bukhar*. New York: Oxford University Press, 2007.

Abdullaev, Sarvar S. *Uzbekistonda etikod erkingligi va Islom*. [The Freedom of Conviction and Islam in Uzbekistan] Ph.D. Diss. Uzbekiston respublikasi Vazirlar Makhkamasi Hozirdagi Toshkent Islam Universiteti, 2002.

Abdurakhimova, Nadira A. "The Colonial System of Power in Turkistan." *International Journal of Islamic Studies*, vol. 34, no. 2 (May 2002).

Abduvakhitov, Abdujabar. "Independent Uzbekistan: A Muslim Community in Development." In *The Politics of Religion in Russia and the New States of Eurasia*. Ed. Michael Bordeaux. New York: M. E. Sharpe, 1995.

Abduvakhitov, Abdujabar. "The Jadid Movement and Its Impact on Contemporary Central Asia." In *Central Asia, Its Strategic Importance and Future Prospects*. Ed. Hafeez Malik. New York: St. Martin's Press, 1994.

Abou Zahab, Mariam, and Olivier Roy. *Islamist Networks: The Afghan-Pakistan Connection*. Translated by John King. New York, Paris: Columbia University Press in association with the Centre d'études et de recherches internationales, 2004.

Abramson, David M. and Elyor E. Karimov. "Sacred Sites, Profane Ideologies: Religious Pilgrimage and the Uzbek State." In *Everyday Life in Central Asia: Past and Present*. Eds. Jeff Sahadeo and Russell G. Zanca. Bloomington, Ind.: Indiana University Press, 2007.

Adams, Laura L. *The Spectacular State: Culture and National Identity in Uzbekistan*. Durham: Duke University Press, 2010.

Agzamkhodzhaev, Saidakbar S. *Turkiston Mukhtorijati: Bor'ba za Svobodu i Nezavisimost'*. [Turkistan's

Autonomy: The Fight for Freedom and Independence] Ph.D. Diss. Akademija Nauk Respubliki Uzbekistan Institut Istorii, 1996.

Ajni, Sadriddin. *The Sands of Oxus: Boyhood Reminiscences of Sadriddin Aini.* Translated by John R. Perry and Rachel Lehr. Costa Mesa, Calif.: Mazda Publishers, 1998.

Akademiya Nauk, USSR, Institut Vostokovedeniya. *Aziatskij Muzej-Leningradskoe Otdelenie Institutat Vostokovedenia Akademiya Nauka SSSR.* [Asian Museum, the Leningrad Separation of the Institute of Eastern Studies, Academy of Sciences, USSR] Moscow: Nauka, 1972.

Akcali, Pinar. "Islam as a 'Common Bond' in Central Asia: Islamic Renaissance Party and the Afghan Mujahideen." *Central Asian Survey*, vol. 17, no. 2 (1998): 267–84.

Akimushkin, O. F. "Materiali Dlya Bibliografii Rabot o Persidskikh Rukopisyakh," [Materials for Bibliographical Work About Persian Manuscripts] *Narodi Azii i Afrikii: Istorii Ekonomika, Kultura*, no. 3 (1963): 165–74. Moscow: Akademiya Nauk SSSR, 1963.

al-Afghani, Jamal ad-Din. *Refutation des materialistes: 3e edition arabe avec introduction et notes.* [The Refutation of the Materialists: Third Arabic Edition with an Introduction and Notes] Translated by A. M. Goichon. Paris: P. Geuthner, 1942.

al-Qazani, Ahmad-Wali, Qurban'ali Khalidi, Allen J. Frank, and Mirkasym Abdulakhatovich Usmanov. *Materials for the Islamic History of Semipalatinsk: Two Manuscripts by Ahmad-Wali al-Qazani and Qurban'ali Khalidi.* Berlin: Das Arabische Buch, 2001.

Ali, Sheikh Jameil. *Sayyid Jamal Al-Din Al-Afghani and the West.* New Delhi, India: Adam Publishers & Distributors, 2002.

Antelava, Natalia. "Popular Kyrgyz imam shot dead." BBC News, August 7, 2006. http://news.bbc.co.uk/2/hi/asia-pacific/5252688.stm.

Association Droits de l'Homme en Asie Central. "The Brief List of Political Prisoners in Uzbekistan." October 2010. Le Mans, France:, 2010.

Atkin, Muriel. "Religious, National, and other Identities in Central Asia." In *Muslims in Central Asia: Expressions of Identity and Change.* Ed. Jo-Ann Gross. Durham and London: Duke University Press, 1992.

Azamatov, Danil' D. "The Muftis of the Orenburg Spiritual Assembly in the 18th and 19th Centuries: The Struggle for Power in Russia's Muslim Institution." In *Muslim Culture in Russia and Central Asia from the 18th to the Early 20th Centuries.* Eds. Anke von Kugelgen, Michael Kemper, and Allen J. Frank, *Inter-Regional and Inter-Ethnic Tensions*, vol. 2, 355–384. Berlin: Klaus Schwarz Verlag, 1998.

Babadjanov, Bakhtiyar. "Debates over Islam in Contemporary Uzbekistan: A View from Within." In *Devout Societies vs. Impious States?: Transmitting Islamic Learning in Russia, Central Asia and China,*

Through the Twentieth Century. Proceedings of an International Colloquium Held in Carré Des Sciences, French Ministry of Research, Paris, November 12–13, 2001. Ed. Stéphane A. Dudoignon. Berlin: Klaus Schwarz Verlag, 2004.

———. "Islam Officiel Contre Islam Politique en Ouzbekistan Aujourd'hui: La Direction Des Musulmans et Les Groups Non-Hanafi." [Official Islam Against Political Islam in Today's Uzbekistan: The Direction of Muslims and the Non-Hanafi Groups] In *Revue d'etudes comparatives Est-Ouest*, vol. 31, no. 3 (2000): 151–64.

———. *Nasihatlik suzim bor. Shayx Sofiy-Tabib Nursafardiy.* [I Have Words of Advice. Sufi Sheikh and Healer Nursafardiy] Tashkent: 2006.

Babadjanov, Bakhtiyar and Muzaffar Kamilov. "Muhammadjan Hindustani and the Beginning of the 'Great Schism' Among Muslims of Uzbekistan." In *Islam in Politics in Russia and Central Asia: Early Eighteenth to Late Twentieth Centuries.* Eds. Stéphane A. Dudoignon and Hisao Komatsu. New York: Kegan Paul, 2001.

Babakhodjaev, M. A. *Respublika Uzbekistan Ocherki Mezhnatsionalnikh i Mezhkonfesionalnikh Otnoshenii, Vneshneiekonomicheskikh Sviazei.* [The Republic of Uzbekistan: Essays on interethnic and interdominational relations and their external economic ties] Tashkent: Elsano, 1996.

Bartold, Vasilii Vladimirovich. Tom 2, chast' 1. *Obshchie raboty po istorii Srednei Azii. Raboty po istorii Kavkaza i vostochnoi Evropy.* [Volume 2, Part 1. Aggregate Works on the History of Central Asia. Works on the History of the Caucusus and Eastern Europe] Moscow: Vostochnoi Literatyry, 1963.

———. *Four Studies on the History of Central Asia.* Translated by Vladimir Minorsky and T. Minorsky. Volume I, Leiden, The Netherlands: E. J. Brill, 1956.

———. *Four Studies on the History of Central Asia.* Translated by Vladimir Minorsky and T. Minorsky. Volume II, Ulugh-Beg. Leiden, The Netherlands: E. J. Brill, 1958.

———. *Four Studies on the History of Central Asia.* Translated by Vladimir Minorsky and T. Minorsky. Volume III, Mir Ali-Shir, A History of the Turkmen People. Leiden, The Netherlands: E. J. Brill, 1962.

Bashiri, Iraj. "Prominent Tajik Figures of the Twentieth Century." www.angelfire.com/rnb/bashiri/TajikFigures/TajikFigures.pdf.

Bayram, Mushfig and John Kinahan. "Uzbekistan: Religious Freedom Survey, August 2008." Forum 18 News Service. www.forum18.org/Archive.php?article_id=1170.

Bennigsen, Alexandre and S. Enders Wimbush. *Mystics and Commissars, Sufism in the Soviet Union.* Berkeley, Calif.: University of California Press, 1985.

Bernd, Radtke and John O'Kane. *The Concept of Sainthood in Early Islamic Mysticism.* Richmond, Surrey, England: Curzon Press, 1996.

Blank, Stephen. *The Sorcerer As Apprentice: Stalin As Commissar of Nationalities, 1917-1924.* Westport, Conn.: Greenwood Press, 1994.

Bobozhonov, B. and Anke von Kügelgen. *Manakib-i Dukchi Ishan: anonim zhiti a Dukchi Ishana predvoditeli a Andizhanskogo vosstanii a 1898 goda.* [Manakib-Dukchi Ishan: An Anonymous Biography of Dukchi Ishan: The leader of the Andijian Uprising of 1898] Tashkent: Daik Press, 2004.

Boukhars, Anouar. "Islam, Jihadism, and Depoliticization in France and Germany." *International Political Science Review*, vol. 30, no. 297 (2009).

Bregel, Yuri. "Barthold and Modern Oriental Studies." *International Journal of Middle East Studies*, vol. 12, no. 3 (November 1980): 385–403.

———. *Turko-Mongol Influences in Central Asia*, Cambridge: University Press, 1991.

Brower, Daniel R. and Edward J. Lazzerini. *Russia's Orient: Imperial Borderlands and Peoples, 1700-1917.* Indiana-Michigan series in Russian and East European Studies. Bloomington: Indiana University Press, 1997.

Buehler, Arthur F. "The Naqshbandiyya in Timurid India: The Central Asian Legacy." *Journal of Islamic Studies*, vol. 7, no. 2 (1996): 208–228.

Carlisle, Donald. "Geopolitics of Uzbekistan." In *Muslim Eurasia: Conflicting Legacies.* Ed. Yaacov Roi. Portland, OR.: F. Cass, 1995.

Chaudet, Didier. "Islamist Terrorism in Greater Central Asia: The 'Al-Qaedaization' of Uzbek Jihadism." *Russie.Nei.Visions*, no. 35 (December 2008).

Chivers, C. J. "The Reach of War: Punishment; Uzbekistan Sentences Militants; Rights Group Questions Trial." *New York Times*, August 25, 2004.

Christmann, Andreas. "Islamic Scholar and Religious Leader: Shaikh Muhammad Sa'id Ramadan al-Buti." In *Islam and Modernity: Muslim Intellectuals Respond.* Eds. John Cooper, Ronald L. Nettler, and Mohamed Mahmoud. New York: I. B. Tauris, 1998.

Clairmonte, Frederick F. "Rise and Fall of Soviet Agriculture." *Economic and Political Weekly*, vol. 24, no. 11 (March 18, 1989): 555–60.

Cole, Juan. R.I. and Deniz Kandiyoti. "Nationalism and the Colonial Legacy in the Middle East and Central Asia: Introduction." *International Journal of Middle East Studies*, vol. 34, no. 2 (May 2002): 189–203.

Collins, Kathleen. "Ideas, Networks, and Islamist Movements, Evidence from Central Asia and the Caucasus." *World Politics*, vol. 60, no. 1, (October 2007): 64–96.

———. "The Logic of Clan Politics: Evidence from the Central Asian Trajectories." *World Politics*, vol. 56, no. 2 (January 2004): 224–61. www.jstor.org/stable/25054256.

Cornell, Svante E. and Regine A. Spector. "Central Asia: More than Islamic Extremists." *Washington Quarterly*, vol. 25, no. 1 (2002): 193–206.

Crews, Robert D. *For Prophet and Tsar: Islam and Empire in Russia and Central Asia*. Cambridge, Mass.: Harvard University Press, 2006.

D'Encausse, Helene Carrere. *Islam and the Russian Empire: Reform and Revolution in Central Asia*. Translated by Quitin Hoare. Berkeley, Calif.: University of California Press and I. B. Tauris & Co. Ltd., 1988.

DeWeese, Devin A. *Islamization and Native Religion in the Golden Horde: Baba Tukles and Conversion to Islam in Historical and Epic Tradition*. University Park, Penn.: Pennsylvania State University Press, 1994.

———. "The Descendants of Sayyid Ata and the Rank of Naqib in Central Asia." *Journal of the American Oriental Society*, vol. 115, no. 4 (October–December 1995): 612–34.

———. ed. *Studies on Central Asian History, In Honor of Yuri Bregel*. Research Institute for Inner Asian Studies, Indiana University. Bloomington: Indiana University Press, 2001.

DeWeese, David. "The Masha'ikh-i Turk and the Khojagan: Rethinking the Links Between The Yasavi and Naqshbandi Sufi Traditions." *Journal of Islamic Studies*, vol. 7, no. 2 (1996): 180–207.

Dietrich, Albert. *Akten des VII. Kongresses fur Arabistik und Islamwissenschaft, Abhandlungen Der Akademie Der Wissenschaften in Gottingen, Philologish-Historische Klasse Dritte Folge*, no. 98, August 1974. [Documents of the 7th Congress for Arabic and Islamic Studies. Essays from the Academy of Sciences in Gottingen, Department of Philology and History, Third Part No. 98] Goettingen: Vandenhoeck & Ruprecht, 1976.

Dor, Remy. "Les islamistes d'Asie centrale: un defi aux etats independants?" [The Islamists of Central Asia: A Challenge to Independent States?] *Cahiers d'Asie centrale*, 15/16. Paris: Maisonneuve & Larose, 2007.

Duderija, Adis. "Islamic Groups and their Worldviews and Identities: Neo-Traditional Salafis and Progressive Muslims." *Understanding Islam*. August 24, 2006. www.understanding-islam.com/reader-articles/worship-and-fasting/islamic-groups-and-their-worldviews-and-identities-neo-traditional-salafis-and-progressive-muslims-8101.

Dudoignon, Stéphane A. "La question scolaire a Boukhara et au Turkestan russe, du 'premier renouveau' a la sovietisation (fin du XVIIIe siecle-1937)." [The Academic Issue in Bukhara and Russian Turkestan From the First Renewal to Sovietization (the End of the XVIII Century to 1937)]. *Cahiers du monde russe*, vol. 37, no. 1 and 2 (1996): 133–210.

———. "Status, Strategies and Discourses of a Muslim "Clergy" under a Christian Law: Polemics about the Collection of the Zakat in Late Imperial Russia." In *Islam in Politics in Russia and Central Asia: Early Eighteenth to Late Twentieth Centuries*. Eds. Stéphane A. Dudoignon and Hisao Komatsu. *Islamic Area Studies*, 3 (2001): 43–76. London: Kegan Paul, 2001.

Eickelman, Dale F., ed. *The Middle East and Central Asia: An Anthropological Approach*. Upper Saddle River, N.J.: Prentice Hall, 1998.

———. *Russia's Muslims Frontiers: New Directions in Cross-Cultural Analysis*. Bloomington: Indiana University Press, 1993.

Fair, C. Christine. "The Militant Challenge in Pakistan." *Asia Policy*, no. 11 (January 2011): 105–137.

Fathi, Habiba. "Ottines: The Unknown Women Clerics of Central Asian Islam." *Central Asia Survey*, vol. 16, no. 1 (1997): 7–43.

Fedtke, Gero. "Jadids, Young Bukharans, Communists and the Bukharan Revolution: From an Ideological Debate in the Early Soviet Union." In *Muslim Culture in Russia and Central Asia from the 18th to the Early 20th Centuries*. Eds. Anke von Kugelgen, Michael Kemper, and Allen J. Frank, *Inter-Regional and Inter-Ethnic Tensions*, vol. 2. Berlin: Klaus Schwarz Verlag, 1998.

Fletcher, Joseph F. and Boris Sergeyev. "Islam and Intolerance in Central Asia: the Case of Kyrgystan." *Europe-Asia Studies*, vol. 54, no. 2 (2002): 251–75.

Frank, Allen J. "Islam and Ethnic Relations in the Kazakh Inner Horde: Muslim Cossacks, Tatar Merchants, and Kazakh Nomads in a Turkic Manuscript, 1870-1910." In *Muslim Culture in Russia and Central Asia from the 18th to the Early 20th Centuries*. Eds. Anke von Kugelgen, Michael Kemper, and Allen J. Frank. *Inter-Regional and Inter-Ethnic Tensions*, vol. 2. Berlin: Klaus Schwarz Verlag, 1998.

Frank, Allen J., and Jahangir Mamatov. *Uzbek Islamic Debates: Texts, Translations, and Commentary*. Springfield, Va.: Dunwoody Press, 2006.

Fredholm, Michael. "Islamic Extremism as a Political Force: A Comparative Study of Central Asian Islamic Extremist Movements." Stockholm: Forum for Central Asian Studies, Stockholm University, 2006.

Frye, Richard Nelson. *The Golden Age of Persia: The Arabs in the East*. New York: Barnes & Noble Books, 1975.

———. *The Heritage of Central Asia from Antiquity to the Turkish Expansion*. Princeton Series on the Middle East. Princeton, N.J.: Markus Wiener Publishers, 1996.

Gafarov, Numandzhon. *Istoria Kulturno-Prosvetitel'skoy Deyatel'nosti Dzhadidov v Bukharskom Emirate*. [The History of the Cultural-Enlightening Activities of the Jihads in the Bukhar Emirate] Tashkent: Khudzhand, 2000.

Geiss, Paul George. *Pre-Tsarist and Tsarist Central Asia: Communal Committment and Political Order in Change*. London, New York: RoutledgeCurzon, Taylor and Francis Ltd., 2003.

Gesink, Indira Falk. "Chaos On The Earth: Subjective Truths versus Communal Unity In Islamic Law and the Rise of Militant Islam" *American Historical Review*, June 2003. www.historycooperative.org/journals/ahr/108.3/gesink.html.

Gibb, H. A. R. *The Arab Conquests in Central Asia*. New York: AMS Press, 1970.

Glasse, Cyril. *The Concise Encyclopedia of Islam*. San Francisco: Harper & Row, 1989.

Gretsky, Sergei. "Russia, Central Asia and Central Asia's Neighbours." In *Russian-American Relations: Islamic and Turkic Dimensions in the Volga-Ural Basin*. Ed. Hafeez Malik. New York: St. Martin's Press, 2000.

Griffin, Michael. *Reaping the Whirlwind: The Taliban Movement in Afghanistan*. London, UK: Pluto Press, 2001.

Grigorovich, Konsichenko Anatolii. *Islamskoye obrasovaniye: Vozmozhnoye budushyee*. [Islamic Education: Potential Future] Kazakhstan: Instituta Filosofiyii Politologii, Ministerstva Obrasovaniya i Nauki Respubliki Kazakhstan.

Gross, Jo-Ann. "The Waqf of Khoja 'Ubayd Allah Ahrar in Nineteenth Century Central Asia: A Preliminary Study of the Tsarist Record." In *Naqshbandis in Western and Central Asia: Change and Continuity*. Ed. Elisabeth Ozdalga. Vol. 9 (1999): 47–60. Istanbul: Swedish Research Institute in Istanbul Transactions, 1999.

———. "The Economic State of a Timurid Sufi Shaykh: A Matter of Conflict or Perception?" *Iranian Studies*, vol. 21, no. 1 and 2. Soviet and North American Studies on Central Asia, (1988): 84-104, 1988.

Gross, Jo-Ann, ed. *Muslims in Central Asia: Expressions of Identity and Change*. Durham and London: Duke University Press, 1992.

Gulitinilbovna, Maxmydova. *Dzhadidskoye Dvizheniye v Turkestane i Eto Vliyane na Razvitiye Nravstvenno-Esteticheskoi Misli*. [The Jadid Movement in Turkestan and its influence on the development of ethnic rights thinking] Akademiya Nauk Respubliki Uzbekistan Institut Filosofii i Prava Imeni I. Muminova, 1996.

Haghayeghi, Mehrdad. "Islam and Democratic Politics in Central Asia." *World Affairs*, vol. 156, no. 4 (Spring 1994): 186–98. www.jstor.org/stable/20672397.

———. *Islam and Politics in Central Asia*. New York: St. Martin's Press, 1995.

Hamid, Tawfiq. "The Development of a Jihadi's Mind." *Current Trends in Islamist Ideology*, vol. 5 (2007).

Human Rights Watch. *Creating Enemies of the State: Religious Persecution in Uzbekistan.* New York: Human Rights Watch, 2004. www.hrw.org/en/reports/2004/03/29/creating-enemies-state.

———. *Burying the Truth: Uzbekistan Rewrites the Story of the Andijan Massacre.* Vol. 17, no. 6, September 2005.

———. *Republic of Uzbekistan, Crackdown in the Farghona Valley: Arbitrary Arrests and Religious Discrimination.* Vol. 10, no. 4, May 1998.

Hunter, Shireen T., ed. *Reformist Voices of Islam: Mediating Islam and Modernity.* Armonk, New York: M.E. Sharpe Inc., 2009.

Hussain, Zahid. *Frontline Pakistan: The Struggle with Militant Islam.* New York Columbia University Press, 2007.

Ibn al-Asir. *Al-Kamil Fi-T-Tarikh: Polnii Svod Istorii.* [The Complete History Set] Uzbekistan: Akademia Nauk Respubliki Uzbekistan Institut Vostokovedenia, 2006.

Ibn Mirza Fazil Churas, Shakh-Makhmud. *Khronika.* [Chronicle] Moscow: Nauka, 1976.

Ilkhamov, Alisher. "Mystery Surrounds Tashkent Explosions." Middle East Research and Information Project. April 15, 2004. www.merip.org/mero/mero041504.

Ilmi-Khal, Mukhtasar. *Vvedenie v Islam.* [An Introduction to Islam] St. Petersburg: Dilia, 2005.

International Crisis Group, "Radical Islam in Central Asia: Responding to Hizb Ut-Tahrir." *ICG Asia Report*, no. 58 (June 30, 2003). Brussels: International Crisis Group, 2003.

———. "Youth in Central Asia: Losing the New Generation." *ICG Asia Report*, no. 66 (October 31, 2003). Brussels: International Crisis Group, 2003.

———. "Central Asia: Islam and the State" *ICG Asia Report*, no. 59 (July 10, 2003). Brussels: International Crisis Group, 2003.

———. "Central Asia: Islamist Mobilisation and Regional Security." *ICG Asia Report*, no. 14 (March 1, 2001). Brussels: International Crisis Group, 2001.

———. "Uzbekistan: The Andijon Uprising." *Asia Briefing*, no. 38 (2005). Bishkek, Brussels, May 25, 2005.

"Iskhan-khan tura ibn Dzzhunaidallak Xvadzha." In *Mizan Az-Zaman.* Eds. Bakhtiyar Babadjanov and Hisao Komatsu. Vol. 2. Tashkent and Tokyo: Institut Vostokovedeniya Akademii Nauk Respubliki Uzbekistan and Islamic Area Studies Project, 2001.

Islam: Na Territorii byvshei Rossiskoi imperii: Entsiklopedicheski slovar. [Islam in the Territories of the Former Russian Empires] Moscow: Izdatelskaya firma, 'Vostochnaya literatura' PAH, 1998.

Islom Dinidagi Okimlar. [Currents of the Islamic Religion] Tashkent: Uzbekiston Respublikasi Oliy va Urta Makhsus Talim Vazirligi, 2006.

Islom, Tarikh va Manaviyat. [Islam, History and Spirituality] Tashkent: Abdulla Kodiriy Nomidagi Khalk Merosi Nashriyoti, 2000.

Islomiy, Khamidkhon. *Sulton ul-Orifin Khoja Ahmad Yassaviy.* Tashkent: Uzbekiston Respublikasi Fanlar Akademijasi "Fan" Nashriyoti, 2005.

Ismoilova, Dilfuzakhon A. *Rol' I Mesto Islama v Obshhestvenno-Politicheskoy i Dukhovnoy Zhizni Narodov Turkestana.* [The Role of Islam in Social-Political and Spiritual Lives of the People of Turkestan] Ph.D. Diss. Akademija Nauk Respubliki Uzbekistan Institut Istorii, 2006.

Johnson, Robert. *Oil, Islam, and Conflict: Central Asia Since 1945.* London: Reaktion Books, 2007.

Johnson, Wallace and Irina Popova, eds. *Central Asian Law: An Historical Overview, A Festschrift for The Ninetieth Birthday of Herbert Franke.* Society for Asian Legal History, University of Kansas. Topeka, Kan.: Jostens, 2004.

Kadirova, Myhisabonu. "Zhitiya Khodzha Akhrar: Opit sistemnovo analiza po rekonstruktsii biografii Khodzha Akhrara i istorii roda Akhraidov." [The Life of Khoja Ahror: The Experience of the System Analysis of the Reconstruction of the Biography of Khoja Ahror and the History of the Role of the Ahrors] Institut Vostokovedeniya imeni Abu Raikhana al-Biruni, Akademiya Nauk Respubliki Uzbekistan. Tashkent: 2007.

Kamp, Marianne. "Pilgrimage and Performance: Uzbek Women and the Imagining of Uzbekistan in the 1920s." *International Journal of Middle East Studies*, vol. 34, no. 2 (May 2002): 263–78.

———. *The New Woman in Uzbekistan: Islam, Modernity, and Unveiling Under Communism.* Seattle: University of Washington Press, 2006.

Kandiyoti, Deniz. "Modernization Without the Market? The Case of the 'Soviet East'" *Economy and Society*, vol. 24, no. 4 (November 1996): 529–42.

———. "Post-Colonianism Compared: Potentials and Limitations in the Middle East and Central Asia." *International Journal of Middle East Studies*, vol. 34, no. 2 (May 2002): 279–97.

Kara, Halim. "Reclaiming Naitional Literary Heritage: The Rehabilitation of Abdurauf Fitrat and Abdulhamid Sulaymon Cholpan in Uzbekistan." *Europe-Asia Studies*, vol. 54, no. 1 (January 2002): 123–42.

Karimov, Eler. "Khozha Ahror." *Obshestvennie Nauki v Uzbekistane* [Social Sciences in Uzbekistan], no. 1. Tashkent, 1990.

Keddie, Nikki R. *Sayyid Jamal Ad-Din: a Political Biography.* Berkeley, Calif.: University of California Press, 1972.

Keddie, Nikki R. and Jamal al-Din Afghani. *An Islamic Response to Imperialism: Political and Religious Writings of Sayyid Jamal Ad-Din "Al-Afghani."* Berkeley, Calif.: University of California Press, 1968.

Kedourie, Elie. *Afghani and 'Abduh; An Essay on Religious Unbelief and Political Activism in Modern Islam.* London: Cass, 1966.

Keller, Shoshana. *To Moscow, Not Mecca: The Soviet Campaign Against Islam in Central Asia, 1917–1941.* London: Praeger, 2001.

Kelsay, John. *Arguing the Just War in Islam.* Cambridge, Mass: Harvard University Press, 2007.

Kendzior, Sarah. "A Reporter Without Borders: Internet Politics and State Violence in Uzbekistan." *Problems of Post-Communism*, vol. 57, no. 1 (January/February 2010): 40–49.

———. "Inventing Akromiya: The Role of Uzbek Propagandists in the Andijon Massacre." *Demokratizatsiya*, vol. 14, no. 4 (Fall 2006): 545–62. www.internationalrelations.com/wbeurasia/Uzbekistan-2007.pdf.

Khakimov, Rafael Stéphane, A. Dudoignon, D. M. Iskhakov, and R. M. Mukhametshin, eds. *Islam v tatarskom mire: istoriia i sovremennost': materialy mezhdunarodnogo simpoziuma, Kazan' 29 aprelya-1 maya 1996g* [Islam in the World of Tatars: History and Modern Times: Materials from an International Symposium in Kazakh April 29–May 1, 1996] Kazan': In-t istorii Akademii Nauk Tatarstana, 1997.

Khakimov, R. S. and R. M. Mukhametshin. "Islam, identichnost' i politika postsovetskom prostranstve: sravnitel'nyi analyz Tsentral'noii Azii i evropeiskoi chasti Rossii." [Islam, Identity and Poltics in the Post-Soviet Space: Comparative Analysis of Central Asia and the European part of Russia] In *Islam, identichnost' i politika v postsovetskom prostranstve: materialy mezhdunarodnoi konferentsii 1–2 apreliya 2004.* [Islam, identity and politics in the Post-Soviet space: Materials from the Kazan international conference, April 1–2, 2004] Kazan': Izd-vo "Master Lain," 2005.

Khalid, Adeeb. *Islam after Communism: Religion and Politics in Central Asia.* Berkeley, Calif.: University of California Press, 2007.

———. "Nation into History: The Origins of National Historiography in Central Asia." In *Devout Societies vs. Impious States?: Transmitting Islamic Learning in Russia, Central Asia and China, Through the Twentieth Century: Proceedings of an International Colloquium, held in Carre Des Sciences, French Ministry of Research, Paris, November 12–13, 2001.* Ed. Stéphane A. Dudoignon. Berlin: Klaus Schwarz Verlag, 2004.

———. "Society and Politics in Bukhara 1868-1920." *Central Asian Survey*, vol. 19, no. 3/4 (2000): 367–96.

———. *The Politics of Muslim Cultural Reform Jadidism in Central Asia.* Berkeley, Calif.: University of California Press, 1998.

Khalidi, Qurban'ali, Allen J. Frank, and Mirkasym Abdulakhatovich Usmanov. *An Islamic Biographical Dictionary of the Eastern Kazakh Steppe, 1770–1912*. Leiden: Brill, 2005.

Khamidov, Alisher. "Officials in Kyrgyzstan Suggest Islamic Militant Group Is Active Gain." Eurasianet. May 13, 2003. www.eurasianet.org/departments/insight/articles/eav051403.shtml.

Khan, Sarfraz. *Muslim Reformist Political Thought: Revivalists, Modernists and Free Will*. London: RoutledgeCurzon, 2003.

Khojiakhmad, Anvar. *Jannat Kaliti* [The Key of Heaven]. Tashkent: Movarounakhr, 1998.

Khudakulov, Abror M. *Prosvetitelskaia Deyatel'nost' Dzhadidov Turkestana*. [The Enlightening Activities of the Jihad of Turkestan] Ph.D. Diss. Institut Istorii Respubliki Uzbekistan, 1995.

Khusnidinov, Zukhriddin, ed. *Islom: Entsiklopediya: A-Kh* [Encylopedia A-Kh] Tashkent: Uzbekistan milliy entsiklopediyasi, 2004.

Khusnidinov, Zukhriddin M. *Uzbekistonda Diniy Bagrikenglikni Mustakhkamlash Omillari Va Muammolari*. [Aspects and Problems of Strengthening Religious Tolerance in Uzbekistan] Ph.D. Diss. Uzbekiston Respublika Vazirlar Makhkamasi Hozoridagi Toshkent Islom Universiteti, 2000.

Kimmage, Daniel. "Analysis: Kazakh Breakthrough On Uzbek Terror Case." Radio Free Europe/Radio Liberty. November 15, 2004. www.rferl.orgcontent/article/1055882.html.

———. "Terror in Uzbekistan: The Aftermath." Radio Free Europe/Liberty Radio Liberty. April 14, 2004. www.rferl.org/content/article/1342160.html.

Klimovitch, Lutsian. *Islam ocherki*. [The Opening of Islam] Moscow: Izdatel'stvo Akademii nauk SSSR, 1962. Association for the Advancement of Central Asian Research. *Journal of Central Asian Studies*, vol. 6, no. 1.

Kocaoglu, Timur. *Turkistanda yenilik hareketleri ve ihtilaller: 1900–1924; Osman Hoca anısına incelemeler*. [Reform movements and revolutions in Turkistan: 1900-1924; Studies in Honor of Osman Khoja] Turquois series, 6. Haarlem: SOTA, 2001.

Komatsu, Hisao. "Dar al-Islam under Russian Rule as Understood by Turkestani Muslim Intellectuals" in *Empire, Islam, and Politics in Central Eurasia*. Ed. Tomohiko Uyama. Sapporo, Japan: Slavic Research Center, Hokkaido University, 2007. http://srch.slav.hokudai.ac.jp/coe21publish/no14_ses/01_komatsu.pdf.

Komilov, Muzaffar. *Movarounakhrda Fikkh Ilmining Rivoji Va Fakih Alouddin al-Samarqandiy*. [The Development of Scientific Work and Fakih Alouddin of Samarkand] Tashkent: Istiqlol, 2006.

Komilov, Majmiddin. *Tasavvur*. [Mysticism] Tashkent: Toshkent Davlat Sharkshunoslik Instituti, 2006.

Kurbanov, Dzhamakul F. *Politicheskaya Bor'ba po Probleme Natsionalnoy Gosudarstvennosti v Period Ustanovlenia Bolshevistskogo Rezhima v Turkestane.* [The Political Fight of the Problem of National Government in the Period of the Establishment of the Bolshevik Regime in Turkestan] Ph.D. Diss. Tashkentski Gosudarstvenniy Institut Vostokovedenia, 1995.

Lamont, James and Farhan Bokhari. "Kabul in Talks with Leading Militants." *Financial Times.* March 23, 2010.

Larson, Christian Nils. *Official Islam in Central Asia: Continuity and Oscillation in the Religio-political Relationship, 1867–2003.* Thesis (M.A.) Bloomington, Ind.: Indiana University, Dept. of Central Eurasian Studies, 2008.

Laruelle, Marlene and Sebastien Peyrouse. *Islam et politique en Ex-URSS.* [Islam and Politics in the Ex-USSR] Paris: IFEAC et l'Harmattan, 2005.

Levi, Scott. "The Ferghana Valley at the Crossroads of World History: The Rise of Khoqand, 1709–1822." *Journal of Global History,* vol. 2, no. 2 (2007): 213–32.

Levi, Scott Cameron and Ron Sela, eds. *Islamic Central Asia: An Anthology of Historical Sources.* Bloomington, Ind.: Indiana University Press, 2010.

Lewis, D. *Rumi. Past and Present, East and West: The Life, Teaching and Poetry of Jalal al-Din Rumi.* Oxford: Oneworld Publications, 2000.

Lewisohn, Leonard, ed. *The Heritage of Sufism, Vol. 1, Classical Persian Sufism from its Origins to Rumi (700–1300).* Oxford: Oneworld Publications, 1999.

———. *The Heritage of Sufism, Vol. 2, The Legacy of Medieval Persian Sufism (1150-1500).* Oxford: Oneworld Publications, 1999.

Lisnyansky, Dina. "Tashayu [Conversion to Shiism] in Central Asia and Russia." *Current Trends in Islamist Ideology,* vol. 8.

Louw, Maria Elisabeth. *Everyday Islam in Post-Soviet Central Asia.* London: Routledge, 2007.

Lubin, Nancy. "Uzbekistan." In *Kazakstan, Kyrgyzstan, Tajikistan, Turkmenistan, and Uzbekistan: Country Studies.* Ed. Glenn E. Curtis. Washington, D.C.: Federal Research Division, Library of Congress, 1996.

Makarov, Dmitri. *Pod'em Radikal'novo Islamizma v Ferganskoi Dolinye v Kontekste Vzaimodeistviya i Inostrannovo Islama.* [The Rise of Islam in the Ferghana Valley in the Context of the Cooperation of 'Local' and 'International' Islam] Moscow: Institut Vostokovedeniya PAH, n.d.

Manaviyat Yulduzlari. [Stars of Spirituality] Tashkent: Abdulla Kodiriy Nomidagi Xalq Merosi Nashriyoti, 2001.

Manz, Beatrice Forbes. *Central Asia in Historical Perspective*. John M. Olin critical issues series. Boulder: Westview Press, 1994.

———. "The Development and Meaning of Chaghatay Identity." In *Muslims in Central Asia: Expressions of Identity and Change*. Ed. Ann Gross. Durham and London: Duke University Press, 1992.

———. *Varieties of Religious Authority and Practice in Central Asia*. Washington, D.C.: NCEEER, National Council for Eurasian and East European Research, 1999.

Martin, Terry. *The Affirmative Action Empire: Nations and Nationalism in the Soviet Union, 1923–1939*. The Wilder House Series in Politics, History, and Culture. Ithaca: Cornell University Press, 2001.

Masanov, N. E., Zh. B. Abylkhozhin, I. V. Erofeeva, A. H. Alekseenko, and G. S. Baratova. *Istoriya Kazakshtana: Narody i Kul'tury*. [History of Kazakhstan: Its Peoples and Culture] Almaty, Kazakhstan: Daik-Press, 2001.

McChesney, R. D. *Central Asia: Foundations of Change*. Princeton, N.J.: Darwin Press, Inc., 1996.

McGlinchey, Eric M. "Divided Faith: Trapped between State and Islam in Uzbekistan." In *Everyday Life in Central Asia: Past and Present*. Eds. Jeff Sahadeo and Russell G. Zanca. Bloomington Ind.: Indiana University Press, 2007.

Megoran, Nick. "The Bell Tolls for Another US-Based NGO in Uzbekistan." Eurasianet. July 10, 2006. www.eurasianet.org/departments/civilsociety/articles/eav071106.shtml.

Melvin, Neil. *Uzbekistan: Transition to Authoritarianism on the Silk Road*. Amsterdam: Overseas Publishers Association, 2000.

Mezhnatsionalnie i Mezhkonfessionalnie Otnoshenia. [Inter-Ethnic and Inter-Religious Relations] Tashkent: Fond Regionalnoi Politiki Respubliki Uzbekistan, 2006.

Miliband, S. D. *Biobibliograficheskii Slovar' Otechestvennikh Vostokovedov s 1917 g. Book 1, A-L*. [The Bibliographic Dictionary of the Domestic Orientalists from 1917] Moscow: Nauka, 1995.

Miloslavskiiy, G. V. and L. V. Negriya, eds. *Islam: entsiklopedicheskii slovar'* [Islam: Encyclopedic Dictionary] Moscow: Nauka, 1991.

Mirzoev, A. M. and M. I. Zand. *Katalog Vostochnykh Rukopisei Akademii Nauk Tadzhiskhoy SSR. Vol. IV*. [The Catalog of Eastern Handwritten Works of the Academy of Science the Tajik USSR] Akademia Nauk Tadzhikistana, Otdel Vostkovedenia i Pis'mennogo Naslediya. Dushanbe: Donish, 1970.

———. *Katalog Vostochnykh Rukopisei Akademii Nauk Tadzhikskoy SSR. Vol. V*. [The Catalog of Eastern Handwritten Works of the Science Academy of the Tajik USSR] Akademia Nauk Tadzhikistana, Odtel Vostkovedenia i Pis'mennogo Nasledija. Dushanbe: Donish, 1970.

Moazzam, Anwar. *Jamal al-Din al-Afghani: A Muslim Intellectual*. New Dehli: Concept Publishing Company, 1984.

Montgomery, David W. "Namaz, Wishing Tress, and Vodka: The Diversity of Everyday Religious Life in Central Asia." In *Everyday Life in Central Asia: Past and Present*. Eds. Jeff Sahadeo and Russell G. Zanca. Bloomington: Indiana University Press, 2007.

Moyne, John A. *Rumi and the Sufi Tradition*. Costa Mesa, Calif.: Mazda, 2009.

Muallifi, Akhmad Lutfijy. *Saodat Asri Qissalari*. [Stories of Centuries of Happiness] Tashkent: Sharq Yulduzi, 2006.

Mukhammad Iunus Khvadzha b. Makhammad Amin-Khvadzha (Ta'ib). *Tukhfa-yi Ta'ib*. Eds. Bakhtiyar Babadjanov, Sh. Kh. Bakhidov, and Hisao Komatsu. Vol. 6. Tashkent and Tokyo: Institut Vostokovedeniya Akademii Nauk Respubliki Uzbekistan and Islamic Area Studies Project, 2002.

Muminov, Ashirbek. "Fundamentalist Challenges to Local Islamic Traditions in Soviet and Post-Soviet Central Asia." In *Empire, Islam, and Politics in Central Eurasia*. Ed. Tomohiko Uyama. Sapporo, Japan: Slavic Research Center, Hokkaido University, 2007.

——. *Xanafiy Ulamolarning Markaziy Movarounnakhr Shahrlari Xayotida Tutgan Urni Va Roli*. [Hanafi Clerics' Place and Role Within Life of the Central Cities of Mawarannahr] Thesis (Ph.D.)— Uzbekiston Respublikasi Vazirlar Makhkamasi Hozirigi Toshkent Islom Universiteti, 2003.

Munavvarov, Zohidullo and Reinhard Krumm. *Gosudarstvo i religiia v stranakh s musul'manskim naseleniem*. [Government and Religion in the Countries with Muslim Populations] Tashkent: Respublikanskii nauchno-prosvetitel'skii tsentr Imama Bukhari, 2004.

Mydans, Seth. "Uzbeks' Anger at Rulers Boils Over." *New York Times*. April 8, 2004. www.nytimes.com/2004/04/08/world/uzbeks-anger-at-rulers-boils-over.html?pagewanted=all&src=pm.

——. "3rd Day of Violence Claims 23 Lives in Uzbekistan." *New York Times*. March 31, 2004. www.nytimes.com/2004/03/31/world/3rd-day-of-violence-claims-23-lives-in-uzbekistan.html.

Nalle, David. "Change and Continuity in Central Asia." *Middle East Journal*, vol. 43, no. 4 (Autumn 1989): 590–96.

National Consortium for the Study of Terrorism and Responses to Terrorism, "Background Report: On the Fifth Anniversary of the 7/7 London Transit Attack." www.start.umd.edu/start/announcements/July07_LondonMetroBombing_2010.pdf.

National Counterterrorism Center. "Islamic Jihad Union (IJU)." www.nctc.gov/site/groups/iju.html.

Naumkin, Vitaly V. *Militant Islam in Central Asia: The Case of the Islamic Movement of Uzbekistan*. Berkeley, Calif.: University of California, Berkeley, 2003.

———. *Radical Islam in Central Asia: Between Pen and Rifle.* Lanham Md.: Rowman & Littlefield, 2005.

———. "Teoriya mezhdunarodnikh otnosheenii i mirovoi politiki. Islamism, etnichnost' i konflikti: O roli simbolicheskoi politiki." [Theory of International Relations and World Politics. Islamism, Ethnicity and Conflicts: On the Roles of Symbolic Politics] *Mezhdunarodnikh otnosheniya i mirovaya politika*, no. 1 (2009).

Nichol, Jim. "Central Asia: Regional Developments and Implications for U.S. Interests." Congressional Research Service, 7-5700. October 12, 2011. www.fas.org/sgp/crs/row/RL33458.pdf.

Northrop, Douglas. *Veiled Empire: Gender and Power in Stalinist Central Asia.* Ithaca and London: Cornell University Press, 2004.

Nursafardiy, Shaikh Sufij-Tabib. *Sufiylik Nursafardiya Talkinida.* [Sufi Nursafardiya in Talkin] Tashkent, 2006.

Obidov, Rakhmatulokh Qori. *Quron Mavzularining Manaviy Tarikhi.* [The History of Ethical Topics of the Quran] Tashkent: Toshkent Islom Universiteti Nashriyot-Matbaa Birlashmasi, 2006.

Olcott, Martha Brill. "A Face of Islam: Muhammad Sodiq Muhammad Yusuf." Carnegie Paper 82. Washington, D.C.: Carnegie Endowment for International Peace, 2007.

———. "Central Asia on Its Own." *Journal of Democracy*, vol. 4, no. 1 (January 1993): 92–103.

———. "Roots of Radical Islam in Central Asia." Carnegie Paper 77. Washington, D.C.: Carnegie Endowment for International Peace, 2007.

———. "Sufism in Central Asia: A Force for Moderation or a Cause of Politicalization?" Carnegie Paper 84. Washington, D.C.: Carnegie Endowment for International Peace, 2007. www.carnegieendowment.org/files/cp84_olcott_final2.pdf.

———. *The Kazakhs.* Second Edition. Stanford: Hoover Institution Press, Stanford University Press, 1995.

———. "Yuri Andropov and the 'National Question'." *Soviet Studies*, vol. 37, no. 1 (January 1985): 103–117.

Olcott, Martha Brill and Bakhtiyar Babadjanov. "The Terrorist Notebooks." *Foreign Policy*, 135, March/April 2003. Washington, D.C.: Carnegie Endowment for International Peace, 2003.

Olcott, Martha Brill and Diora Ziyaeva. "Islam in Uzbekistan: Religious Education and State Ideology." Carnegie Paper 91. Washington, DC: Carnegie Endowment for International Peace, 2008.

Ortikova, Dilbar. *Real'nyy mneniya nravstvennye tsennosti Islama v otnoshenii k zhenshchine.* [The Factual and Moral Value of Islam in Relation to Women] Ph.D. Diss. Tashkent: Tashkentskiy Gosudarstvennyy Universitet, 1993.

Peyrouse, Sebastien. "The Rise of Political Islam in Soviet Central Asia." *Current Trends in Islamist Ideology*, vol. 5. Washington, D.C: Hudson Institute, 2007.

Poliakov, Sergeii Petrovich and Martha Brill Olcott. *Everyday Islam: Religion and Tradition in Rural Central Asia*. Armonk, N.Y.: M.E. Sharpe, 1992.

Privratsky, Bruce. *Muslim Turkistan, Kazan Religion and Collective Memory*. Surrey, UK: Curzon Press, 2001.

Prozorov, S. M. *Islam na territorii byvsheii Rossiiskoi imperii: entsiklopedicheskii slovar'*. [Islam in the Territories of the Former Russian Empire: An Encyclopedic Dictionary] First Edition. Moskva: Vostochnaya literatura, 1998.

———. *Islam na territorii byvsheii Rossiiskoi imperii: entsiklopedicheskii slovar'*. [Islam in the Territories of the Former Russian Empire: An Encyclopedic Dictionary] Second Edition. Moskva: Vostochnaya literatura, 1999.

Pyatibratova, Alla. "Kyrgyz Mufti Fends Off Extremism Charges: Leading Muslim Leader Denies Claims that He's a Key Figure in Hizb ut-Tahrir Movement." Institute for War & Peace Reporting. February 21, 2005. http://iwpr.net/report-news/kyrgyz-mufti-fends-extremism-charges.

Quttb, Sayyid and M. A. Salahi. *In the Shade of the Qur'an*. London: MWH London Publishers, 1979.

Rasanayagam, Johan. *Islam in Post-Soviet Uzbekistan: The Morality of Experience*. New York: Cambridge University Press, 2011.

Rashid, Ahmed. *Jihad: The Rise of Militant Islam in Central Asia*. New Haven: Yale University Press, 2002.

Reichmuth, Stefan. "The Interplay of Local Developments and Transnational Relations in the Islamic World: Perceptions and Perspectives." In *Muslim Culture in Russia and Central Asia from the 18th to the Early 20th Centuries*. Eds. Anke von Kugelgen, Michael Kemper, and Allen J. Frank. *Inter-Regional and Inter-Ethnic Tensions*, vol. 2: 6–37. Berlin: Klaus Schwarz Verlag, 1998.

Rizaev, Shukhrat. *Jadid Dramasi*. [The Drama of Jadid] Tashkent: Sharq, 1997.

Roi, Yaacov. *Islam in the CIS: A Threat to Stability?* London: Royal Institute of International Affairs, Russia and Eurasia Programme, 2001.

———. *Islam in the Soviet Union*. New York: Columbia University Press, 2000.

Rorlich, Azade-Ayse. *The Volga Tatars: A Profile in National Resilience*. Stanford, Calif.: Hoover Institution Press, Stanford University, 1986.

Rotar, Igor. "Kyrgyzstan: Imam's Killing Seen as Attack on Independent Islam." Forum 18 News Service. August 24, 2006. www.forum18.org/Archive.php?article_id=835.

———. "The Islamic Movement of Uzbekistan: A Resurgent IMU?" *Terrorism Monitor*, vol. 1, no. 8 (May 2005). Washington, D.C.: Jamestown Foundation, 2005.

———. "Uzbekistan: Mahalla and Mullah Block Jehovah's Witness Registration." Forum 18 News Service. December 1, 2005. www.forum18.org/Archive.php?article_id=698.

———. "Uzbekistan: Exiled Imam Denies Links to Arrested Tashkent Muslims." Forum 18 News Service. April 12, 2006. www.forum18.org/Archive.php?article_id=758.

———. "Tajikistan Brands "Bayat" A Terrorist, Religious, Extremist, Organization." Eurasia Daily. http://eurasiadaily.org/article.php?article_id=2370419.

Roy, Olivier. *Globalized Islam: The Search for a New Ummah*. New York: Columbia University Press, 2004.

Sadr Ziyaa', Sharif Jan Makhdum, R. Shukurov, M. Shukurov, and Edward Allworth. *The Personal History of a Bukharan Intellectual: The Diary of Muhammad Sharif-I Sadr-I Ziya*. Brill's Inner Asian Library, vol. 9. Leiden: Brill, 2004.

Sageman, Marc. *Understanding Terror Networks*. Philadelphia: University of Pennsylvania Press, 2004.

Saidazimova, Gulnoza. "Uzbekistan: Dissident Imam Reaches Safety After Eight Years in Hiding." Radio Free Europe/Radio Liberty. March 16, 2006. www.rferl.org/content/article/1066744.html.

Sanderson, Thomas M., Daniel Kimmage, and David A. Gordon. "From the Ferghana Valley to South Waziristan: The Evolving Threat of Central Asian Jihadists." Washington, D.C.: Center for Strategic and International Studies. March 2010. http://csis.org/files/publication/100324_Sanderson_FerghanaValley_WEB_0.pdf.

Saralaeva, Leila. "Kyrgyz Passport Scam: Corruption Within Passport System May Jeopardise Reforms Aimed at Curbing Counterfeit Travel Document Trade." Institute for War and Peace Reporting. February 21, 2005. http://iwpr.net/report-news/kyrgyz-passport-scam.

Sardar, Zianddin and Merryl Wyn Davies. *No Nonsense Guide to Islam*. Oxford: New Internationalist Press, 2007.

Sartori, Paolo. "When a Mufti Turned Islamism into Political Pragmatism: Sadreddin-Khan and the Struggle for an Independent Turkestan." *Cahiers d'Asie centrale*, no. 15/16 (2007): 118–39. http://asiecentrale.revues.org/index61.html.

Schimmel, Annemarie. *Mystical Dimensions of Islam*. Chapel Hill: The University of North Carolina Press, 1975.

Schneider-Deters, Winfried and Zahidulla Munavvarov. *Islam i svetskoe gosudarstvo*. [Islam and the Secular State] Tashkent: International Fund of al-Imam al-Bukhari, 2003.

Schoeberlein, John. "Islam in the Ferghana Valley: Challenges for New States." In *Islam in Politics in Russia and Central Asia: Early Eighteenth to Late Twentieth Centuries*. Eds. Stéphane A. Dudoignon and Hisao Komatsu. Islamic Area Studies, vol. 3: 323–40. London: Kegan Paul, 2001.

Semenov, A. A. *Sobranie Vostochnykh Rukopisey Akademii Nauk Uzbekskoy SSR. Vol. II.* [The Collection of Eastern Handwritten Works of the Uzbek SSR's Academy of Science] Akademia Nauk Uzbekskoy SSSR, Institut Vostkovedenia. Tashkent: Izdatel'stvo Akademii Nauk USSR, 1954.

———. *Sobranie Vostochnykh Rukopisey Akademii Nauk Uzbekskoy SSR. Vol. III.* [The Collection of Eastern Handwritten Works of the Uzbek SSR's Academy of Sciences] Akademia Nauk Uzbekskoy SSR, Institut Vostkovedenia. Tashkent: Izdatel'stvo Akademii Nauk USSR, 1955.

———. *Sobranie Vostochnykh Rukopisey Akademii Nauk Uzbekskoy SSR. Vol. IV.* [The Collection of Eastern Handwritten Works of the Uzbek SSR's Academy of Sciences] Akademia Nauk Uzbekskoy SSR, Institut Vostkovedenia. Tashkent: Izdatel'stvo Akademii Nauk USSR, 1957.

———. *Sobranie Vostochnykh Rukopisey Akademii Nauk Uzbekskoy SSR. Vol. VII.* [The Collection of Eastern Handwritten Works of the Uzbek SSR's Academy of Science] Akademia Nauk Uzbekskoy SSR, Institut Vostkovedenia. Tashkent: Izdatel'stvo Akademii Nauk USSR, 1964.

———. *Sobranie Vostochnykh Rukopisey Akademii Nauk Uzbekskoy SSR. Vol. VIII.* [The Collection of Eastern Handwritten Works of the Uzbek SSR's Academy of Science] Akademia Nauk Uzbekskoy SSR, Institut Vostkovedenia. Tashkent: Izdatel'stvo Akademii Nauk USSR, 1967.

Shaykh Hakim. *Moinuddin Chishti. Sufiyskoe Tselitel'stvo.* [The Book of Sufi Healing] Moscow: Izdatelstvo Dilia, 2004.

Siddique, Abubakar. "IMU's Evolution Branches Back To Central Asia." Eurasianet. December 6, 2010. www.eurasianet.org/node/62514.

Sovremennye Etnokulturnye Protsessy v Makhallyakh Tashkenta. [Contemporary Ethnocultural Processes in the Neighborhoods of Tashkent] Tashkent: Izdatelstvo Fan Akademii Nauk Respubliki Uzbekistan, 2005.

Splidsboel-Hansen, Flemming."The Official Russian Concept of Contemporary Central Asian Islam: The Security Dimension." *Europe-Asia Studies*, vol. 49, no. 8 (1997).

Starr, S. Frederick, Baktybek Beshimov, Inomjon I. Bobokulov, and P. D. Shozimov. *Ferghana Valley: The Heart of Central Asia*. Armonk, N.Y.: M.E. Sharpe, 2011.

Strachota, Kryzsztof and Maciej Falkowski. *Jihad vs. The New Great Game*. Warsaw, Poland: Center for European Studies, 2010.

Subhan, John A. *Sufism: Ego Svyatie i Svyatini.* [Sufism: Its Saints and Shrines] Moscow: Izdatelstvo Dilia, 2005.

Subtelny, Maria Eva. "The Cult of Holy Places: Religious Practices Among Soviet Muslims" *Middle East Journal*, vol. 43, no. 4 (Autumn 1989).

Sujman, Makhmat. *Musulmoning Chuntak Kitobi.* [A Muslim's Pocket Book] Ankara: Dienat Ishlari Boshkarmasi, 1995.

"Tajikistan: Influential Islamic Politician Remembered." Radio Free Europe/Radio Liberty. August 10, 2006. www.rferl.org/content/article/1070492.html.

Ta'lim Tizimi. [The Educational System] Tashkent: Uzbekiston musulmonari idorasi, 2003.

Tishkov, Valery. *Ethnicity, Nationalism, and Conflict in and After the Soviet Union.* London: Sage Publications, 1997.

Togan, Isenbike. "The Khafi, Jahri Controversy in Central Asia Revisted." In *Naqshbandis in Western and Central Asia: Change and Continuity.* Ed. Elisabeth Ozdalga. Vol. 9: 17–45. Istanbul: Swedish Research Institute in Istanbul Transactions, 1999.

Turkestanskiy literaturnyy sbornik' vy pol'zy prokazhennykh'. [A Collection of Turkestan's Literature, Published to Support Leporosy] Saint Petersburg: Turkestanskogo Okruzhango Upravleniya Rossiyskago Obshchestva Krasnago Kresta, 1900.

United States High Commissioner for Refugees. "After Andijan: Tensions Mount in Central Asia." Refugees, no. 143, issue 2 (2006).

———. *International Protection Considerations Regarding Asylum-Seekers and Refugees from the Republic of Uzbekistan.* Geneva: United Nations High Commissioner for Refugees, March 2006.

U.S. Department of State, Bureau of Democracy, Human Rights, and Labor. "2000 Annual Report on International Freedom: Uzbekistan." www.state.gov./www/global/human_rights/irf/irf_rpt/irf_uzbekist.html.

U.S. Department of State, Office of Research. Opinion Analysis: "Central Asians Differ on Islam's Political Role, but Agree on a Secular State." Washington, D.C.: U.S. Department of State, 2000.

U.S. Department of State. "2010 Human Rights Report: Uzbekistan." April 8, 2011. www.state.gov/documents/organization/160482.pdf.

———. "Uzbekistan: International Religious Freedom Report 2007." www.state.gov/g/drl/rls/irf/2007/90237.htm.

U.S. Department of the Treasury."Treasury Designates Leadership of the IJU Terrorist Group." U.S. Department of the Treasury Press Center. June 18, 2008. www.treasury.gov/press-center/press-releases/Pages/hp1035.aspx.

Usmankhodzhaev, Amirsaidkhan. *Zhizn muftiev Babakhanovykh: sluzhenie vozrozhdeniiu Islama v Sovetskom Soiuze.* [Lives of the Muftis of the Babakhanov Family: Serving the Revival of Islam in the Soviet Union] Moscow: Medina Publishing, 2008.

Uyama, Tomohiko. "Empire, Islam, and Politics in Central Eurasia." *Slavic Eurasian Studies*, no. 14. Sapporo: Slavic Research Center, Hokkaido University, 2007.

"Uzbekistan: Stifled Democracy, Human Rights in Decline." Hearing before the Commission on Security and Cooperation in Europe, One Hundred and Eighth Congress, Second Session. June 24, 2004. Washington, D.C.: U.S. Government Printing Office, 2004.

"Uzbeks Shut Religious Bookstores." Eurasianet. March 30, 2011. www.eurasianet.org/node/63189.

Vatikiotis, P. J. "Muhammed Abduh and the Quest for a Muslim Humanism." *Arabica*, no. 1 (January 1957): 55–72.

Venturi, Franco. *Roots of Revolution: A History of the Populist and Socialist Movements in Nineteenth Century Russia.* Translated from the Italian by Francis Haskell. New York: Grosset & Dunlap, 1966.

"Visit to Uzbekistan of the Exiled Mufti." Eurasianet. August 17, 2004. www.eurasianet.org/resource/uzbekistan/press_digest/digest2.1.shtml.

Vostokovednye Fondy Krupneyshikh Bibliotek Sovetskogo Soyuza: Stat'i i Soobshheniya. [The Eastern Fund of the Largest Library of the Soviet Union] Akademia Nauk SSSR Institut Narodov Aziil. Moscow: Izdatel'stvo Vostochnoy Literatury, 1963.

Whitlock, Monica. "After Andijan: Tensions Mount in Central Asia." *Refugees*, no. 143, issue 2, 2006.

———. *Land Beyond the River: The Untold Story of Central Asia.* New York: Thomas Dunne Books, 2003.

Wigen, Einar. "Islamic Jihad Union: al-Qaida's Key to the Turkic World?" Norwegian Defence Research Establishment (FFI). February 23, 2009. www.ffi.no/no/Rapporter/09-00687.pdf.

Wilcox, Lynn. *Sufizm i psikhologiya.* [Sufism and Psychology] Moscow and St. Petersburg: Dilya, 2005.

Witter, David. "Uzbek Militancy in Pakistan's Tribal Region." Institute for the Study of War. January 27, 2011. www.understandingwar.org/files/BackgrounderIMU_web.pdf.

Woehrlin, William. *F. Chernyshevskii: The Man and the Journalist.* Cambridge, Mass.: Harvard University Press, 1971.

Yakubov, Oleg. *The Pack of Wolves: The Blood Trail of Terror: A Political Detective Story.* Moscow: Veche Publishers, 2000.

Yalcin, Resul. *The Rebirth of Uzbekistan: Politics, Economy, and Society in the Post-Soviet Area.* Reading, UK: Garnet Publishing Ltd., 2002.

Yilmaz, Ihsan. "Predicaments and Prospects in Uzbek Islamism: A Critical Comparison with the Turkish Case." Ankara, Turkey: International Strategic Research Orgnanization, 2008.

Yurchak, Alexei. *Everything Was Forever, Until It Was No More: The Last Soviet Generation.* Information Series. Princeton, N.J. and Oxford, UK: Princeton University Press, 2006.

Zahad, Mariam Abou and Olivier Roy. *Islamist Networks: The Afghan-Pakistan Connection.* Translated from the French by John King. New York, Paris: Columbia University Press in association with Centre d'Etudes et de Recherches International, 2004.

Zemtsov, Ilya. *Chernenko, the Last Bolshevik: The Soviet Union on the Eve of Perestroika.* New Brunswick, N.J.: Transaction Publishers, 1989.

Zenkovsky, Serge Alexander. *Pan-Turkism and Islam in Russia.* Cambridge, Mass.: Harvard University Press, 1967.

Zhenshchina i Obshhestvo. [Women and Society] Tashkent: Fond Regionalnoy Politiki Respubliki Uzbekistan, 2006.

Zhuraevich, Minavarov Sobirzhon. *Idei Svobodomysliya v Tvorchestve Uzbekskikh Prosvetiteli Kontsa XIX i Nachala XX Vekov.* [The Idea of Free-Thinking in the Creative Works of Uzbek Enlightening Figures from the End of the Nineteenth to the Beginning of the Twentieth Century] Tashkent: Tashkentskii Gosudarstvenii Universitet, 1998.

Zvezda Vostoka. *Al'manax.* [Almanacs] 2002.

INDEX

Abbasid Empire, 2
Abd Allah (qori), 101
Abd as-Samad (Mullah), 84
Abduh, Muhammad, 11, 13, 45
Abdukadir (Margiloniy), 257, 267
Abdullaev, Mukhtarkhon, 119, 200, 219
Abdurahmonjon, Eshon, 95
Abdurashid domla (Qozi), 93
Abdurashidkhanov, Munavvar qori, 47, 53
Abduvali (qori)
    Andijan radicals and, 231–234
    beliefs of, 224
    break from Hanafi tradition, 92, 103
    disappearance of, 8, 198, 223, 245, 289
    film of, 275, 277, 298
    hujra of, 104–105, 235
    mufti quest, 115–117
    students and study groups of, 15, 17
    support of Tajik fighters, 21
adat (customary law), 27, 31
Adolat, 73, 192, 239–241, 242, 250
al-Afghani, (Sayyid) Jamal ud-Din ("al-Afghani"), 11, 132

Ahl-i Hadith, 13, 81–84
Ahl-i Quran, 84, 86, 88, 102, 273, 275
Ahmadjon, (Hojji) Makhdum, 94–95, 96–97, 99–100
Ahror Vali (Khoja), Ubaydalla, 4, 31
Akramiya movement
    Andijan unrest and, 22–23, 83, 288
    anti-religious legislation and, 203
    as "extremist" organization, 192, 312
    Muhammad Sodiq opposition to, 122, 126
Akramov, Rahimjon, 248, 255–256
alem al-ulama (learned of the learned), 34
Alim Khan, (Emir) Muhammad, 22
Aloutdinov, Nodirkhon (domla) [Nodirkhon domla], 89–90
Al-Qaeda, 1, 5, 254, 283, 284, 287, 290
Andijan unrest (May 2005), 22–23, 83, 122, 288, 293–294
Andijan Uprising of 1898, 41, 195–196, 269
Andropov, Yuri, 69, 80
Asadulloh, Eshon (Shaykh), 99
Astrakhanid dynasty, 4
Awadi, Fahmi, 15

Ayni, Sadriddin, 94

Babadjanov, Bakhtiyar, 31–36, 42–43, 83–84, 86, 87, 89, 93, 95, 96, 101, 104, 116, 120–121, 132, 195–196, 207–212, 218–219, 232–234, 236, 241, 243, 246, 255, 258–259, 263
Bahadirov, Royiq, 207
Baisun (Boysun), 136, 137–139, 142–149
Bakhromov, (Mufti) Abdurashid (qori), 116, 119, 235, 316
al-Banna, Hassan, 14, 87, 103
Barnaev, Abdulahad, 243, 244–245
Basmachi Movement, 13, 39, 53, 56, 142, 220
Behbudi, Mahmud (Khoja), 47, 49
Bek, Madamin, 39, 53
Berke Khan, 3
Bobo, Abd ar-Rahmanjon (Makhdum vi-Andaki) [Makhdum Bobo vi-Andaki], 95
Bobokhon, Eshon Ibn Abdulmajidkhon (Mufti), 14, 61, 72, 85–88, 109
Bobokhon, Ziyauddin (Mufti), 66, 79, 85–89, 93
Bobokhonov, Shamsuddin (Mufti), 72, 85, 105, 110, 115, 117, 235
Bolshevik Revolution, 51–57
Brezhnev, Leonid, 15, 62, 67, 148–153
Bukhara, Emirate of, 9, 10, 34, 51, 136, 143
Bukharan People's Republic, 54, 56
al-Bukhari, (Khoja) Abu Abdullah Muhammad ibn Ismail ibn Ibrahim. *See* Khoja Ismail al-Bukhari
al-Bukhari, Said Ahmad Vali Kulakduz Khoja, 215
al-Buti, Muhammad Said Ramadan, 128, 132

"The Call," 22, 269
Chernenko, Konstantin, 80
Chingis Khan, 34

Dalilov, Saifullo, 256
dar al-harb (*Dar al-kufr*), 4, 39, 52
dar al-Islam, 4, 12, 35, 38–39, 41, 52
davat, 23, 76, 129, 208, 209, 236, 238, 259
DMU, 13
Dukchi Ishan, 41–44, 196, 231

Fahriddinov, Ruhiddin, 237, 292
Faqiri (Ismail bin Ibrahim), 98–99, 100
al-Farabi, Abu Nasr Muhammad, 2
Ferghana Valley, 17, 19, 21, 38–43, 83–84, 114, 116–118, 135–136, 139, 140–141, 161–162, 168, 172–173, 177, 179, 199, 217, 255

Gafurov, Abdurauf, 243–244
Gafurov, Bobojon, 93
Gasprinski, Ismail, 46–49
Ghijduvani, Abd al-Khaliq, 30, 195
Ghofur qori, 88
Gorbachev, Mikhail, 18, 69–71, 78, 80, 111, 153–154
Gulen, Fethullah, 220. *See also* Nurchi (Gulen) movement
Gumbaz mosque, 59, 244–245

Hadiths and Life (Muhammad Sodiq), 126, 131
Hakimjon qori. *See* Abdulhakim Vosiev
Hamadani, (Hazrat) Abu Yaqub Yusuf [Khoja Yusuf Hamadani], 4, 30
Hanafi *mazhab*, 1–2, 305

Hanafi traditionalism, 90–95
Hazrat Bobo Muhammad, 94, 99
Hazrat Hasan. *See* Ponomarev, (Hazrat) Hasan Akhmadajanovich (al-Kizilajari)
Hindustani, Muhammadjon Rustamov
    Hanafi "traditionalism" and, 14, 90–95
    influence of, 8, 15, 92–93, 102
    Rahmatulla-alloma and, 224–225
    Salim Hajji and, 86
    student views of, 103
    Ziyauddin Bobokhon and, 79
Hizb ut-Tahrir, 93, 122, 124, 129, 131, 192, 202, 291, 299, 302, 306, 312
Homidov, Ayubkhon, 104
"Hujum" campaign, 57
Husayniya Sufi movement, 100–101
Husniddinov, Zuhriddin, 211

Ibrahim (Hazrat), 79, 99, 101, 307
Ikramov, Akmal, 145, 154
Imam Ismail al-Bukhari Islamic Institute (Tashkent), 66
al-Islahiyah, 45
Islamic "extremism," 1, 6, 131, 189
    Adolat and, 239–241
    Gulen schools and, 220
    Uzbek definition/criminalization of, 192–193, 201, 203, 239
Islamic fundamentalism, 14, 201, 210, 229, 230, 307
Islamic Jihad Union (IJU), 193, 203, 287, 290
Islamic Movement of Uzbekistan (IMU) (*Uzbekiston islomiy haraqati*), 5, 17, 22, 53, 73, 193, 200, 203, 227, 234, 251, 253–285
    end of, 283–285

NATO bombing of camps, 287
oath, 278–281
propaganda materials, 268–272
reasons for joining, 272–278
suicide missions, 281–283
training facilities, 258–269
Turkey and, 258
Islamic radicalism, 6, 16, 20–21, 239–251.
    See also "Wahhabis"
    Abduvali qori and Andijan radicals, 231–234
    Adolat, 239–241
    Akramiya movement and, 288
    anti-religious policies and, 199–200
    de-secularization and, 134
    in Ferghana Valley, 117–119
    Hakimjon qori and, 102–105, 292
    Hanafi groups and, 309
    Hindustani *versus* young radicals, 227–231
    Hizb ut-Tahrir and, 299
    ideological divides and, 114–115
    Karimov and, 247
    Muhammad Sodiq and, 122–123
    in Namangan, 239–247
    Namangan meeting, 247–251
    Obidkhon qori and, 234–239
    politicization of Islam and, 311–312
    repression and, 311
    Sufism as counterbalance to, 309
    Tashkent Islamic University and, 210–211
    Umarkhon domla and, 241–243
Islamic Renaissance Party (IRP) [Tajikistan], 21, 72, 92, 112, 245, 250, 253
Islamic Revival Party (*Islom uygonish partiyasi*) [Uzbekistan], 192

Islamic unification message, 131–134
Islom adolati, 240–241, 242, 244, 246, 248–249
Islom lashkarlari, 192, 200, 239–240, 241, 247, 250
Islom militsiyasi, 240
Ixtiloflar haqida (Muhammad Sodiq), 15

Jadid movement (*Usul-isautiyya jadidiyya* or *Usul-u jadid*), 11, 45, 84
Jahriya, 101
Jamal, (Khoja) Ishan, 84
Jamoas, 77, 236–237, 292
Jihadist movements, 5, 284, 287, 320
Jome (Gumbaz) Mosque (Namangan), 59

Kamalov, (Imam) Muhammad Rafik, 293, 295, 299
Kamalov, Sodikjon (qori) [Kamalludin], 19, 295–296, 299
Karimov, Islam, 5–7, 73–74
    Andijan uprising and, 294
    eventual successor to, 315
    IMU and, 253, 270–272
    insular nature of policies of, 319
    Islamic Jihad Union and, 290
    Islamic radicals and, 227
    Muhammad Sodiq and, 110, 185
    Namangan meeting, 247–250
    national ideology, 193, 206
    policies toward Islam, 41, 175, 194, 199–200, 243–244, 308–310
    terrorist attacks, response to, 202
    Uzbek clashes with Kyrgyzstan and, 19–20, 23–24
Karomatov, Hamidulla, 211

Kasymov, Abdulatif (Andijoni), 93
Kasymov, Muhammad Sodiq (Andijoni), 92
Khakimdjanov, (Mullah) Yunus (qori) [Yunus qori], 84
Khamidov, Khayrullo, 123
Khattab, 256
ibn al-Khattab, Umar Khimmatzoda, Muhammad-Sharif, 19
Khodjaev, Faizulla, 97, 145, 154
Khoja Ismail al-Bukhari, 139, 164
Khrushchev, Nikita, 15, 62, 66–67, 93, 148
Kimsanbai-azhi, 93
Kokand Autonomy government, 12–13
al-Kubra, Najm ad-Din, 3, 29
Kubrawiya Sufi movement, 29
Kuva, 140–141, 142, 143, 146–147, 154

Mangit dynasty, 4, 34
Mansur, Alauddin, 273
Mansurov, Abdulaziz, 105, 202
Marifat va manaviyat (enlightenment and spirituality), 207
al-Marjani, Shihab ad-Din, 84
al-Maturidi (Imam) Muhammad Abu Mansur, 195
Maududi, Sayyid Abul Ala, 15, 16, 87, 103, 228
mazhab, 49, 131, 133
Mir-i Arab Madrasa (Bukhara), 14, 61, 88–89, 109, 241
Mirsaidov, Shukrullo, 243
Mirzaev, Abduvali (qori). *See* Abduvali (qori)
Muhammad Ali (domulla) (Andijani), 109
Muhammad Sadik Mamyusuf [or Mamayusupov]. *See* Muhammad Sodiq Muhammad Yusuf (Sheikh)

Muhammad Sodiq Muhammad Yusuf
    (Sheikh), 8, 15, 19, 21, 67, 72, 74, 75,
    88, 92, 107–134
  biographical sketch, 109–110
  Islamic unification message, 131–134
  major works of, 125–131
  as *mufti*, 110–119
  as speaker and writer, 119–124
Mujaddidiya, 33, 39, 95, 99
Abd as-Samad (Mullah), 84
ibn Musa, (Hazrat) Bobo Muhammad
    (al-Khorazmi). *See* Hazrat Bobo
    Muhammad
Muslim Brotherhood, 15, 133, 192, 209
"Muslimness," (*musulmonchilik*) 154–158

al-Kubra, Najm ad-Din, 3, 27, 29
Namangani, Juma [Juma Khojaev], 17, 200,
    224, 227, 246, 254, 257, 259, 267,
    280, 284, 285, 287
Namangan meeting, 247–251
namaz, 83, 113, 146, 147, 148, 151, 155, 156,
    158, 161, 162, 176
Naqshaband, Baha ud-Din Bukhari, 4, 30–31
Naqshabandiya Sufi movement, 3, 9, 30–34,
    43–44, 96–98
an-Nasafi, Najm ad-Din Abu Hafs Umar ibn
    Muhammad ibn Ahmad, 27
National Reconciliation Agreement
    (Tajikistan), 22, 253
Navoi, Alisher, 161, 181
Nazarov, Obidkhon (qori), 21, 77, 224,
    234–239, 288
Nodirkhon domla, 89–90
Nurchi (Gulen) movement, 192, 203
Nuri, Sayid Abdulloh, 19, 21, 92, 94

Nursi, Said. *See* Nurchi (Gulen) movement
Omar, Mullah, 285
Ortikov, Dovudkhon, 102, 245–247
Ozal, Turgut, 24, 219

Ponomarev, (Hazrat) Hasan Akhmadajanovich
    (al-Kizilajari), 84
Pulat, Abdurahim, 258

Qadimist (traditionalist) clerics, 47, 49
Qadiriya Sufi movement, 3, 39, 101–102, 246
Qalandariya Sufi movement, 39
Quqoni, Ismoil (qori), 92
Quran
  adat law *versus*, 31
  Ahl-i Quran movement and, 83, 84
  commentaries on, 15, 94, 103, 115, 232
  Hindustani's study & teaching of, 92, 93
  on internal strife and polytheism, 127
  Muhammad Sodiq and, 115, 118, 125, 129
  radical interpretation of, 224, 225
  religious instruction in, 16–17, 27, 39,
    49, 61, 66, 77, 81–82, 84, 87–88, 102,
    162, 176–177, 196, 215, 236
  Salafiya interpretation of, 45, 307
  Uzbek demand for copies of, 20
  Uzbek translation of, 83, 93, 265,
    273–274, 312
Qurbon hayit (*Eid al-Adha*), 63, 143, 185
Qutb, Sayyid, 15, 16, 87, 103, 115, 232

Rafikov, Burgutali, 243
Rahmatulla-alloma, 92, 103, 104, 105, 223,
    224, 225, 226, 228–229, 231
Rahmon, Emomali, 22, 200, 289, 297

Ramazan hayit (*Eid ul-Fitr*), 63
Ramzi. *See* Ravnaqi, Faizallah Makhdum Khodjaev (Shakhrisabzi) [pseudonym Ramzi]
Rashidov, Sharaf, 68, 136, 150, 153
Ravnaqi, Faizallah Makhdum Khodjaev (Shakhrisabzi) [pseudonym Ramzi], 97–98, 100
Religion Is Edification (Muhammad Sodiq), 125, 127–131
Rumi, Jalal ad-Din, 91, 95

Sabir, Muhammad-Ali (Madali). *See* Dukchi Ishan
Sabircha-domulla, 84
SADUM (Spiritual Administration of the Muslims of Central Asia)
    Abdurauf Gafurov and, 243–244
    Bobokhon family and, 85–90
    clerical training and, 65–66
    creation and design of, 13, 61–62
    Eshon Bobokhon and, 14
    Muhammad Sodiq and, 19, 72, 109–115
    policy changes, 72–73
    religious instruction and, 19, 65–66, 79–80, 92
    role of *taqlid* and, 78
    Soviet anti-religious policies and, 63–64, 153, 250
    Ziyauddin Bobokhon and, 13, 93
Salafiya, 11, 13–14, 45, 49, 81–84
    Ahl-i Hadith, 82–84
    Ahl-i Quran movement, 83
    Hazrat Hasan and, 84
    Sabircha-domulla, 84
    Shami (domulla) al-Tarabulsi, 13, 81–83, 84, 85
    Yunus qori, 84
Salim Hajji (Khujandi), 86–87
Samanids, 2–3
Sattiev, Ismail, 88–89, 109
Sattimov, Abduhakim (Hakimjon), 245
Seljuk dynasty, 3
Shafi *mazhab*, 1–2, 265
"Shahid Abu Dujon" (film), 283
shahids, 129, 280, 282, 288, 291, 297–298
Shaybanid dynasty, 4
ibn Sino (Abu Ali al-Husayn ibn Abdullah ibn Sino) [Avicenna], 2
Sirhindi, Ahmad, 33, 100
Solih, Muhammad, 219–220, 258
Soviet rule
    early years of, 142–148
    Gorbachev's anti-corruption campaign, 153–154
    Khrushchev and Brezhnev years, 148–153
    Stalin period, 12–14, 57–61, 76–77, 137, 145–146, 147, 231
SOVNARKOM (Council of People's Commissars), 54, 55
Spiritual Administration of the Muslims of Central Asia and Kazakhstan. *See* SADUM (Spiritual Administration of the Muslims of Central Asia)
Stalin, Joseph, 12–14, 57–61, 76, 91
Sufism
    Central Asia's legacy of, 29–33
    emphasis of, 195
    history of, 2–3
    intellectual *versus* folk practices, 34
    Khoja Ahror and, 195
    leaders of, 96–100

lineages, 100–102
politicalization of, 33
religiously inspired unrest and, 40–44
role of, in Uzbekistan's future, 307–309
Sharia and, 95, 246
Uzbekistan and, 28
Sunni Islam, 2, 131–133, 269, 313

Taaba, 192
Tablighi Jamaat, 192
Taib, Muhammad Yunus bin Muhammad Amin, 38–39
Tajikistan civil war, 21–22, 121, 137, 159, 186–189, 199, 224
rise of the IMU and, 253–258
Taliban, 254, 257
taqlid, 14, 78
taqlidchis, 86, 224
al-Tarabulsi, Shami (domulla) [Said ibn Muhammad ibn Abd al-Wahid ibn Ali al-Asali al-Tarabulsi], 13, 81–83, 84, 85
tariqas, 28, 52, 53
Tashkent Islamic University, 197, 208, 210–213
Tavba, 73, 245
ibn Taymiya (Sheikh ul-Islam), 82
"Ten Lessons on Jihad," 258
"Them" ("Ular") (film), 238, 275, 278–279
Throne of Suleiman (Osh), 63
Tilla Sheikh Mosque, 116, 235, 238
Timur (Emir), 3, 28, 30, 63
Tova, 140, 141–142, 149, 152, 155, 156, 158, 160–161, 167, 169, 177, 178–179, 184–185
Transoxiana (Mawarannahr), 2, 29, 33

Tukhtaboy Vacha Mosque, 234–235
Turajonzoda, Akbar, 94, 255–256
Turkestan Autonomous Soviet Socialist Republic, 53, 56
Turkestan Commission of the Central Committee of the Communist Party, 54
Turkestani, (Sheikh) Abd al-Wahid, 100–101
Turkipoen, 139–140, 147, 150–151, 154–156, 162–163, 165, 175, 183–185

Umarkhon domla, 241–243, 245, 247–248
United Tajik Opposition, 255
Usul-u jadid, 56
Uzbekistan
education and Islam, 173–178, 207–218
global environment and, 24–25
Islamic-inspired violence in, 289–293
Islamic revival in, 159–173
legislating religious behavior in, 199–203
Muslim identity in, 203–207
national ideology of, 193–199
radicalism in, 223–227
religion and state ideology, 23–24, 184–186
rise of Jihadist groups in, 20–23
role of women in, 178–183
Tajik civil war and, 186–189
Uzbek Soviet Socialist Republic, 5, 53

Vosiev, Abdulhakim (Margiloniy) (Hakimjon qori), 84, 102–105

al-Wahhab, Muhammad ibn Abd, 133, 228
"Wahhabis," 6, 24, 87, 93, 105, 119, 188, 195, 229, 242, 274
Women, role of, 178–183

Yasawi, (Khoja) Ahmad, 3–4, 29, 30, 33, 161
Yasawiya Sufi movement, 29, 97, 101
Young Bukhara Party, 51
Yovkochev, Shuhrat, 212
Yuldoshev, Abduvali, 284
Yuldoshev, Akrom [Akram Yuldashev], 83, 122
Yuldoshev, Tohir [Tahir Yuldashev], 200,
    224, 227, 240, 242, 244–249, 254,
    256–259, 265, 268–273, 277–281,
    284–285
Yunus qori, 84

Ziyoev, Mirzo, 275
Zokirjon domla, 241

ABOUT THE AUTHOR

Martha Brill Olcott is a senior associate with the Russia and Eurasia Program at the Carnegie Endowment in Washington, D.C. and co-director of the al-Farabi Carnegie Program on Central Asia in Almaty, Kazakhstan.

Olcott specializes in the problems of transitions in Central Asia and the Caucasus as well as the security challenges in the Caspian region more generally. She has followed interethnic relations in Russia and the states of the former Soviet Union for more than twenty-five years and has traveled extensively in these countries and in South Asia. She is the author of *Central Asia's Second Chance* and *Kazakhstan: Unfulfilled Promise?*

CARNEGIE ENDOWMENT FOR INTERNATIONAL PEACE

The Carnegie Endowment for International Peace is a private, nonprofit organization dedicated to advancing cooperation between nations and promoting active international engagement by the United States. Founded in 1910, its work is nonpartisan and dedicated to achieving practical results.

Carnegie is pioneering the first global think tank, with flourishing offices now in Washington, Moscow, Beijing, Beirut, and Brussels. These five locations include the centers of world governance and the places whose political evolution and international policies will most determine the near-term possibilities for international peace and economic advance.

In 2011 the Carnegie Endowment for International Peace and al-Farabi National University established the al-Farabi Carnegie Program on Central Asia, which aims to generate a deeper dialogue between policy institutes, business leaders, and governments in Kazakhstan and the Central Asia region, and to engage international audiences on a wide range of issues.

OFFICERS

Jessica T. Mathews, *President*
Paul Balaran, *Executive Vice President and Secretary*
Tom Carver, *Vice President for Communications and Strategy*
Charles Gauvin, *Chief Development Officer*
Thomas Carothers, *Vice President for Studies*
Marwan Muasher, *Vice President for Studies*
Douglas H. Paal, *Vice President for Studies*
George Perkovich, *Vice President for Studies*

BOARD OF TRUSTEES

Richard Giordano, *Chairman*
Stephen R. Lewis, Jr., *Vice Chairman*
Kofi A. Annan
Paul Balaran
Bill Bradley
Gregory Craig
William H. Donaldson
Mohamed A. El-Erian
Harvey V. Fineberg
Donald V. Fites
Chas W. Freeman, Jr.
James C. Gaither
William W. George

Patricia House
Linda Mason
Jessica T. Mathews
Raymond McGuire
Zanny Minton Beddoes
Sunil Bharti Mittal
Catherine James Paglia
J. Stapleton Roy
Vanessa Ruiz
Aso O. Tavitian
Shirley M. Tilghman
Daniel Vasella
Rohan Weerasinghe